Social Epistem
Essential Read...

Social Epistemology:
Essential Readings

EDITED BY
Alvin I. Goldman and Dennis Whitcomb

UNIVERSITY PRESS

2011

Oxford University Press, Inc., publishes works that further
Oxford University's objective of excellence
in research, scholarship, and education.

Oxford   New York
Auckland   Cape Town   Dar es Salaam   Hong Kong   Karachi
Kuala Lumpur   Madrid   Melbourne   Mexico City   Nairobi
New Delhi   Shanghai   Taipei   Toronto

With offices in
Argentina   Austria   Brazil   Chile   Czech Republic   France   Greece
Guatemala   Hungary   Italy   Japan   Poland   Portugal   Singapore
South Korea   Switzerland   Thailand   Turkey   Ukraine   Vietnam

Published by Oxford University Press, Inc.
198 Madison Avenue, New York, New York 10016

www.oup.com

Oxford is a registered trademark of Oxford University Press

Social epistemology: essential readings /edited by Alvin I. Goldman and Dennis Whitcomb.
p.   cm.
ISBN 978-0-19-533461-6 (pbk.: alk. paper)—ISBN 978-0-19-533453-1 (hardcover: alk. paper)
1. Social epistemology. I. Goldman, Alvin I., 1938-II. Whitcomb, Dennis.
BD175.S622   2011
121—dc22   2010004045

1 3 5 7 9 8 6 4 2

Printed in the United States of America
on acid-free paper

Table of Contents

IV. JUDGMENT AGGREGATION

V. SYSTEMS DESIGN

Acknowledgments

The following essays have been published previously:

Chapter 1. Alvin I. Goldman, "A Guide to Social Epistemology," is a reprinted and slightly updated version of "Systems-oriented Social Epistemology," in *Oxford Studies in Epistemology*, T. Gendler and J. Hawthorne (eds.), Oxford University Press, 2009.

Chapter 2. Paul Boghossian, "Epistemic Relativism Defended." In Paul Boghossian, *Fear of Knowledge*, Oxford University Press, 2006, pp. 58–80.

Chapter 3. Miranda Fricker, "Rational Authority and Social Power: Towards a Truly Social Epistemology." In *Proceedings of the Aristotelian Society* 98, pt. 2 (1988), 159–77. Reprinted by courtesy of the editor of the Aristotelian Society, © 1988.

Chapter 6. Alvin I. Goldman, "Experts: Which Ones Should You Trust?" In *Philosophy and Phenomenological Research* 63, 1 (2001), 85–110.

Chapter 7. Richard Feldman, "Reasonable Religious Disagreement." In *Philosophers without Gods*, Louise Antony (ed.), Oxford University Press, 2007, pp. 194–214.

Chapter 8. Adam Elga, "Reflection and Disagreement." Reprinted with very light revisions from *Noûs* 41, 3 (2007), 478–502.

Chapter 9. Thomas Kelly, "Peer Disagreement and Higher Order Evidence." Significantly abridged version of "Peer Disagreement and Higher Order Evidence," in *Disagreement*, Richard Feldman and Ted Warfield (eds.), Oxford University Press, forthcoming.

Chapter 10. Christian List, "Group Knowledge and Group Rationality." *Episteme* 2, 1 (2005), 25–38. Edinburgh University Press, euppublishing.com.

Chapter 11. Philip Pettit, "Groups with Minds of Their Own." In *Socializing Metaphysics*, Frederick Schmitt (ed.), Rowman and Littlefield, 2004, pp. 167–93.

Chapter 12. Larry Laudan, "Thinking about Error in the Law." In Larry Laudan, *Truth, Error, and Criminal Law: An Essay in Legal Epistemology*, Cambridge University Press, 2007, pp. 1–26. © Larry Laudan 2006. Reprinted with the permission of Cambridge University Press.

Chapter 14. Cass R. Sunstein, "Deliberating Groups versus Prediction Markets (or Hayek's Challenge to Habermas)." In *Episteme* 3, 3 (2006), 192–213. Edinburgh University Press, euppublishing.com.

Chapter 15. Kevin J. S. Zollman, "The Communication Structure of Epistemic Communities." Reprinted with light revisions from *Philosophy of Science* 74, 5, 574–87. University of Chicago Press. Copyright 2007 by the Philosophy of Science Association.

Contributors

Alvin I. Goldman is Board of Governors Professor of Philosophy and Cognitive Science, Rutgers University.

Paul Boghossian is Silver Professor of Philosophy, New York University.

Miranda Fricker is Reader in Philosophy, Birkbeck College, University of London.

Jennifer Lackey is Associate Professor of Philosophy, Northwestern University.

Sanford C. Goldberg is Professor of Philosophy, Northwestern University.

Richard Feldman is Professor of Philosophy and Dean of the College, University of Rochester.

Adam Elga is Associate Professor of Philosophy, Princeton University.

Thomas Kelly is Associate Professor of Philosophy and George H. and Mildred F. Whitfield University

Preceptor in the Humanities, Princeton University.

Christian List is Professor of Political Science and Philosophy, London School of Economics and Political Science.

Philip Pettit is Laurence S. Rockefeller University Professor of Politics and Human Values, Princeton University.

Larry Laudan is Researcher, National Autonomous University of Mexico.

Don Fallis is Associate Professor of Information Resources and Library Science and Adjunct Associate Professor of Philosophy, University of Arizona.

Cass R. Sunstein is Felix Frankfurter Professor of Law, Harvard Law School.

Kevin J. S. Zollman is Assistant Professor of Philosophy, Carnegie Mellon University.

Social Epistemology:
Essential Readings

Introduction

Dennis Whitcomb

Epistemology is social in a number of ways, and it has been so for a long time, at least since Plato.[1] In recent years, the social aspects of epistemology have been the subject of increasing (and increasingly sophisticated) philosophical attention. Social epistemology is a blooming discipline, full of exciting work on topics old and new. This book brings some central parts of this work together in one place, making them accessible to students and researchers alike. We have collected work under five headings: conceptions of social epistemology, trust in testimony and experts, reasonable peer disagreement, judgment aggregation, and social-system design.

Part I represents three approaches to social epistemology. In chapter 1, Alvin Goldman provides an overview of social epistemology that divides it into three categories. The first category, "individual doxastic agent social epistemology," concerns individual belief-forming agents and how they should respond to social sources of evidence, such as evidence from the testimony of others. The second category, "collective doxastic agent social epistemology," concerns collective belief-forming agents, such as juries and committees, which are themselves constituted by other agents. How should these collective agents go about forming their beliefs? The third category, "systems-oriented social epistemology," concerns entire social systems such as legal adjudication systems and systems of peer review for academic research. Systems-oriented social epistemology evaluates these systems epistemically in terms of how they influence their members' beliefs. This tripartite classification of social epistemology is reflected in the structure of the current volume (beginning with part II). Individual social epistemology is represented by parts II and III, collective social epistemology by part IV, and systems-oriented social epistemology by part V. Thus, chapter 1 serves as an organizing piece for (most of) the volume as a whole.[2]

In chapter 2, Paul Boghossian considers the problem of epistemic relativism as it arises in social systems. Different communities seem to have different "epistemic systems"—that is, different systems of rules or principles about the conditions under which belief is justified. One system of rules may imply that perceptual evidence outweighs evidence from religious texts when the two conflict; another system may imply the opposite. What could make one such system better or more correct than another? One might answer: *nothing*. Developing that answer, each epistemic system might be considered right on its own terms, with no system being objectively superior to any other. Although Boghossian does not endorse this relativist view, he formulates, motivates, and explores it in a charitable spirit. In chapter 3, Miranda Fricker lays out a different approach to social epistemology, one that gives the field a particularly tight connection to political philosophy. Following Edward Craig, she stresses our need to find "good informants," people who will tell us the truth.[3] Various societal norms of credibility can be viewed as arising to fulfill this need. However, these norms often distribute credibility *unjustly*, assigning it only to the powerful. By focusing on this kind of epistemic injustice, Fricker adds a new political dimension to the field; and she does so from a classical truth-centered starting point.

Part II focuses on the branch of social epistemology most widely discussed in recent years, namely, the epistemology of testimony. Under what conditions are testimony-based beliefs justified? Must a hearer first confirm the reliability of informants before taking them at their word? Or is she justified in trusting them right away, without first checking up on them? When testimony-based beliefs *are* justified, what is it that *makes* them justified? Is it simply a matter of the hearer's evidence for the reliability of the informant, or is something else involved—something like one's interpersonal relationship with an informant, or even the mere fact that he invites one to trust him? Jennifer Lackey explores these and related issues in chapter 4. She gives an opinionated overview of this terrain, ultimately arguing for her own hybrid position. In chapter 5, Sanford Goldberg pushes beyond the question of when and why one is justified in believing what other people assert. He takes up the related question of when and why one is justified in *disbelieving* what other people *don't* assert. Consider, for example, the proposition that Mars was destroyed by a comet last week. If this proposition were true, someone or some media channel would have asserted it by now in a prominent place; and so, plausibly, one is justified in disbelieving it. Goldberg inquires into the general conditions under which one can obtain this kind of justification for disbelieving, and then goes on to explore some theoretical upshots of the results. In chapter 6, Alvin Goldman inquires into how novices should decide what to believe on a given topic when experts on that topic disagree. Given that they are novices, how can they tell which experts are the most trustworthy? Goldman explores several attempts to resolve this conundrum, for example, by having the novice inquire into the past track records of the experts she knows to disagree, or by having her zero in on a majority expert opinion by consulting a number of *additional* experts. Goldman delineates these proposals and several others and weighs the relative merits of all of them.

Part III presents the problem of disagreement among *peers*. Let's say that your "peers" (on a given topic) are those people who are your equals in terms of reasoning ability, exposure to relevant evidence, and reasoning effort heretofore invested. Suppose you are in the presence of someone you know to be a peer on a topic such as whether God exists or whether the next president will be a Republican. What should you do on learning that you and your peer have conflicting beliefs? Should you adopt your peer's belief, stick with your own, split the difference by assigning equal credence to both options, or what? In certain domains such as the religious and the political, it is sometimes said that the proper response to peer disagreement is to recognize that "reasonable people can disagree" and leave it at that. But can peers (as defined) really be reasonable when they disagree? In chapter 7, Richard Feldman argues to the contrary: since peers share the same evidence, and a given batch of evidence justifies exactly one doxastic attitude (belief, disbelief, or agnosticism) toward a proposition, peers cannot reasonably disagree.

In chapter 8, Adam Elga addresses many of the same issues within a framework that evaluates *degrees* of belief. He develops a version of the position that when you believe someone to be your peer, you should give her view the same weight you give your own. He defends this position from a number of objections and extends its scope to include cases in which disputing parties do *not* take themselves to be peers. In chapter 9, Thomas Kelly argues that Elga's "equal weight view" gives too much probative force to peer opinion. In place of the equal weight view, Kelly develops what he calls the "total evidence view," according to which peer opinion has some probative force but less than the equal weight view assigns it.

These essays on peer disagreement theorize about what individuals should believe in various social scenarios. A different sort of social epistemology theorizes not about what *individual* agents should believe but (in line with Goldman's "collective doxastic agent social epistemology") about what *group agents* should believe. Part IV concerns this issue: what a group should believe, as opposed to what individuals should believe. In chapter 10, Christian List explores the issue from a formal point of view. He begins by introducing the theory of "judgment aggregation," the theory of how group judgments should be made on the basis of the judgments of the individuals who compose a group. After introducing some striking difficulties and impossibility results for commonsensical "majority vote" proposals, he launches into an analysis of several interesting judgment aggregation methods with respect to two epistemic desiderata: rationality and knowledge. On both of these desiderata, different methods perform differently in different circumstances. Nonetheless, there are some informative results that bear on which judgment aggregation methods best promote group rationality and knowledge—or so List argues. Now you might doubt that groups themselves can make judgments at all, let alone rational judgments or judgments amounting to knowledge. In chapter 11, Philip Pettit rejects these doubts. Since certain kinds of groups can implement rational judgment aggregation methods, Pettit claims, these groups can have a kind of rational unity that is sufficient for making judgments and indeed sufficient for these groups to have minds of their own. These groups can even be, in an important sense, *persons*.

Finally, part V focuses on social structures such as legal systems and, in line with Goldman's "systems-oriented social epistemology," evaluates these systems epistemically in terms of how they influence the beliefs of their members. In chapter 12, Larry Laudan explores the epistemology of the contemporary American criminal trial system. He starts by identifying a number of epistemologically significant aspects of that system. Then he argues that current rules about the admissibility of evidence are epistemically suboptimal, leading to numerous errors that could be avoided via the adoption of different rules. In chapter 13, Don Fallis explores one of the largest contemporary instances of mass collaboration for epistemic purposes: Wikipedia. He compares Wikipedia to traditional encyclopedias such as *Britannica* and to other information sources, judging them all along a number of epistemic dimensions such as reliability and fecundity. His assessment is balanced but largely positive and in favor of Wikipedia over more traditional encyclopedic information sources. In chapter 14, Cass Sunstein explores two systems through which people can form their beliefs on the basis of interactions within groups: deliberation and prediction markets. Deliberation is the familiar process of group discussion. Prediction markets facilitate widespread betting on the truth of a given proposition, and people use the bets to estimate the probability that the proposition is true. These markets have been remarkably successful, indeed so successful that Sunstein argues that they should often be used instead of deliberation. In chapter 15 (the final chapter), Kevin Zollman explores the extent to which scientists should share their results with one another. He argues via computer simulations of alternative procedures that in an important class of cases it is best to *restrict* information sharing. His main idea is that when everyone shares information with everyone else, misleading initial research results can polarize the community on mistaken views, and such polarization can be avoided through information restriction. He thus connects social epistemology quite closely with philosophy of science.

Zollman is not the only author here to connect his work to other fields. Laudan and Goldman (in both of his essays) also relate their themes to the philosophy of science. Pettit makes similar connections to metaphysics and the philosophy of mind; Fricker to feminist philosophy and political philosophy; Feldman to the philosophy of religion; and so forth. These connections provide an inflow and outflow of ideas that bring new insights to all the branches of study involved. Social epistemology is a richly linked node in the network of contemporary thought. Yet it is still a branch of *epistemology*. All the work in this book takes central epistemological topics such as the pursuit of truth as its starting point. From this starting point new routes are charted. Unseen problems get seen, unrecognized alliances get recognized, and unmade proposals get made; theoretical progress ensues. This book brings some of that progress together, in the hope that it will generate more of the same.

Notes

Thanks to Alvin Goldman for helpful comments on multiple drafts of this introduction.

1 Plato's *Republic* theorizes about the division of cognitive labor, and his *Charmides* addresses the epistemology of expert testimony. On the topic of trust in experts, see chapter 6. On the problem of division of cognitive labor, see Philip Kitcher, *The Advancement of Science* (Oxford: Oxford University Press, 1993), chap. 8. For a journal issue devoted to the history of social epistemology, see *Episteme* 7, no. 1 (February 2010).

2 For Goldman's extended work in systems–oriented social epistemology, see his *Knowledge in a Social World* (Oxford: Oxford University Press, 1999).

3 See Edward Craig, *Knowledge and the State of Nature: An Essay in Conceptual Synthesis*. (Oxford: Oxford University Press, 1990).

I

CONCEPTIONS OF SOCIAL EPISTEMOLOGY

1

A Guide to Social Epistemology*

Alvin I. Goldman

1. LAYING THE GROUNDWORK FOR SOCIAL EPISTEMOLOGY

Social epistemology (SE) is an expanding sector of epistemology. There are many directions of expansion, however, and the rationales for them may vary. To illustrate the scope of SE, consider the following topics that have occupied either whole issues or single articles in *Episteme*:

1. Testimony
2. Peer disagreement
3. Epistemic relativism
4. Epistemic approaches to democracy
5. Evidence in the law
6. The epistemology of mass collaboration (e.g., Wikipedia)
7. Judgment aggregation

How can SE be characterized so that all of these topics fit under its umbrella? Why does each topic qualify as epistemology and in what respects is it social? This essay begins by proposing a tripartite division of SE. Under this classification scheme the first variety of SE is highly continuous with traditional epistemology, whereas the second and third varieties diverge from the tradition to a lesser or greater extent. The divergences are not so great, however, as to disqualify their inclusion under the SE heading. After explaining the proposed classification, the essay examines in greater depth the third variety of SE, *systems-oriented* SE, which is the least familiar and most adventurous form of SE.[1]

I shall not formulate any unique characterization of either "epistemology" or "social" with which to delineate the three types of SE. The basic idea, however, is that epistemology involves the evaluation, from an epistemic perspective, of various "decisions" or "choices" by epistemic agents, or, in the case of the systems approach, the evaluation of alternative social systems from an epistemic standpoint. There are variations in the identities of the agents and systems, as well as in the precise terms and grounds of evaluation. All modes of evaluation are *epistemic*, but several kinds and structures of epistemic evaluation are admissible. For greater systematization, I introduce four parameters and possible settings of these parameters.

The four parameters are the following: (1) the *options* from which agents or systems make choices or selections; (2) the type of *agent* or *system* that makes the choices or selections; (3) the sources of *evidence* used in making doxastic choices; and (4) the kinds of *epistemic outcomes, desiderata*, or *norms* used in the evaluations.

Types of Options

In moral philosophy the objects of evaluation are typically overt actions or conduct, such as making a charitable gift or committing a theft. In epistemology, by contrast, the usual "acts" that comprise the target of evaluation are certain mental "choices," namely, adopting some doxastic attitude toward a proposition. For example, agents choose to believe, reject, or withhold judgment on the question of whether there is extra-terrestrial intelligence. (In speaking here of "choices" or "acts," I do not mean voluntary or deliberate choices. Belief and rejection are not, for the most part, voluntary affairs.) There is more than one way to delineate doxastic options. There is the tripartite classification listed above—belief, rejection, and withholding—and there are richer ranges of options, for example, graded beliefs or subjective probabilities, which can be represented as points on the interval $[0, 1]$. Mainstream epistemology seeks principles for selecting doxastic attitudes under varying evidential conditions. Thus, both mainstream epistemology and significant parts of SE are interested in epistemic norms for doxastic choice. In addition to doxastic options, however, epistemology may be concerned with (1) choices of whether or what to *assert*, (2) choices of whether and how to *search* for evidence, and (3) choices among alternative *institutions, arrangements*, or *characteristics* of social systems that influence epistemic outcomes. None of these types of choices or options is purely mental. Type (3) options are crucial to the third variety of SE, systems-oriented SE, on which this article concentrates.

Although epistemology acquires its original impetus from questions about particular beliefs, it usually proceeds by focusing on broad categories of belief, for example, belief based on induction, or belief based on perception, memory, or testimony. Similarly, although SE may examine the epistemic properties of specific social systems, for example, the American criminal trial system, SE can be expected to ascend to more theoretical levels as well, by studying the epistemic consequences of more abstract features of social systems, such as how they employ (or decline to deploy) expertise or how they encourage or discourage various forms of communication or divisions of cognitive labor.

Types of Agents or Systems

The epistemic agents in mainstream epistemology are always individuals. This holds, too, in one branch of SE. But if the epistemic agents are individuals, it may be asked, how does this variety of epistemology qualify as social? Something beyond the nature of the agent must qualify it as social. We return to this "something" below. A second type of SE takes group agents as its subject matter, collective entities that make doxastic choices or decisions. The third species of SE takes epistemic systems as its subject matter. An epistemic system is a social system that houses a variety of procedures, institutions, and patterns of interpersonal influence that affect the epistemic outcomes of its members. Epistemic systems and their properties can arise and evolve in many ways. Some might be deliberately designed; others might emerge through ill-understood forms of historical evolution. Systems of legal adjudication, for example, are sometimes devised at a constitutional stage. Such systems can be designed with an explicit concern for truth-promoting or error-minimizing properties. Other epistemic systems and their properties are the products of social processes that are difficult to pinpoint. Whatever the historical process of establishment, theorists and practitioners can engage in the epistemic appraisal of such systems. This is what interests us here.

Types of Evidential Sources

One way of presenting traditional epistemology uses the terminology of epistemic "sources." Standard examples of such sources are perception, memory, reasoning, and introspection. These sources can be sources of knowledge, of justification, or of evidence. In this article, the primary interest is sources of *evidence*. What a person perceives or seems to perceive provides evidence for the truth or falsity of external-world propositions, such as whether there is a persimmon on the table. A long-neglected evidential source has become prominent in recent decades, namely testimony, or the statements one hears (or reads) from other persons. If another person testifies to the truth of P, a hearer acquires a new source of prima facie evidence for P. The precise circumstances in which testimony provides prima facie evidence is a central question in the field, but not something this article seeks to resolve here. To the extent that mainstream epistemology largely ignored testimony for a long period, the field remained largely or wholly nonsocial. Contemporary mainstream epistemology, however, regards testimony as an important source of evidence. So a certain portion of contemporary epistemology is already squarely social. This segment of current mainstream epistemology is the first variety of SE distinguished here (see section 2 for details).

Epistemically Valuable States

Epistemology assesses doxastic and other choices as comparatively good or bad, proper or improper, from an epistemic point of view. So there must be schemes of epistemic valuation for making these assessments or

judgments. A scheme of epistemic valuation may appeal to a set of fundamental epistemic values, which might include (1) having true beliefs, (2)
avoiding errors, (3) having justified beliefs, (4) having rational beliefs (or
partial beliefs), and (5) having knowledge. This article adopts an ecumenical approach to SE, in which any of these states of affairs can be taken as
fundamentally valuable from an epistemic standpoint.[2] We also admit
both consequentialist and nonconsequentialist approaches to epistemic
norms and valuations. Systems-oriented SE adopts a predominantly consequentialist framework, in which states of affairs such as (1)-(5) are
treated as valued outcomes that epistemic systems can promote or impede
to a greater or lesser extent. Systems that generate better sets of epistemic
outcomes merit higher epistemic ratings than alternatives. Nonconsequentialist approaches are also used, however, including ones that appeal
to formal theories or models (e.g., the probability calculus) to articulate
norms of rationality.

Some comments are in order about the methodologies available to SE
(although methodology is not one of our four specified parameters). Our
general approach to methodology is again ecumenical. Social epistemology
employs both informal and formal methodologies. It examines epistemic
concepts and phenomena by traditional analytical techniques, as well as by
using formal approaches like the axiomatic method or mathematical modeling and computer simulation. Finally, empirical methodologies are emi-
nently appropriate in assessing epistemic outcomes of alternative epistemic
institutions. The admissibility of empirical methods indicates that SE is not
confined to armchair or a priori methodologies. Thus, disciplines outside
philosophy can make important contributions to SE.

2. FIRST VARIETY OF SE: INDIVIDUAL DOXASTIC AGENTS (IDAS) WITH SOCIAL EVIDENCE

With our four parameters in place, we can turn to characterizations of the
three types of SE. Agents in the first variety of SE are individuals, and the
options from which they choose are doxastic attitudes. Call these agents
individual doxastic agents (IDAs). Doxastic choice by IDAs is, of course,
the primary topic of traditional epistemology. What is initially puzzling is
how part of *SE* can take individuals as its targets of analysis. Isn't SE's
mission to go "beyond" individuals?

We have already responded to this question. In evaluating an IDA's
doxastic choices, one commonly considers her evidence. Most evidential
sources have little or nothing to do with other people, but some evidential
sources do involve them. What qualifies the first sector of SE as social is
that it addresses doxastic choices made in the light of social evidence.
What is social evidence? For present purposes, evidence possessed by an
agent is social evidence if it concerns acts of communication by others, or

traces of such acts such as pages of print or messages on computer screens. In addition, social evidence can consist in other people's doxastic states that become known to the agent.

The terms of evaluation for IDA SE are quite inclusive. It studies any of the following questions: Under what conditions are social-evidence-based beliefs *justified* (or *warranted*)? Under what conditions are they *rational*? And under what conditions do they qualify as *knowledge*?

One issue in the justification category is whether testimony is a basic or derived source of evidence. According to David Hume (1977), the evidential worth of testimony arises from personally verifying earlier testimonial claims, remembering those verifications, and drawing inductive inferences from the earlier cases to the present instance of testimony. This is a reductionist view of the evidential power of testimony; it reduces such power to the combined power of observation, memory, and induction. An early antireductionist position was defended by another eighteenth-century Scottish philosopher, Thomas Reid (1983). Antireductionism holds that there is a separate and independent principle of testimonial justification, a principle to the effect that one is prima facie justified in trusting someone's testimony even without prior knowledge or justified belief about the testifier's competence and sincerity, and without prior knowledge of the competence and sincerity of people in general.[3] Whether one adopts a reductionist or antireductionist position, an epistemological question of justification is on the table. And since the justification is based on the testimony of another person, a social source of evidence, the topic belongs to the province of IDA SE.[4] (For treatments of the topic of testimony, see chapters 4 and 5 here.)

The generic notion of testimony may be subdivided into a variety of special categories. For example, one might consider the special case of a layperson hearing testimony from an expert. How much deference should the layperson accord to the expert? Another serious problem arises when one hears testimony from many different people, including many experts, some of whom might disagree with one another. How can a layperson, L, justifiably determine which speaker has superior expertise and therefore deserves greater credence? (On the problem of choosing between experts, see chapter 6 here.) To determine comparative expertise, L might try to assess the speakers' past track records. But can she justifiably establish past track records, since verifying someone's track record in a specialized domain requires intellectual training in that domain, which is precisely what a layperson lacks?

Another much-discussed problem of social evidence is peer disagreement (see Feldman and Warfield in press). This is usually discussed under the heading of rationality or reasonability. Is it is ever reasonable for two intellectual peers, who take themselves to be such peers, to disagree with one another on a given proposition? For present purposes, two people count as peers (with respect to a given question or proposition) if they share the same relevant evidence and have comparable intellectual skills pertinent to that proposition. If each recognizes the other as a peer, how can they knowingly maintain different attitudes toward the target proposition? Shouldn't each recognize that her peer is as likely to be right as she is, and shouldn't she therefore continually adjust her credence in the peer's direction until they converge on the same attitude? (Feldman 2007), Elga (2007), and Christensen (2007) roughly agree with this approach, whereas others—Kelly (in press), Sosa (2010), and Lackey (2010)—reject it. Whatever one's theoretical answer, the problem remains in the province of IDA SE, because it concerns doxastic choices for each agent given her social evidence about the peer's opinion (as well as her own). (Three of the foregoing contributions to the problem of peer disagreement appear here as chapters 7, 8, and 9.)

The problem acquires wider scope when we go beyond the special case of peers and consider how weights should be assigned to other people's viewpoints in general. On learning that someone else—peer or nonpeer—has a different opinion from yours, how should you revise or update your credence in the target proposition? This is a special case of the general question of what doxastic attitude to adopt in light of one's total evidence. What others think is part of one's total evidence, a *social* part of that evidence.[5]

3. SECOND VARIETY OF SE: COLLECTIVE DOXASTIC AGENTS (CDAS)

The next variety of SE departs more from the mainstream by positing *collective doxastic agents* (CDAs) and investigating their distinctive properties. For example, it explores the prospects of collective doxastic agents having *rational* doxastic attitudes toward sets of related propositions. A collective epistemic agent has members, or constituents, who are themselves epistemic agents. Like their members, CDAs make *judgments*— collective, or aggregate, judgments—about the truth-values of propositions. Such collective judgments are presumably determined by the collective's members' judgments. Collective doxastic agents can accept propositions, reject them, or suspend judgment about them.[6] What makes CDA epistemology *SE* is the collective nature of the agents under study. In this case, the type of evidence used plays no role in the classification. Doxastic decision-making by CDAs qualifies as social whether the evidence used is social or nonsocial.

Many philosophers in recent years have defended the plausibility of treating collective entities as subjects of propositional attitudes (Bratman 1993; Gilbert 1989; Pettit 2003; Schmitt 1994; Searle 1995; Tuomela 1990).[7] In this article, the only interest is in collective factual judgments, that is, *doxastic* attitudes. In everyday life and public affairs, something like doxastic states are often ascribed to collective entities. We speak of governments, courts, juries, commissions, corporations, and even political campaigns as "thinking," "endorsing," or "denying" the truth of specified propositions. A football team might be described as being "confident" of winning an upcoming game; the Council of Economic Advisors might be described as "expecting" the recession to be short-lived. In 2007 the Intergovernmental Panel on Climate Change issued a public statement rating the likelihood levels of various propositions, including propositions about the impact of humans on climate change. Some propositions were rated as "very likely," others as "likely," and still others as "more likely than not." Such statements seemingly express levels of credence or confidence by the panel, or commission, as a whole, qua collective doxastic agent.

Christian List and Philip Pettit (2002, forthcoming) have spearheaded a new research paradigm that focuses on the epistemological properties of collective agents. They dub this general area of research "judgment aggregation." Several kinds of epistemological questions can be asked about collective agents. One question is how collective judgments or attitudes are related to their members' judgments: must they be responsive, in specified ways, to members' judgments? Another question is how aggregate judgmental rationality is related to member judgmental rationality.

Special problems of rationality emerge when we reflect on the rationality of aggregate judgments. Even reasonable-looking aggregation functions like majority rule can generate an inconsistent set of aggregate judgments over a set of related propositions despite the fact that each individual's judgment set over the same propositions is consistent. To illustrate this, consider the interconnected set of three propositions—P, "If P then Q," and Q—and consider a group with three members who make judgments about each proposition. Assume that the collective judgment is determined by majority vote of the members on each proposition. It can easily happen that each member (A, B, and C) has a consistent set of attitudes toward the three propositions, yet two members accept P, two accept "If P then Q," and two reject Q. In these circumstances, the group's aggregate judgments across the three propositions will be inconsistent (see fig. 1.1).[8]

Thus, inconsistency—hence irrationality—arises more easily for collective attitudes than individual attitudes, even under an attractive judgment aggregation function (in this case, proposition-wise majority rule).

What are the prospects for finding a judgment aggregation function that avoids this kind of scenario, a mapping from profiles of individual

	A	B	C	Group
P	Yes	Yes	No	Yes
If P then Q	Yes	No	Yes	Yes
Q	Yes	No	No	No

Figure 1.1.

judgments into collective judgments that always outputs a rational set of collective judgments when the input is a profile of individual judgment sets that are all rational? A number of impossibility theorems in this territory have been proved. Here is one such theorem due to Dietrich and List (2009).

First, here are some standard conditions (constraints) on a plausible aggregation function:

1. *Universal domain.* The aggregation function accepts as admissible input any possible profile of fully rational individual judgment sets.
2. *Collective rationality.* The aggregation function generates as outputs fully rational collective judgment sets.
3. *Consensus preservation.* If all individuals submit the same judgment set, this is also the collective one.
4. *Independence (systematicity).* The collective judgment on "p" depends only on the individual judgments on "p" (and the pattern of dependence is the same across propositions).

   Theorem: Any function satisfying the conditions of universal domain, collective rationality, consensus preservation, and independence (systematicity) is a dictatorship.

Assuming that dictatorship is an unacceptable aggregation function for collective agents, it follows that there is no acceptable judgment aggregation function. This is a surprising and unsettling result, though it is not clear what its epistemically normative consequences are, or should be. Just as epistemologists may disagree about how to resolve skeptical paradoxes, social epistemologists may disagree in deciding how to react to this CDA "paradox." At a minimum, however, this is interesting fodder for SE. Moreover, since the methodology used in studying this type of phenomenon is a formal methodology, that is, the axiomatic method, it is an example of formal methods currently being utilized in SE. (A more detailed exposition of judgment aggregation theory appears as chapter 10, and a "metaphysical" defense of collective agency appears as chapter 11.)

4. THIRD VARIETY OF SE: SYSTEMS-ORIENTED (SYSOR) SE

As previously indicated, a third type of SE would study a class of entities I shall call *epistemic systems*. These social systems are to be studied in terms of their effects on epistemic outcomes. Thus, the third variety of SE is a *systems-oriented* variety, which I shall call the SYSOR conception of SE. This form of SE departs fairly substantially from the tradition. As mentioned earlier, "epistemic system" designates a social system that houses social practices, procedures, institutions, and/or patterns of interpersonal influence that affect the epistemic outcomes of its members. The outcomes typically involve IDAs as doxastic agents, but in special cases could involve CDAs. Epistemic systems themselves are not usually CDAs, although it is not precluded that some entities might qualify as both. Even if an epistemic system coincides with a CDA, however, analyzing and appraising it *as* an epistemic system would belong to a different sector of SE from treating it as a CDA.

Paradigm cases of epistemic systems are formal institutions with publicly specified aims, rules, and procedures. Not all epistemic systems, though, are formal in this sense. Among social systems, formal or informal, some have a fairly explicit aim of promoting positive epistemic outcomes in their members. These systems include science, education, and journalism. The core mission of each of these systems is to elevate its community's level of truth possession, information possession, knowledge possession, or possession of justified or rational belief. The legal trial is another institution for which truth determination is a core mission. In each case, SE would examine the system in question to see whether its mode of operation is genuinely conducive to the specified epistemic ends. In addition, SE would identify alternative organizational structures that might be epistemically superior to the existing systems. Systems-oriented SE would proceed in a similar fashion even with systems that do not regard epistemic improvement as their primary mission.

For a concrete illustration of how SYSOR SE might proceed, consider legal adjudication. Historically, many different traditions have evolved by which societies assign responsibility for criminal acts or property damage. In the European countries and their one-time colonies, two major traditions can be identified: the common-law (English) system and the civil-law (Continental) system, also called, respectively, the adversarial system and the inquisitorial system. One thing that SYSOR SE might do is compare these general systems in terms of epistemic outcomes. In the common-law tradition, the course of a trial proceeding is substantially managed by attorneys (including the prosecutor) who represent the contending parties, with a judge who serves as arbiter and a lay jury that serves as "fact-finder." In the Continental tradition, criminal trials are primarily conducted by a panel of professional judges (sometimes a combination of professional and lay judges), who jointly play several roles: investigator, interrogator, judge, and jury, all rolled into one.

Another difference is that the common-law system has highly detailed rules of evidence, many of which bar the admission of certain types of evidence despite their acknowledged relevance and reliability. Some of these exclusionary rules are rationalized on epistemic grounds, as promoting the aim of truth determination. Evidence might be excluded on the ground that it would excessively bias jurors, or that the exclusion of its type (e.g., hearsay evidence) might lead to the production of "better" (more probative) evidence. Whether such rules achieve their intended epistemic ends—for example, fewer false verdicts—is open to question. Laudan (2006) makes a lively assault on the American system's large-scale adoption of exclusionary rules. (The general rationale for Laudan's critique appears in chapter 12.) This critical assessment from an epistemic perspective is an instance of SYSOR SE, whether pursued by philosophers (like Laudan) or legal scholars.

5. INVESTIGATION, COMMUNICATION, AND TRUST

The remainder of this article explores additional topics that SYSOR SE might tackle and methods it might employ.[10] In some cases, we shall find, SYSOR SE overlaps to some extent with other disciplines or subdisciplines.

Consider a community with a shared interest in moving to a new location. Perhaps their present ecology has deteriorated through drought, fire, or other natural calamities. The community must first identify a desirable new location. How should it proceed? Like honeybee colonies, they might send out scouts in many directions to survey resettlement prospects and report on their findings. The community (the system) has various options on how to divide its cognitive labor in the search process. It might send single scouts, or messengers, in each of numerous directions. Or it might send teams of scouts, either because a team is needed for defense against enemies or because single individuals cannot provide accurate enough appraisals of a potential site. Perhaps no individual has the expertise to provide accurate (enough) reports on more than one or two dimensions. Or individuals might have biases that render their reports untrustworthy. For example, someone might have relatives who own land in a certain direction. His family would profit if the community locates there, and his report might be biased accordingly. The community must choose the structure and composition of the search team in order to maximize (or satisfice) the quality of information received.

Analogous choices with significant epistemic consequences are made in a variety of social systems. Edwin Hutchins (1995) analyzes the communication network used in ship navigation. He offers a vivid illustration of distributed cognition, in which visual bearings of landmarks are made by certain members of the crew, whose reports are forwarded to higher levels of decision-making within the vessel. The overall operation is called the *fix cycle*, consisting of two major epistemic tasks: determining the present position of the ship and projecting its future position. The organization of ship navigation is a carefully designed social epistemic system, in which assigned roles and carefully honed expertise are relied on to achieve designated epistemic ends. The general theory of how to distribute search or investigation operations, and how communication networks can optimally be built on them, is a prime topic for SYSOR SE. At the theoretical level this topic intersects with distributed artificial intelligence.

Ship navigation is not a traditional topic for epistemology. A more common topic, science, can also be approached as a social system. The institutional features of science—its reward structure, for example—provide one window on its epistemic characteristics. The sociologist Robert Merton (1973) noted that institutional science uses a *priority rule* to reward its members, so that honors and prizes (e.g., Nobel prizes) are awarded to the *first* individual(s) to discover or establish a major scientific fact. This reward system can influence investigational choices made by scientists, as Philip Kitcher (1993) observes (see also Strevens 2003). Does this incentivizing feature of science have good or bad epistemic consequences? Kitcher argues that scientists with "sullied" motives—those who are driven by a quest for priority rather than a "disinterested" goal of helping the scientific community—will actually do better in terms of the community achieving its epistemic ends. If so, this is a case in which (in Adam Smith's famous metaphor) an "invisible hand" brings about good outcomes for society as a whole even when actors—in this case scientists—pursue their private ends.[11]

The pooling of informational resources is a pervasive practice throughout society. It is obvious, however, that people do not invariably convey accurate or sincere information to their peers. Epistemic incompetence and private interest often lead to inaccurate, insincere, deceptive, or incomplete information. To assist people in deciding whom to trust as an informant, some types of people are often designated "reliable informants." People who possess certain "indicator properties," in William Craig's (1990) terminology, are said to be worthy of credence and trust. Others do not merit such trust, at least not to the same degree. According to Steven Shapin (1994), *being a gentleman* in seventeenth-century England was a positive marker of epistemic trustworthiness or credibility. Gentlemen were regarded as distinctively reliable informants because they were generally considered to have no need, in virtue of their social position, to lie or dissemble.

However, assigning indicator properties is a fallible process. Socially selected indicator properties may or may not correlate with genuine credibility, that is, truthfulness. Those who possess these properties may not really be so credible, and those who lack them may nonetheless merit high credibility. Critics can properly challenge prevailing indicator properties of a given social system. This is one possible application of SE. Several feminist epistemologists have weighed in on this issue, pointing to failed systems that wrongly deny epistemic credibility to large groups of people, for example, females in general. Miranda Fricker (1998, 2007) characterizes this phenomenon as "epistemic injustice," because social denial of a due credibility commonly results in many disadvantages. Elizabeth Anderson (2006) argues that an important aspect of democracy is to make optimal use of *all* of society's epistemic resources, without ignoring some voices for prejudicial reasons. She adopts an epistemic approach to democracy, in which democracy is fundamentally an epistemic engine.

Is it always inappropriate, then, for society to assign markers of reliability or credibility? This goes too far, I would argue. It would seem to exclude entirely proper activities such as making public the "scorecards" of financial advisors who predict the rise and fall of markets or equities. And it might exclude the journalistic practice of "fact-checking" the political campaign statements of candidates for office. Surely these are not objectionable activities. It may be replied that these examples concern the track records of particular individuals, not the legitimacy of general markers of credibility to be used in the absence of individualized information. But are general markers of credibility to be rejected as a blanket rule? Credentials like education and professional training commonly serve as indicators of competence and credibility. Such indicators are fallible, to be sure, but won't social systems have better epistemic prospects if their members have clues to others' reliability? Aren't some clues better than none at all?

6. EXPERT TESTIMONY IN THE LAW

Similar issues are encountered in connection with experts and expertise. Reliance on expertise is a pervasive feature of epistemic systems, but distinguishing between genuine and faux expertise is fraught with difficulty. This section looks at problems associated with expertise in the legal sphere. Later we shall see how the cyber-era has ushered in critiques of reliance on experts and proposed replacements for such reliance.

In systems of legal adjudication, several types of actors play important roles in the identification and deployment of putative expertise, especially scientific expertise. When prosecutors seek to introduce forensic testimony into court, it is up to a judge's discretion whether to admit such testimony. Consider forensic evidence, such as fingerprint evidence and breath-analysis evidence, to which forensic scientists are prepared to testify. Many species of forensic evidence are entrenched in the legal system and the public's mind, so jurors give high credence to what forensic witnesses say. How reliable is this evidence? And how good are judges in deciding which kinds of forensic evidence and whose forensic testimony is of sufficiently high quality? Do judges make well-informed decisions to admit or exclude such evidence? What are their guidelines for deciding which forensic witnesses and methods should be admitted?

Latent fingerprint evidence was long considered forensic science's gold standard, but it has lately become rather tarnished, as Jennifer Mnookin (2008) explains.[12] It has been subject to increasing scrutiny, including numerous challenges to its reliability. The method of fingerprint examiners, explains Mnookin, offers less than meets the eye; its empirical validation is shockingly limited. Latent fingerprint examiners employ the methodology known as ACE-V, which stands for "analysis," "comparison," "evaluation," and "verification." This sounds methodical, but what does it really come to? Given a pair of prints for comparison, one found at a crime scene and one taken from a suspect, an examiner looks at them closely ("analysis"), notes both similarities and potential differences ("comparison"), and then evaluates these similarities and possible differences to reach a conclusion about whether they came from the same source ("evaluation"). A second examiner reanalyzes the same pair of prints ("verification"), though in many jurisdictions the second examiner has full knowledge of the original examiner's conclusion, so that verification is hardly independent!

Fingerprint examiners insist that ACE-V is a scientific method and offers a reliable methodology; and many courts have agreed. As Mnookin notes, however, merely labeling a process of careful looking a "methodology" does not make it one, nor does labeling it "scientific" tell us anything about its validity or error rate. In fact, fingerprint examination lacks any formalized specifications of what is required to declare a match: no minimum number of points of resemblance, and so on. Moreover, fingerprint examiners employ no statistical information, and have no statistically validated standard to justify how many characteristics must be the same on two prints to warrant a conclusion of a "match." There is a shocking lack of empirical research to substantiate the claim of reliability for their so-called method.[13] Why do judges allow such testimony into court? What guidelines are they using? They are supposed to be governed by, *Daubert v. Merrell Dow* (509 U.S. 579), the U.S. Supreme Court decision of 1993 in which the Court delineated judges' responsibilities vis- -vis scientific evidence in federal courts. The Court said that trial court judges must serve as gatekeepers to assure that proffered evidence is genuinely reliable and based on scientific validity. There are two problems here. First, judges may not be well prepared by virtue of their training to make such assessments of scientific validity and expertise. Second, the guidelines offered in this Supreme Court ruling (and others that followed in its wake, attempting to provide clarification) are of questionable adequacy. A substantial body of legal literature criticizes the clarity and adequacy of *Daubert*. The *Daubert* criteria and their progeny are a theoretical hodgepodge, drawing on a wide assortment of philosophers and theorists of science of divergent opinion and debatable, questionable credentials.[14] In short, many commentators argue that the theory is a morass (see Brewer 1998, Haack 2003). Thus, there is reason for grave doubts about the soundness of the relevant part of the legal epistemic system: at the level of fingerprint examiners, at the level of judges, and at the level of the reigning criteria for admissibility. It cannot be said that a sound system for handling science-based testimony in the law is in place. The kind of critique lawyers like Mnookin perform belongs in the SYSOR category of SE. Although her critique is not spelled out specifically in terms of epistemic *outcomes*, she does highlight the centrality of a method's *reliability* as a standard for its admissibility as scientific evidence.

There are other problems afflicting expert forensic testimony in the courts. According to Roger Koppl and colleagues (2008), crime laboratories are part of an institutional structure that probably fosters bias.

Forensic laboratories have a monopoly position on the analysis of any evidence sent to them: once a given laboratory receives and analyzes such a body of evidence, it is unlikely that any other laboratory will examine it. A further serious problem is that crime laboratories are dependent for their business on the police, and therefore have a powerful incentive to "give" the police what they want, namely, testimony of "matches" rather than "nonmatches." This does not bode well for the truth-seeking rationale of the criminal trial system. Koppl et al. therefore propose to break the monopoly structure of crime laboratories' relationship with police by periodically and randomly requiring evidence to be sent to more than one laboratory. This would change the institutional setting in which crime lab reports are produced, and a game-theoretic analysis suggests that it could reduce the existing bias toward matches.

The foregoing discussion registers three worries about self-proclaimed experts. First, their expertise may be far more modest than they claim. Second, systems that utilize proffered experts may have poor methods for discriminating better ones from worse. Third, systems may hide experts' liabilities from the very decision-making agents who rely on their testimony.

Some writers register even more radical doubts about experts and expertise. They regard expertise as a myth or masquerade, behind which ideology rules. Critiques of this sort can be found in the literatures of social theory and cultural studies.[15] These more radical doubts are not pursued here—since I have my own doubts about the epistemological bases of these doubts. Nevertheless, worries raised in the bulk of this section provide reasons to explore the prospects for epistemic systems that reduce reliance on experts. As it happens, dispensing with experts is currently advocated in many arenas, especially in systems using digital technologies. These are the subjects of the next section.

7. POOLING INFORMATION *VIA* THE INTERNET

In this section I do not challenge the reality of expertise or deny the possibility of identifying the experts (see Goldman 2001). Instead I consider the claim that what experts know (often) pales by comparison to the knowledge dispersed in society at large. By harvesting this dispersed knowledge, a social epistemic engine can foster better epistemic consequences than it can by relying on a small group of experts. Mass collaboration implemented on the Internet enables democratic epistemic systems to reap significant epistemic bounty. This theme is especially prominent among Web utopians.

The basic idea behind the contemporary version of this approach is often credited to Friedrich Hayek (1945), an economist and political theorist. A key economic question for Hayek was how to incorporate the unorganized and dispersed knowledge that exists in society, which is far greater than that held even by well-chosen experts. Hayek argued that free economic markets offer the best hope of surpassing such experts' knowledge. A model for the best solution, he suggested, is the price system. Prices in a well-functioning economic market act as an astonishingly concise and accurate signaling device. They incorporate the dispersed knowledge and also publicize it, because the price itself operates as a signal to all.

Using the Internet, such ideas have been realized via *prediction markets*. Just as horse race odds are set by wagers on an upcoming race, prices in a prediction market are set by bets about the occurrence of a selected future event. These bets reflect widely dispersed information and perspectives concerning the target event. As George Bragues (2009) reports, prediction markets now exist for elections, weekend movie box office receipts, snowfall amounts, scientific discoveries, disease outbreaks, and earthquakes. In a recent empirical test, two Web sites, based on major polls as well as two prediction markets, predicted the outcome of the 2008 U.S. presidential election on the night before the election. Averaging the polls yielded quite accurate predictions of Barack Obama's victory, but the two prediction markets did even better (Bragues 2009). InTrade gave Obama a 364–174 margin in the Electoral College, missing the actual margin by just 1. Iowa Electronic Markets priced in a prediction of seven percentage points for the popular vote margin, coming within 0.2 points of the actual spread. Such successes suggest that prediction markets are a remarkably accurate way of extracting the best available information from a large number of people and probably exceed the capacities of single experts or teams of experts.[16] (An analysis of the comparative advantages of prediction markets over other methods of pooling information—such as group deliberation—appears in chapter 14.)

A more familiar instance of Internet-based mass collaboration is the online encyclopedia Wikipedia. Wikipedia is a species of wiki, a Web site that allows any user to add material and to edit and delete what previous users have done. Bol Leuf and Ward Cunningham (the originator of the wiki concept) explain the rationale behind wikis in explicitly democratic terms: "Wiki is *inherently democratic*—every user has exactly the same capabilities as any other user" (Leuf and Cunningham 2001: 15). Evidently, this is intended to be the antithesis of an expertise-based mechanism or institution, which is more "elitist."

How should the Wikipedia system be evaluated based on current evidence? How does it compare with the traditional encyclopedia-construction system, of which *Britannica* is the best current product? A preeminent strength of Wikipedia is its speed in constructing entries, exploiting an enormous army of volunteers. What about accuracy? *Nature* compared four pairs of articles on various scientific topics (Giles 2005). Here are some data from the study (Magnus 2009):

1. *Britannica* had a mean error per article of 3.0, with a standard deviation of 2.4.
2. Wikipedia had a mean error per article of 3.9, with a standard deviation of 3.5.
3. Wikipedia contained more entries than *Britannica* with zero errors, but two Wikipedia articles were worse than the worst of *Britannica*.

In addition to having more errors overall, Wikipedia's entries varied in accuracy more than *Britannica*'s entries.

What general characteristics of Wikipedia might make its entries generally accurate, hence productive of epistemically good outcomes (e.g., true beliefs)? The key idea is that errors can be quickly found and corrected in Wikipedia because such a large number of people are working to remove them. As Don Fallis (2008) points out, however, this story is not completely satisfying. Just as errors can be easily corrected, they can also be easily introduced (either intentionally or unintentionally). Another popular story of why Wikipedia should be very reliable is that it is an example of the "wisdom of crowds" (Surowiecki 2004). Surowiecki presents examples of large groups whose average guess about various quantities—for example, the weight of a fat ox in a livestock exhibition— was extremely accurate. Similarly, when contestants on *Who Wants to Be a Millionaire* call for the assistance of the studio audience, the audience gets the right answer approximately 91 percent of the time (4). Surowiecki argues that groups will be reliable when they are large, independent, and diverse. This is in line with the Condorcet jury theorem. Does this apply to Wikipedia? True, a large number of people contribute to Wikipedia, but typically only a few of these people work on any given entry (Sunstein 2006: 152). Second, it is not clear how diverse or independent are the contributors to any specific entry. Third, the examples of the wisdom of crowds involve *aggregation*, that is, either averaging or taking a majority vote of the independent viewpoints. Wikipedia entries, by contrast, are rarely determined in this fashion. Entries are usually edited by single individuals, and the form of an entry at each moment is a function of whoever was the last person to edit it. The last editor can therefore be a self-appointed dictator (Sunstein 2006: 158). So the claim that Wikipedia is especially "democratic" is open to debate. (Fallis provides a detailed assessment of the epistemic properties of Wikipedia in chapter 13.)

Another social arena in which the "democracy" of the Web might vie with expert-based systems for superior epistemic outcomes is reporting the news. Traditional news media make extensive use of experts, particularly journalists professionally trained to ferret out the news and commissioned by their news organization to report what they learn. The chief competitor of the traditional media is the blogosphere, a set of Web-based platforms that invite all comers to contribute their thoughts on the affairs of the day. With the eroding economic climate for (print) newspapers, many of which have already closed their operations, it is widely agreed that we are witnessing a transition from one kind of epistemic system for news dissemination to a very different kind. What are the consequences for the quality of epistemic outcomes?

Richard Posner (2005) argues that the takeover of the journalism function by the blogosphere is not inimical to the prospects of public knowledge. He puts the point primarily in terms of error detection:

> [T]he blogosphere as a whole has a better error-correction machinery than the conventional media do. The rapidity with which vast masses of information are pooled and sifted leaves the conventional media in the dust. Not only are there millions of blogs, and thousands of bloggers who specialize, but, what is more, readers post comments that augment the blogs, and the information in those comments, as in the blogs themselves, zips around blogland at the speed of electronic transmission.
>
> This means that corrections in blogs are also disseminated virtually instantaneously, whereas when a member of the mainstream media catches a mistake, it may take weeks to communicate a retraction to the public.
>
> The charge by mainstream journalists that blogging lacks checks and balances is obtuse. The blogosphere has *more* checks and balances than the conventional media, only they are different. The model is Friedrich Hayek's classic analysis of how the economic market pools enormous quantities of information efficiently despite its decentralized character, its lack of a master coordinator or regulator, and the very limited knowledge possessed by each of its participants. (10–11)

However, Posner ignores (or underplays) a crucial ingredient: investigative reporting. When there are no longer conventional journalistic enterprises, which hire reporters to investigate matters that require months of research, who will undertake this investigation? Where corruption and other public harms are under way, whether in government, business, or you name it, who will unearth these facts and disseminate them? The matter might be formulated in terms of the epistemological metaphor of "foundations" of knowledge. There cannot be "corrections" that defeat or undermine an initial journalistic story unless such a story is first reported by somebody. Unless we are content to let bloggers fabricate whatever comes into their heads, we need initial stories to be based on firsthand observation, or searching interviews with people who have observed the relevant incidents (or ongoing practices) firsthand. People involved in corruption or other practices inimical to the public good have powerful incentives to remain silent. They will also try to silence anybody who works with them who might otherwise be willing to disclose relevant information. Traditionally, investigative reporters are the people paid and trained to unearth such facts. Abuses of the political system were uncovered by such reporters in the United States in many of the crucial annals of political history of the last fifty years (Watergate being one of the most famous). How would bloggers serve this function? So it is doubtful that the blogosphere, qua social system, can adequately replace the traditional media in terms of epistemic outcomes. The blogosphere free rides on the conventional media by picking up their reportage and commenting on it. But if all of the conventional media disappear, including news-gathering agencies of all sorts (newspapers, wire services, and so on), how will the blogosphere supplant them with unpaid amateurs (Goldman 2008)?

The Web is a platform that enormously enhances speech opportunities, a feature of cyberspace widely extolled by theorists and enthusiasts. But a closer look may reveal some problems. Freedom of speech, while rightly associated with democratic values, does not automatically solve all problems of public knowledge. Much depends on how such speech is consumed by the listening (or reading) public. To use the terminology of "social evidence," the ready availability of the Internet implies that there is a vast array of social evidence on offer. But who will encounter which sectors of that evidence, and what use will they make of it? That is an important determinant of the distributed epistemic outcomes.

Cass Sunstein (2008) points to the problem of people increasingly making use of personally designed communication packages, a type of package Nicholas Negroponte refers to as "the Daily Me." The components of such a package are fully chosen in advance. When a consumer exercises this sort of control over content, with a corresponding decrease in the power of general interest intermediaries to select the content, the consumer's prior tastes and points of view greatly narrow the evidence encountered. When reading a city or international newspaper, one comes across stories on topics one didn't set out to read. This is educational. It is like walking down a public street where one might encounter not only like-minded friends engaged in activities similar to one's own but a heterogeneous variety of people engaged in a wide array of activities. A system of perfect individual control of the news reduces exposure to the "public sphere," which is important to epistemic outcomes. Reduced exposure to the public sphere may be a worrisome side effect of the communicational ascendance of the Web, says Sunstein.

8. COMPUTER SIMULATIONS OF SOCIAL EPISTEMIC SYSTEMS

At the end of section 1, I commented on the multiplicity of methodologies that might help ply the enterprise of SE. Among these methodologies is mathematical modeling, possibly accompanied by computer simulations that study the consequences of certain assumptions about successive interactions among individual epistemic agents. This section provides a brief and superficial overview of the work being done using this methodology.

Computer simulation is a widely used technique in social science, where investigators seek to model what transpires in systems of interacting agents. In the present case, as befits SE, the interest focuses on what transpires in a *search for truth* by the various agents when they receive independent evidence concerning the truth they are after and also revise their beliefs on learning of the beliefs of selected others. It is the dynamics of these belief changes over time—and their changing relation to the truth—that interests SE investigators. In particular, under what varieties of assumptions do the several agents converge on the truth? What proportion of the agents approach the truth, and how quickly? For example, in one model —the "bounded-confidence" model—it is assumed that agents assign positive weights only to other people whose opinions are "not too far away" from their own opinions.

The best known models of opinion dynamics are due to Rainer Hegselmann and Ulrich Krause (2006, 2009). In their models, the truth the agents are after is a numerical value of some parameter. So the belief states of the agents consist of single numerical beliefs. This suggests straightforward ways an agent may revise his belief in light of other agents' beliefs and the evidence he receives. For example, he could take the arithmetic mean of those beliefs and the evidence, which also comes in the form of a number.

Riegler and Douven (2009) study types of epistemic interaction between agents capable of having richer belief states. These agents tend to have numerous beliefs, many of them of a nonnumerical nature, which are typically interconnected. Thus, they study truth-seeking agents where the truth is a theory rather than a numerical value, and where the agents receive evidence in varying degrees of informativeness about the truth. Computer simulations are then used to determine how fast and accurately such populations are able to approach the truth under differing combination of settings of the key parameters of the model, for example, the degree of informativeness of the evidence. Here is one conclusion Riegler and Douven draw from their results. Being open to interaction with other agents and giving some weight to their beliefs helps agents, on average, track the truth more accurately; such openness also slows them down more in getting within a moderately close distance of the truth than when they go purely by the evidence. Of course, this kind of effect depends on the settings of the parameters. But this illustrates how exploring interesting assumptions about social epistemic systems can illuminate the likely upshots in terms of epistemic outcomes. (Chapter 15 exemplifies the computer simulation approach to social epistemic systems by applying it to patterns of evidence distribution within populations of scientists.)

9. RELATIVISM VERSUS OBJECTIVISM ABOUT JUSTIFICATIONAL OUTCOMES

Our illustrations of SYSOR SE have focused heavily on how social systems can influence epistemic outcomes by influencing the body of social evidence that an individual encounters. Some critics might object, however, that I have ignored a very different way epistemic systems can influence epistemic outcomes. In addition to the *causal* impact epistemic systems can have on people's epistemic outcomes (via social evidence), they can have a *constitutive* impact on such outcomes. This needs some explaining.

Focus on the justificational dimension of epistemic outcomes (justified beliefs, unjustified beliefs, and so forth). Assume that a belief's justificational status is a function of whether it conforms to the governing set of epistemic *norms*, norms that permit belief in light of the agent's evidential situation (see Conee and Feldman 2008, Feldman and Conee 1985, Goldman 2009). Throughout this article, up to this juncture, I have assumed that there is an objectively correct set of norms that does not vary across cultures or communities. This objectively correct set of norms, in conjunction with the agent's situation, determines whether her beliefs are justified or unjustified. However, this assumption may be disputed. Critics may contend that there are no universally correct norms, only "local" norms, tacitly endorsed by this or that society or culture. (Of course, norms may overlap with one another across localities to any degree.) Because (1) a belief's justifiedness is a function of epistemic norms, (2) local norms are the only norms there are, and (3) local norms are a function of epistemic systems (which construct or create such norms), whether and when an agent's belief is justified depends *constitutively* on a local epistemic system. It is not merely *causally* influenced by such a system or systems. So say the critics.[17] (A rationale for this viewpoint is considered in chapter 2.)

There is no conflict, of course, between the two different ways epistemic systems can influence epistemic outcomes. There can be both causal and constitutive influence. Epistemic outcomes of the justificational type may partly be constituted by justificational norms, in the sense that whether a given belief is justified is partly a matter of justificational norms (perhaps local norms of a social epistemic system). But whether that belief occurs at all may be a causal upshot of other features of a social epistemic system. There is no inconsistency or incompatibility here.

Furthermore, some of the types of epistemic outcome I have delineated—specifically, the veritistic type—are not even partly constituted by epistemic norms. That a belief is true or false is not a function of whether the agent's choice of that belief in her situation conforms to local norms or to objective norms. Thus, true and false beliefs are positive and negative epistemic outcomes (respectively) that can be employed in epistemic consequentialism without worrying about the status of the governing epistemic norms.

Still, this does not help with the justification-related outcomes (or the rationality-related ones). We still face choices, it would seem, between an objectivist approach and a relativist approach, the former favoring appeal to objectively correct norms and the latter favoring appeal to local norms (norms of the agent's own community or culture). However, why not be ecumenical? Assuming there are both objectively correct norms and local norms, why not offer theorists who wish to evaluate epistemic systems the option of using either objectivist norms or local (relativist) norms? This would not trivialize the evaluations to be made. Judging an agent's doxastic choices by the norms of her own culture or community does not guarantee her the highest grades. She may not always conform to her own culture's norms. Moreover, if we assume that justified *belief* is a superior epistemic outcome to justified suspension of judgment (or justified degree of belief 0.60), it is not a trivial task to achieve high-grade justificational outcomes (even judged by one's own culture's norms). Doing so will depend on obtaining the kind of evidence that entitles one to full belief under the governing norms.

The possibility of local norms having been raised, however, readers may feel that it would set standards too high to evaluate epistemic systems by outcomes defined by different norms, namely, objective ones. If a person is acculturated in one set of norms, is it reasonable or fair to judge her doxastic choices by entirely different norms? This is particularly problematic because objective epistemic norms may not be accessible to her, and may require habits of mind that don't come "naturally."

Here is a third possible approach to justificational outcomes. We can mark the first two approaches by speaking of L-justifiedness (local justifiedness) and O-justifiedness (objective justifiedness). We can formulate a sort of "compromise" between the two by introducing a concept that uses only the terminology of O-justifiedness, but in a way that makes indirect reference to L-justifiedness.

Suppose an agent absorbs her culture's epistemic norms by heeding remarks of her parents and teachers. Assume, plausibly enough, that objectively correct norms allow a person's beliefs to be based on the testimony of such elders (who have usually proved trustworthy in the past). Then the agent may well be O-*justified* in believing that her local norms are *correct*, even if this is false.[18] What shall we say, then, about those of the agent's beliefs that conform to local norms but violate objective norms? Well, we have to say that they are L-justified but O-*un*justified. At the same time, we can add that she is O-justified in *believing* that she is O-justified in believing P ($J_oJ_o(P)$). This is a matter of *iterative* O-justifiedness. Notice that being O-justified in *believing* that one is O-justified does not entail *being* O-justified (just as being O-justified in believing P does not entail P, for any random proposition P). Iterative O-justifiedness is a third type of justifiedness that is plausibly regarded as a species of positive epistemic value (see Goldman forthcoming). We can add it to the list of types of justifiedness that can figure in epistemic outcomes.

A concrete illustration may help. The astronomer-physicist Galileo believed that heavenly bodies moved, because he could see such motion through his telescope. But the movement of heavenly bodies contradicted Scripture. So Cardinal Bellarmine, voicing the viewpoint of the prevailing culture, denied the thesis of movement. In the historical story, the cardinal declined even to look through Galileo's telescope, because he thought he had a better source of evidence about the makeup of the heavens, namely Holy Scripture itself. For illustrative purposes, however, let's amend the story so that the cardinal looks through the telescope. This is an instructive revision, because now the cardinal's evidence is very similar to Galileo's. Yet Bellarmine does not believe what he sees. How shall we appraise the justificational statuses of the two opponents? Bellarmine's belief that the heavenly bodies do not move is L-justified, assuming that local norms instruct one to believe in the dicta of Scripture. This belief is also iteratively O-justified, assuming that the objective norms instruct one to believe what one's elders say and that the cardinal's elders said that Scripture is an objectively correct guide to belief. What about Galileo? Assuming that objectively correct norms imply that science should be the guide to belief and that observation is a core part of science, Galileo is objectively justified (given the evidence of his eyes, when looking through the telescope) in believing that heavenly bodies do move. But he is not L-justified in believing this; and it is doubtful whether he is iteratively O-justified in believing this. (This depends on further details about Galileo that I won't pursue.) So each agent's belief has some kind of justifiedness property, but the properties differ from one another. Some lend themselves to one or another brand of relativism; others do not (Goldman 2010a).

Which is the most important justifiedness property? That's a question I won't try to settle here. Indeed, this entire discussion is a bit of a digression in terms of the tripartite conception of SE. Some philosophers, however, regard it as critically important to SE.[19] So it should not be ignored or swept under the rug.

11. CONCLUSION

This article began by delineating three distinct but equally legitimate varieties of SE. It then highlighted the third of these—SYSOR SE— because it is the least developed or widely understood variety. Systems-oriented SE is a flexible form of epistemological consequentialism that evaluates social epistemic systems in terms of their impact on epistemic outcomes. This variety of SE raises many issues of theoretical interest. But it also demonstrates that ethics is not the only sector of philosophy that can make helpful contributions toward solving real-world problems and therefore invites an applied subfield, namely, *applied ethics*. There is room in philosophical space for a substantial field of *applied epistemology* as well.

Notes

* This essay was originally published under the title "Systems-oriented Social Epistemology." I am grateful to the following people for valuable comments and suggestions: Christian List, Jennifer Lackey, Dennis Whitcomb, Frank Jackson, Don Fallis, and Holly Smith. Talks based on earlier versions of this essay were presented

at the conference "The Epistemology of Liberal Democracy," University of Copenhagen, Denmark, and in a symposium on SE at the annual meeting of the Pacific Division of the American Philosophical Association, Vancouver, 2009.

1   In a companion essay (Goldman, 2010b), I present a slightly different tripartite taxonomy of approaches to SE. The three conceptions of SE presented there are called "revisionist," "preservationist," and "expansionist."

2   *Knowledge in a Social World* (Goldman 1999) concentrated on a "veritistic" approach to SE, highlighting true belief and error avoidance as the fundamental epistemic values. Neither justifiedness, nor rationality, nor knowledge in the strong sense played important roles in that treatment. This essay, by contrast, assigns no priority to the veritistic scheme of valuation. It is often invoked in illustrating the systems-oriented approach, but in principle any plausible form of epistemic valuation is admissible.

3   In the modern era, Coady (1973, 1992) was perhaps the first to argue for antireductionism. Burge (1993) defends a particularly strong form of it.

4   Not all theorists of testimony agree that a hearer's reason for believing a speaker's testimony is that the testimony constitutes *evidence*. On the "assurance" view, advocated by Moran (2006) and Faulkner (2007), the reason for belief arises from the speaker's "assuming responsibility" for the hearer's belief. I disagree with this alternative approach, and endorse the social evidence interpretation. This is not a weighty matter here, however. Sympathizers with the assurance view might simply be asked to allow a terminological stipulation that extends the notion of "evidence" to the social act of assuming responsibility.

5   Lehrer and Wagner (1981) offer a specific approach to this subject. Each agent should start with a weight assignment (a measure of respect) to himself and every other agent. Then the agent should form a new opinion by taking a weighted average of all agents' opinions from the initial stage. Finally, each agent should iterate this procedure for higher-order weights, where weights are held constant. These proposals of iteration and weight constancy are controversial. The spirit of the approach, however, fits the present variety of SE insofar as it presents principles for a single agent's rational treatment of social evidence (the other agents' opinions).

6   Perhaps CDAs can also have graded beliefs, or subjective probabilities. Dietrich and List (2009) present a general theory of propositional-attitude aggregation that encompasses graded beliefs of collective agents as well as binary beliefs.

7   Related publications outside philosophy treat the epistemic properties of collections of infrahuman animals, for example, the "intelligence" of swarms, flocks, herds, schools, and colonies of social insects and other species (Conradt and List 2009; Kennedy and Eberhart 2001).

8   Specifically, the inconsistency arises under the aggregation function of proposition-wise majority voting.

9   See Goldman (1999) for a defense of the thesis that each of these enterprises (science, education, journalism, and legal adjudication) have *true belief* promotion (and error avoidance) as their core aim(s). Others may prefer to emphasize *justified* or *rational* belief as the primary aim. Yet others may prefer the core aim of *knowledge* promotion. These distinctions are unimportant under the present ecumenical approach, which does not privilege any one of these choices. Whitcomb (2007) offers a unified account of epistemic values in terms of the preeminent good of knowing. On his approach, other epistemic values like true belief and justified belief attain their respective statuses in virtue of their "closeness" to knowledge. He calls this approach *epistemism*.

10 Some readers might be uncomfortable with our tripartite structure of SE, feeling that it is a heterogeneous and disunified assemblage, with little claim to being a "natural" discipline or subdiscipline. Our structure, however, closely parallels a similar assemblage of inquiries that also spans philosophy and the theoretically oriented social sciences. I have in mind here—following the suggestion of Christian List—the field of rational choice theory. The three branches of rational choice theory are decision theory, social choice theory, and game theory, and these branches bear striking parallels with our three branches of SE. This is especially true if we consider the new form of game theory called "mechanism-design theory." Like the IDA branch of SE, decision theory studies decision-making by *individuals*. Like the CDA branch of SE, social choice theory studies the relationship between *collective* preference orderings and individual preference orderings. Mechanism-design theory earned economics Nobel prizes for three economists in 2007. It aims to design social systems, institutions, or arrangements that yield some antecedently specified social desideratum, as judged by efficiency or another goal-maximizing standard. Mechanism designers try to devise a "game form" that would best achieve a specified goal under realistic assumptions about the players' preferences and rationality. In all of these areas of rational choice theory, there is the common theme of evaluating decisions, preferences, or institutions (game forms) in terms of rationality—in this case *practical* rather than *epistemic* rationality. This assemblage of inquiries strikes one as a reasonably homogeneous and unified assemblage. So I see little reason to despair of the notion that SE, as presently described, is similarly well-motivated and well-integrated. Of course, the proof of the pudding is in the eating. As SE continues to grow, practitioners will see how well it works as a unified (sub)discipline. There is already a fair amount of consensus—among practitioners—that it does so work.

11 A somewhat similar invisible hand theme is struck by Goldman and Shaked (1991), who show that under certain assumptions about the motives of scientific investigators and the credit-assignment practices of their peers, investigators driven by a credit-earning motive will do about as well as investigators driven by a pure truth-revelation motive in advancing scientists' truth acquisition.

12 Latent fingerprints are finger marks not immediately visible to the naked eye. Technicians use fingerprint powder, fuming, and other techniques to expose them and then analyze them.

13 Shortly after Mnookin's article was published, a report was issued by the National Academy of Sciences that contained very similar conclusions (about many parts of forensic science). The executive summary of the full report stated: "there is a notable dearth of peer-reviewed, published studies establishing the scientific basis and validity of many forensic methods" (National Academy of Sciences, 2009: S-6).

14 The National Academy of Sciences report on forensic science, addressing the impact of the *Daubert* ruling on forensic science testimony in the courts, remarks: "*Daubert* and its progeny have engendered confusion and controversy" (National Academy of Sciences 2009: S-8).

15 For an overview, see Turner (2000). [?? The references for chap. 1 do include the Turner reference.] Some theorists are suspicious of expertise because of an apparent tension between it and liberal or democratic principles. Feyerabend (1978) argued that public science education is merely a form of state propaganda for a faction of so-called experts. Postmodernists and cultural studies

writers, following Foucault, argue that expert claims about reality are the products of discursive structures that were originally expressions of patriarchy, racism, and the like.

16 For discussion, see Sunstein (2006: 129–145).

17 It may be objected that I do not correctly characterize these critics in saying that they deny that there are any universally correct epistemic norms. Don't they accept as universally correct the following norm: "X's belief that P is justified if and only if it meets the norms of X's own society"? Well, perhaps they would accept this statement. But this is not a good example of what I mean by an epistemic norm. For better examples, see Goldman (2009).

18 Suppose that she never conceptualizes a distinction between cultural norms and objective norms. Everyone in her culture just assumes that the epistemic norms they accept are correct norms. The prospect of there being other norms that are "really" correct is never contemplated and never raised.

19 This is because a number of philosophers have thought that a properly socialized epistemology should be a relativistic epistemology. For a recent statement of this kind of position, see Kusch (2002).

References

Anderson, E. (2006). "The Epistemology of Democracy." *Episteme* 3(1–2): 8–22.

Bragues, G. (2009). "Prediction Markets: The Practical and Normative Possibilities for the Social Production of Knowledge." *Episteme* 6(1): 91–106.

Bratman, M. (1993). "Shared Intention." *Ethics* 104: 97–113.

Brewer, S. (1999). "Scientific Expert Testimony and Intellectual Due Process." *Yale Law Journal* 107: 1535–681.

Burge, T. (1993). "Content Preservation." *Philosophical Review* 102: 457–88.

Christensen, D. (2007). "Epistemology of Disagreement: The Good News." *Philosophical Review* 166: 187–217.

Coady, C. A. J. (1973). "Testimony and Observation." *American Philosophical Quarterly* 10: 149–55.

———. (1992). *Testimony: A Philosophical Study*. Oxford: Oxford University Press.

Conee, E., and Feldman, R. (2008). "Evidence." In Q. Smith, ed., *Epistemology: New Essays* (pp. 83–104). Oxford: Oxford University Press.

Conradt, L., and List, C. (2009). "Introduction: Group Decisions in Humans and Animals." *Philosophical Transactions of the Royal Society B* 364: 719–742.

Craig, E. (1990). *Knowledge and the State of Nature*. Oxford: Oxford University Press.

Dietrich, F., and List, C. (2009). "The Aggregation of Propositional Attitudes: Towards a General Theory." In T. Gendler and J. Hawthorne, eds., *Oxford Studies in Epistemology, vol. 3* (pp. 215–234). Oxford: Oxford University Press.

Elga, A. (2007). "Reflection and Disagreement." *Nous* 41(3): 478–502.

Fallis, D. (2008). "Toward an Epistemology of *Wikipedia*." *Journal of the American Society for Information Science and Technology* 59: 1662–674.

Faulkner, P. (2007). "What Is Wrong with Lying?" *Philosophy and Phenomenological Research* 75(3): 535–57.

Feldman, R. (2007). "Reasonable Religious Disagreement." In L. Antony, ed., *Philosophers without God* (pp. 194-214). Oxford: Oxford University Press.

Feldman, R., and Conee, E. (1985). "Evidentialism." *Philosophical Studies* 48: 15–34.

Feldman, R., and Warfield, T., eds. (in press). *Disagreement*. Oxford: Oxford University Press.

Feyerabend, P. (1978). *Science in a Free Society*. London: New Left Books.

Fricker, M. (1998). "Rational Authority and Social Power: Towards a Truly Social Epistemology." *Proceedings of the Aristotelian Society* 98(2): 159–77.

———. (2007). *Epistemic Injustice: Power and the Ethics of Knowing*. Oxford: Oxford University Press.

Gilbert, M. (1989). *On Social Facts*. London: Routledge.

Giles, Jim. (2005). "Internet Encyclopaedias Go Head to Head." *Nature* 438: 900–901.

Goldman, A. I. (1999). *Knowledge in a Social World*. Oxford: Oxford University Press.

———. (2001). "Experts: Which Ones Should You Trust?" *Philosophy and Phenomenological Research* 63: 85–109.

———. (2008). "The Social Epistemology of Blogging." In J. van den Hoven and J. Weckert, eds., *Information Technology and Moral Philosophy* (pp. 83–104). Cambridge: Cambridge University Press.

———. (2009). "Internalism, Externalism, and the Architecture of Justification." *Journal of Philosophy* 106(6): 309–338.

———. (2010a). "Epistemic Relativism and Reasonable Disagreement." In R. Feldman and T. Warfield, eds., *Disagreement* (pp. 187–215). Oxford: Oxford University Press.

———. (2010b). "Why Social Epistemology Is Real Epistemology." In D. Pritchard, A. Haddock, and A. Millar, eds., *Social Epistemology*. Oxford: Oxford University Press.

Goldman, A. I., and Shaked, M. (1991). "An Economic Model of Scientific Activity and Truth Acquisition." *Philosophical Studies* 63: 31–55.

Haack, S. (2003). "Disentangling Daubert: An Epistemological Study in Theory and Practice." *APA Newsletter on Philosophy and Law* 31: 118–22.

Hayek, F. (1945). "The Use of Knowledge in Society." *American Economic Review* 35: 519–30.

Hegselmann, R., and Krause, U. (2006). "Truth and Cognitive Division of Labour: First Steps towards a Computer Aided Social Epistemology." *Journal of Artificial Societies and Social Simulation* 9(3). http://jasss.soc.surrey.ac.uk/9/3//10.html.

———. (2009). "Deliberative Exchange, Truth, and Cognitive Division of Labour: A Low-resolution Modeling Approach." *Episteme* 6(2):

Hume, D. (1977). *An Enquiry Concerning Human Understanding*. Ed. E. Steinberg. Indianapolis: Hackett.

Hutchins, E. (1995). *Cognition in the Wild*. Cambridge, MA: MIT Press.

Kelly, T. (in press). "Peer Disagreement and Higher Order Evidence." In R. Feldman and T. Warfield, eds., *Disagreement*. Oxford: Oxford University Press.

Kennedy, J., and Eberhart, R. (2001). *Swarm Intelligence*. San Diego: Academic Press.

Kitcher, P. (1993). *The Advancement of Science*. New York: Oxford University Press.

Koppl, R., Kurzban, R., and Kobilinsky, L. (2008). "Epistemics for Forensics." *Episteme* 5(2): 141–59.

Kusch, M. (2002). *Knowledge by Agreement*. Oxford: Oxford University Press.

Lackey, J. (2010). "A Justificationist View of Disagreement's Epistemic Significance." In A. Haddock, A. Millar, and D. Pritchard, eds., *Social Epistemology*. Oxford: Oxford University Press.

Laudan, L. (2006). *Truth, Error, and Criminal Law: An Essay in Legal Epistemology*. Cambridge: Cambridge University Press.

Lehrer, K., and Wagner, C. (1981). *Rational Consensus in Science and Society*. Dordrecht: Reidel.

Leuf, B., and Cunningham, W. (2001). *The Wiki Way: Quick Collaboration on the Web*. Boston: Addison-Wesley.

List, C. (2005). "Group Knowledge and Group Rationality." *Episteme* 2(1): 25–38.

List, C., and Pettit, P. (2002). "The Aggregation of Sets of Judgments: An Impossibility Result." *Economics and Philosophy* 18: 89–110.

———. (forthcoming). *Group Agents: The Possibility, Design, and Status of Corporate Agents*. Oxford: Oxford University Press.

Magnus, P. D. (2009). "On Trusting *Wikipedia*." Episteme 6(1): 74–90.

Merton, R. K. (1973). *The Sociology of Science*. Chicago: University of Chicago Press.

Mnookin, J. (2008). "Of Black Boxes, Instruments, and Experts: Testing the Validity of Forensic Science." *Episteme* 5(3): 344–58.

Moran, R. (2006). "Getting Told and Being Believed." In J. Lackey and E. Sosa, eds., *The Epistemology of Testimony* (pp. 272-306). Oxford: Oxford University Press.

National Academy of Sciences. (2009). *Free Executive Summary of Strengthening Forensic Science in the United States: A Path Forward*. Washington, DC: National Academies Press.

Pettit, P. (2003). "Groups with Minds of Their Own." In F. Schmitt, ed., *Socializing Metaphysics* (pp. 167-93). Lanham, MD: Rowman and Littlefield. Posner, R. (2005, July 31). "Bad News." *New York Times Book Review*, pp. 1–11.

Reid, T. (1983). Essay on the Intellectual Powers of Man, in R. Beanblossom and K. Lehrer, eds., *Thomas Reid's Inquiry and Essays*. Indianapolis: Hackett.

Riegler, A., and Douven, I. (2009). "Extending the Hegselmann-Krause Model III: From Single Beliefs to Complex Belief States." *Episteme* 6(2): 145-63.

Schmitt, F. (1994). "*The Justification of Group Beliefs*." In F. Schmitt, ed., *Socializing Epistemology* (pp. 257-87). Lanham, MD: Roman and Littlefield.

Searle, J. (1995). *The Construction of Social Reality*. New York: Free Press.

Shapin, S. (1994). *A Social History of Truth*. Chicago: University of Chicago Press.

Sosa, E. (2010). "The Epistemology of Disagreement." In A. Haddock, A. Millar, and D. Pritchard, eds., *Social Epistemology*. Oxford: Oxford University Press.

Strevens, M. (2003). "The Role of the Priority Rule in Science." *Journal of Philosophy* 100(2): 55–79.

Sunstein, C. R. (2006). *Infotopia: How Many Minds Produce Knowledge*.[correct] Oxford: Oxford University Press.

———. (2008). "Democracy and the Internet." in J. van den Hoven and J. Weckert, eds., *Information Technology and Moral Philosophy* (pp. 93–110). Cambridge: Cambridge University Press.

Surowiecki, J. (2004). *The Wisdom of Crowds*. New York: Doubleday.

Tuomela, T. (1990). "Can Collectives Have Beliefs?" In L. Haaparanta, M. Kusch, and I. Niiluoto, eds., special issue, *Acta Philosophica Fennica*.

Turner, S. (2006). "What Is the Problem with Experts?" in E. Selinger and R. P. Crease, eds., *The Philosophy of Expertise* (pp. 159–86). New York: Columbia University Press.

Whitcomb, D. (2007). "An Epistemic Value Theory." Ph.D. diss., Rutgers University.

2

Epistemic Relativism Defended

Paul Boghossian

INTRODUCTION

If the argument of the previous two chapters is correct, we have no choice but to think that the world out there is what it is largely independently of us and our beliefs about it. There are many facts that we did not have a hand in shaping. If we want to have a true conception of the way the world is, our beliefs need to accurately reflect those mind-independent facts.

Of course, the world doesn't just inscribe itself onto our minds. In trying to get at the truth, what we do is try to figure out what's true from the evidence available to us: we try to form the belief that it would be most *rational* to have, given the evidence.

But is there just *one* way of forming rational beliefs in response to the evidence? Are facts about justification universal or might they vary from community to community?

Just as there are moral relativists who think that there are no universal moral facts, so there are *epistemic relativists* who think that there are no universal epistemic facts, that facts about what belief is justified by a given item of evidence can vary from community to community. If these latter philosophers are right, then different people may rationally arrive at opposed conclusions, even as they acknowledge all the same data; or so it would appear.

A proponent of equal validity, then, can easily agree with our negative assessment of fact-constructivism, for he can hope to make good on a constructivist view of rational belief. He can forego the idea that *all* facts vary from social context to social context while maintaining the much weaker thesis that facts about rational belief do.

Just as before, of course, a constructivist view of rational belief had better assume an explicitly relativistic form, if it is to avoid the problem of disagreement; and I shall henceforth assume that it does. As we shall see, in contrast with the case of fact-constructivism, there looks to be a powerful argument in support of a relativistic view of rational belief.

Once again, we turn to Richard Rorty for the most vivid exposition of the view. But first, some potted astronomical history.

RORTY ON CARDINAL BELLARMINE

Up until the sixteenth century, the dominant view of the universe was that it was a closed space, bounded by a spherical envelope, with the earth at its center and the celestial bodies, including the stars, the sun and the planets, revolving around it. This geocentric view of the universe was elaborated with great ingenuity by Ptolemy and his followers into a complex astronomical theory that was able to predict the movements of the heavenly bodies with remarkable accuracy.

Nevertheless, by the time Copernicus turned his attention to the study of the heavens, astronomers had compiled a large mass of detailed observations, principally concerning the locations of the planets and the precession of the equinoxes, that the Ptolemaic view could not comfortably account for.

In 1543, Copernicus published his *De Revolutionibus* which proposed that the known astronomical observations could be explained better by supposing that the earth rotated on its own axis once a day and revolved around the sun once a year. Several decades later, Galileo, using one of the first astronomical telescopes, produced dramatic evidence in favor of Copernicus' theory. The Copernican view suggested that the planets should resemble earth, that earth is not the only center around which heavenly bodies revolve, that Venus would exhibit phases and that the universe is vastly larger than had previously been supposed. When Galileo's telescope revealed mountains on the moon, the moons of Jupiter, the phases of Venus and a huge number of previously unsuspected stars, the stage seemed set for a radical reconception of the universe.

For his efforts, Galileo is summoned to Rome in 1615, to defend his views against the charge of heresy.[1] The Vatican's case was prosecuted by the infamous Cardinal Bellarmine, who when invited by Galileo to look through his telescope to see for himself, is reputed to have refused, saying that he had a far better source of evidence about the make-up of the heavens, namely, the Holy Scripture itself.

Commenting on this incident, Rorty writes:

> But can we then find a way of saying that the considerations advanced against the Copernican theory by Cardinal Bellarmine—the scriptural description of the fabric of the heavens—were "illogical or unscientific?" . . . [Bellarmine] defended his view by saying that we had excellent independent (scriptural) evidence for believing that the heavens were roughly Ptolemaic. Was his evidence brought in from another sphere, and was his proposed restriction of scope thus "unscientific?" What determines that

Scripture is not an excellent source of evidence for the way the heavens are set up?[2]

Rorty answers his own questions as follows:

So the question about whether Bellarmine . . . was bringing in extraneous "unscientific" considerations seems to me to be a question about whether there is some antecedent way of determining the relevance of one statement to another, some "grid" (to use Foucault's term) which determines what sorts of evidence there could be for statements about the movements of planets.

Obviously, the conclusion I wish to draw is that the "grid" which emerged in the later seventeenth and eighteenth centuries was not there to be appealed to in the early seventeenth century, at the time that Galileo was on trial. No conceivable epistemology, no study of the nature of human knowledge, could have "discovered" it before it was hammered out. The notion of what it was to be "scientific" was in the process of being formed. If one endorses the values . . . common to Galileo and Kant, then indeed Bellarmine was being "unscientific." But, of course, almost all of us . . . are happy to endorse them. We are the heirs of three hundred years of rhetoric about the importance of distinguishing sharply between science and religion, science and politics, science and philosophy, and so on. This rhetoric has formed the culture of Europe. It made us what we are today. We are fortunate that no little perplexity within epistemology, or within the historiography of science, is enough to defeat it. But to proclaim our loyalty to these distinctions is not to say that there are "objective" and "rational" standards for adopting them. Galileo, so to speak, won the argument, and we all stand on the common ground of the "grid" of relevance and irrelevance which "modern philosophy" developed as a consequence of that victory. But what could show that the Bellarmine-Galileo issue "differs in kind" from the issue between, say, Kerensky and Lenin, or that between the Royal Academy (circa 1910) and Bloomsbury?[3]

In these arresting passages, Rorty expresses the central tenets of a constructivist/relativist view of justified belief.[4] Galileo asserts that he has evidence which justifies belief in Copernicanism. Bellarmine denies this, claiming that he has a better source of evidence about the make-up of the heavens than Galileo's observations, namely, the Holy Scripture itself. According to Rorty, there is no fact of the matter about which of these antagonists is right, for there are no absolute facts about what justifies what. Rather, Bellarmine and Galileo are operating with fundamentally different *epistemic systems*—fundamentally different "grids" for determining "what sorts of evidence there could be for statements about the movements of planets." And there is no fact of the matter as to which of their systems is "correct"—a fact that some epistemology might discover—just as there is no fact that can help settle the political dispute between the Mensheviks and the Bolsheviks or the aesthetic dispute between members of the Bloomsbury Group and the Royal Academy.

Rorty acknowledges that, having come to adopt Galileo's system, we now reject Bellarmine's and call it "unscientific" and "illogical." According to Rorty, however, this is just a sophisticated form of name-calling: all we're doing is expressing our preference for Galileo's system and rejecting Bellarmine's: there can be no "objective . . . standards" by virtue of which Galileo's system is better than Bellarmine's, more accurately reflective of the objective facts about justification. If our judgments about what it's "rational" to believe are to have any prospect of being true, we should not claim that some belief (e.g. Copernicanism) is justified absolutely by the available evidence (e.g. Galileo's observations), but only that it is justified relative to the particular epistemic system that we have come to accept.

Notice that this relativistic view is untouched by the arguments of the previous chapters because it proposes only to relativize facts about justified beliefs and not all facts as such.

And notice, also, how concessive such a view can afford to be to the objectivism about facts that we were insisting on in the previous chapter. Sure, there may be a fact of the matter about whether the heavens are Copernican or Ptolemaic. But there is no absolute fact of the matter, such a relativist may argue, about which of those views it would be most rational for someone to have. The only absolute truths in the vicinity are truths about what is permitted by this or that epistemic system, with different people finding different epistemic systems attractive.

If such a constructivist/relativistic view of justification could be sustained, it would look to give immediate support to the idea that there are many radically different, yet equally valid ways of knowing the world.[5] Moreover, and as I have already mentioned, there appears to be a seductively powerful argument in its support. I propose, therefore, to devote considerable attention to it in the next three chapters.

EPISTEMIC SYSTEMS AND PRACTICES

Galileo, Rorty says, "won the argument, and we all stand on the common ground of the "grid" of relevance and irrelevance which "modern philosophy" developed as a consequence of that victory." Let us begin by taking a closer look at the "grid" on which we, post-Galileans, are supposed to stand.

Just about any reader of this book, I conjecture, will recognize the following to be a principle that he or she relies upon in forming beliefs, or in assessing the beliefs of others:

> (Observation-dog) If it visually appears to a thinker S that there is a dog in front of him, then S is prima facie justified in believing that there is a dog in front of him.

Several points are in order, even with respect to such a simple example. First, the actual principle we endorse is nothing as straightforward as

Observation-dog. Various other conditions—some pertaining to the state
of the thinker's visual apparatus, others pertaining to the environmental
circumstances—would also have to be satisfied. If, for example, we have
reason to distrust the operation of our senses on a given occasion, or if the
lighting conditions are poor, we would not think it justified to believe that
there is a dog in front of us, even if it so seemed. So when I say that we
endorse a principle that permits belief on the basis of observation, I mean
something that is subject to a number of complicated provisos, something
more like:

> (Observation-dog 2) If it visually seems to S that there is a dog in front of
> him, and circumstantial conditions D obtain, then S is prima facie justified
> in believing that there is a dog in front of him.

Second, there is, of course, nothing special about beliefs involving dogs.
Rather, we take there to be a certain range of propositional contents—
observable contents—belief in which is reasonably secured on the basis of
observation:

> (Observation) For any observational proposition p, if it visually seems to S
> that p and circumstantial conditions D obtain, then S is prima facie justified
> in believing p.

It is not easy to be precise about which propositional contents are
observational in this sense, but our commitment to the existence of some
such distinction is clear enough (propositions about the shapes of middle-
sized objects count, whereas those about sub-atomic particles don't).

Finally, and as we have just seen, it is hard to say, even as a purely
descriptive matter, precisely which epistemic principles we operate with.
In their full detail, these principles are enormously complicated and even
philosophers who have worked on the topic for years would be hard
pressed to formulate them in a way that is free of counterexamples. In
what sense, then, could we say that these rules constitute *our* epistemic
practice?

Clearly, the idea is not that we *grasp* Observation explicitly, as we
would some ordinary proposition; rather, the idea is that we *operate
according to* Observation: it is *implicit* in our practice, rather than explicit
in our formulations. We operate according to this principle even if we
are unable to say, if asked, exactly which principle it is that we are following. The phenomenon is by no means confined to the case of knowledge. Our *linguistic* behavior is equally under the control of an enormously
complex system of principles of which we lack as yet a fully adequate
representation.[6]

Observation is an example of a "generation" principle—it generates a
justified belief on the basis of something that is not itself a belief but
rather a perceptual state. Many of the epistemic principles we operate
with are "transmission" principles, principles that prescribe how to move
from some justified beliefs to other justified beliefs.

One example of such a transmission principle has to do with moving across what we take to be *deductively valid* inferences, inferences which are such that, if their premises are true, their conclusions must be true as well. For example:

> (Modus Ponens-rain) If S justifiably believes that it will rain tomorrow, and justifiably believes that if it rains tomorrow the streets will be wet tomorrow, S is justified in believing that the streets will be wet tomorrow.

Another example is given by the principle of conjunction-elimination:

> (Conjunction-elimination-rain) If S justifiably believes that it will be cold and rainy tomorrow, then S is justified in believing that it will be cold tomorrow.

More generally, we endorse the principle that thinkers are justified in believing the obvious logical consequences of beliefs they are justified in having.

> (Deduction) If S is justified in believing p and p fairly obviously entails q, then S is justified in believing q.

(As before, a large number of delicate qualifications would have to be entered for this to capture the exact principle we operate with, but they will not matter for our purposes.)[7]

Although much of our reasoning is deductive, much of it isn't and couldn't be. If we ask how we know that whenever it rains the streets get wet, the answer is *experience:* it's a regularity that we've observed. But as David Hume pointed out, our experience only speaks to what has been true about the past and to what has been true in our immediate vicinity. When we use our experience with rain to predict how things will be tomorrow when it rains, or when we use it to form beliefs about how things are in places far away from us, we are not reasoning deductively but rather *inductively*. The claim

Whenever it has rained in the past the streets have become wet does not logically entail

Whenever it rains in the future, the streets will get wet. It is not, strictly speaking, a logical contradiction to maintain that, although wet streets have always succeeded rain in the past they will fail to do so in the future. That prospect may seem bizarre, but it is not self-contradictory. Rather, our assumption is that our experience with rain here and now gives us a good but non-conclusive reason for forming beliefs about rain there and then. We may express our practice here through the principle of

> (Induction) If S has often enough observed that an event of type A has been followed by an event of type B, then S is justified in believing that all events of type A will be followed by events of type B.

Needless to say by now, Induction, as stated, is very rough and stands in need of various qualifications that need not detain us.

Between them, Observation, Deduction and Induction specify a significant portion, even if not the whole, of the *fundamental* principles of our ordinary, "post-Galilean" epistemic system. (The way of fixing beliefs that we call "science" is in large part a rigorous application of these ordinary, familiar principles.) By a "fundamental" principle, I mean a principle whose correctness cannot be derived from the correctness of other epistemic principles. Since the distinction between fundamental and derived epistemic principles is important to what follows, let me dwell on it for a moment.

Suppose that by using some of the ordinary epistemic principles I have been describing, I conclude that Nora is a very reliable guide to what live music might be available on any given evening in New York. Every time I have asked her, she has turned out to have all the information at her fingertips and it has always been accurate as verified by observation and so forth. On that basis, I would be justified in operating according to a new epistemic principle:

(Nora) Regarding propositions about what live music is available on any given evening in NY, if Nora says that p to S then S is justified in believing p.

Clearly, though, my endorsement of this principle would not be fundamental to my epistemic system but would rather derive from my acceptance of these other principles: were it not for them, I would not have come to accept Nora.

Observation, by contrast, seems not to be like that: its status seems rather to be basic and underived. Any evidence in support of Observation, it would seem, would have to rely on Observation itself.

In what follows, we shall naturally be especially interested in the fundamental principles, in those that can be justified, if at all, only by appeal to themselves.

Some philosophers would insist on recognizing yet further fundamental principles in our ordinary epistemic system:

(Inference to the best explanation) If S justifiably believes that p, and justifiably believes that the *best explanation* for p is q, then S is justified in believing q.

Others will want to incorporate various assumptions about the role of *simplicity* in our thinking. Others still will want to complicate the picture further by talking not so much about belief but about *degrees of belief*, and about the role that assumptions about probability play in fixing them.

We could go much further in attempting to fill in this picture of our ordinary epistemic system; but we don't need to for present purposes. We already have enough with which to engage the relativist's claim that there are no absolute facts about what justifies what, but only relational facts about what is allowed or forbidden by particular epistemic systems.

Let us return briefly to the dispute between Galileo and Cardinal Bellarmine. It is not immediately clear from Rorty's description how we should characterize the alternative epistemic system to which Bellarmine is said to adhere. A plausible suggestion would be that among its fundamental principles is the following:

> (Revelation) For certain propositions p, including propositions about the heavens, believing p is prima facie justified if p is the revealed word of God as claimed by the Bible.

[handwritten margin note: what might be accepted by some cultures.]

And so, since the Bible apparently says that the heavens are Ptolemaic, that is what we are justified in believing. In contrast, I take it, *we* would think that even the ostensibly revealed word of God should give way to the theories that were arrived at through such principles as Observation, Induction, Deduction and inference to the best explanation.

Very few ordinary (non-fundamentalist) members of contemporary Western society would advocate substituting the Scriptural view of the heavens for the picture disclosed by science. Nor would we regard with equanimity anyone who would.

Rorty acknowledges that we do not take a tolerant view of the disagreement to which these two conceptions give rise. He echoes Wittgenstein who says in his *On Certainty:*

> 611. Where two principles really do meet which cannot be reconciled with one another, then each man declares the other a fool and a heretic.[8]

He insists, however, that all this rhetorical heat simply covers up the fact that there is no system-independent fact in virtue of which one epistemic system could be said to be more correct than any other.

WITTGENSTEIN AND THE AZANDE

The wider context for the passage from Wittgenstein just quoted is the following series of remarks from *On Certainty:*

> 608. Is it wrong for me to be guided in my actions by the propositions of physics? Am I to say I have no good ground for doing so? Isn't precisely this what we call a "good ground"?

> 609. Supposing we met people who did not regard that as a telling reason. Now, how do we imagine this? Instead of the physicist, they consult an oracle. (And for that we consider them primitive.) Is it wrong for them to consult an oracle and be guided by it?—If we call this "wrong" aren't we using our language-game as a base from which to *combat* theirs?

> 610. And are we right or wrong to combat it? Of course there are all sorts of slogans which will be used to support our proceedings.

> 611. Where two principles really do meet which cannot be reconciled with one another, then each man declares the other a fool and a heretic.

612. I said I would "combat" the other man,—but wouldn't I offer him *reasons*? Certainly, but how far would they go? At the end of reasons comes *persuasion*. (Think what happens when missionaries convert natives.)

Although Wittgenstein presents his community of oracle consulters as though it were merely imaginary, he was intimately familiar, through the writings of anthropologists like James G. Frazer and E. E. Evans-Pritchard, with real-life examples.[9]

Look at the case of Azande studied by Evans-Pritchard. According to his account, there are many respects in which the Azande are just like ordinary Westerners, sharing many of our ordinary beliefs about the world. For example, they believe that the shadow cast by a granary can provide relief from summer heat, that termites are capable of eating away at the legs of granaries so that they sometimes fall down unexpectedly, and that large, heavy objects falling on someone can injure them.

However, when a granary falls on someone who is sheltering under it, the Azande don't talk about these natural causes but attribute the misfortune rather to witchcraft. On their view, all calamities are to be explained by invoking witchcraft.

A witch, the Azande further believe, is a (typically male) member of their own community who has a special witchcraft substance in his belly. This substance, they maintain, is transmitted by a male witch to all his male descendants and can be detected visually in post-mortem examinations. If a witch attack is particularly serious, an effort is made to determine who might have been responsible.

To answer this question, a close kinsman of the victim takes the name of a possible suspect to an oracle and a "yes/no" question is put to him. Simultaneously, a small amount of poison is administered to a chicken. Depending on how the chicken dies, the oracle is able to say whether the answer to the question is positive or negative. This procedure is followed not only with respect to questions about witchcraft, but with respect to most questions that are of significance to the Azande.

It looks, then, as though with respect to a significant range of propositions—who caused this calamity? Will it rain tomorrow? will the hunt be successful?—the Azande employ a significantly different epistemic principle than we would. Instead of reasoning via explanation, induction and so forth, they seem to employ the principle:

(Oracle) For certain propositions p, believing p is prima facie justified if a Poison Oracle says that p.

This practice certainly seems to contrast with our own epistemic procedures; whether it amounts to a fundamental alternative to our epistemic system is a question to which I shall return; for now, I will simply go along with the assumption that it is.

Some scholars have maintained that the Azande differ from us in another important respect as well—they have a different deductive *logic* from ours.

Recall the Azande belief that witchcraft substance is inherited patrilineally. It would seem to follow from this that one clear-cut case of witchcraft identification is all it would take to establish that an entire lineage of people have been or will be witches. The reasoning would proceed by modus ponens. If x is a witch, then all of x's patrilineal male descendants are witches. x is a witch (independently confirmed, let's suppose, by the oracle or by a post-mortem). Therefore, all of these male descendants must be witches as well.

The Azande, however, do not seem to accept these inferences. As Evans-Pritchard put it:

> To our minds it appears evident that if a man is proven a witch the whole of his clan are ipso facto witches, since the Zande clan is a group of persons related biologically through the male line. Azande see the sense of this argument but they do not accept its conclusions, and it would involve the whole notion of witchcraft in contradiction were they to do so.[10]

Apparently, the Azande accept only that the close paternal kinsmen of a known witch are also witches. Some scholars have concluded from this that the Azande employ a different logic from ours, one that involves rejecting unqualified use of modus ponens.[11]

DEFENDING EPISTEMIC RELATIVISM

Let us accept for now the claim that Azande and the Vatican circa 1630 represent the use of *fundamentally* different epistemic systems: their underived epistemic principles diverge from ours.

Let us also accept that these systems are what I shall call *genuine* alternatives to ours: on a given range of propositions and fixed evidential circumstances, they yield *conflicting* verdicts on what it is justified to believe. (It's important to add this condition at this point, for we want to make sure that the epistemic systems that concern us not only differ from each other but that they rule on the justifiability of a given belief in mutually incompatible ways.)

Using the template we developed in the previous chapter, we can formulate epistemic relativism as follows:

Epistemic Relativism:
A. There are no absolute facts about what belief a particular item of information justifies. (Epistemic non-absolutism)
B. If a person, S's, epistemic judgments are to have any prospect of being true, we must not construe his utterances of the form
"E justifies belief B"
as expressing the claim.
E justifies belief B
but rather as expressing the claim:

*According to the epistemic system C, that I, S, accept, information
E justifies belief B.* (Epistemic relationism)

C. There are many fundamentally different, genuinely alternative
   epistemic systems, but no facts by virtue of which one of these
   systems is more correct than any of the others. (Epistemic
   pluralism)

Now, there are many prima facie puzzling aspects to epistemic relativism
as so formulated—but I propose not to dwell on them now but to come
back to them after we have had a chance to appreciate the positive case
that can be made in its favor. In marked contrast with a relativism about
facts in general, which as we saw is very difficult to defend, I believe that
a very strong prima facie case can be made for epistemic relativism. It is
given by the following argument:

Argument for Epistemic Relativism

1. If there are absolute epistemic facts about what justifies what,
   then it ought to be possible to arrive at justified beliefs about
   them.
2. It is not possible to arrive at justified beliefs about what absolute
   epistemic facts there are. Therefore,
3. There are no absolute epistemic facts. (Epistemic non-absolutism)
4. If there are no absolute epistemic facts, then epistemic relativism
   is true. Therefore,
5. Epistemic relativism is true.

This argument is evidently valid; the only question is whether it is sound.

I propose immediately to sidestep the premise 4. Since the issues it
raises are subtle and potentially distracting, I am simply going to grant it
for the purposes of this discussion. Let me explain.

According to epistemic relativism, as I have construed it, when we say
something of the form

($) "E justifies belief B"

we intend to be making a factual judgment capable of being assessed as
true or false. Since according to non-absolutism, there is no unrelativized
fact of that form for the sentence to report, the relativist urges us to
reconstrue such judgments as making only relational judgments about
what various epistemic systems require or permit.

However, as we had occasion to note in the previous chapter, there
have been philosophers, who have thought that normative statements
in general—and so epistemic statements in particular—are not in the
business of making factual judgments. According to these philosophers,
judgments of the form ($) are rather to be understood as expressing the
thinker's states of mind—according to Allan Gibbard's well-known proposal, for example, as expressing the thinker's acceptance of a system of

norms that permits believing B under conditions E.[12] We may call such philosophers *expressivists* about epistemic judgments. An expressivist in this sense may well want to accept epistemic non-absolutism; but he would resist the second clause of the relativist's view which recommends reconstruing epistemic judgments as relational judgments.

Now, the question whether there really is such an expressivist option in the epistemic case or elsewhere and the question whether it amounts to a compelling view of normative judgments, are large questions that I cannot hope to enter into here.[13] For the purpose of giving the epistemic relativist the strongest possible hand, I propose simply to grant premise 4 for the purposes of this discussion. Thus, I will take it that epistemic relativism will have been secured once we have made a plausible case for epistemic non-absolutism. The question I shall consider is whether such a case is forthcoming.

Let us turn our attention then to the two premises on which the case for non-absolutism depends, beginning with the first. According to this premise, if there are absolute epistemic facts, it must be possible to come to have justified beliefs about what those facts are.

It is possible to hear this as making a stronger claim than is actually intended.

It is not crucial to the first premise that we be able to know which absolute epistemic facts obtain in their full detail. Perhaps the norms that specify when a belief is justified are so extraordinarily complicated that it would take an enormous idealization of our actual powers to figure out what they are in full detail. It is enough for the purposes of this premise that we be able to know them in rough approximation, that we be able to rule out *radical* alternatives, even if we are unable to decide between two very close contenders.

When the first premise is qualified in this way, it seems hardly to need any defense. Whenever we confidently judge that some belief is justified on the basis of a given piece of information, we are tacitly assuming that such facts are not only knowable but that they are known. And in doing epistemology, we not only assume that they are knowable, we assume that they are knowable a priori. Indeed, what would be the interest of an absolutism about epistemic truths which combined that absolutism with the affirmation that those truths are necessarily inaccessible to us? (Compare: what would be the interest of an absolutism about moral truths which combined it with the affirmation that those absolute truths are necessarily inaccessible to us?)

Suppose, then, that we grant the first premise, either because it seems plausible, or because we so define epistemic absolutism that it already includes the (rough) epistemic accessibility of facts about justification. Still, why should we grant the argument's second premise, that such facts are not knowable?

Consider a situation in which a disagreement arises about what the absolute epistemic facts are. We encounter Bellarmine, or the Azande, and

[Handwritten margin note: equivocation! (Jund K)]

they question whether our view of those facts is correct. They say we are mistaken to think that Galileo's observations justify Copernicanism. We, for our part, think they are mistaken to deny it. If there really were a fact of the matter here, we have said, we ought to be able to settle it one way or the other. How, though, could we show them the error of their views?

Our first move, of course, would be to show that our judgment that Such-and-so considerations justify Copernicanism follows from the general epistemic principles that we accept, from our epistemic system. But that just pushes the crucial question back. Why think that our epistemic system is correct and theirs isn't? How do we now tackle that question?

To show them—or ourselves, for that matter—that our system is correct and theirs wrong, we would have to *justify* the principles of our system over theirs, we would have to offer them some *argument* that demonstrated the objective superiority of our system over theirs. But any such argument would require using an epistemic system, relying on the cogency of some epistemic principles and not others. Which system should we use?

Well, naturally, we would use ours. We take ours to be the correct system; we think theirs is mistaken. That's exactly what we are trying to show. We could hardly hope to show that we are justified in thinking our system correct by justifying it with the use of a system that doesn't yield justified verdicts.

But also naturally, *they* would use *their* system to decide which of us is right.

Suppose now that we each discover that our own principles decide in favor of themselves and against the other practice. This is not exactly a foregone conclusion since some sets of principles will be *self-undermining*, ruling against themselves, and others may be *tolerant* of some degree of divergence.[14] But it is a very likely outcome for any sufficiently well-developed epistemic system.

On that scenario, then, we will have two self-supporting practices that are at odds with each other. Will we have shown anything substantive; could we really claim to have demonstrated that our principles are correct, and theirs not? Is either one of us in a position to call the other "wrong"?

Think of what Wittgenstein says:

> Is it wrong for them to consult an oracle and be guided by it?—If we call this "wrong" aren't we using our language-game as a base from which to *combat* theirs?

If we persist in calling them wrong, Wittgenstein is saying, we are simply *insisting* on the superiority of our practice over theirs; we could not honestly claim to have rationally demonstrated that their system is mistaken.

Now, there are two different ways of hearing this charge of Wittgenstein's, one of which is less threatening to epistemic absolutism than the other.

On the less threatening interpretation, we could understand him to say: well, although you may have shown something about the superiority of your system over your opponents', your demonstration is dialectically ineffective: your opponents will remain thoroughly unpersuaded and they would have every right to do so since your demonstration begs the question against them. You may have shown something substantive by *your* lights, but not by *theirs*.

To this objection, the objectivist could reasonably reply: perhaps you are right, but if so that is their problem. It's not my fault that they are so far gone that my perfectly reasonable arguments are unable to reach them.

But there is another more potent reading of Wittgenstein's charge according to which our argument would not have shown anything about the correctness of our own system, even *by our own lights*, and not just by the lights of our opponents.

The point is that *we ourselves* seem to acknowledge that we cannot hope to demonstrate the correctness of an epistemic system by using *that very system*. As Richard Fumerton has put it,

> . . . there is no philosophically interesting notion of justification or knowledge that would allow us to use a kind of reasoning to justify the legitimacy of using that reasoning.[15]

Fumerton is surely onto something. If we really do take our confrontation with an alien epistemic system to throw our system into doubt, and so to call for a genuine justification of that system, how could we possibly hope to advance that project by showing that our system is ruled correct by itself? If we have reason to doubt whether our principles yield genuinely justified beliefs, why should we be comforted by the fact that we can construct an argument in their favor that relies on them? To doubt them is precisely to doubt the value of the beliefs that are arrived at on their basis.

If these considerations are right, then it looks as though, *even by our own lights*, we cannot hope to settle the question which epistemic system is correct, once it has been raised. We consequently seem to have to concede that, if there are objective facts about justification, those facts are in principle unknowable.[16]

And with that the relativist's argument goes through. The most that any epistemic practice will be able to say, when confronted by a fundamentally different, genuine alternative, self-supporting epistemic practice, is that it is correct by its own lights, whereas the alternative isn't. But that cannot yield a *justification* of the one practice over the other, without begging the question. If the point is to decide which of the two practices is better than the other, self-certification is not going to help. Each side will be able to provide a *norm-circular* justification of its own practice; neither side will be able to provide anything more. With what right, then, could either party claim to have a superior conception of rational or justified belief? We seem left with no choice but to say, as Wittgenstein does in his *Philosophical Inves tigations*:

> If I have exhausted the justifcations I have reached bedrock, and my spade is turned. Then I am inclined to say: "This is simply what I do."[17]

Notes

1 For a gripping account of this episode in the history of thought, see Giorgio de Santillana, *The Crime of Galileo* (Chicago: University of Chicago Press, 1955).

2 Richard Rorty, *Philosophy and the Mirror of Nature* (Princeton: Princeton University Press, 1981), 328–9.

3 ibid. 330–1.

4 There are other positions in the literature that have claimed this label. In this book, I shall concentrate on the sort of epistemic relativism that Rorty describes in this passage—a relativism that insists on relativizing epistemic judg-ments to the background epistemic conceptions employed by diverse thinkers, to their respective "grids" of epistemic relevance and irrelevance, in Rorty's language. I will have something to say about alternative formulations in the next chapter.

5 The relativist should avoid the trap of saying that this is because such a view would show that there are many radically different, yet equally *rational*, ways of knowing the world, for that would amount to endorsing a use of "rational" that is absolute—whereas the relativist view on offer is precisely that we cannot sensibly speak of what is rational, period, but only of what is rational relative to this or that accepted epistemic system.

6 I have been talking about our following norms or principles. It is more common to talk about our following *rules*, which are expressed by imperatives of the form "If C, do A", rather than principles, which are typically expressed by indicative sentences. I cannot here explain why I have avoided rule-talk, except to say that there are many things that we call rules—such as the rule for castling in chess—which are expressed by indicatives rather than imperatives.

7 For some discussion of the qualifications that might be needed see Gilbert Harman, "Rationality," in his *Reasoning, Meaning, and Mind* (Oxford: Clarendon Press, 1999), 9–45, and Gilbert Harman, *Changes in View: Principles of Reasoning* (Cambridge, Mass.: The MIT Press, 1986), ch. 1.

8 Ludwig Wittgenstein, *On Certainty*, ed. G. E. M. Anscombe and G. H. von Wright, trans. Denis Paul and G. E. M. Anscombe (Oxford: Basil Blackwell, 1975).

9 See James G. Frazer, *The Golden Bough: A Study in Magic and Religion*, 3rd edn. reprint of the 1911 edn. (New York: Macmillan, 1980) and E. E. Evans-Pritchard, *Witchcraft, Oracles and Magic among the Azande* (Oxford: Clar-endon Press, 1937).

10 Evans-Pritchard, *Witchcraft, Oracles and Magic among the Azande*, 34.

11 David Bloor, *Knowledge and Social Imagery*, 2nd edn. (Chicago, University of Chicago Press, 1991), 138–40.

12 Allan Gibbard, *Wise Choices, Apt Feelings: A Theory of Normative Judgement* (Cambridge, Mass.: Harvard University Press, 1990).

13 For some discussion, see my "How are Objective Epistemic Reasons Possible?" *Philosophical Studies* 106 (2001): 1–40.

14 It's an interesting question how tolerance should be construed. See, for example, Thomas Kelly, "The Epistemic Significance of Disagreement," in *Oxford Studies in Epistemology*, ed. John Hawthorne and Tamar Szab'O Gendler (Oxford: Oxford University Press, forthcoming).

15 Richard Fumerton, *Metaepistemology and Skepticism* (Lanham, Md.: Row-man & Littlefield, 1995), 180.

16 In presenting this pro-relativist argument, I am deliberately eliding certain important distinctions—we will return to those distinctions in the next chapter.

17 Ludwig Wittgenstein, *Philosophical Investigations*, trans. G. E. M. Anscombe (Oxford: Blackwell, 1953), para. 217.

3

Rational Authority and Social Power: Towards a Truly Social Epistemology

Miranda Fricker

ABSTRACT *This paper explores the relation between rational authority and social power, proceeding by way of a philosophical genealogy derived from Edward Craig's Knowledge and the State of Nature. The position advocated avoids the errors both of the "traditionalist" (who regards the socio-political as irrelevant to epistemology) and of the "reductivist" (who regards reason as just another form of social power). The argument is that a norm of credibility governs epistemic practice in the state of nature, which, when socially manifested, is likely to imitate the structures of social power. A phenomenon of epistemic injustice is explained, and the politicizing implication for epistemology educed.*

I

> Knowledge is a collective good. In securing our knowledge we rely upon others, and we cannot dispense with that reliance. That means that the relations in which we have and hold our knowledge have a moral character, and the word I use to indicate that moral relation is *trust*—Steven Shapin.[1]

The relations of trust which Shapin speaks of here have a political character as well as a moral one. Their political character derives from the fact that epistemic subjects are socially constituted individuals who stand in relations of power. Through his study of seventeenth-century gentlemanly culture (particularly as manifested in the person of Robert Boyle), Shapin investigates a historical phase of the connection between trust and social power. I propose to explore the relation between rational authority and social power, proceeding not by way of history but primarily by way of a philosophical genealogy. I end with a suggestion about what that genealogy reveals about the relation between knowledge and power.

In epistemology it can too often seem as if a concern with truth and rationality were wholly disconnected from any concern with power and the social identities of the participants in epistemic practices. For the most part the tradition provides us with a clinically asocial conception of the knowing subject, with the result that epistemology tends to proceed as if socio-political considerations were utterly irrelevant to it. At another extreme, there are many "end-of-epistemology" and postmodernist theorists (treated either as an occult tendency or as the new orthodoxy—depending on the company one keeps) who tell us to abandon reason and truth as universal norms on the grounds that they are mere functions of power as it is played out in the drama of epistemic practice. Whereas on the traditionalist view social power is seen as wholly *irrelevant* to the rational, on the postmodernist view reason tends to be *reduced* to social power. One might venture a diagnosis: that both the traditionalist and reductivist camps make the same mistake of thinking it is an all or nothing situation, so that if social power is involved in rational proceedings in any but the most superficial of ways, then it is all up with rationality. (The respective mindsets of two people engaged in a heated argument about whether or not *God is dead* are very much closer together than either is to that of the person trapped in the middle wishing they could all find a different way of talking.)

These characterizations of traditionalist and reductivist extremes are somewhat artificial, of course, although I think they are not quite caricatures. They serve to delineate two contrasting and equally mistaken conceptions of how rational authority and social power are related. I shall present a different conception of the relation, which explains, firstly, why socio-political matters are a proper concern in epistemology; and, secondly, why the very possibility of bringing a politicized critical perspective to bear requires that rational authority and social power be firmly distinguished. The first point is addressed to those who are inclined towards the position I have called traditionalist; the second to those inclined towards the position I have characterized as reductivist. My final remarks about the relation between knowledge and social power may be more disruptive to traditionalism, while still supplying no grist to the reductivist mill.

II

Who knows? Reductivism about reason stands or falls with the question whether there can be a characterization of rational authority which is genuinely independent of social power. If we want to see at what point and in what way social power enters into epistemic practice, and if we want to see to what extent it *must* enter in, then it will be a useful heuristic to imagine a minimal epistemic practice in a situation that is minimally social. In *Knowledge and the State of Nature*, Edward Craig presents a philosophical genealogy that provides a "practical explication" of the concept of knowledge through an exploration of its fundamental role in our lives. His innovative account provides an excellent framework within which to pursue the question of how social power and rational authority are related.[2]

Craig's *practical* approach[3] to explaining the concept of knowledge is not to explore in the abstract the meaning of the word "know", as in the traditional epistemological project. Instead he imagines a minimal case of the actual situations in which we employ the concept—an epistemic "state of nature" in which we must seek true beliefs in order to survive. By taking this approach, conducted from the perspective of the inquirer, he aims to identify those features of the concept of knowledge which crucially distinguish it from that of true belief:

> We take some prima facie plausible hypothesis about what the concept of knowledge does for us, what its role in our life might be, and then ask what a concept having that role would be like, what conditions would govern its application.[4]

Craig suggests that human beings have a fundamental need to acquire true beliefs, for without an ability to acquire them we would surely perish. The point arises from the quite general thought that epistemic subjects are *agents*, whose attempts at causal intervention in the world can only be effective if they (to a sufficient degree) form true beliefs about what will happen if. . . . This basic need for truth drives our practice, leading us to seek out "good informants"—people who will tell us the truth as to whether *p*—in order to multiply our epistemic resources. We inevitably develop a collective strategy such that the information available from the different vantage points of fellow inquirers is pooled. In this way we are driven towards an essentially co-operative practice that enables us to benefit not only from our own eyes and ears, but also from the eyes and ears of fellow inquirers.

That the minimal epistemic practice in the state of nature is cooperative gives it an ethical dimension. And Craig characterizes the relevant co-operative attitude by reference to our capacity for empathy and to "the special flavour of situations in which human beings treat each other as subjects with a common purpose, rather than as objects from which services, in this case true belief, can be extracted".[5] But the trusting, co-operative attitude towards one's fellow inquirers can only serve its purpose if it is discriminating. There must be some public means of distinguishing good informants. Broadly (and introducing terms (i) and (ii) of my own), the good informant is distinguished by three features:

i) competence
ii) trustworthiness
iii) indicator-properties.

What I call "competence" is specified counterfactually in Craig's account, so that the good informant as to whether p must believe that p if p is the case, and not believe that p if *not-p* is the case, across those possible worlds that are relevant to the predicament of the inquirer.[6] I make "trustworthiness" the name of Craig's requirement that "[c]hannels of communication between [informant and inquirer] . . . should be open".[7] This covers the informant's accessibility, speaking the same language, willingness to part with the information, and possession of a good track-record of non-deception (the paradigm counter example being Matilda who told such dreadful lies). One could of course add any number of other requirements, such as that the informant should convey the information in an organized, not too long-winded, not too technical form, etc. As Craig makes clear, quite what is required will vary from context to context. His concern, and the present concern, is with characterizing the prototypical case.

Indicator-properties are prototypically detectable by the inquirer, and indicate that the potential informant is "likely to be right about p".[8] But someone's being "right about p" can be ambiguous between their *believing* truly that p and their *telling* truly that p. Craig explains being "right about p" simply in terms of having "a true belief on the matter",[9] so that the guarantee that the good informant tells one what she (truly) believes has to come from the independent requirement that "channels of communication" be open. His account has it that, in my terms, the good informant must be recognizable as competent with respect to p, but need not be recognizable as trustworthy with respect to p. On this point I depart from Craig, however. For, surely, what the inquirer needs is someone he can pick out as likely to *tell* him truly whether p—someone likely to be able *and* willing to give him the information he wants. So the method of investigating knowledge from the inquirer's perspective should (or, at least, can) be taken to require that not only the informant's competence be recognizable, but also her trustworthiness. I therefore adapt the account accordingly:[10] indicator-properties are such as to signal the presence of both competence and trustworthiness.

Knowledge, then, is enshrined in the figure of the good informant. Our concept of knowledge as distinct from mere true belief arises from the fundamental human imperative to identify people who will tell one the truth about p. It is important to appreciate that Craig is not suggesting that the requirement of being a good informant is to be slotted into a set of necessary and sufficient conditions for knowledge. On the contrary, his practical explication is intended as a methodological alternative to the project of analysis. (It is obvious that being a good informant cannot be a necessary condition for knowing, since we can readily think up examples where a person knows something but cannot constitute a good informant on the matter. Perhaps they have a track-record of lying, or error, or perhaps they have an evident motivation for deception.[11])

The good-informant account is offered as an account of the "common core"[12] of the concept of knowledge, in order to bring to light the fundamental point that the concept has in our lives. Cases where we attribute knowledge whether *p* to people who nonetheless cannot qualify as good informants whether *p* present perfectly *bona fide* uses of the concept; but such uses are parasitic upon the prior practice of good-informing, which dramatizes the core of what it is to *know*.

III

Methodological note. It is at the best of times difficult to grasp the status of state-of-nature stories. They are notorious for providing a blank canvas onto which a philosopher may paint the image of his personal theoretical predilections; yet they also provide a unique format for identifying a start-ing point (say, a set of basic human needs) and telling a narrative story from which a theory may emerge. We tend to see plausibility as a wel-come constraint on philosophical whim. But why we should want plausi-bility from a state-of-nature account of the provenance of a concept can seem puzzling. If "plausible" means "likely to be true", then it has an inap-propriately empirical ring for a manifestly made-up story that is quite properly composed from the armchair.

The matter becomes clearer if we concentrate on the distinction between the historian's question "how has X actually come about?" and the philosopher's modal question "how is it possible that X has come about?". Answers to the first are candidates for true explanations of X; answers to the second are candidates for providing philosophical *under-standing* of X. The understanding will be brought by what we might call the *how-possibly?* explanation. But, clearly, not any such explanation will bring philosophical understanding—it must be a good one to do that. And we tend to think that a good one is (at least) a plausible one. But if so then "plausible" cannot in this context mean "likely to be true", for most state-of-nature explanations would fail *that* test.

There are many and various things which determine whether a *how-possibly?* explanation is philosophically illuminating, but one thing we may want when we say we want plausibility is a certain relation between the *how-possibly?* explanation and actuality; between (if I may) genealogy and history. A good genealogical explanation of the concept of knowledge helps us understand how, and in what respects, our actual epistemic prac-tices are the contingent social manifestations of our most basic epistemic predicament. So it helps us understand to what extent features of our actual practice are necessary, and to what extent they are contingent. This will in turn explain how some kinds of criticism of our practice are worth making, and how some are senseless. (In particular, it explains why some kinds of political criticism of the norms surrounding rational authority are worth making, and why others can never be genuinely political: where the norm in question is necessary, political criticism is at best futile.)

When we engage in genealogical story-telling, then, we give a *how-possibly?* explanation of something, designed to increase our understanding of it. The genius of using the state-of-nature format in the arena of epistemology is that it allows one to tell a narrative story about X (e.g. the concept "know") even where we find it otherwise barely intelligible that there could have been a narrative development towards X.[13] In such cases the state of nature is a unique heuristic device. It allows one to tell a story which is plausible (in the revised sense), philosophically illuminating, and yet quite false, known to be false, and perhaps even necessarily false (for instance, if the idea of a progression towards X were conceptually impossible).

Craig gives a state-of-nature explanation of a creature which progresses, provided it has sufficient intellectual capacity, from a purely subjective consciousness of "food, here, now", towards a capacity for concepts as of an objective world, so that it comes to distinguish food here, food soon, food over there, and so on. This capacity for conceptualization is explained by reference to the advantages that would accrue if it were able causally to interact with and manipulate the world to its own advantage.[14] Now this transition from no capacity for conceptualization towards such a capacity is one which we do not normally know how to present as a *progression*. The capacity for conceptualization—for meaning—seems indivisible. Perhaps we are given a brilliantly suggestive metaphor—' [l]ight dawns gradually over the whole'[15]—but we may still not feel that in itself this amounts to any explanation. By contrast, appeal to the state of nature offers a means of genuine explanation—*how-possibly?* explanatio—which provides for philosophical understanding.

If Craig's account shows that the fundamental human need to form a collective strategy for the pursuit of truth is a feature of any epistemic practice, then the implications which may be drawn from the basic features of that strategy are necessary[16] features of epistemic practice. Next it will be suggested that some of these necessary features take on a distinctly political character as soon as we move away from the minimally social state of nature to the fully social setting in which epistemic practices are actually conducted.

IV

The social manifestation of the norm of credibility. The key requirements of the good informant (competence, trustworthiness, and indicator-properties) demonstrate that the notion of the good informant has external and internal aspects. There is the (external) requirement that the good informant tells one truly whether *p*, and there is the (internal) requirement that the inquirer is able to identify the informant as a good one. Competence and trustworthiness together supply the former; indicator-properties supply the latter.

It will be convenient to introduce two shorthand terms. Let it be that if someone is both competent and trustworthy, then she has *rational authority*. And let it be that someone who possesses indicator-properties has *credibility*. (Someone who has both rational authority and credibility is a good informant.) The fact that the concept of the good informant has this structure immediately raises the possibility of two sorts of mismatch between rational authority and credibility. There is the possibility of someone's being rationally authoritative without being recognized as such; and there is the possibility of someone's seeming to be rationally authoritative when she is not. The latter possibility will be called *mere* credibility.

Either kind of mismatch may come about as a result of the fact that credibility is only defeasibly correlated with rational authority: its presence does not guarantee rational authority; its absence does not guarantee lack of it. Even in the state of nature there will be occasions when someone who has rational authority with respect to a question lacks credibility nonetheless. The person who has a track-record of failing to tell between the poisonous and the non-poisonous red berries, but who recently learned the secret of distinguishing them, will not gain credibility with respect to red-berry-edibility until he has established a reformed track-record. If, on the other hand, someone is falsely reputed to have a good track-record of distinguishing the berries, then she has *mere* credibility regarding red-berry-edibility. More sinisterly, someone might be *merely* credible as a result of deliberately feigning the indicator-properties—perhaps she spread the false rumour of her red-berry expertise. In the social world (as in the state of nature) knowledge provides a means to gaining certain things one might need or want. For instance, it serves entry into many jobs, especially lucrative or prestigious ones. If knowledge is in this sense a power, then so is the mere appearance of knowledge. So there is a direct motivation (depending upon how grave the risk of being found out) for imposture: for someone's pretending to know when he doesn't.[17]

These ways in which rational authority and credibility can come apart illustrate that any practice of good-informing is both innocently fallible and vulnerable to deliberate individual corruption. Neither of these will be the chief concern here, however.

The chief concern will be with a tendency for corruption that is equally inherent in epistemic practice, but which is political and structural in character. It need not grow from any deliberate manipulation of the norms governing the practice.

To bring out the political dimension, a distinction must first be made between indicator-properties as they have so far been discussed, which are such that they do in fact reliably indicate rational authority; and what we might call *working-indicator-properties*, which are those properties actually used in a given practice to indicate rational authority, and which may or may not be so reliable. The norm of credibility governs who is picked out as a good informant: it tells us to attribute rational authority to all and only those potential informants who possess relevant indicator-properties. When that norm is socially manifested in a particular historical and cultural setting, it will guide practice so that rational authority is attributed to all and only those who possess the relevant working-indicator-properties. Further, a state-of-nature story need only mention indicator-properties that signal rational authority with respect to particular questions—whether p, whether q. . . . But in the social context our practice will include attributions of rational authority which are more general, and even completely non-specific in scope. (One example of a wholly non-specific credibility might be that which once accrued to people of noble birth—a credibility institutionalized in a form of government in which the authority of members of the Second House derives solely from their heredity.)

Craig is surely right to characterize the basic epistemic practice in the state of nature in terms of a certain co-operative ethic where, in treating each other as (potential) good informants, inquirers treat each other as ends-in-themselves rather than as mere means from which to acquire truths. But the co-operative ethic is likely to be compromised when epistemic practice is transplanted from the state of nature to the socially and politically complex setting in which we actually live. Only the minimal co-operative ethic is required to get epistemic practice off the ground; thereafter there is plenty of room for parasitic practices of misinformation, imposture, and the political kind of epistemic dysfunctionality whose possibility and structure I shall attempt to outline.

Recall the two components of rational authority—competence and trustworthiness—of which the good informant must bear the marks (sc. the working-indicator-properties sufficient for credibility). What relation might we expect these to bear to social power and powerlessness? Access to institutions of education is manifestly influenced by various dimensions of social power—nowadays principally class, and (through its connection with class) race. Crudely, you have to be rich to go to what tend to be considered the best schools; and the most over-stretched state schools tend to be in the most socially deprived areas. Does this system lead to corruption in the operation of the norm of credibility? The answer will depend on how far there is a phenomenon of credibility-overspill such that the property of having had a private education is taken to indicate more competence and/or more trustworthiness than is in fact due; and conversely for those who lack the property.

In a significant range of contexts, the position of powerlessness may place one under general suspicion of being motivated to deceive, in a way which the position of powerfulness does not. Further, powerlessness diminishes one's ability to protest one's trustworthiness—especially if it would be at the expense of the reputation of someone more powerful. In the state of nature we only have to entertain socio-politically neutral indicator-properties such as "looking in the right direction". But when considering epistemic practice in the social context, where perceptual knowledge is only one of the many kinds of information we trade in, there are many other working-indicator-properties of both competence and trustworthiness that will stand in need of ongoing critical assessment.

Things may be especially complicated if the knowledge that we seek is about contested social phenomena. If someone in a relevantly powerless position is asked for information on something apparently simple, such as "what happened at the annual general meeting?", it may be that if she attempts to convey her perception of the interactions that went on in the meeting, she will find she lacks what Lorraine Code has suggestively named the "rhetorical space" that her answer requires. In particular, if she needs to give an answer whose intelligibility depends on her interlocutor's appreciating a certain interpretive perspective on such things, she may find that her credibility goes missing when that perspective is not forthcoming. Code quotes from Patricia Williams' account of attempting to make a complaint about a racist incident:

> [Williams] observes: "I could not but wonder . . . what it would take to make my experience verifiable. The testimony of an independent white bystander?" And she comments on "how the blind application of principles of neutrality . . . acted either to make me look crazy or to make the reader participate in old habits of cultural bias".[18]

The foregoing reflections might lead one to suspect that—as a countervailing force against the fundamental imperative to trade co-operatively in truths—there is likely to be some social pressure in the direction of the norm of credibility's favouring the powerful in its control over who is picked out as credible, and thus in who is picked out as a good informant. There is likely (at least in societies recognizably like ours) to be some social pressure on the norm of credibility to imitate the structures of social power. Where that imitation brings about a mismatch between rational authority and credibility—so that the powerful tend to be given *mere* credibility and/or the powerless tend to be wrongly denied credibility—we should acknowledge that there is a phenomenon of *epistemic injustice*.

That there is likely to be a corrupting sort of social pressure on the norm of credibility remains an empirical conjecture. Broadly speaking, it is a historical question; so perhaps it is to history we should look in support of the claim. Steven Shapin's account of the culture of gentlemanly veracity in seventeenth-century England provides a compelling historical illustration. In Shapin's study we see the requirements of the good informant made socially manifest in the person of the seventeenth-century gentleman. Shapin tells us that the gentleman was, quite literally, accorded privileged *competence*, even in matters of perception:

> The first consideration implicated in the culture of gentlemanly veracity was rarely given explicit treatment in the practical ethical literature of early modern Europe. Nevertheless, it was an absolutely fundamental feature of the practical assessment of testimony, and one which might assist in

discriminating the worth of testimony from gentle and nongentle sources. This was the ascription to gentlemen of *perceptual competence*.[19]

Trustworthiness, too, is made socially concrete in the figure of the gentleman. He enjoyed the economic and social independence brought by social advantage, and this elevated social position meant he was generally free from the sorts of beholdenness that might be thought to, and might actually, provide motivations for deceiving others. Further, the question of non-deception was sured up by a code of gentlemanly honour. Not only did his social privilege mean he was seen to have little to gain from deception; it meant he stood to lose a great deal if he were seen to flout the code—a noble track-record was worth protecting.

It seems, then, that there was a time in England when being a gentleman was a key working-indicator-property of rational authority, not with respect to any particular question or range of questions, but generally. If being a gentleman was a positive indicator of rational authority; being nongentle and/or female was a negative indicator. Seventeenth-century women's economic and social dependence meant that their supposed lack of rational authority—like that of nongentle men—went for the most part without saying:

> There were powerful institutions of exclusion that affected the cultural and political role of women, as well as of nongentle men. But precisely because those institutional systems were so effective, and because the justifications overwhelmingly picked out dependence as a disqualifying circumstance, the *literate culture* of early modern England was not nearly so significantly marked by identifications of gender disabilities as it was by commentary on "ignobility," "servility," and "baseness".[20]

Not that Elizabethan versifiers were exactly silent on the subject:

> A woman's face is full of wiles,
> Her tears are like the crocadill . . .
> Her tongue still chats of this and that,
> Than aspen leaf it wags more fast;
> And as she talks she knows not what,
> There issues many a truthless blast.[21]

That was then; the pressures on the norm of credibility today are naturally quite different from those of the seventeenth-century. But the suggestion that there is likely to be some such pressure is general. In the present day, consider the effect of the relations of power surrounding (and partially constituting) gender which can lead to the withholding of credibility from, say, a woman putting her views at a professional meeting; or those surrounding class and race that may undermine the credibility of, say, a black person being questioned by the police. As Code says:

> [T]he rhetorical spaces that a society legitimates generate presumptions of credibility and trust that attach differentially according to how speakers and interpreters are positioned within them.[22]

V

Assessing epistemic practice: veritism and epistemic justice. I purport to have shown, adapting Craig's framework, that the norm of credibility is a fundamental norm of any epistemic practice. In the minimal practice in the state of nature, there is an overwhelming practical imperative to operate with working-indicator-properties that do reliably indicate rational authority, since there is an overwhelming imperative to trade in truths and not falsehoods. But once the practice is up and running, and once we transpose our story to the social world, other forces come into play to place pressure in the opposite direction. New forms of competition and self-interest mean that individuals and institutions have something to gain from seeming rationally authoritative when they are not, and from others' seeming not rationally authoritative when they are. But, more importantly, there is likely to be pressure on the norm of credibility itself to imitate structures of social power in such a way that the working-indicator-properties will tend to pick out the powerful and not the powerless. This will amount to an epistemic injustice to the extent that it also brings about a mismatch between credibility and rational authority. Where this sort of injustice has developed, the mechanism which enables us to discriminate good informants has deteriorated into a mechanism of (unfair) *epistemic discrimination.*

A perfect correlation between rational authority and credibility would be the mark not only of an epistemic practice successfully geared to truth, but also of a practice which is epistemically just. It is not surprising that this is so, for epistemic injustice will typically be obstructive to the achievement of truth. This casts a new and politicized light on what Alvin Goldman calls the "veritistic" assessment of practices (assessment for truth).[23]

Goldman has laudably drawn attention to the social practices whereby information is produced and disseminated. The project of theorizing about such practices he calls a project of "social epistemology". But what the foregoing considerations show is that social identity and relations of power are likely to be highly relevant to how "verific" a given practice is. For every potential informant from whom a discriminatory set of indicator-properties (wrongly and wrongfully) withholds credibility, there are truths which could have and should have been transmitted, but were not. In such a case, the potential informant is epistemically discriminated against, and the injustice involves a veritistic failure.

It is wholly consonant with the good-informant account to think of epistemic practices as primarily assessable veritistically. The present point is that the veritist cannot ignore all matters political, because epistemic discrimination will be an important factor in how verific a given practice may be. Even leaving the aim of epistemic justice *qua* justice aside, if our only aim were truth, then typically a tendency towards epistemic discrimination should still be militated against.

To give a proper account of epistemic discrimination is too big a task for the present paper. But a brief comparison with discrimination in the arena of employment may be instructive. Sometimes a person's ethnicity, gender, class, religion, sexual orientation etc. will be a relevant factor in how well she or he is likely to do a job. It will be a legitimate consideration. Possible examples are a person's gender in rape crisis counselling, or the ethnicity of a social worker in an ethnically specific community.

Similarly, categories of social identity will sometimes be legitimately taken into account in determining whether someone is credible in a given case. That is, it will sometimes be legitimate for categories of social identity to be positive or negative working-indicator-properties. The property of being a practising Catholic may be a positive indicator-property for rational authority as to questions of Catholic teaching; or, the property of being poor may be a negative indicator-property for rational authority as to which private schools are considered the more academic. Sometimes we might seek knowledge of the nature of a certain kind of social experience itself (of being a single parent, of being super-rich), in which case a first resort must be to find someone who has had that experience. (This is the social analogue of the standard perceptual inquiry in the state of nature: ask someone who was there.)

When it comes to assessing an epistemic practice for discrimination, we must make judgements of relevance, just as we must in the employment context. If someone is deemed unsuitable for a job, or not credible with respect to some question, on the basis of *mere* social identity (i.e. without his identity having a relevant bearing on whether he would do the job well, or give true information as to whether p) then there is unfair discrimination.

The realization that any epistemic practice is characterized by a reliance on working-indicator-properties provides for two new ways of assessing epistemic practice. Firstly, it explains why veritistic assessment must be sensitive to the anti-verific effects which relations of power can have, via their possible influence upon the norm of credibility. Secondly, it introduces a political standard via the possibility of a distinctively epistemic variety of injustice, whereby some people are effectively denied and/or others given credibility owing to their mere social identity. When people suffer this sort of injustice, they are prevented from exercising their ability to participate in epistemic practice. They are wrongly disbarred from being valued *qua* knowers, and from reaping the practical advantages which that can bring. Epistemology will not be truly socialized until it has been appropriately politicized.

VI

Credibility at the core of what it is to "know". I said at the outset that the reductivist position stands or falls with the question whether we can formulate a conception of rational authority which is independent of social power. The state-of-nature story does this: rational authority is just competence plus trustworthiness. Thus the good-informant approach to explicating the concept of knowledge demonstrates the falsity of the reductivist conception of reason as mere social power by another name. Indeed, insofar as the reductivist's ambitions may be to politicize epistemology, she should appreciate that the conceptual distinction between rational authority and credibility is positively confirmed whenever we bring a political perspective to bear. The possibility of identifying a given set of working-indicator-properties as discriminatory depends on being able to say that they manifest the norm of credibility so as to attribute rational authority where it should not, and/or withhold it where it should not. If rational authority were the same as the power to appear rationally authoritative, then there could be no genuine notion of discrimination, and the political perspective in epistemology would have been lost before it was won.

We are now in a position to see a sense in which the relation between *knowledge* and social power runs deep. Recall the position of women and nongentle men in seventeenth-century England. It seems they have no chance of credibility, and *pro tanto* they cannot qualify as good informants. We might say that their status as knowers is undermined by the relation which their social identities bear to the working-indicator-properties. Less-than- good informants can only be knowers parasitically, in virtue of the concept's having undergone a process which Craig calls "objectivisation", whereby it acquires other uses owing to our having come to regard that which the concept picks out—knowledge—as independent of the practical context in which it arose.[24] Knowers are fundamentally participants in the spread of knowledge; less-than-good informants cannot play that core role.

The point must be handled with care. Of course women and nongentle men had knowledge; they had plenty. Lack of social power can never deprive one of *that* (sympathizers with reductivism, please note). Moreover, it would doubtless have been no secret that they could give much better information on many matters than some of the gentlemen they had to kow-tow to. The good-informant account is not at all in conflict with any of this; it has our ordinary concept of knowledge as its object, and does not (could not possibly) change its extension. However, the very fact that it is indeed our ordinary concept whose core is explicated in terms of a practice of good-informing means that the political aspects of such a practice demand the attention of the epistemologist. The account shows that when structures of power influence working-indicator-properties so that some people are systematically denied credibility because of their mere social identity, then epistemic practice inflicts a kind of injustice which it is *intrinsically* prone to—for the norm from which the discrimination is likely to arise is a necessary one. But now the point is that when people are unjustly denied credibility, they are thereby unjustly denied the opportunity to participate in the spread of knowledge—the "original" practice from which the concept of knowledge arises. This means that the epistemic injustice to which they are subject is not only a matter of their credibility being undermined, but also their status as knowers.

Because the dependence on credibility is established at the core of the concept of knowledge, questions of social power are shown to be profoundly relevant in epistemology. Equally, however—and precisely because the connection between knowledge and social power is established so far down—it cannot disturb our practice at ground level, which has us readily and rightly attribute knowledge (when we are in a position to do so) to those whose lack of credibility disqualifies them from acting as good informants.

VII

Conclusion. The foregoing considerations show, firstly, that the traditionalist is wrong to think of all things socio-political as mere external interferences in epistemic practice, and therefore wrong to think of them as irrelevant to epistemology. Secondly, they show that the reductivist is equally wrong: the very possibility of bringing a political perspective to bear on epistemic practice presupposes the distinction between rational authority and the power merely to seem rationally authoritative. Thirdly, they suggest that knowledge is connected at core—only at core—with structures of social power, through its necessary dependence on the norm of credibility. The ever-present risk that the norm of credibility will be socially manifested in a discriminatory manner is not a political accident to be noted somewhere on the periphery of the epistemology of testimony. It amounts to a politicization of epistemology more generally, for the perpetual risk of epistemic injustice arises from the role which, at core, the concept of knowledge plays in our lives.[25]

Birkbeck College
Malet Street
London WC1E 7HX
m.fricker@philosophy. bbk.ac. uk

Notes

1 *A Social History of Truth—Civility and Science in Seventeenth-Century England* (Chicago/London: University of Chicago Press, 1994) p. xxv. I am grateful to John Dupré for suggesting Shapin's book to me.

2 Edward Craig, *Knowledge and the State of Nature—An Essay In Conceptual Synthesis* (Oxford: Clarendon Press, 1990). The politicizing purpose for which I adapt Craig's framework is not Craig's.

3 Bernard Williams takes a similar approach in chapter 2 of *Descartes: The Project of Pure Enquiry* (London: Penguin, 1978); see especially pp. 37–41. And in *The Community of Knowledge* (Aberdeen: Aberdeen University Press, 1986)

Michael Welbourne places the "commoning" of information at the centre of an account of knowledge.

4   Craig, op. cit. p. 2.

5   op. cit. p. 36. The ethical point is connected with the distinction between a "source of information" and an "informant"; op. cit. chapter V.

6   This range of possible worlds is slightly narrower than that set by Nozick, because for those nearby possible worlds which the inquirer already knows are not the actual world, the fact that the potential informant would "track" p in them is irrelevant; op. cit. pp. 20–23.

7   op. cit. p. 85

8   op. cit. p. 85, and *passim*.

9   op. cit. p. 18–19, and *passim*.

10   Some of Craig's formulations encourage me in this. For instance: "It is not just that we are looking for an informant who *will tell* us the truth about p; we also have to be able to pick him out, distinguish him from others to whom we would be less well advised to listen" (op. cit. p. 18; italics added). If we recognize that someone "will tell us the truth", then we recognize not only that he has a true belief, but also that he can be trusted to impart it to us.

11   op. cit. p. 82.

12   op. cit. p. 88.

13   This point was made by Bernard Williams in a lecture, "Truth and Truthfulness", delivered to The London Consortium, Birkbeck College, London, May 1997.

14   op. cit. p. 83.

15   Ludwig Wittgenstein, *On Certainty* §141.

16   Or almost necessary: "[State-of-nature] explanations work by identifying certain human needs and arguing that the practices are a necessary (*or at the least a highly appropriate*) response to them . . ." (op. cit. p. 89; italics added). In addition, we should perhaps make explicit the proviso that the epistemic practices under consideration are those that would be recognizably human ones.

17   I thank Adam Morton for this point, made when I presented Ian earlier version of this paper at the Departmental Seminar at the University of Bristol. I am indebted to all those present on that occasion for helpful discussion.

18   Lorraine Code, *Rhetorical Spaces—essays on gendered locations* (London/ NY: Routledge, 1995) p. 69. The quotation is from "Incredulity, Experientialism, and the Politics of Knowledge", whose themes—and especially the discussion of how stereotyping affects credibility—are highly relevant to those discussed here.

19   Shapin op. cit. p. 75; original italics.

20   op. cit. p. 88.

21   Humfrey Gifford, in Norman Ault ed. *Elizabethan Lyrics*, (NY: Capricorn Books, 1960); quoted in Shapin, op. cit. p. 89.

22   Code, op. cit. p. 60.

23   See, for example, Alvin Goldman, *Epistemology and Cognition* (Cambridge MA/London: Harvard University Press, 1986); and Alvin Goldman and James C. Cox "Accuracy in Journalism: An Economic Approach" in Schmitt, Frederick F. ed. *Socializing Epistemology—The Social Dimensions of Knowledge* (Maryland/London: Rowman & Littlefield Publishers, Inc., 1994) pp. 189–215; also Goldman, *Knowledge In A Social World* (Oxford: Oxford University Press, forthcoming).

24   op. cit. pp. 88–97.

25   I am grateful to Jennifer Hornsby for immensely helpful comments on an earlier draft.

II

TRUST IN TESTIMONY AND EXPERTS

4

Testimony

Acquiring Knowledge from Others

Jennifer Lackey

Virtually everything we know depends in some way or other on the testimony of others—what we eat, how things work, where we go, even who we are. We do not, after all, perceive firsthand the preparation of the ingredients in many of our meals, or the construction of the devices we use to get around the world, or the layout of our planet, or our own births and familial histories. These are all things we are told. Indeed, subtracting from our lives the information that we possess via testimony leaves them barely recognizable. Scientific discoveries, battles won and lost, geographical developments, customs and traditions of distant lands—all of these facts would be completely lost to us. It is, therefore, no surprise that the importance of testimony, both epistemological and practical, is nearly universally accepted.

Less consensus, however, is found when questions about the nature and extent of our dependence on the word of others arise. Is our justified reliance on testimony fundamentally basic, for instance, or is it ultimately reducible to perception, memory, and reason? Is trust, or some related interpersonal feature of our social interaction with one another, essential to the acquisition of beliefs that are testimonially justified? Is testimonial knowledge necessarily acquired through transmission from speaker to hearer? Can testimony generate epistemic features in its own right? These are the questions that will be taken up in this essay and, as will become clear, their answers have far-reaching consequences for how we understand our place in the social world.

1. TESTIMONY AND TESTIMONY-BASED BELIEF

The central focus in the epistemology of testimony is not on the nature of testimony itself, but instead on how justified belief or knowledge is acquired on the basis of what other people tell us. Because of this, those interested in the epistemology of testimony often embrace a very broad notion of what it is to testify, one that leaves the distinction between reliable and unreliable (or otherwise epistemically good and bad) testimony for epistemology to delineate.[1] So, for instance, Elizabeth Fricker holds that the domain of testimony that is of epistemological interest is that of "tellings generally" with "no restrictions either on subject matter, or on the speaker's epistemic relation to it."[2] Similarly, Robert Audi claims that in accounting for testimonial knowledge and justification, we must understand testimony as "people's telling us things."[3] And Ernest Sosa embraces "a broad sense of testimony that counts posthumous publications as examples . . . [and] requires only that it be a statement of someone's thoughts or beliefs, which they might direct to the world at large and to no one in particular."[4]

Despite the virtues of these broad conceptions of what it is to testify, however, there is reason to think that, as stated, they are too broad. In particular, there is a difference between entirely *noninformational expressions of thought* and *testimony.* For instance, suppose that you and I are walking down the street and I say, "Ah, it is indeed a lovely day." Suppose further that such a statement, though it expresses my thought that it is indeed a lovely day, is neither offered nor taken as conveying information; it is simply a conversational filler, comparable to a sigh of contentedness.[5] Or suppose that as my young daughter glides across the ice on her new skates for the first time, I shout, "You can do it!" While my assertion here is surely an expression of my thought that Catherine has the capacity to ice skate, its function in this context is merely to encourage her to accomplish a difficult task, similar to clapping or cheering. There is no intention on my part to convey information, nor is Catherine apt to acquire information, from my words of encouragement. In both cases, it is doubtful that these statements should qualify as testimony, despite the fact that they are "tellings" or expressions of thought. Otherwise put, the concept of testimony is intimately connected with the notion of conveying information, and thus those statements that function as *mere* conversational fillers and cheers should fail to qualify as instances of testimony. A more precise account of the nature of testimony, then, should be formulated as a speaker's making an act of communication—which includes statements, nods, pointing, and so on—that is intended to convey the information that *p* or is taken as conveying the information that *p*.[6]

Moreover, clearly not everything we learn from the testimony of others qualifies as *testimonially based.* For instance, suppose that I say that ten people have spoken in this room today and you, having counted the previous nine, come to know that ten people have spoken in this room today.[7] Here, my statement may certainly be causally relevant with respect to your forming this belief, but your knowledge is based on your having heard and counted the speakers in the room today, thereby rendering it perceptual in nature. Or suppose that I sing "I have a soprano voice" in a soprano voice and you come to know this entirely on the basis of hearing *causally based vs based on content?*

my soprano voice.[8] Again, the resulting knowledge is perceptual in nature
since it is based on your hearing my soprano voice rather than on what I
testified to. What is of import for distinctively testimonial justification or
knowledge is that a hearer form a given belief *on the basis of the content
of a speaker's testimony*. This precludes cases such as those above—where
a belief is formed entirely on the basis of features *about* the speaker's
testimony—from qualifying as instances of *testimonial* justification or
knowledge.

how does this clear up the distinction

There are also intermediate cases in which a hearer has relevant background information and uses it to derive knowledge from the statement
of a speaker. For example, suppose that you know from past experience
that I report that there is no coffee in the carafe only when there is some.
Now when I report to you that there is no coffee in the carafe, you may
supplement my testimony with your background information and hence
derive knowledge that there is coffee in the carafe. Because the epistemic
status of beliefs formed in these types of cases relies so heavily on memory
and inference, the resulting justification and knowledge are only partially
testimonially based. Hence, such beliefs typically fall outside the scope of
theories purporting to capture only those beliefs that are entirely based
on testimony.

2. NONREDUCTIONISM AND REDUCTIONISM

One of the central questions in the epistemology of testimony is how,
exactly, hearers acquire justified beliefs from the testimony of speakers.
Answers to this question have traditionally fallen into one of two camps:
nonreductionism or *reductionism*. According to nonreductionists—whose
historical roots are typically traced to the work of Thomas Reid—testimony
is a *basic* source of justification, on an epistemic par with sense perception,
memory, inference, and the like. Given this, nonreductionists maintain
that, so long as there are no relevant undefeated defeaters, hearers can be
justified in accepting what they are told *merely* on the basis of the testimony of speakers.[9] So, for instance, Tyler Burge writes that "[a] person is
entitled to accept as true something that is presented as true and that is
intelligible to him, *unless there are stronger reasons not to do so*." Similarly,
Matthew Weiner argues that "[w]e are justified in accepting anything that
we are told unless there is positive evidence against doing so." And Robert
Audi claims that "gaining testimonially grounded knowledge normally
requires *only having no reason for doubt about the credibility of the attester*."
In all of these passages, we find endorsements of nonreductionism.[10]

refer to notebook

There are two central kinds of defeaters that are typically taken to be
relevant to the nonreductionist's view. First, there are what we might call
psychological defeaters. A psychological defeater is a doubt or belief that is
had by S, and indicates that S's belief that *p* is either false or unreliably

formed or sustained. Defeaters in this sense function by virtue of being *had* by S, regardless of their truth-value or epistemic status.[11] Second, there are what we might call *normative defeaters*. A normative defeater is a doubt or belief that S ought to have, and indicates that S's belief that *p* is either false or unreliably formed or sustained. Defeaters in this sense function by virtue of being doubts or beliefs that S *should have* (whether or not S does have them) given the presence of certain available evidence.[12] The underlying thought here is that certain kinds of doubts and beliefs contribute epistemically unacceptable *irrationality* to doxastic systems and, accordingly, justification can be defeated or undermined by their presence.

Moreover, a defeater may itself be either defeated or undefeated. Suppose, for instance, that Harold believes that there is a bobcat in his backyard because he saw it there this morning, but Rosemary tells him, and he thereby comes to believe, that the animal is instead a lynx. Now, the justification Harold had for believing that there was a bobcat in his backyard has been defeated by the belief he acquires on the basis of Rosemary's testimony. But since psychological defeaters can themselves be beliefs, they, too, are candidates for defeat. For instance, suppose that Harold consults a North American wildlife book and discovers that the white tip of the animal's tail confirms that it was indeed a bobcat, thereby providing him with a *defeater-defeater* for his original belief that there was a bobcat in his backyard. And, as should be suspected, defeater-defeaters can also be defeated by further doubts and beliefs, which, in turn, can be defeated by further doubts and beliefs, and so on. Similar considerations involving reasons, rather than doubts and beliefs, apply in the case of normative defeaters. When one has a defeater for one's belief that *p* that is not itself defeated, one has what is called an *undefeated defeater* for one's belief that *p*. It is the presence of undefeated defeaters, not merely of defeaters, that is incompatible with testimonial justification.

In contrast to nonreductionism, reductionists—whose historical roots are standardly traced to the work of David Hume—maintain that, in addition to the absence of undefeated defeaters, hearers must also possess *nontestimonally based positive reasons* in order to be justified in accepting the testimony of speakers. These reasons are typically the result of induction: for instance, hearers observe a general conformity between reports and the corresponding facts and, with the assistance of memory and reason, inductively infer that certain speakers, contexts, or types of reports are reliable sources of information. In this way, the justification of testimony is *reduced* to the justification for sense perception, memory, and inductive inference.[13]

There are two different versions of reductionism. According to *global reductionism*, the justification of *testimony as a source of belief* reduces to the justification of sense perception, memory, and inductive inference. Thus, in order to be justified in accepting the testimony of speakers, hearers must possess nontestimonally based positive reasons for believing *offer a quick fix learning about field beyond our capacities, but it becomes obvious (is that a problem?)*

that *testimony is generally reliable.* According to local reductionism, which is the more widely accepted of the two versions, the justification of *each instance of testimony* reduces to the justification of instances of sense perception, memory, and inductive inference. So, in order to be justified in accepting the testimony of speakers, hearers must have nontestimonially based positive reasons for accepting *the particular report in question.* For instance, Paul Faulkner writes:

> Given that a speaker's intentions in communicating need not be informative and given the relevance of these intentions to the acquisition of testimonial knowledge . . . [i]t is doxastically irresponsible to accept testimony without *some background belief in the testimony's credibility or truth.* In the case of perception and memory, rational acceptance requires only the absence of defeating background beliefs. In the case of testimony, rational acceptance requires the presence of supporting background beliefs.
>
> This demand of responsibility may be expressed as a criterion of justification. *An audience is justified in forming a testimonial belief if and only if he is justified in accepting the speaker's testimony.*[14]

Similarly, Elizabeth Fricker maintains, "In claiming that a hearer is required to assess a speaker for trustworthiness, I [mean] . . . that the hearer should be discriminating in her attitude to the speaker, in that she should be continually evaluating him for trustworthiness throughout their exchange, in the light of the evidence, or cues, available to her. This will be partly a matter of her being disposed to deploy background knowledge which is relevant, partly a matter of her monitoring the speaker for any tell-tale signs revealing likely untrustworthiness."[15]

Both nonreductionism and reductionism have been subject to various objections, objections that opponents use to motivate their own preferred views. The central problem raised against nonreductionism is that it is said to sanction gullibility, epistemic irrationality, and intellectual irresponsibility.[16] For given that, on such a view, hearers can acquire testimonially justified beliefs in the complete absence of any relevant positive reasons, randomly selected speakers, arbitrarily chosen postings on the Internet, and unidentified telemarketers can be trusted, so long as there is no negative evidence against such sources. Yet surely, the opponent of nonreductionism urges, accepting testimony in these kinds of cases is a paradigm of gullibility, epistemic irrationality, and irresponsibility.

Against reductionism, it is frequently argued that young children clearly acquire a great deal of knowledge from their parents and teachers and yet it is said to be doubtful that they possess—or even could possess— nontestimonially based positive reasons for accepting much of what they are told.[17] For instance, an eighteen-month-old baby may come to know that the stove is hot from the testimony of her mother, but it is unclear whether she has the cognitive sophistication to have reasons for believing her mother to be a reliable source of information, let alone for believing that testimony is generally reliable. Given this, reductionists—of both the global and the local stripes—may be hard pressed to explain how such young subjects could acquire all of the testimonial knowledge they at least seem to possess.

Objections are also raised that are specific to each kind of reductionism. Against the global version, two main problems arise. The first is that in order to have nontestimonially based positive reasons that testimony is generally reliable, one would have to be exposed not only to a wide-ranging sample of reports but also to a wide-ranging sample of the corresponding facts. But both are said to be problematic. With respect to the reports, most of us have been exposed only to a very limited range of reports from speakers in our native language in a handful of communities in our native country. This limited sample of reports provides only a fraction of what would be required to legitimately conclude that testimony is *generally* reliable. With respect to the corresponding facts, a similar problem arises: the observational base of ordinary epistemic agents is simply far too small to allow the requisite induction about the reliability of testimony. As C. A. J. Coady says:

> it seems absurd to suggest that, individually, we have done anything like the amount of field-work that [reductionism] requires. . . . [M]any of us have never seen a baby born, nor have most of us examined the circulation of the blood nor the actual geography of the world nor any fair sample of the laws of the land, nor have we made the observations that lie behind our knowledge that the lights in the sky are heavenly bodies immensely distant nor a vast number of other observations that [reductionism] would seem to require.[18]

Moreover, with many reports, such as those involving complex scientific, economic, or mathematical theories, most of us simply lack the conceptual machinery needed to properly check the reports against the facts. Global reductionism, then, is said to ultimately lead to skepticism about testimonial knowledge, at least for most epistemic agents.

A second objection raised against global reductionism is that it is questionable whether there even is an epistemically significant *fact of the matter* regarding the general reliability of testimony. To see this, consider, for instance, the following epistemically heterogeneous list of types of reports, all of which are subsumed under "testimony in general": reports about the time of day, what one had for breakfast, the achievements of one's children, whether one's loved one looks attractive in a certain outfit, the character of one's political opponents, one's age and weight, one's criminal record, and so on. Some of these types of reports may be generally highly reliable (e.g., about the time of day and what one had for breakfast), generally highly unreliable (e.g., about the achievements of one's children, the looks of one's loved ones, and the character of one's political opponents), and generally very epistemically mixed, depending on the speaker (e.g., about one's age, weight, and criminal record). Because of this epistemic heterogeneity, it is doubtful not only whether "testimony" picks out an epistemically interesting or unified *kind* but also whether it even makes sense to talk about testimony being a *generally reliable source.* As Elizabeth Fricker says, "looking for generalisations about the reliability or otherwise of testimony . . . as a homogenous whole, will not be an enlightening project. Illuminating generalisations, if there are any, will be about particular types of testimony, differentiated according to subject matter, or type of speaker, or both. . . . [W]hen it comes to the probability of accuracy of speakers' assertions, and what sorts of factors warrant a hearer in trusting a speaker, *testimony is not a unitary category*."[19]

Against the local version of reductionism, it is argued that most ordinary cognitive agents do not seem to have enough information to possess relevant positive reasons in all the cases where testimonial knowledge appears present. For instance, it is argued that most cognitive agents frequently acquire testimonial knowledge from speakers about whom they know very little.[20] For instance, on arriving in Chicago for the first time, I may receive accurate directions to Navy Pier from the first passerby I see. Most agree that such a transaction can result in my acquiring testimonial knowledge of Navy Pier's whereabouts, despite the fact that my positive reasons for accepting the directions in question—if indeed I possess any—are scanty at best.

The direction some recent work on testimony has taken is to avoid the problems afflicting nonreductionism and reductionism by developing qualified or hybrid versions of either of these views.[21] For instance, in an effort to avoid the charges of gullibility and epistemic irresponsibility, some nonreductionists emphasize that hearers must be "epistemically entitled" to rely on the testimony of speakers or that they need to "monitor" incoming reports, even though such requirements do not quite amount to the full-blown need for nontestimonially based positive reasons embraced by reductionists.[22] And some reductionists, trying to account for the testimonial knowledge of both young children and those hearers who possess very little information about their relevant speakers, argue that positive reasons are not needed during either the "developmental phase" of a person's life—which is when one is acquiring concepts and learning the language, relying in large part on one's parents and teachers to guide the formation of one's belief system; or when hearers are confronted with "mundane testimony": testimony about, for instance, a speaker's name, what she had for breakfast, the time of day, and so on.[23] On this view of reductionism, then, while positive reasons remain a condition of testimonial justification, such a requirement applies only to hearers in the "mature phase" of life who are encountering "nonmundane testimony." Such qualified or hybrid views of both nonreductionism and reductionism often encounter either variations of the very same problems that led to their development, or altogether new objections.[24]

Arguably, a more promising strategy for solving the problems afflicting nonreductionism and reductionism should, first, include a necessary condition requiring nontestimonially grounded positive reasons for testimonial justification. This avoids the charges of gullibility, epistemic irrationality, and intellectual irresponsibility facing the nonreductionist's view. Second, the demands of such a condition should be weakened so that merely some positive reasons, even about the type of speaker, or the kind of report, or the sort of context of utterance, are required. This avoids the objections facing the reductionist's position that young children cannot satisfy such a requirement and that beliefs formed on the basis of the testimony of those about whom we know very little cannot be justified. Third, additional conditions should be added for a complete account of testimonial justification, such as the need for the reliability of the speaker's statement. This frees the positive reasons requirement from shouldering all of the justificatory burden for testimonial beliefs, thereby enabling the weakening of its content discussed above.[25]

3. THE INTERPERSONAL VIEW OF TESTIMONY

An alternative family of views has been growing in popularity in recent work in the epistemology of testimony, one that provides a radically different answer to the question of how testimonial beliefs are justified. Though there are some points of disagreement among some of the members of this family, they are united in their commitment to at least three central theses. First, and perhaps most important, the *interpersonal relationship* between the two parties in a testimonial exchange should be a central focus of the epistemology of testimony. Second, and closely related, certain features of this interpersonal relationship—such as the speaker *offering her assurance* to the hearer that her testimony is true, or the speaker *inviting the hearer to trust* her—are (at least sometimes) actually *responsible for conferring epistemic value* on the testimonial beliefs acquired. Third, the epistemic justification provided by these features of a testimonial exchange is *nonevidential* in nature. For ease of discussion, I shall call the general conception of testimony characterized by these theses the *interpersonal view of testimony* (IVT).[26]

One of the central motivations for the IVT is a perceived failure of existing views of testimony—particularly those that regard a speaker's testimony that p as merely *evidence* for a hearer to believe that p—to adequately account for the import of the interpersonal relationship between the speaker and the hearer in a testimonial exchange. For instance, in discussing such evidential views of testimonial justification, Edward Hinchman says, "[w]hen you have evidence of a speaker's reliability you don't need to trust her: you can treat her speech act as a mere assertion and believe what she says on the basis of the evidence you have of its truth. You can ignore the fact that she's addressing you, inviting you. You can *treat her as a truth-gauge*."[27] In a similar spirit, Richard Moran maintains that "if we are inclined to believe what the speaker says, but then learn that he is *not*, in fact, presenting his utterance as an assertion whose truth he stands behind, then what *remains are just words*, not a reason to believe anything . . . the utterance as [a] phenomenon, loses the epistemic import we thought it had."[28] According to proponents of the IVT, then, a significant aspect of true communication is missing when a speaker is treated as a mere truth gauge, offering nothing more than words.

In contrast, proponents of the IVT argue that speakers should be regarded as agents who enter into interpersonal relationships with their hearers. For instance, according to Moran's version of the IVT—the *assurance view*—a speaker's testimony that p is understood as the speaker giving her *assurance* that p is true. Since assurance can be given only when it is freely presented as such, Moran claims that a speaker freely assumes responsibility for the truth of p when she asserts that p, thereby providing the hearer with an *additional* reason to believe that p, different in kind from anything given by evidence alone. In a similar spirit, Hinchman argues:

> How can I entitle you to believe what I tell you? One way is by influencing the evidence available to you, perhaps by making an assertion or otherwise manifesting a belief, which still makes you epistemically responsible for the belief I want you to form. Another is by inviting you to trust me, thereby taking part of that responsibility onto my own shoulders. These two ways of giving an epistemic entitlement work very differently. When a speaker tells her hearer that p . . . she acts on an intention to give him an entitlement to believe that p that derives not from evidence of the truth of "p" but from his mere understanding of the act she thereby perform . . . unlike acts of mere assertion, acts of telling give epistemic warrant directly.[29]

Now, whereas Moran claims that the assurance of truth that the speaker gives to the hearer is the nonevidential feature of their interpersonal relationship that confers epistemic value on testimonial beliefs, Hinchman's *trust view* maintains that this feature is *the speaker's invitation to the hearer to trust her*.

There is, however, a central problem afflicting the IVT, which can be cast in terms of a dilemma. The first horn is that if the view in question is genuinely interpersonal, it is epistemologically impotent. To see this, notice that a natural question to ask the proponents of the IVT is what the precise connection is between *a speaker's giving a hearer assurance of the truth of her utterance* or *a speaker's inviting a hearer to trust her* and *the truth itself*. Otherwise put, what is the *epistemic* value of such interpersonal features? By way of answering this question, Moran says, "the speaker, in presenting his utterance as an *assertion*, one with the force of *telling* the audience something, presents himself as *accountable* for the truth of what he says, and in doing so he offers a kind of guarantee for this truth."[30] But even if a speaker explicitly offers her hearer a guarantee of the truth of her assertion, what does this actually have to do with the *truth itself*? For instance, consider Beatrice, a radically unreliable believer who consistently offers assertions to her hearers that she sincerely believes to be true but that are wholly disconnected from the truth. Now since Beatrice presents herself as accountable for the truth of what she says, Moran claims that the hearer in question is thereby provided with a guarantee of the truth of what Beatrice says. But what does this so-called guarantee amount to? Nearly every time Beatrice offers an assertion to a hearer, it turns out to be false. In this way, she is what we might call a reliably unreliable testifier. Moreover, notice that the point brought out by this case is not merely that a speaker can give her assurance that p is true but be wrong on a particular occasion; rather, the point is that a speaker can repeatedly give her assurance that various propositions are true and yet consistently offer utterances that fail to be reliably connected with the truth in any way. A "guarantee" of truth that nearly always turns out to be false, however, is a far cry from anything resembling a genuine guarantee. Thus, as it stands, the assurance view, though genuinely interpersonal, is epistemologically impotent. For, in the absence of distinctively epistemic conditions placed on the testimonial exchange, a speaker can give assurance and thereby a justified belief to a hearer even when she shouldn't be able to (because, e.g., she is a radically unreliable testifier). If the assurance view is going to be a genuine contender in the epistemology of testimony, however, it simply cannot float free from all that is epistemic.

Aware of the sort of problem afflicting the assurance view, Hinchman adds the following crucial amendment to his trust view:

> Trust is a source of epistemic warrant just when it is epistemically reasonable. Trust is epistemically reasonable when the thing trusted is worthy of the trust—as long as there is no evidence available that it is untrustworthy. Assuming satisfaction of this negative evidential condition . . . when an epistemic faculty is trustworthy by serving as a reliable guide to the truth, it makes available an entitlement to believe what it tells you whose basis lies simply in the fact that you trust it.[31]

In order for the acceptance of an invitation to trust to confer epistemic justification directly on a testimonial belief acquired, then, the following two conditions must be satisfied:

1. the speaker's testimony must serve as a reliable guide to the truth, and
2. the hearer cannot have any relevant undefeated defeaters (i.e., "evidence available" that the speaker trusted "is untrustworthy") for accepting the invitation to trust the speaker.

Now, as should be clear, the addition of these two conditions puts the trust view of testimony on the epistemological map. In particular, by virtue of placing epistemic conditions on both the speaker and the hearer in a testimonial exchange, the trust view avoids the debilitating objection that it is simply impotent for the epistemology of testimony.

However, here is where the second horn of the dilemma afflicting the IVT emerges: if the IVT is not epistemologically impotent, then neither is it genuinely interpersonal. In other words, while it is true that the addition of conditions (1) and (2) renders the trust view a genuine contender in the epistemology of testimony, it does so at the cost of making trust itself *epistemically superfluous*. To see this, consider the following case. Abraham and Belinda, thinking they are alone in their office building, are having a discussion about the private lives of their coworkers. During the course of their conversation, Abraham tells Belinda that their boss is having an affair with the latest intern hired by the company, Iris. Unbeknownst to them, Edgar has been eavesdropping on their conversation, and so he, like Belinda, comes to believe solely on the basis of Abraham's testimony—which is in fact both true and epistemically impeccable—that their boss is having an affair with Iris. Moreover, Belinda and Edgar not only have the same relevant background information about both Abraham's reliability as a testifier and the proffered testimony, they also are properly functioning recipients of testimony who possess no relevant undefeated defeaters. Now, according to all versions of the IVT, Belinda's testimonial belief in the case of the eavesdropper possesses epistemic value that Edgar's does not. For while Abraham offered Belinda his assurance that his testimony is true and invited Belinda to trust him, neither is true of the relationship between Abraham and eavesdropping Edgar. Because of this, the epistemic value of Edgar's belief about the affair between the boss and intern Iris is inferior to, or at least different from, that of Belinda's belief with the same content.

But if Belinda and Edgar are equally properly functioning as recipients of testimony, have the same relevant background information, both about Abraham as a testifier and about the proposition to which he is testifying, and form their beliefs about the boss and Iris solely on the basis of Abraham's testimony, then what could distinguish their beliefs epistemically? According to Hinchman's view, the central difference between these two cases is that Belinda's, but not Edgar's, justification for believing the boss and Iris are having an affair is acquired simply by recognizing Abraham's intention to give her an entitlement to hold this belief. That these two justifications are epistemologically different is apparently evidenced by the purported fact that, were Belinda and Edgar both to refuse to treat Abraham's telling as a source of epistemic justification, Abraham "is entitled to feel slighted" by Belinda's refusal but not by Edgar's. For Abraham has "tendered an invitation to [Belinda] to trust [him] and explicitly been rebuffed," whereas Edgar was tendered no such invitation and thus cannot slight Abraham in this way.[32] The thought underlying these remarks is that there are certain expectations that come along with invitations and, accordingly, certain attitudes that follow from their being rejected or accepted.

There are, however, at least two central problems with this response. First, it is not at all clear that the difference cited by Hinchman between situations involving the invited and the noninvited in fact hold. For instance, suppose that after the scenario envisaged in this case, Abraham and Edgar are later talking at a dinner party and Edgar confesses both that he eavesdropped on Abraham's conversation with Belinda and that he has no relevant information about the boss and Iris other than what Abraham reported to Belinda. Suppose further that Abraham then asks, "So what do you think about the boss and Iris?" and Edgar responds, "Oh, I don't believe that the boss and Iris are having an affair." Wouldn't Abraham be entitled to feel slighted by Edgar's refusal to believe what he reported, even if he did not issue a specific invitation to trust him? Indeed, it is not at all clear that Abraham would, or should, feel more slighted by Belinda's refusal to believe him than by Edgar's, for both are revealing in their refusals their belief that Abraham is somehow untrustworthy, either in general or with respect to the topic at hand. It may even be the case that Abraham is entitled to feel *more* slighted by Edgar's refusal to believe him than by Belinda's if we suppose, for instance, that Abraham regards Edgar, but not Belinda, as a friend.

The second, and more important, problem with the above response is that, even if Hinchman is correct about the purported differences between the situations involving the invited and the noninvited, being entitled to the reactions in question lacks any *epistemological* significance and hence fails to establish that there is an *epistemologically relevant difference* between justification from telling and justification from mere asserting. In particular, Abraham's being entitled to feel slighted should Belinda, but not Edgar, refuse his invitation to trust and Belinda's, but not Edgar's, being entitled to feel resentment should Abraham prove untrustworthy do not bear in any way on the truth-conduciveness or epistemic rationality of the testimonial beliefs in question. For notice: Abraham's inviting Belinda but not Edgar to trust him does not make it more likely that the testimonial belief in question is true for Belinda but not for Edgar—they are both receiving testimony with the same degree of reliability, the same kind of truth-tracking, the same amount of proper functioning, and so on. Moreover, Belinda and Edgar have the same relevant background information about both Abraham's reliability as a testifier and the proffered testimony, so it is not more rational for Belinda to form the relevant belief than it is for Edgar. Of course, a situation may be envisaged in which Belinda but not Edgar has had a deep friendship with Abraham since childhood and, because of this, has more reasons to trust Abraham's testimony. But this doesn't show that interpersonal features of a relationship can affect the epistemic value of testimonial beliefs; all it shows is that a hearer who possesses *more evidence* for the trustworthiness of a given speaker can acquire a testimonial belief that is more justified than a hearer who does not—an obvious point, but one that fails to support the IVT.

What these considerations show is that interpersonal features are not capable of adding epistemic value to testimonial beliefs. This is made clear in the eavesdropping case: there does not seem to be anything epistemically significant about the fact that, though Belinda and Edgar both learned about the boss's affair from Abraham's testimony, only the former was *told* this. Indeed, the counterintuitive consequences of the IVT quickly proliferate: if you are addressing a particular room of people at a conference, surely the epistemic value of the belief that I acquire on the basis of your testimony does not differ from those acquired by the audience members merely because I overhear your talk from the hallway. Or if you write a book with the intended audience being Democrats, the fact that a Republican reads it should not, by itself, affect the epistemic status of the testimonial beliefs that are thereby acquired. Interpersonal features, then, do not add any epistemic value to testimonial beliefs that is not already contributed by the truth-conducive grounding in question, thereby rendering such features epistemologically impotent.

Thus, while the addition of conditions (1) and (2) places the trust view on the epistemological map, trust itself turns out to be epistemically superfluous. For the reason it is no longer an utter mystery how justification could be conferred through the acceptance of an invitation to trust is because conditions (1) and (2) do all the epistemic work. When a hearer acquires a justified belief that p from a speaker's telling her that p, this is explained through both the speaker's reliability as a testifier with respect to p and the hearer's rationality as a recipient of the testimony. In providing the *epistemic* explanation of the hearer's newly acquired justified belief, then, trust simply drops out of the picture. Once trust becomes epistemically superfluous, however, the trust view ceases to even represent a version of the IVT. For the interpersonal relationship between the two parties in a testimonial exchange is not the central focus of the epistemology of testimony on such a view, nor are features of this interpersonal relationship responsible for conferring epistemic value on the testimonial beliefs acquired—the reliability of the speaker's testimony and the rationality of the hearer's acceptance of the testimony are doing all of the epistemic work.

The upshot of these considerations, then, is that there is a general dilemma confronting the proponent of the IVT: either the view of testimony in question is genuinely interpersonal but not epistemological, or it is genuinely epistemological but not interpersonal. Either way, the IVT fails to provide a compelling alternative to existing theories in the epistemology of testimony.

4. TESTIMONY AS THE TRANSMISSION OF KNOWLEDGE

Most views in the current literature on testimony are built around a central thesis, which we may call the *transmission view* (TV). The basic thought expressed by TV is that a testimonial exchange involves a speaker's knowledge being *transmitted* to a hearer.[33] There are two dimensions to

TV; one is a *necessity* thesis (TVN) and the other is a *sufficiency* thesis (TVS). More precisely:

TVN: For every speaker, A, and hearer, B, B knows that *p* on the basis of A's testimony that *p* only if A knows that *p*.[34]

TVS: For every speaker, A, and hearer, B, if (1) A knows that *p*, (2) B comes to believe that *p* on the basis of the content of A's testimony that *p*, and (3) B has no undefeated defeaters for believing that *p*, then B knows that *p*.[35]

Support for this view, particularly for TVN, derives from a purported analogy between testimony and memory. While memory is thought to be capable of only *preserving* knowledge from one time to another—and cannot therefore *generate* new knowledge—testimony is said to be capable of only *transmitting* knowledge from one person to another. So, for instance, just as I cannot know that *p* on the basis of memory unless I nonmemorially knew that *p* at an earlier time, the thought underlying this picture of testimonial knowledge is that a hearer cannot know that *p* on the basis of testimony unless the speaker who provided the testimony herself knows that *p*. Similarly, just as my knowing that *p* at an earlier time may be sufficient, in the absence of present undefeated defeaters, for me to memorially know that *p* now, it is said that a speaker's knowing that *p* may also be sufficient, in the absence of undefeated defeaters, for a hearer to know that *p* on the basis of her testimony.

Recently, however, objections have been raised to both dimensions of TV, thereby calling into question the widely accepted view that transmission lies at the heart of the epistemology of testimony.[36] There are two general types of counterexamples that have been raised to TVN. The first type involves speakers who fail to believe, and hence know, a proposition to which they are testifying but nevertheless reliably convey the information in question through their testimony. For instance, suppose that a devout creationist who does not believe in the truth of evolutionary theory nonetheless researches the topic extensively and on this basis constructs extremely reliable lecture notes from which she teaches her third-grade students. In such a case, the teacher seems able to reliably teach to her students that *Homo sapiens* evolved from *Homo erectus*, thereby imparting knowledge to her students that she fails to possess herself. The second type of counterexample that has been raised to TVN involves speakers who have an undefeated defeater for believing a proposition to which they are testifying, but nevertheless reliably convey such a proposition through their testimony without transmitting the defeater in question to their hearers. For instance, suppose that a speaker in fact possesses her normal visual powers, but she is the subject of a neurosurgeon's experiments, and the surgeon falsely tells her that implantations are causing malfunction in her visual cortex. While she is persuaded that her present visual appearances are an entirely unreliable guide to reality and thereby possesses a doxastic defeater for the corresponding beliefs, she continues to place credence in her visual appearances. On the basis of her in fact reliable visual experience, then, she forms the true belief that there is a badger in a nearby field and then later reports this fact to her friend without communicating the neurosurgeon's testimony to him. In such a case, the speaker reliably conveys the content of her visual experience to her hearer, but not her doxastic defeater, thereby imparting knowledge she does not have herself. Both types of cases, then, show that TVN is false.[37]

There are also two general types of counterexamples that have been raised to TVS. The first type of case shows that, for reasons having to do specifically with the *hearer*, a hearer's belief may fail to be an instance of knowledge even though the hearer has no relevant undefeated defeaters, the speaker from whom it was acquired has the knowledge in question, and the speaker testifies sincerely. For instance, suppose that a hearer is compulsively trusting so that she accepts whatever she is told, regardless of the amount or kind of evidence there is to the contrary. In such a case, the hearer simply is not a properly functioning recipient of testimony. In particular, she is so constituted that the knowledge in question cannot be passed to her, even though she does not possess any relevant defeaters. The second type of counterexample to TVS shows that, for reasons having to do specifically with the *speaker*, a hearer's belief may fail to be an instance of knowledge even though the hearer has no relevant undefeated defeaters, the speaker from whom it was acquired has the knowledge in question, and the speaker testifies sincerely. For instance, suppose that a speaker in fact knows that there was a raccoon in the park this morning because she saw one there, but she is such that she would have reported to her hearer that there was such a raccoon even if there hadn't been one. In such a case, the speaker's belief is an instance of knowledge, and yet because she is an unreliable testifier, the belief that the hearer forms on the basis of her testimony is not an instance of knowledge. Once again, both types of counterexamples show that TVS is false.[38]

One of the central conclusions that the above considerations motivate is the replacement of TV with conditions focusing on the *statements* of speakers rather than on their states of believing or knowing. More precisely, TV may be replaced with the following *statement view* (SV) of testimony:

> SV: For every speaker, A, and hearer, B, B knows that p on the basis of A's testimony that p only if (1) A's statement that p is reliable or otherwise truth-conducive, (2) B comes to truly believe that p on the basis of the content of A's statement that p, and (3) B has no undefeated defeaters for believing that p.[39]

Further conditions may be needed for a complete view of testimonial knowledge, such as the need for positive reasons embraced by reductionists. But regardless of what is added to SV, such a view avoids the problems afflicting TV. Moreover, because hearers can acquire testimonial knowledge from speakers who do not possess the knowledge in question themselves, SV reveals that testimony is not merely a transmissive epistemic source, as has been traditionally assumed, but can instead generate epistemic features in its own right.

Notes

1 For a narrow view that builds the epistemology of testimony directly into its nature, see Coady (1992). For views of the nature of testimony with other types of restrictions, see Ross (1975) and Graham (1997).

2 Fricker (1995, pp. 396–97).

3 Audi (1997, p. 406).

4 Sosa (1991, p. 219).

5 Of course, the situation would be entirely different if, for instance, I were offering this statement to my blind friend with the intention of conveying information about the weather.

6 For a full development of this view, see Lackey (2006c, 2008).

7 This type of example is found in Sosa (1991).

8 This is a variation of an example found in Audi (1997).

9 Proponents of various versions of nonreductionism include Austin (1979), Welbourne (1979, 1981, 1986, 1994), Evans (1982), Reid (1983), Ross (1986), Hardwig (1985, 1991), Coady (1992, 1994), Burge (1993, 1997), Plantinga (1993), Webb (1993), Dummett (1994), Foley (1994), McDowell (1994), Strawson (1994), Williamson (1996, 2000), Goldman (1999), Schmitt (1999), Insole (2000), Owens (2000, 2006), Rysiew (2002), Weiner (2003), Goldberg (2006), and Sosa (2006). Some phrase their views in terms of knowledge, others in terms of justification or entitlement, still others in terms of warrant. Audi (1997, 1998, 2006) embraces a nonreductionist view of testimonial knowledge, but not of testimonial justification. Stevenson (1993), Millgram (1997), and Graham (2006) defend restricted versions of nonreductionism.

10 Burge (1993, p. 467, emphasis added); Weiner (2003, p. 257); Audi 1998, p. 142, emphasis added).

11 For various views of what I call psychological defeaters see, for example, BonJour (1980, 1985), Nozick (1981), Pollock (1986), Goldman (1986), Plantinga (1993), Lackey (1999, 2006b, 2008), Bergmann (1997, 2004), and Reed (2006).

12 For discussions involving what I call normative defeaters, approached in a number of different ways, see BonJour (1980, 1985), Goldman (1986), Fricker (1987, 1994), Chisholm (1989), Burge (1993, 1997), McDowell (1994), Audi (1997, 1998), Williams (1999), Lackey (1999, 2006b, 2008), BonJour and Sosa (2003), Hawthorne (2004), and Reed (2006). What all these discussions have in common is simply the idea that evidence can defeat knowledge (justification) even when the subject does not form any corresponding doubts or beliefs from the evidence in question.

13 Proponents of different versions of reductionism include Hume (1977), Fricker (1987, 1994, 1995, 2006), Adler (1994, 2002), Lyons (1997), Lipton (1998), and Van Cleve (2006). Lehrer (2006) develops a qualified reductionist/nonreductionist view of testimonial justification.

14 Faulkner (2000, 587–88, first emphasis added).

15 Fricker (1994, pp. 149-50).

16 See, for instance, Fricker (1987, 1994, 1995), Faulkner (2000, 2002), and Lackey (2006a, 2008).

17 See, for instance, Audi (1997). For a response to this objection, see Lackey (2005, 2008).

18 Coady (1992, p. 82).

19 Fricker (1994, p. 139, emphasis added).

20 See, for instance, Webb (1993), Foley (1994), Strawson (1994), and Schmitt (1999). For a response to this objection, see Lackey (2006a, 2008).

21 See, for instance, Fricker (1995, 2006a), Faulkner (2000), Goldberg (2006, 2008), and Lehrer (2006).

22 See Goldberg (2006) and Goldberg (2008), respectively, for these qualifications to a nonreductionist view.

23 See Fricker (1995) for these modifications to reductionism.

24 See, for instance, Insole (2000), Weiner (2003), and Lackey (2008).

25 For a detailed development of this strategy, see Lackey (2008).

26 Proponents of the IVT include Ross (1986), Hinchman (2005), Moran (2006), and Faulkner (2007).

27 Hinchman (2005, p. 580, emphasis added).

28 Moran (2006, p. 283, second emphasis added).

29 Hinchman (2005, pp. 563–64).

30 Moran (2006, p. 283, original emphasis).

31 Hinchman (2005, pp. 578–79, emphasis added).

32 Hinchman (2005, pp. 565–66). It should be noted that Hinchman restricts this claim to cases in which the hearer refuses to accept the speaker's telling in ways that manifest mistrust in the speaker herself. For instance, a speaker may not be entitled to feel slighted if a hearer refuses to accept her telling about the time of day merely because he doubts the accuracy of her watch (rather than the trustworthiness of her word).

33 For the sake of simplicity, I shall here focus on the TV only in terms of knowledge. However, it should be noted that such a view is widely endorsed with respect to other epistemic properties, such as justification, warrant, entitlement, and so on.

34 Proponents of different versions of TVN include Welbourne (1979, 1981, 1986, 1994), Hardwig (1985, 1991), Ross (1986), Burge (1993, 1997), Plantinga (1993), McDowell (1994), Williamson (1996, 2000), Audi (1997, 1998, 2006), Owens (2000, 2006), Reynolds (2002), Faulkner (2006), and Schmitt (2006).

35 Proponents of different versions of TVS include Austin (1979), Welbourne (1979, 1981, 1986, 1994), Evans (1982), Fricker (1987), Coady (1992), McDowell (1994), Adler (1996, 2006), and Owens (2000, 2006). Burge (1993), Williamson (1996, 2000), and Audi (1997) endorse qualified versions of this thesis.

36 See, for instance, Lackey (1999, 2003, 2006b, 2008), Graham (2000), and Goldberg (2001, 2005).

37 Both types of cases are developed in far more depth and detail in Lackey (1999, 2008). The second sort of case is adapted from one found in Goldman (1986), though it is used by Goldman for quite different purposes.

38 Both types of cases are developed in far more depth and detail in Lackey (2006c, 2008).

39 For a detailed defense of SV, see Lackey (2006b, 2008).

References

Adler, Jonathan E. (1994) "Testimony, Trust, Knowing." *Journal of Philosophy* 91: 264–75.

———. (2002) *Belief's Own Ethics*. Cambridge, MA: MIT Press.

Audi, Robert. (1997) "The Place of Testimony in the Fabric of Knowledge and Justification." *American Philosophical Quarterly* 34: 405–22.

———. (1998) *Epistemology: A Contemporary Introduction to the Theory of Knowledge*. London: Routledge.

———. (2006) "Testimony, Credulity, and Veracity." In Jennifer Lackey and Ernest Sosa (eds.), *The Epistemology of Testimony*. Oxford: Oxford University Press: 25–49.

Austin, J.L. (1979) "Other Minds." In Austin, *Philosophical Papers*, 3rd ed. Oxford: Oxford University Press.

Bergmann, Michael. (1997) "Internalism, Externalism and the No-defeater Condition." *Synthese* 110: 399–417.

———. (2004) "Epistemic Circularity: Malignant and Benign." *Philosophy and Phenomenological Research* 69: 709–27.

BonJour, Laurence. (1980) "Externalist Theories of Epistemic Justification." *Midwest Studies in Philosophy* 5: 53–73.

———. (1985) *The Structure of Empirical Knowledge*. Cambridge, MA: Harvard University Press.

Burge, Tyler. (1993) "Content Preservation." *Philosophical Review* 102: 457–88.

———. (1997) "Interlocution, Perception, and Memory." *Philosophical Studies* 86: 21–47.

Chisholm, Roderick M. (1989) *Theory of Knowledge*. 3rd ed. Englewood Cliffs, N.J.: Prentice-Hall.

Coady, C.A.J. (1992) *Testimony: A Philosophical Study*. Oxford: Clarendon Press.

———. (1994) "Testimony, Observation and 'Autonomous Knowledge.'" In Bimal Krishna Matilal and Arindam Chakrabarti (eds.), *Knowing from Words*. Dordrecht: Kluwer Academic: 225–50.

Dummett, Michael. (1994) "Testimony and Memory." In Bimal Krishna Matilal and Arindam Chakrabarti (eds.), *Knowing from Words*. Dordrecht: Kluwer Academic: 251–72.

Evans, Gareth. (1982) *The Varieties of Reference*. Oxford: Clarendon Press.

Faulkner, Paul. (2000) "The Social Character of Testimonial Knowledge." *Journal of Philosophy* 97: 581–601.

———. (2002) "On the Rationality of Our Response to Testimony." *Synthese* 131: 353–70.

———. (2006) "On Dreaming and Being Lied To." *Episteme* 3: 149–59.

———. (2007) "What Is Wrong with Lying?" *Philosophy and Phenomenological Research* 75: 535–57.

Foley, Richard. (1994) "Egoism in Epistemology." In Frederick F. Schmitt (ed.), *Socializing Epistemology: The Social Dimensions of Knowledge*. Lanham, MD: Rowman and Littlefield: 53–73.

Fricker, Elizabeth. (1987) "The Epistemology of Testimony." *Proceedings of the Aristotelian Society*, supp. 61: 57–83.

———. (1994) "Against Gullibility." In Bimal Krishna Matilal and Arindam Chakrabarti (eds.), *Knowing from Words*. Dordrecht: Kluwer Academic: 125–61.

———. (1995) "Telling and Trusting: Reductionism and Anti-reductionism in the Epistemology of Testimony." *Mind* 104: 393–411.

———. (2006a) "Knowledge from Trust in Testimony Is Second-hand Knowledge." *Philosophy and Phenomenological Research* 73: 592–618.

———. (2006b) "Testimony and Epistemic Autonomy." In Jennifer Lackey and Ernest Sosa (eds.), *The Epistemology of Testimony*. Oxford: Oxford University Press: 225–50.

Goldberg, Sanford C. (2001) "Testimonially Based Knowledge from False Testimony." *Philosophical Quarterly* 51: 512–26.

———. (2005) "Testimonial Knowledge through Unsafe Testimony." *Analysis* 65: 302–11.

———. (2006) "Reductionism and the Distinctiveness of Testimonial Knowledge." In Jennifer Lackey and Ernest Sosa (eds.), *The Epistemology of Testimony*. Oxford: Oxford University Press: 127–44.

———. (2008) "Testimonial Knowledge in Early Childhood, Revisited." *Philosophy and Phenomenological Research* 76: 1–36.

Goldman, Alvin I. (1986) *Epistemology and Cognition*. Cambridge, MA: Harvard University Press.

———. (1999) *Knowledge in a Social World*. Oxford: Clarendon Press.

Graham, Peter J. (1997) "What Is Testimony?" *Philosophical Quarterly* 47: 227–32.

———. (2000) "Conveying Information." Synthese 123: 365–92.

———. (2006) "Liberal Fundamentalism and Its Rivals." In Jennifer Lackey and Ernest Sosa (eds.), *The Epistemology of Testimony*. Oxford: Oxford University Press: 93–115.

Hardwig, John. (1985) "Epistemic Dependence." *Journal of Philosophy* 82: 335–49.

———. (1991) "The Role of Trust in Knowledge." *Journal of Philosophy* 88: 693–708.

Hawthorne, John. (2004) *Knowledge and Lotteries*. Oxford: Oxford University Press.

Hinchman, Edward S. (2005) "Telling as Inviting to Trust." *Philosophy and Phenomenological Research* 70: 562–87.

Hume, David. (1977) *An Enquiry Concerning Human Understanding*. Ed. Eric Steinberg. Indianapolis: Hackett.

Insole, Christopher J. (2000) "Seeing Off the Local Threat to Irreducible Knowledge by Testimony." *Philosophical Quarterly* 50: 44–56.

Lackey, Jennifer. (1999) "Testimonial Knowledge and Transmission." *Philosophical Quarterly* 49: 471–90.

———. (2003) "A Minimal Expression of Nonreductionism in the Epistemology of Testimony." *Noûs* 37: 706–23.

———. (2005) "Testimony and the Infant/Child Objection." *Philosophical Studies* 126: 163–90.

———. (2006a) "It Takes Two to Tango: Beyond Reductionism and Nonreductionism in the Epistemology of Testimony." In Jennifer Lackey and Ernest Sosa (eds.), *The Epistemology of Testimony*. Oxford: Oxford University Press: 160–89.

———. (2006b) "Learning from Words." *Philosophy and Phenomenological Research* 73: 77–101.

———. (2006c) "The Nature of Testimony." *Pacific Philosophical Quarterly* 87: 177–97.

———. (2008) *Learning from Words*. Oxford: Oxford University Press.

Lehrer, Keith. (2006) "Testimony and Trustworthiness." In Jennifer Lackey and Ernest Sosa (eds.), *The Epistemology of Testimony*. Oxford: Oxford University Press: 145–59.

Lipton, Peter. (1998) "The Epistemology of Testimony." *Studies in History and Philosophy of Science* 29: 1–31.

Lyons, Jack. (1997) "Testimony, Induction and Folk Psychology." *Australasian Journal of Philosophy* 75: 163–78.

McDowell, John. (1994) "Knowledge by Hearsay." In Bimal Krishna Matilal and Arindam Chakrabarti (eds.), *Knowing from Words*. Dordrecht: Kluwer Academic: 195–224.

Millgram, Elijah. (1997) *Practical Induction*. Cambridge, MA: Harvard University Press.

Moran, Richard. (2006) "Getting Told and Being Believed." In Jennifer Lackey and Ernest Sosa (eds.), *The Epistemology of Testimony*. Oxford: Oxford University Press: 272–306.

Nozick, Robert. (1981) *Philosophical Explanations*. Cambridge, MA: Belknap Press.

Owens, David. (2000) *Reason without Freedom: The Problem of Epistemic Normativity*. London: Routledge.

———. (2006) "Testimony and Assertion." *Philosophical Studies* 130: 105–29.

Plantinga, Alvin. (1993) *Warrant and Proper Function*. Oxford: Oxford University Press.

Pollock, John. (1986) *Contemporary Theories of Knowledge*. Totowa, N.J.: Rowman and Littlefield.

Reed, Baron. (2006) "Epistemic Circularity Squared? Skepticism about Common Sense." *Philosophy and Phenomenological Research* 73: 186–97.

Reid, Thomas. (1983) "Essay on the Intellectual Powers of Man." In Ronald E. Beanblossom and Keith Lehrer (eds.), *Thomas Reid's Inquiry and Essays*. Indianapolis: Hackett.

Reynolds, Steven L. (2002) "Testimony, Knowledge, and Epistemic Goals." *Philosophical Studies* 110: 139–61.

Ross, Angus. (1986) "Why Do We Believe What We Are Told?" Ratio 28: 69–88.

Ross, James. (1975) "Testimonial Evidence." In Keith Lehrer (ed.), *Analysis and Metaphysics: Essays in Honor of R.M. Chisholm*. Dordrecht: Reidel: 35–55.

Rysiew, Patrick. (2002) "Testimony, Simulation, and the Limits of Inductivism." *Australasian Journal of Philosophy* 78: 269–74.

Schmitt, Frederick F. (1999) "Social Epistemology." In John Greco and Ernest Sosa (eds.), *The Blackwell Guide to Epistemology*. Oxford: Blackwell: 354–82.

———. (2006) "Testimonial Justification and Transindividual Reasons." In Jennifer Lackey and Ernest Sosa (eds.), *The Epistemology of Testimony*. Oxford: Oxford University Press: 193–224.

Sosa, Ernest. (1991) *Knowledge in Perspective: Selected Essays in Epistemology*. Cambridge: Cambridge University Press.

———. (2006) "Knowledge: Instrumental and Testimonial." In Jennifer Lackey and Ernest Sosa (eds.), *The Epistemology of Testimony*. Oxford: Oxford University Press: 116–23.

Stevenson, Leslie. (1993) "Why Believe What People Say?" *Synthese* 94: 429–51.

Strawson, P.F. (1994) "Knowing from Words." In Bimal Krishna Matilal and Arindam Chakrabarti (eds.), *Knowing from Words*. Dordrecht: Kluwer Academic: 23–27.

Van Cleve, James. (2006) "Reid on the Credit of Human Testimony." In Jennifer Lackey and Ernest Sosa (eds.), *The Epistemology of Testimony*. Oxford: Oxford University Press: 50–74.

Webb, Mark Owen. (1993) "Why I Know About As Much As You: A Reply to Hardwig." *Journal of Philosophy* 110: 260–70.

Weiner, Matthew. (2003) "Accepting Testimony." *Philosophical Quarterly* 53: 256–64.

Welbourne, Michael. (1979) "The Transmission of Knowledge." *Philosophical Quarterly* 29: 1–9.

———. (1981) "The Community of Knowledge." *Philosophical Quarterly* 31: 302–14.

———. (1986) *The Community of Knowledge*. Aberdeen: Aberdeen University Press.

———. (1994) "Testimony, Knowledge and Belief." In Bimal Krishna Matilal and Arindam Chakrabarti (eds.), *Knowing from Words*. Dordrecht: Kluwer Academic: 297–313.

Williams, Michael. (1999) *Groundless Belief: An Essay on the Possibility of Epistemology*. 2nd ed. Princeton: Princeton University Press.

Williamson, Timothy. (1996) "Knowing and Asserting." *Philosophical Review* 105: 489–523.

———. (2000) *Knowledge and Its Limits*. Oxford: Oxford University Press.

5

"If That Were True I Would Have Heard about It by Now"

Sanford C. Goldberg

1. CASES

Over lunch, you and a friend are having a discussion about U.S. foreign policy. She raises the question whether weapons of mass destruction (WMDs) have been found in Iraq. You say that they have not. (You reason that if such weapons had been found, you would have heard about it by now.)

As his mind is wandering, the thought occurs to Smith (out of the blue) that the president announced a new major change in foreign policy last week. Believing that if the president had done so he (Smith) would have heard about it by now, Smith forms the belief that the president did not announce a new major foreign policy change last week.

Listening to the locals discuss the goings-on of various Hollywood celebrities, McSorley overhears a particularly juicy tidbit regarding Toothy Thompson, a famous celebrity who is nearly universally regarded (including by McSorley) as a person of high integrity. According to the speaker, Toothy has actually led the life of a degenerate who has barely escaped legal prosecution on various occasions. Given Toothy's reputation, McSorley rejects the testimony: McSorley thinks to herself that if any of this were true, she would have heard about it by now (from some more familiar source).

The phenomenon illustrated in these cases is rather common. In them, the fact that a subject has never come across a piece of testimony to the effect that *p* is used as support for her belief in not-*p*. This support can take the form of a reason that offers (further) support for believing something she believed all along (the WMD case); it can take the form of a reason supporting the formation of a belief she did not previously have (the change in foreign policy case); or it can take the form of a reason to disbelieve some piece of presently observed testimony opposing a belief she presently has (the Toothy Thompson case). I do not claim that these options are exhaustive.

Regarding these kinds of case, various questions emerge. Under what conditions is this sort of reasoning offered? Under what conditions is there justification for a belief formed on the basis of this sort of reasoning? Under what conditions does this sort of reasoning justify the repudiation of a piece of testimony to the contrary? And what does this tell us about the nature of testimony? Of our reliance on our peers? Or of the organization of our epistemic communities?

2. EPISTEMIC COVERAGE

I begin first with the descriptive task, that of saying when it is that reasoning of the above sort is offered.

First, it is clear that in a typical case a hearer will reason in the way above—using the silence of a standard source (the newspaper; a trusted blog) to form or sustain a belief, or to repudiate a piece of testimony to the contrary—only if she presupposes and/or explicitly believes certain things. In particular, the hearer will believe or presuppose that the proposition in question concerns a subject matter regarding which there is some subgroup (or subgroups) of members of her community (the standard source(s)) who regularly report about such matters; that the standard source is, or is likely to be, reliable in uncovering and subsequently publicizing truths about such matters; that such a source had sufficient time to discover the relevant facts and report on them; that she herself (the hearer) would likely have come across such a report had one been made; and that she has not come across such a report. If the hearer fails to believe or presuppose any of these five things, she is not likely to reason in the way indicated. (Or if she does, it would appear that her doing so is unjustified; more on this in section 4.)

Let us call a belief that is supported by this sort of reasoning—whether the belief is one that is newly formed or sustained, and whether the supporting reasoning was explicit or only implicit—a *coverage-supported* belief. Although I will have more to say on the matter below, for now I simply note that the relevant notion of coverage is seen in the believer's reliance on a source to be both reliably apprised of the facts in a certain domain, and reliably disposed to report on the obtaining of facts in that domain (when those facts are known by the source).

The sort of reliance exhibited by our hearer toward her standard source in cases of coverage-supported belief is not often discussed in connection with the epistemology of testimony. That literature is primarily focused on such questions as: Under what conditions is a hearer justified in accepting another speaker's say-so? And under what conditions does a hearer acquire *knowledge* through such acceptance? We might say that, in asking such questions, we are examining our need (as hearers) for the reliable consumption of reliable testimony.[1] In the case above, by contrast, we are going beyond this to examine a *further* type of reliance. I will designate this further type *coverage-reliance.* A hearer *H* exhibits coverage-reliance toward some source(s) in domain *D* when she relies on the existence of sources who are such that, if *p* is a true proposition in *D*, one or more of the sources will publicize or broadcast that *p*, in such a way that *H* herself will come across the report.

The existence of coverage-based belief makes clear how the discussion in the epistemology of testimony has been almost universally one-sided. The literature has been devoted almost exclusively to issues pertaining to what we might call the "soundness" of the testimonial belief-fixing process, which is to say, (1) the reliability and trustworthiness of testimonies that are offered, and (2) the reliability of hearers in distinguishing reliable from unreliable testimonies.[2] What the literature has not focused on—indeed, what it has not been so much as raised as an issue to be investigated—are issues pertaining to *coverage*, to what we might call the "completeness" of testimony within one's epistemic community. By focusing on these issues, we can bring to the fore yet another way the phenomenon of testimony pushes us ever more in the direction of an irreducibly social epistemology.

3. TESTIMONY TRANSITIONS

It will be helpful to have some more terminology on the table. Testimonial belief is acquired through one's endorsement of the testimony, where this endorsement is a matter of believing the attested content on the basis of the speaker's having so attested.[3] Such cases instantiate what I will call a "testimony-to-truth" transition: the move is from the observing of a piece of testimony that *p*, to the (formation of a) belief in the truth of *p*. In saying this I do not mean that this transition is consciously undertaken, or that the hearer herself would articulate the transition as the basis of her belief. The point, rather, concerns the epistemic ground of the belief. The nature of this ground is brought out by the sort of *ex post facto* rationalization that could be offered (by an epistemologist, if not by the subject herself) for the subject's testimonial belief. The rationalization itself displays relations of epistemic dependence holding among pieces of information within a given subject's epistemic perspective. Stripped to its basics, such a rationalization would involve something like the following inference:[4]

1. *S* testified that *p*.
2. If *S* testified that *p*, then *p*.

Therefore,

3. *p*.

What I am calling the "testimony-to-truth" transition is manifested in the conditional statement (2). Epistemologists interested in testimony typically focus on issues pertaining to (2), and to a hearer's entitlement to rely on (2). Such questions include: Does (2), or something like it, derive from a basic epistemological principle, or does it stand in need of further (presumably empirical) justification?[5] And: Under what conditions is a hearer entitled to employ or rely on (2) on a given occasion? I will not address these questions here; versions of them are addressed at length in the epistemological literature on testimony. My present point is one on which all parties to the debate should agree: that in an ex post facto rationalization of a testimonial belief, something like this stripped-down inference will be present. In this way we can say that the process involved in testimonial belief-fixation instantiates the testimony-to-truth transition.

Now consider what we might call the phenomenon of *coverage-supported belief*, where one forms or sustains a belief in the negation of a proposition, on the basis of the fact that one's preferred source(s) has/have not (yet) so attested. What sort of ex post facto rationalization might a coverage-supported belief receive? Here I focus on a "pure" case: one where the belief in the negation-proposition is justified solely on the basis of coverage considerations (e.g. no other information is brought to bear on the likely truth of the negation-proposition in question).[6] Stripped to its basics, a rationalization in such a "pure" case would involve something like the following inference:

4. None among the trusted sources Σ testified that p.
5. If p, then one among the trusted sources Σ testified that p.

Therefore,

6. It is not the case that p.

Here, what I would call the "truth-to-testimony" transition is manifested in the conditional (5).

It may seem curious that the truth-to-testimony conditional (5) is in the material mode. After all, the reasoning in cases of coverage-supported belief typically involves the subjunctive conditional (witness the title of this essay). To some degree this sense of curiosity can be alleviated by noting that (5) follows from the claim, at the heart of coverage-supported belief, that all (relevant) truths are/have been reported. It is also worth noting a parallel with the testimony-to-truth conditional. The reason we want trustworthy (reliable; competent; what-have-you) testimony is that we want it to be the case that we can come to know something about the world through accepting another's relevant say-so on the matter; and this, in turn, requires the truth of a conditional to the effect that if our source asserted that p, then p. Of course, the property of trustworthiness itself is not best characterized in terms of this material conditional. Trustworthiness appears to be more robustly modal: we would say that a piece of testimony is trustworthy (reliable; competent) when it is such that (e.g.) it *wouldn't* be offered if it *were* false.[7] We want testimony to have this property precisely because we want the transition, from the observation of a piece of testimony to the truth of the proposition attested to, to be warranted. In precisely the same fashion, I acknowledge that coverage is a more robustly modal property than that captured in the material conditional in (5); but the reason we care that our community exhibit coverage (when we form coverage-supported belief) is that we want it to be the case that the transition, from the absence of (observed) testimony to the effect that p to not-p, is itself warranted. It is this transition that is captured by the material conditional (5).

It is perhaps unsurprising that, to date, the epistemology of testimony literature has focused on the testimony-to-truth transition. As noted, this transition is instantiated whenever one forms the belief that p through one's acceptance of testimony that p. What I would like to do in the remainder of this essay is to frame the issues I see arising from the (implicit) employment of the truth-to-testimony transition. Regarding this transition, we can ask questions analogous to those asked in connection with the testimony-to-truth transition. These questions include the following. Under what conditions is one epistemically entitled to rely on the truth of (5)? Under what conditions (if any) does one's reliance on (5), together with one's failure to have observed any of the trusted sources attest to p, suffice to underwrite one's justified belief (or knowledge) that not-p—supposing that one does not have such justified belief (or knowledge) through other sources?[8] In pursuing these questions, I hope to deepen our appreciation for the ways in which beliefs supported by *the noted absence* of particular testimony, like beliefs supported by the *presence* of testimony, demand an epistemological account that is interestingly social.

4. COMMUNITY AND INDIVIDUAL

Under what conditions is a hearer epistemically entitled to rely on the truth of the truth-to-testimony conditional, (5), in the course of belief-fixation? I want to approach this question by answering another question first: What sort of facts (regarding one's community and one's place in it) would render it epistemically fruitful for a hearer to rely on the truth-to-testimony conditional? We might then answer our original question by saying that a hearer is entitled to rely on this conditional when she is entitled to believe that things are this way.

We do well to recall the points made above (in section 2) in connection with what is presupposed in the typical case by a hearer exhibiting coverage-reliance. Regarding the conditions on one's community, we noted that the hearer presupposes that the proposition in question concerns a subject matter regarding which there is some subgroup of members of her community (the standard source) who can be relied on to report about such matters; and that the standard source is, or is likely to be, both timely and reliable in uncovering and subsequently publicizing all relevant truths about such matters.

Let us begin with the presupposition that some subgroup of members of the subject's community regularly report about such matters. (Call this the *source-existence* condition.) This subgroup might be one that is traditionally recognized by virtually everyone in the community (the traditional print and TV media, for example). Or it might be that the subgroup in question is one that is specific to the subject herself (a group of her friends, say, whose members are particularly interested in, and disposed to publicize to the others what they have learned about, some subject matter).

The interesting question concerns the timeliness and reliability of the reports they make. Here what is important is that if there were a relevant truth, one or more of the sources would discover it and make it known in a timely fashion. What "timely fashion" amounts to will depend on the nature of the case. Thus, the average citizen expects the goings-on in the nation's capital to be reported daily, whereas she harbors no such expectation for the goings-on in the Physics Department at State U. Alternatively, our expectations of the timeliness of reports might be formed on the basis of (our beliefs regarding) the particular source in question. So, for example, you expect your (daily) newspaper to be delivered on a daily basis, but you probably expect the news from a neighbor down the street on a much less regular basis (indeed, the intervals between these reports might not be regular at all), and for some reports—say that of an angry mob invading one's town, pitchforks in hand—one typically does not expect any relevant reports at all unless such an incident has been observed.[9] In still other cases the expectations may be the effect of some sort of ongoing coordination between two or more parties: I might give you the standing directive to report to me as soon as you observe any developments in the recent negotiations between labor and management (and we might agree to revise this directive, under various conditions, to make it more general, or more specific, in various ways).

Thus we see that, in addition to the source-existence condition—there must be a source that regularly reports on the facts in the domain in question—there is a second presupposition that amounts to a condition on the community: the relied-on source must be, or be likely to be, timely and reliable in uncovering and subsequently publicizing truths about the domain in which the subject is exhibiting coverage-reliance. Let D be a domain of interest to subject H, let p be any true proposition in D regarding whose truth H might take an interest, and let a be some source on whom H could rely on matters pertaining to D. Then we can formulate the *reliable coverage* (CR) condition as follows:

(CR) a is *coverage-reliable* in D relative to $H =_{\text{def}}$

It is likely that a (1) will investigate and reliably determine whether p, (2) will be reliable in reporting the outcome of that investigation, and (3) will satisfy both of the previous two conditions in a timely manner.

With this as our basic notion, we can then go on to define other, related notions. For example, in many cases a subject does not rely on any *particular* source, but instead relies on the fact that the relevant information would be publicized by *some source or other*. We can capture this notion in terms of generic coverage-reliance (GC), as follows:

(GC) There is generic coverage-reliability in D relative to $H =_{\text{def}}$
    There is some source or other in H's community that is coverage-reliable in D relative to H.

And I am confident that there will be other notions in the vicinity worth capturing. (I leave this for future work.)

As it is formulated (CR) captures what we might call a *nonattuned* sort of coverage-reliance, one in which the subject H coverage-relies on a source, a, who may or may not know that H is so relying, and who (even if a knows that H is so relying) may or may not know H's specific informational needs and expectations. But there can be other cases with a source that is attuned to the scope and informational needs and expectations of its audience; and such a source will be one that can explicitly aim to render itself coverage-reliable relative to that audience. I offer the following as capturing this notion of "attuned" coverage-reliance (AC):

(AC) a exhibits *attuned* coverage-reliability in D relative to $H =_{\text{def}}$
    (1) a has knowledge of both the scope of the audience ϕ that relies on it for (some of) their informational needs, and the information-relevant expectations that members of ϕ have with respect to a itself; (2) H is in ϕ; and (3) for any true proposition p in D, if it is reasonable for a to suppose, *both* that (i) members of ϕ would be interested in the truth of p, *and* that (ii) members of ϕ are likely to rely on a for the information whether p, then it is likely that a (a) will (investigate and) reliably determine whether p, (b) will be reliable in reporting the outcome of that investigation, and (c) will satisfy both of the previous two conditions in a timely manner.

What is more, we might distinguish the attuned coverage-reliability captured by (AC) from a sort of coverage-reliability where the scope and informational expectations of the relevant audience are *common knowledge*, possessed by both members of the audience and by the source itself (and where both sides know this of the other side, etc.). The difference between *common-knowledge coverage reliability* (as we might call it) and the sort of case captured by (AC) is that in the common-knowledge case the fact of attunement is known to both sides, not just to the source.

We have been exploring the conditions on the subject's community, if her coverage-reliance tendencies are to be epistemically fruitful. What can we say regarding the conditions on the coverage-relying subject, H, herself? Once again we can begin with one of the presuppositions listed in section 2: (The subject presupposes that) she herself must be likely to have come across whatever relevant reports were offered by the source(s) on whom she was relying. (I will call this the *reception condition*.) To be sure, the subject can satisfy the reception condition without having to receive the relevant reports directly from the source itself: it may be that there is a more extensive chain of communication linking her to the source. So long as the communication chain is itself both sufficiently reliable (preserving whatever relevant content there was in the original report(s)), sufficiently complete (passing on all of the relevant reports), and sufficiently well publicized (reaching at least some of the places where the subject is likely to encounter the transmitted message), the subject is likely to come across the reports from the source(s) on which she is relying.

There are other presuppositions concerning *H* herself: to date, she must not have encountered any report attesting to the truth of the proposition in question, over a period of time long enough to allow for the discovery and reporting of any relevant fact. We can break this up into two conditions, the *silence* condition (no relevant report observed) and the *sufficient time* condition (time was sufficient for the source to discover and publicize relevant information, had there been any).[10]

We have, then, what I submit are five jointly sufficient conditions on the epistemic fruitfulness of coverage-supported belief: the source-existence condition, the coverage-reliance condition, the reception condition, the silence condition, and the sufficient time condition.[11] But precisely what is the relevance of these conditions to the justification of coverage-supported belief? On the assumption that a belief can be justified without being true, we need not suppose that all five conditions must be true in order for a coverage-supported belief to be justified. Rather, the plausible initial proposal is that a coverage-supported belief is justified so long as the subject is (or would be) justified in believing that each of the conditions holds. With this, of course, we are staring in the face of some vexed matters about the nature of justification generally (and perhaps of testimonial justification in particular). For example, need the subject, *H*, have *positive reasons* to regard these five conditions as satisfied? Or does it suffice that her coverage-supported beliefs are, for example, reliable—as they would be if she were disposed to form coverage-supported beliefs only when these conditions are in fact satisfied (under conditions in which she has no reasons to think that they are not satisfied)? This issue, of course, is a special case of a much larger question, concerning the nature of justification itself: does something like reliability suffice for justification, or does justification require the presence of some sort of adequate positive reasons? Although my sympathies lie with the reliabilist, I do not have the space to address the larger question here;[12] I can only suggest how matters will be seen according to whether one's theory of justification is reasons-centered or reliabilist—or, more generally, internalist or externalist.

freedom of subject!

Our question concerns the conditions on a subject's epistemic entitlement to rely on the truth of the truth-to-testimony conditional, (5),
in the course of the fixation of a coverage-supported belief. Suppose one
is an epistemic internalist regarding justification. Then it would seem
that justification for coverage-supported belief is not a matter of one's
sensitivity (in the fixation of coverage-supported belief) to the actual
satisfaction of the five conditions above so much as it is a matter of one's
reasons for thinking that these conditions are satisfied in the present
case: one's coverage-supported belief is justified if and only if these reasons are adequate.

Such a view puts all of the epistemic burden on the hearer, rather than
on her community: if her coverage-supported belief is to be justified,
she must have good reasons to think that there is a relevant coverage-
reliable source whose reports she would likely have come across by now.
It is tempting to suppose that, on such a view, there will be no need
to acknowledge any distinctly social dimension to the epistemology of
coverage-supported belief. Though tempting, such a conclusion should
be resisted. For even if one's theory of justification is reasons-centered
and internalist, one ought to acknowledge that facts regarding one's community can affect the full epistemological assessment of a coverage-
supported belief—if not in connection with justification, then in
connection with some other epistemological status.[13] This can be brought
out in connection with pairs of cases, alike as to the hearers' reasons and
the proper functioning of their cognitive processes, but differing in the
satisfaction of one or more of the five conditions noted above. My claim
is that in such cases, the hearer's coverage-supported beliefs are not
equally well-off, epistemologically speaking—and that this epistemic difference must be accounted for in terms of differences in the social context of their coverage-supported beliefs.

The following example is meant to illustrate. Let Don and Don* be
doppelgängers, both of whom form the coverage-supported belief that
the president has not announced any new major policy initiative. (Neither has heard mention of such an initiative, and each reasons that if the
president had announced a new major policy initiative, he would have
heard about it by now.) Both Don and Don* would avow the very same
reasons for thinking that the five coverage conditions are satisfied in their
respective cases; and both are in excellent cognitive condition, with their
faculties working properly. In fact, the cases are exactly alike, save with
the following difference: whereas the sources on which Don is relying for
coverage continue to operate efficiently and well, as they always have, the
sources on which Don* is relying for coverage, though historically as reliable as those on which Don is relying, are (unbeknownst to anyone
except the sources themselves) in serious disarray, and have not been
operating efficiently or reliably for the past two weeks. To be sure, all of
this has escaped Don*'s (and virtually everyone else's) notice: Don* is
nonculpably ignorant of these facts. But the result is that, although it is

true that the president has not announced any new major policy changes, if he had—and this could easily have happened—the sources on which Don* was relying for coverage would have failed to report it.

Now I submit that Don*'s coverage-related belief is less well-off, epistemically speaking, than is Don's; and I submit that this point should be granted even by those epistemic internalists who regard Don's and Don*'s respective coverage-related beliefs as on a par, justification-wise. It might appear that the difference between these cases is to be chalked up to Gettier considerations (Don*'s belief being Gettierized, whereas Don's belief is not). But the point I wish to make, regarding a difference in epistemic goodness between their respective coverage-related beliefs, could be made in a different case, where it is clear that the epistemic differences between the twins' beliefs is not to be chalked up to Gettierization. Suppose that, instead of being in serious disarray, the sources on which Don* is relying for coverage are only slightly worse off than those on which Don is relying for coverage. As it might be: Don's sources would pick up and report on all of the facts that Don*'s sources would pick up and report on, and then a few more as well (which would escape the notice of Don*'s sources). Here it should still seem clear that Don*'s coverage-related beliefs are not quite as well-off, epistemically speaking, as are Don's—and yet there should be no temptation to ascribe this difference to Gettier considerations.[14] (We can imagine that this difference in the coverage-reliability of their respective sources makes for a difference in the reliability of their respective coverage-supported beliefs, but this difference does not make for a difference at the level of knowledge—both know, or fail to know.) This is the sort of difference, I submit, that reflects the distinctly *social* contribution in coverage-reliance cases—even for those who favor an internalist, reasons-based theory of justification.[15]

Of course, the social dimension of the epistemology of coverage-supported belief will be even clearer if one's theory of justification is not internalist. To see this it will be helpful to work with a standard externalist theory of justification. I propose to use standard reliabilism regarding justification, according to which

> (JR) A belief is justified iff it is formed and sustained through processes that are (generally) reliable.

Given (JR), coverage-based beliefs are justified iff they are formed and sustained through processes that are (generally) reliable. And it would seem that they are formed through processes that are (generally) reliable iff H is disposed to form coverage-supported beliefs only when the five conditions above are satisfied.

In spelling out the reliabilist picture here, it is interesting to focus exclusively on the coverage-reliability condition. (This will enable us to bring out what the reliabilist might see as the epistemic significance of the different sorts of coverage-reliability I mentioned above.) Let us suppose that, in general, sources are more likely to be coverage-reliable when they are attuned to the informational needs of their audience—that is, when the case is one satisfying (AC). In that case, there may be a difference, justification-wise, between cases satisfying (CR) but not (AC), and cases satisfying the more demanding (AC). Assuming that we have a situation in which the beliefs in both cases attain a degree of (general) reliability that suffices for justification, beliefs in both cases will be justified; but beliefs formed under (AC)-conditions will in general be better off, justification-wise, than those formed under (CR). What is more, these results do not depend on H's having justified beliefs regarding her sources: so long as she is in fact disposed to rely on sources that in fact are coverage-reliable (and the other conditions are satisfied), her coverage-supported beliefs will be justified. Or so it would seem on a standard externalist (reliabilist) framework.

It is worth making the same point from a slightly different perspective. Many reliabilists will want to know what explains H's reliance (in a given situation) on a source that in fact is coverage-reliable relative to H. If the explanation is dumb luck—perhaps there were many sources that were not coverage-reliable on the topic at hand, H just happened to rely on one that was—many reliabilists will hold that H's connection to the truth is still too lucky to count as reliable in the relevant sense. (This might be the analogue, for coverage-supported belief, of what Goldman's barn façade case is for perceptual belief.) But now suppose that the sources in Σ (the set of sources available to H) are not merely coverage-reliable, but *attunedly* so (and so satisfy (AC)). In that case the explanations for H's success in relying on a source that is in fact coverage-reliable might be the high percentage of attuned coverage-reliable sources in Σ—where this might be explained, in turn, in terms of the (social and economic) pressures for coverage-reliability in the various domains regarding which people in H's community assign a high utility to having reliable and (relatively) complete information. In this case even the more demanding reliabilist has grounds for regarding as justified the beliefs H forms or sustains through coverage-reliance on sources in Σ. For even if H herself does not have explicit reasons for regarding as coverage-reliable the various sources on whom she relies for coverage, even so—this being a case of *attuned* coverage-reliability—those sources aim to satisfy the informational needs of subjects like H, and they have a profile of what those needs are. Here, the burden (on ensuring that the conditions on justified coverage-supported belief are satisfied) is not entirely H's; on the contrary, *her sources themselves* assume some of this burden, since (as part of their very aim as information-sources) they assume the burden of rendering themselves coverage-reliable to those who rely on them.

It would seem, then, that justification-internalists and -externalists alike should agree that there is a social dimension to the epistemology of coverage-supported belief. To be sure, the two sides will account for this dimension differently. The main disagreement will concern whether social considerations can affect a belief's status as justified, in a way that is independent of being represented in the subject's belief corpus itself: the externalist can accept such a view, while an internalist will dispute it. What is more, while an internalist might have no grounds for treating cases as distinct according to whether the coverage reliance at play is attuned, the externalist may well want to do so, on grounds pertaining to the difference in reliability in cases of attuned versus nonattuned coverage-reliability.

5. THE SOCIAL EPISTEMOLOGY OF COVERAGE:
SOME REMAINING QUESTIONS

Let us step back and review our phenomenon from the perspective of social epistemology. I propose two notions, both of which emerge from the foregoing discussion of the epistemology of coverage, and both of which are naturally construed as notions from a social epistemology. These are the notions of *newsworthiness* and of *epistemic environments*.

Let us begin with the notion of *newsworthiness*. Above we asked after the conditions under which coverage-reliance is to be an epistemically fruitful way of forming or sustaining belief. Although it does not say so explicitly, it is reasonable to think that the coverage-reliability condition—one of the conditions in our jointly sufficient set—requires that there be a meshing between the propositions regarding whose truth community members *assume* there to be adequately reliable coverage in the community, and the propositions regarding whose truth there actually *is* adequately reliable coverage in the community. It is here that the notion of *newsworthiness* can be of service: the individual's sense of what is newsworthy must eventuate in judgments[16] that agree, more or less, with the standards of newsworthiness that inform the investigative and publishing decisions of the relevant news group(s) in her epistemic community.

It should be clear that one's sense of newsworthiness is relevant to the justification of one's coverage-supported belief: a subject whose sense of newsworthiness is radically different from that of the sources on which she is relying risks forming coverage-related beliefs in propositions regarding which she has no reliable coverage. Following this, I suggest that the notion of newsworthiness has an important, and heretofore largely neglected, role to play in epistemology. The relevant notion is the one possessed not just by those who *report* the news but also by those who *consume* it—at least if the latter hope to be able to exploit the coverage they receive. The relevant point here is simply that the individual's notion must be *synchronized* with the notion of those who are or would be most likely to acquire and disseminate the information in question. No doubt, this process of synchronization is one that develops over time, as an interplay between consumers and producers of news. Individual consumers develop a sense of the sorts of media (and other information-transmitters) with which they regularly interact, of the sorts of news that these sources regularly report, and of the communication channels through which it is reported. But that process can also work the other way, as when the demand for news in a certain domain is unmet, leading to existing media (and other transmission sources) extending what they consider newsworthy and to the creation of new media designed specifically to fill the lacuna. (I take it that the Internet, and the relatively recent phenomenon of blogging, has only sped up this media-spawning process.)

Much more work could be done investigating the epistemic dimension of the evolution (within a community) of the notion of newsworthiness. I submit that this work would capture part of the *cognitive* dimension of the epistemology of coverage—that part of such epistemology that takes stock of the beliefs and presuppositions of the participating parties (hearers and sources alike). However, the considerations discussed in section 4 also suggest that part of the epistemology of coverage will not be in cognitive terms at all, but instead will have to do with features of how well placed, information-wise, an individual is within her community. Here we see the relevance of the notion of an *epistemic environment*.

Epistemic environments can be evaluated along various dimensions. But if we restrict our attention to coverage-reliance, two such dimensions are particularly salient. Once again, these dimensions reflect the main types of role played by community and individual in the process of coverage reliance.

One of these dimensions concerns an attempt to assess the coverage that is provided within that community. How many domains D are such that one or more community groups exist that take an active interest in discovering and reporting the facts in D? Within such a domain, how likely is it that if p is true, one or more of these community groups will discover and publicize that p? What is the nature of the publication process? (Is it through traditional media? On the Internet? Etc.)

The second dimension along which to assess an epistemic environment (for the purpose of characterizing coverage-reliance in that community) regards the factors relating to the likelihood that a community member interested in knowing whether p will come across relevant reports made within her community (access assessment). How accessible is the source publication? How likely is it that an individual with informational interests not served by the mainstream media (newspapers, TV) will find those more specific news groups devoted to meeting informational needs of the sort she has? How efficient and reliable are the reporters "downstream" in the chain of communication—those who observe either a firsthand or a secondhand report and go on to report to others what they've heard? Are there any institutions or social practices that can serve as correctives, either when a false report is transmitted along a chain of communication or when a true report has its contents distorted in transmission? How effective are these corrective institutions or social practices? One can imagine assessing both the relative information-saturation of a community and the reliability of any arbitrary communication one comes across in that community.

These remarks are abstract in the extreme, and any successful assessment of the epistemology of coverage will have to descend from the heights of such abstraction to take a look at the details of particular cases. But as we do, it is worth keeping the big picture in mind. Take any information-rich community, where there are groups dedicated to the investigation and reporting of facts in some domain. In any such community, it can come to pass that community members begin to rely on one or more of these groups for what they know in that domain, in the sense that such groups are the main, and perhaps the only, source that the individual has regarding information in the domain in question. It can also come to pass that individuals will begin to rely on such groups for adequate (reliable) coverage. Such a moment presents both an epistemic opportunity and a danger.

The opportunity lies in having some epistemically adequate way to separate the informational wheat from the chaff in our information-rich society. Take cases where the information we receive involves something we cannot independently confirm (at least not without great cost and effort). In such cases it may well be an epistemically wise policy not just to accept *everything* the "sanctioned" sources tell us (unless there is/are positive reason(s) not to) but also to accept *only* information from such sources (unless there is/are positive reason(s) to accept information from a not-yet-recognized source). However, no sooner is such a policy formulated than we see the very real possibility for abuse by the powerful interests at play in the dissemination of news—which brings us to the danger.

The danger is threefold. For one thing, the coverage-relying individual runs the risk of committing the fallacy of ignorance: believing not-p merely because she has not come across evidence (testimony) that p.[17] For another, an individual who exhibits coverage-reliance toward a particular source, and who begins to rely uncritically on that source for what she knows in a given domain, risks forming beliefs in a way that reflects the vested interests of her source—and these may not amount to a disinterested interest in truth (so to speak). Finally, an individual who exhibits coverage-reliance toward a particular source can become blind to new or unrecognized but still reliable sources of information, when these offer reports going beyond what the relied-on sources have said about some matter. In this respect, the individual is both persisting in retaining false belief in the face of what is in fact a reliable indication to the contrary and losing out on an opportunity to acquire reliable information.

I see the epistemology of coverage as assessing how well individuals and communities manage these risks as they aim to reap the benefits of their information-saturated environment.

6. CONCLUSION

In standard discussions of the epistemology of testimony, it has been noted that hearers aim to acquire testimony-based beliefs from testimony that satisfies the testimony-to-truth conditional,

(2) If S testified that p, then p.

But here I have been suggesting that something close to the converse is also a desirable feature of the institution of testimony. In particular, we want to be in an epistemic community where the newsworthy propositions satisfy the coverage (or truth-to-testimony) conditional,

(5) If p, then one among the trusted sources Σ testified that p.

While it has been clear to everyone working in epistemology that there is something epistemologically beneficial with being in a community whose members regularly satisfy (2), it has been less remarked—though it should be equally clear—that there is something epistemologically beneficial with being in a community that satisfies (5) as well. It is not for nothing that the *New York Times* presents itself as publishing "*All* the News That's Fit to Print."

Notes

*I would like to thank Frank Döring for suggesting to me the interest (for social epistemology) of reasoning involving "If that were true, I would have heard about it by now"; and for a helpful discussion of such cases. (Any flaws in the account I have suggested for such cases are mine, not Frank's.) I would also like to thank the members in the audience at the conference "Social Epistemology," Stirling University, where I presented a paper on a similar theme; Jessica Brown, Igor Douven, Miranda Fricker, Alvin Goldman, Peter Graham, Klemens Kappell, Jon Kvanvig, Jennifer Lackey, Peter Lipton, Nenad Miscevic, Alan Millar, Erik Olsson, Duncan Pritchard, Ernie Sosa, and Finn Spicer, for particular comments on that paper; and a special thanks to Jasper Kallestrup, who served as my commentator at that conference.

1 This is not quite right, but for reasons that need not further detain us here. See Goldberg (2005, 2007).

2 Regarding the latter, see Goldberg and Henderson (2007), and Goldberg (2007: chap. 1).

3 This characterization is linguistically restrictive in that it requires that testimonial belief be belief in the attested content. If one thinks that testimonial belief is belief in any content presented-as-true (whether or not that content is identical to the content attested to), then this characterization would have to be modified. I assume that this could be done, but I will not attempt to do so here.

4 In saying this I do *not* mean that the testimonial belief is epistemically inferential. In fact in Goldberg (2006b) I argue against such a thesis (though the present argument does not depend on that conclusion). The point of the inference in (1)–(3) is rather to capture the epistemic dependence of the hearer's belief on

the epistemic goodness of a piece of testimony—a goodness that should support the conditional in (2).

5 I take it that questions regarding the need to modify (2) (to include further antecedent conditions—such as the sincerity, competence, etc. of the speaker) would fall here. For the suggestion that (2) will have to be modified in this way, see Fricker (1987: 73).

6 It may well be that in actual fact there are no pure cases: for any proposition there will always be background information, beyond the facts pertaining to coverage, that bear on the likely truth of the negation-proposition. If this is so, then my characterization above of a "pure" case will have no application, but instead can be considered an ideal that real cases will only approximate.

7 This characterization of testimonial goodness is endorsed by people of differing ideological orientation: see e.g. Fricker (1994: 132) and Graham 2000 (to name just two of the many who could be named).

8 There are other comparisons to be made between these two "transitions." For example, it is arguable that the testimony-to-truth transition brings with it a transmission of epistemic properties, from speaker's testimony to hearer's testimony-based belief. This is not true in the case of the truth-to-testimony transition: arguably, there is no transmission of epistemic properties from the speaker's silence to the hearer's coverage-based belief. This point, which I owe to Jasper Kallestrup, is interesting and worthy of further pursuit elsewhere.

9 I thank Jessica Brown for indicating the need for discussion of this last sort of case.

10 It may be that the satisfaction of the sufficient time condition falls out of the satisfaction of the reliable coverage condition: after all, the latter contains a condition on the "timely" publication of news. At worst, including the sufficient time condition as part of my set of jointly sufficient conditions introduces a harmless redundancy in the account. At best it allows us to distinguish reasonable expectations of timeliness from any particular subject's expectations on this score. Having such a distinction would allow us to say that there could be a source that is coverage-reliable with respect to any reasonable expectation of timeliness, but where a given subject relying on that source has unreasonable expectations on the timeliness of the reports. (To be sure, we would then have to characterize yet another notion of coverage-reliability—one formulated in terms of "reasonable" expectations for the timely manner of reporting. But so be it.)

11 In conversation Jasper Kallestrup has suggested that if these conditions are to be jointly sufficient, we need a sixth condition, to the effect that had *H* gotten reliable testimony on the matter at hand he would have believed it. Kallestrup thinks this is needed since it renders *H*'s coverage-based belief appropriately sensitive to the fact at hand. I am uncertain of this (if only because I am uncertain whether sensitivity is relevant to justification, as opposed to knowledge—and it is justification I am speaking about here). But for the sake of argument, those who think Kallestrup is correct are welcome to read this condition into my account.

12 See Goldberg (2007: pt. 2).

13 I have argued for a similar claim in connection with accounts of the justified acceptance of testimony: even if one's account holds that a subject is not justified in accepting testimony unless she has adequate positive reasons to do so, even so, one ought to acknowledge the relevance of the social dimension to a full epistemic appraisal of testimony-based belief. See Goldberg (2006a;

2007: chaps. 5, 6; forthcoming). The point is also nicely made in Faulkner (2000).

14 See Goldberg (forthcoming), where an argument of this sort is developed at much greater length—albeit in connection with testimonial (rather than coverage-supported) belief.

15 Those who favor an internalist, reasons-based theory of justification might describe this as a difference in *warrant*, or total truth-conducive support. That would be fine with me. My only point is that this difference is an epistemically relevant one.

16 By "eventuate in judgments" I do not mean that the individual herself must actually make the judgments in question. Rather, I mean that her sense of news-worthiness can be represented as a commitment to various "principles" of news-worthiness that, when applied to her descriptions of the current situation, entail newsworthiness judgments—and these judgments can then be compared to the judgments entailed by the standards employed by the sources on which she relies.

17 I am speaking loosely in speaking of testimony as evidence. In fact, I think testimony is not happily conceived of as evidence in any standard sense; see Goldberg (2006b).

Work Cited

Audi, R. 1982: "Believing and Affirming." *Mind* 91, 115–20.

Burge, T. 1993: "Content Preservation." *Philosophical Review* 102:4, 457–88.

Coady, C. 1992: *Testimony: A Philosophical Study*. Oxford: Oxford University Press.

Faulkner, P. 2000: "The Social Character of Testimonial Knowledge." *Journal of Philosophy* 97:11, 581–601.

Fricker, E. 1987: "The Epistemology of Testimony." *Proceedings of the Aristotelian Society*, supp. 61, 57–83.

———. 1994: "Against Gullibility." In B. Matilal and A. Chakrabarti, eds., *Knowing from Words* (Amsterdam: Kluwer Academic), 125–61.

Goldberg, S. 2005: "Testimonial Knowledge from Unsafe Testimony." *Analysis* 65:4, 302–11.

———. 2006a: "Reductionism and the Distinctiveness of Testimonial Knowledge." In J. Lackey and E. Sosa, eds., *The Epistemology of Testimony* (Oxford: Oxford University Press, 2006), 127–44.

———. 2006b: "Testimony as Evidence." *Philosophia* 78, 29–52.

———. 2007: *Anti-Individualism: Mind and Language, Knowledge and Justification.* Cambridge: Cambridge University Press.

Goldberg, S., and Henderson, D. 2007: "Monitoring and Anti-reductionism in the Epistemology of Testimony." *Philosophy and Phenomenological Research* 72:3, 600–617.

Graham, P. 2000: "Conveying Information." *Synthese* 123:3, 365–92.

Reid, T. 1872/1993: *The Complete Works of Thomas Reid*. Ed. Sir William Hamilton. (Edinburgh: Maclachlan and Stewart.)

Ross, A. 1986: "Why Do We Believe What We Are Told?" *Ratio* 28:1, 69–88.

6

Experts: Which Ones Should You Trust?

Alvin I. Goldman

1. EXPERTISE AND TESTIMONY

Mainstream epistemology is a highly theoretical and abstract enterprise. Traditional epistemologists rarely present their deliberations as critical to the practical problems of life, unless one supposes—as Hume, for example, did not—that skeptical worries should trouble us in our everyday affairs. But some issues in epistemology are both theoretically interesting and practically quite pressing. That holds of the problem to be discussed here: how lay persons should evaluate the testimony of experts and decide which of two or more rival experts is most credible. It is of practical importance because in a complex, highly specialized world people are constantly confronted with situations in which, as comparative novices (or even ignoramuses), they must turn to putative experts for intellectual guidance or assistance. It is of theoretical interest because the appropriate epistemic considerations are far from transparent; and it is not clear how far the problems lead to insurmountable skeptical quandaries. This paper does not argue for flat-out skepticism in this domain; nor, on the other hand, does it purport to resolve all pressures in the direction of skepticism. It is an exploratory paper, which tries to identify problems and examine some possible solutions, not to establish those solutions definitively.

The present topic departs from traditional epistemology and philosophy of science in another respect as well. These fields typically consider the prospects for knowledge acquisition in "ideal" situations. For example, epistemic agents are often examined who have unlimited logical competence and no significant limits on their investigational resources. In the present problem, by contrast, we focus on agents with stipulated epistemic constraints and ask what they might attain while subject to those constraints.

Although the problem of assessing experts is non-traditional in some respects, it is by no means a new problem. It was squarely formulated and addressed by Plato in some of his early dialogues, especially the *Charmides*.

In this dialogue Socrates asks whether a man is able to examine another man who claims to know something to see whether he does or not; Socrates wonders whether a man can distinguish someone who pretends to be a doctor from someone who really and truly is one (*Charmides* 170d-e). Plato's term for posing the problem is *techné*, often translated as "knowledge" but perhaps better translated as "expertise" (see Gentzler 1995, LaBarge 1997).[1]

In the recent literature the novice/expert problem is formulated in stark terms by John Hardwig (1985, 1991). When a layperson relies on an expert, that reliance, says Hardwig, is necessarily *blind*.[2] Hardwig is intent on denying full-fledged skepticism; he holds that the receiver of testimony can acquire "knowledge" from a source. But by characterizing the receiver's knowledge as "blind", Hardwig seems to give us a skepticism of sorts. The term "blind" seems to imply that a layperson (or a scientist in a different field) cannot be *rationally justified* in trusting an expert. So his approach would leave us with testimonial skepticism concerning rational justification, if not knowledge.

There are other approaches to the epistemology of testimony that lurk in Hardwig's neighborhood. The authors I have in mind do not explicitly urge any form of skepticism about testimonial belief; like Hardwig, they wish to expel the specter of skepticism from the domain of testimony. Nonetheless, their solution to the problem of testimonial justification appeals to a minimum of *reasons* that a hearer might have in trusting the assertions of a source. Let me explain who and what I mean.

The view in question is represented by Tyler Burge (1993) and Richard Foley (1994), who hold that the bare assertion of a claim by a speaker gives a hearer prima facie reason to accept it, quite independently of anything the hearer might know or justifiably believe about the speaker's abilities, circumstances, or opportunities to have acquired the claimed piece of knowledge. Nor does it depend on empirically acquired evidence by the hearer, for example, evidence that speakers generally make claims only when they are in a position to know whereof they speak. Burge, for example, endorses the following Acceptance Principle: "A person is entitled to accept as true something that is presented as true and that is intelligible to him, unless there are stronger reasons not to do so" (1993: 467). He insists that this principle is not an empirical one; the "justificational force of the entitlement described by this justification is not constituted or enhanced by sense experiences or perceptual beliefs" (1993: 469). Similarly, although Foley does not stress the a priori status of such principles, he agrees that it is reasonable of people to grant *fundamental* authority to the opinions of others, where this means that it is "reasonable for us to be influenced by others even when we have no special information indicating that they are reliable" (1994: 55). Fundamental authority is contrasted with *derivative* authority, where the latter is generated from the hearer's *reasons for thinking* that the source's "information, abilities, or circumstances put [him] in an especially good position" to make an accurate claim (1994: 55). So, on Foley's view, a hearer need not have such reasons about a source to get prima facie grounds for trusting that source. Moreover, a person does not need to acquire empirical reasons for thinking that people generally make claims about a subject only when they are in a position to know about that subject. Foley grants people a fundamental (though prima facie) epistemic right to trust others even in the absence of any such empirical evidence.[3] It is in this sense that Burge's and Foley's views seem to license "blind" trust.

I think that Burge, Foley, and others are driven to these sorts of views in part by the apparent hopelessness of reductionist or inductivist alternatives. Neither adults nor children, it appears, have enough evidence from their personal perceptions and memories to make cogent inductive inferences to the reliability of testimony (cf. Coady 1992). So Burge, Foley, Coady and others propose their "fundamental" principles of testimonial trustworthiness to stem the potential tide of testimonial skepticism. I am not altogether convinced that this move is necessary. A case might be made that children are in a position to get good inductive evidence that people usually make claims about things they are in a position to know about.

A young child's earliest evidence of factual reports is from face-to-face speech. The child usually sees what the speaker is talking about and sees that the speaker also sees what she is talking about, e.g., the furry cat, the toy under the piano, and so forth. Indeed, according to one account of cognitive development (Baron-Cohen 1995), there is a special module or mechanism, the "eye-direction detector", that attends to other people's eyes, detects their direction of gaze, and interprets them as "seeing" whatever is in the line of sight.[4] Since seeing commonly gives rise to knowing, the young child can determine a certain range of phenomena within the ken of speakers. Since the earliest utterances the child encounters are presumably about these *speaker- known* objects or events, the child might easily conclude that speakers usually make assertions about things within their ken. Of course, the child later encounters many utterances where it is unclear to the child whether the matters reported are, or ever were, within the speaker's ken. Nonetheless, a child's early experience is of speakers who talk about what they apparently know about, and this may well be a decisive body of empirical evidence available to the child.

I don't want to press this suggestion very hard.[5] I shall not myself be offering a full-scale theory about the justification of testimonial belief. In particular, I do *not* mean to be advancing a sustained defense of the reductionist or inductivist position. Of greater concern to me is the recognition that a hearer's evidence about a source's reliability or unreliability can often *bolster* or *defeat* the hearer's justifiedness in accepting testimony from that source. This can be illustrated with two examples.

As you pass someone on the street, he assertively utters a sophisticated mathematical proposition, which you understand but have never
previously assessed for plausibility. Are you justified in accepting it from
this stranger? Surely it depends partly on whether the speaker turns out
to be a mathematics professor of your acquaintance or, say, a nine-year-
old child. You have prior evidence for thinking that the former is in a
position to know such a proposition, whereas the latter is not. Whether
or not there is an a priori principle of default entitlement of the sort
endorsed by Burge and Foley, your empirical evidence about the identity of the speaker is clearly relevant. I do not claim that Burge and
Foley (etc.) cannot handle these cases. They might say that your recognition that the speaker is a math professor *bolsters* your *overall* entitlement to accept the proposition (though not your prima facie
entitlement); recognizing that it is a child *defeats* your prima facie entitlement to accept the proposition. My point is, however, that your evidence about the properties of the speaker is crucial evidence for your
overall entitlement to accept the speaker's assertion. A similar point
holds in the following example. As you relax behind the wheel of your
parked car, with your eyes closed, you hear someone nearby describing
the make and color of the passing cars. Plausibly, you have prima facie
justification in accepting those descriptions as true, whether this prima
facie entitlement has an a priori or inductivist basis. But if you then
open your eyes and discover that the speaker is himself blindfolded and
not even looking in the direction of the passing traffic, this prima facie
justification is certainly defeated. So what you empirically determine
about a speaker can make a massive difference to your overall justifiedness in accepting his utterances.

The same obviously holds about two putative experts, who make
conflicting claims about a given subject-matter. Which claim you
should accept (if either) can certainly be massively affected by your
empirical discoveries about their respective abilities and opportunities
to know the truth of the matter (and to speak sincerely about it).
Indeed, in this kind of case, default principles of the sort advanced by
Burge and Foley are of no help whatever. Although a hearer may be
prima facie entitled to believe each of the speakers, he cannot be entitled *all things considered* to believe both of them; for the propositions
they assert, we are supposing, are incompatible (and transparently incompatible to the hearer). So the hearer's all-things-considered justifiedness vis-à-vis their claims will depend on what he empirically learns
about each speaker, or about the opinions of other speakers. In the rest
of this paper I shall investigate the kinds of empirical evidence that a
novice hearer might have or be able to obtain for believing one putative expert rather than her rival. I do not believe that we need to settle
the "foundational" issues in the general theory of testimony before
addressing this issue. This is the working assumption, at any rate, on
which I shall proceed.[6]

2. THE NOVICE/EXPERT PROBLEM VS.
THE EXPERT/EXPERT PROBLEM

There are, of course, degrees of both expertise and novicehood. Some novices might not be so much less knowledgeable than some experts. Moreover, a novice might in principle be able to turn himself into an expert, by improving his epistemic position vis-à-vis the target subject-matter, e.g., by acquiring more formal training in the field. This is not a scenario to be considered in this paper, however. I assume that some sorts of limiting factors—whether they be time, cost, ability, or what have you—will keep our novices from becoming experts, at least prior to the time by which they need to make their judgment. So the question is: Can novices, while remaining novices, make justified judgments about the relative credibility of rival experts? When and how is this possible?

There is a significant difference between the novice/expert problem and another type of problem, the expert/expert problem. The latter problem is one in which experts seek to appraise the authority or credibility of other experts. Philip Kitcher (1993) addresses this problem in analyzing how scientists ascribe authority to their peers. A crucial segment of such authority ascription involves what Kitchen calls "calibration" (1993: 314–22). In *direct* calibration a scientist uses his own opinions about the subject-matter in question to evaluate a target scientist's degree of authority. In *indirect* calibration, he uses the opinions of still other scientists, whose opinions he has previously evaluated by direct calibration, to evaluate the target's authority. So here too he starts from his own opinions about the subject-matter in question.

By contrast, in what I am calling the novice/expert problem (more specifically, the novice/2-expert problem), the novice is not in a position to evaluate the target experts by using his own opinion; at least he does not think he is in such a position. The novice either has no opinions in the target domain, or does not have enough confidence in his opinions in this domain to use them in adjudicating or evaluating the disagreement between the rival experts. He thinks of the domain as properly requiring a certain expertise, and he does not view himself as possessing this expertise. Thus, he cannot use opinions of his own in the domain of expertise—call it the *E-domain*—to choose between conflicting experts' judgments or reports.

We can clarify the nature of the novice/expert problem by comparing it to the analogous listener/eyewitness problem. (Indeed, if we use the term "expert" loosely, the latter problem may just be a species of the novice/expert problem.) Two putative eyewitnesses claim to have witnessed a certain crime. A listener—for example, a juror—did not himself witness the crime, and has no prior beliefs about who committed it or how it was committed. In other words, he has no personal knowledge of the event. He wants to learn what transpired by listening to the testimonies of the eyewitnesses. The question is how he should adjudicate between their testimonies if and when they conflict. In this case, the E-domain is the domain of propositions concerning the actions and circumstances involved in the crime. This E-domain is what the listener (the "novice") has no prior opinions about, or no opinions to which he feels he can legitimately appeal. (He regards his opinions, if any, as mere speculation, hunch, or what have you.)

It may be possible, at least in principle, for a listener to make a reasonable assessment of which eyewitness is more credible, even without having or appealing to prior opinions of his own concerning the E-domain. For example, he might obtain evidence from others as to whether each putative witness was really present at the crime scene, or, alternatively, known to be elsewhere at the time of the crime. Second, the listener could learn of tests of each witness's visual acuity, which would bear on the accuracy or reliability of their reports. So in this kind of case, the credibility of a putative "expert's" report can be checked by such methods as independent verification of whether he had the opportunity and ability to see what he claims to have seen. Are analogous methods available to someone who seeks to assess the credibility of a "cognitive" expert as opposed to an eyewitness expert?

Before addressing this question, we should say more about the nature of expertise and the sorts of experts we are concerned with here. Some kinds of experts are unusually accomplished at certain skills, including violinists, billiards players, textile designers, and so forth. These are not the kinds of experts with which epistemology is most naturally concerned. For epistemo-logical purposes we shall mainly focus on cognitive or intellectual experts: people who have (or claim to have) a superior quantity or level of knowledge in some domain and an ability to generate new knowledge in answer to questions within the domain. Admittedly, there are elements of skill or know-how in intellectual matters too, so the boundary between skill expertise and cognitive expertise is not a sharp one. Nonetheless, I shall try to work on only one side of this rough divide, the intellectual side.

How shall we define expertise in the cognitive sense? What distinguishes an expert from a layperson, in a given cognitive domain? I'll begin by specifying an objective sense of expertise, what it is to *be* an expert, not what it is to have a reputation for expertise. Once the objective sense is specified, the reputational sense readily follows: a reputational expert is someone widely believed to be an expert (in the objective sense), whether or not he really is one.

Turning to objective expertise, then, I first propose that cognitive expertise be defined in "veritistic" (truth-linked) terms. As a first pass, experts in a given domain (the E-domain) have more beliefs (or high degrees of belief) in true propositions and/or fewer beliefs in false propositions within that domain than most people do (or better: than the vast majority of people do). According to this proposal, expertise is largely a comparative matter. However, I do not think it is wholly comparative. If the vast majority of people are full of false beliefs in a domain and Jones exceeds them slightly by not succumbing to a few falsehoods that are widely shared, that still does not make him an "expert" (from a God's-eye point of view). To qualify as a cognitive expert, a person must possess a substantial body of truths in the target domain. Being an expert is not simply a matter of veritistic superiority to most of the community. Some non-comparative threshold of veritistic attainment must be reached, though there is great vagueness in setting this threshold.

Expertise is not all a matter of possessing accurate information. It includes a capacity or disposition to deploy or exploit this fund of information to form beliefs in true answers to new questions that may be posed in the domain. This arises from some set of skills or techniques that constitute part of what it is to be an expert. An expert has the (cognitive) know-how, when presented with a new question in the domain, to go to the right sectors of his information-bank and perform appropriate operations on this information; or to deploy some external apparatus or data-banks to disclose relevant material. So expertise features a propensity element as well as an element of actual attainment.

A third possible feature of expertise may require a little modification in what we said earlier. To discuss this feature, let us distinguish the *primary* and *secondary* questions in a domain. Primary questions are the principal questions of interest to the researchers or students of the subject-matter. Secondary questions concern the existing evidence or arguments that bear on the primary questions, and the assessments of the evidence made by prominent researchers. In general, an expert in a field is someone who has (comparatively) extensive knowledge (in the weak sense of knowledge, i.e., true belief) of the state of the evidence, and knowledge of the opinions and reactions to that evidence by prominent workers in the field. In the central sense of "expert" (a strong sense), an expert is someone with an unusually extensive body of knowledge on both primary and secondary questions in the domain. However, there may also be a weak sense of "expert", in which it includes someone who merely has extensive knowledge on the secondary questions in the domain. Consider two people with strongly divergent views on the primary questions in the domain, so that one of them is largely right and the other is largely wrong. By the original, strong criterion, the one who is largely wrong would not qualify as an expert. People might disagree with this as the final word on the matter. They might hold that anyone with a thorough knowledge of the existing evidence and the differing views held by the workers in the field deserves to be called an expert. I concede this by acknowledging the weak sense of "expert".

Applying what has been said above, we can say that an expert (in the strong sense) in domain D is someone who possesses an extensive fund of knowledge (true belief) and a set of skills or methods for apt and successful deployment of this knowledge to new questions in the domain. Anyone purporting to be a (cognitive) expert in a given domain will claim to have such a fund and set of methods, and will claim to have true answers to the question(s) under dispute because he has applied his fund and his methods to the question(s). The task for the layperson who is consulting putative experts, and who hopes thereby to learn a true answer to the target question, is to decide who has superior expertise, or who has better deployed his expertise to the question at hand. The novice/2-experts problem is whether a layperson can *justifiably* choose one putative expert as more credible or trustworthy than the other with respect to the question at hand, and what might be the epistemic basis for such a choice?[7]

3. ARGUMENT-BASED EVIDENCE

To address these issues, I shall begin by listing five possible sources of evidence that a novice might have, in a novice/2-experts situation, for trusting one putative expert more than another. I'll then explore the prospects for utilizing such sources, depending on their availability and the novice's exact circumstance. The five sources I shall discuss are:

(A)   Arguments presented by the contending experts to support their own views and critique their rivals' views.
(B)   Agreement from additional putative experts on one side or other of the subject in question.
(C)   Appraisals by "meta-experts" of the experts' expertise (including appraisals reflected in formal credentials earned by the experts).
(D)   Evidence of the experts' interests and biases vis-à-vis the question at issue.
(E)   Evidence of the experts' past "track-records".

In the remainder of the paper, I shall examine these five possible sources, beginning, in this section, with source (A).[8]

There are two types of communications that a novice, N, might receive from his two experts, E_1 and E_2.[9] First, each expert might baldly state her view (conclusion), without supporting it with any evidence or argument whatever. More commonly, an expert may give detailed support to her view in some public or professional context, but this detailed defense might only appear in a restricted venue (e.g., a professional conference or journal) that does not reach N's attention. So N might not encounter the two experts' defenses, or might encounter only very truncated versions of them. For example, N might hear about the experts' views and their support from a second-hand account in the popular press that does not go into many details. At the opposite end of the communicational spectrum, the two experts might engage in a full-scale debate that N witnesses (or reads a detailed reconstruction of). Each expert might there present fairly developed arguments in support of her view and against that of her opponent. Clearly, only when N somehow encounters the experts' evidence or arguments can he have evidence of type (A). So let us consider this scenario.

We may initially suppose that if N can gain (greater) justification for believing one expert's view as compared with the other by means of their arguments, the novice must at least understand the evidence cited in the experts' arguments. For some domains of expertise and some novices, however, even a mere grasp of the evidence may be out of reach. These are cases where N is an "ignoramus" vis-à-vis the E-domain. This is not the universal plight of novices. Sometimes they can understand the evidence (in some measure) but aren't in a position, from personal knowledge, to give it any credence. Assessing an expert's evidence may be especially difficult when it is disputed by an opposing expert.

Not every statement that appears in an expert's argument need be epistemically inaccessible to the novice. Let us distinguish here between *esoteric* and *exoteric* statements within an expert's discourse. Esoteric statements belong to the relevant sphere of expertise, and their truth-values are inaccessible to N—in terms of his personal knowledge, at any rate. Exoteric statements are outside the domain of expertise; their truth-values may be accessible to N—either at the time of their assertion or later.[10] I presume that esoteric statements comprise a hefty portion of the premises and "lemmas" in an expert's argument. That's what makes it difficult for a novice to become justified in believing any expert's view on the basis of arguments per se. Not only are novices commonly unable to assess the truth-values of the esoteric propositions, but they also are ill-placed to assess the support relations between the cited evidence and the proffered conclusion. Of course, the proponent expert will claim that the support relation is strong between her evidence and the conclusion she defends; but her opponent will commonly dispute this. The novice will be ill-placed to assess which expert is in the right.

At this point I wish to distinguish *direct* and *indirect argumentative justification*. In direct argumentative justification, a hearer becomes justified in believing an argument's conclusion by becoming justified in believing the argument's premises and their (strong) support relation to the conclusion. If a speaker's endorsement of an argument helps bring it about that the hearer has such justificational status vis-à-vis its premises and support relation, then the hearer may acquire "direct" justification for the conclusion via that speaker's argument.[11] As we have said, however, it is difficult for an expert's argument to produce direct justification in the hearer in the novice/2-expert situation. Precisely because many of these matters are esoteric, N will have a hard time adjudicating between E_1's and E_2's claims, and will therefore have a hard time becoming justified vis-à-vis either of their conclusions. He will even have a hard time becoming justified in trusting one conclusion *more* than the other.

The idea of indirect argumentative justification arises from the idea that one speaker in a debate may demonstrate dialectical superiority over the other, and this dialectical superiority might be a plausible *indicator*[12] for N of greater expertise, even if it doesn't render N directly justified in believing the superior speaker's conclusion. By dialectical superiority, I do not mean merely greater debating skill. Here is an example of what I do mean.

Whenever expert E_2 offers evidence for her conclusion, expert E_1 presents an ostensible rebuttal or defeater of that evidence. On the other hand, when E_1 offers evidence for her conclusion, E_2 never manages to offer a rebuttal or defeater to E_1's evidence. Now N is not in a position to assess the truth-value of E_1's defeaters against E_2, nor to evaluate the truth-value or strength of support that E_1's (undefeated) evidence gives to E_1's conclusion. For these reasons, E_1's evidence (or arguments) are not directly justificatory for N. Nonetheless, in "formal" dialectical terms, E_1 seems to be doing better in the dispute. Furthermore, I suggest, this dialectical superiority may reasonably be taken as an indicator of E_1's having superior expertise on the question at issue. It is a (non-conclusive) indicator that E_1 has a superior fund of information in the domain, or a superior method for manipulating her information, or both.

Additional signs of superior expertise may come from other aspects of the debate, though these are far more tenuous. For example, the comparative quickness and smoothness with which E_1 responds to E_2's evidence may suggest that E_1 is already well familiar with E_2's "points" and has already thought out counterarguments. If E_2's responsiveness to E_1's arguments displays less quickness and smoothness, that may suggest that E_1's prior mastery of the relevant information and support considerations exceeds that of E_2. Of course, quickness and smoothness are problematic indicators of informational mastery. Skilled debaters and well-coached witnesses can appear better-informed because of their stylistic polish, which is not a true indicator of superior expertise. This makes the proper use of indirect argumentative justification a very delicate matter.[13]

To clarify the direct/indirect distinction being drawn here, consider two different things a hearer might say to articulate these different bases of justification. In the case of direct argumentative justifiedness, he might say: "In light of this expert's argument, that is, in light of the truth of its premises and the support they confer on the conclusion (both of which are epistemically accessible to me), I am now justified in believing the conclusion." In indirect argumentative justifiedness, the hearer might say: "In light of the way this expert has argued—her argumentative *performance*, as it were—I can infer that she has more expertise than her opponent; so I am justified in inferring that her conclusion is probably the correct one."

Here is another way to explain the direct/indirect distinction. Indirect argumentative justification essentially involves an *inference to the best explanation*, an inference that N might make from the performances of the two speakers to their respective levels of expertise. From their performances, N makes an inference as to which expert has superior expertise in the target domain. Then he makes an inference from greater expertise to a higher probability of endorsing a true conclusion. Whereas *indirect* argumentative justification essentially involves inference to the best explanation, direct argumentative justification need involve no such inference. Of course, it *might* involve such inference; but if so, the topic of the explanatory inference will only concern the objects, systems, or states of affairs under dispute, not the relative expertise of the contending experts. By contrast, in indirect argumentative justifiedness, it is precisely the experts' relative expertise that constitutes the target of the inference to the best explanation.

Hardwig (1985) makes much of the fact that in the novice/expert situation, the novice lacks the expert's reasons for believing her conclusion. This is correct. Usually, a novice (1) lacks all or some of the premises from which an expert reasons to her conclusion, (2) is in an inferior position to assess the support relation between the expert's premises and conclusions, and (3) is ignorant of many or most of the defeaters (and "defeater-defeaters") that might bear on an expert's arguments. However, although novice N may lack (all or some of) an expert's reasons R for believing a conclusion p, N *might* have reasons R* for believing *that* the expert has good reasons for believing p; and N might have reasons R* for believing that one expert has *better* reasons for believing her conclusion than her opponent has for hers. Indirect argumentative justification is one means by which N might acquire reasons R* without sharing (all or any) of either experts' reasons R.[14] It is this possibility to which Hardwig gives short shrift. I don't say that a novice in a novice/2-expert situation invariably has such reasons R*; nor do I say that it is easy for a novice to acquire such reasons. But it does seem to be possible.

4. AGREEMENT FROM OTHER EXPERTS: THE QUESTION OF NUMBERS

An additional possible strategy for the novice is to appeal to further experts. This brings us to categories (B) and (C) on our list. Category (B) invites N to consider whether other experts agree with E_1 or with E_2. What proportion of these experts agree with E_1 and what proportion with E_2? In other words, to the extent that it is feasible, N should consult the numbers, or degree of consensus, among all relevant (putative) experts. Won't N be fully justified in trusting E_1 over E_2 if almost all other experts on the subject agree with E_1, or if even a preponderance of the other experts agree with E_1?

Another possible source of evidence, cited under category (C), also appeals to other experts but in a slightly different vein. Under category (C), N should seek evidence about the two rival experts' relative degrees of expertise by consulting third parties' assessments of their expertise. If "meta-experts" give E_1 higher "ratings" or "scores" than E_2, shouldn't N rely more on E_1 than E_2? Credentials can be viewed as a special case of this same process. Academic degrees, professional accreditations, work experience, and so forth (all from specific institutions with distinct reputations) reflect certifications by other experts of E_1's and E_2's demonstrated training or competence. The relative strengths or weights of these indicators might be utilized by N to distill appropriate levels of trust for E_1 and E_2 respectively.[15]

I treat ratings and credentials as signaling "agreement" by other experts because I assume that established authorities certify trainees as competent when they are satisfied that the latter demonstrate (1) a mastery of the same methods that the certifiers deem fundamental to the field, and (2) knowledge of (or belief in) propositions that certifiers deem to be fundamental facts or laws of the discipline. In this fashion, ratings and conferred credentials ultimately rest on basic agreement with the meta-experts and certifying authorities.

When it comes to evaluating specific experts, there is precedent in the American legal system for inquiring into the degree to which other experts agree with those being evaluated.[16] But precedented or not, just how good is this appeal to consensus? If a putative expert's opinion is joined by the consensual opinions of other putative experts, how much warrant does that give a hearer for trusting the original opinion? How much evidential worth does consensus or agreement deserve in the doxastic decision-making of a hearer?

If one holds that a person's opinion deserves prima facie credence, despite the absence of any evidence of their reliability on the subject, then numbers would seem to be very weighty, at least in the absence of additional evidence. Each new testifier or opinion-holder on one side of the issue should add weight to that side. So a novice who is otherwise in the dark about the reliability of the various opinion-holders would seem driven to agree with the more numerous body of experts. Is that right?

Here are two examples that pose doubts for "using the numbers" to judge the relative credibility of opposing positions. First is the case of a guru with slavish followers. Whatever the guru believes is slavishly believed by his followers. They fix their opinions wholly and exclusively on the basis of their leader's views. Intellectually speaking, they are merely his clones. Or consider a group of followers who are not led by a single leader but by a small elite of opinion-makers. When the opinion-makers agree, the mass of followers concur in their opinion. Shouldn't a novice consider this kind of scenario as a possibility? Perhaps (putative) expert E_1 belongs to a doctrinal community whose members devoutly and uncritically agree with the opinions of some single leader or leadership cabal. Should the numerosity of the community make their opinion more credible than that of a less numerous group of experts? Another example, which also challenges the probity of greater numbers, is the example of rumors. Rumors are stories that are widely circulated and accepted though few of the believers have access to the rumored facts. If someone hears a rumor from one source, is that source's credibility enhanced when the same rumor is repeated by a second, third, and fourth source? Presumably not, especially if the hearer knows (or justifiably believes) that these sources are all uncritical recipients of the same rumor.

It will be objected that additional rumor spreaders do not add credibility to an initial rumor monger because the additional ones have no established reliability. The hearer has no reason to think that any of their opinions is worthy of trust. Furthermore, the rumor case doesn't seem to involve "expert" opinions at all and thereby contrasts with the original case. In the original case the hearer has at least some prior reason to think that each new speaker who concurs with one of the original pair has *some* credibility (reliability). Under that scenario, don't additional concurring experts increase the total believability of the one with whom they agree?

It appears, then, that greater numbers should add further credibility, at least when each added opinion-holder has positive initial credibility. This view is certainly presupposed by some approaches to the subject. In the Lehrer-Wagner (1981) model, for example, each new person to whom a subject assigns "respect" or "weight" will provide an extra vector that should push the subject in the direction of that individual's opinion.[17] Unfortunately, this approach has a problem. If two or more opinion-holders are totally *non-independent* of one another, and if the subject knows or is justified in believing this, then the subject's opinion should not be swayed—even a little—by more than one of these opinion-holders. As in the case of a guru and his blind followers, a follower's opinion does not provide any additional grounds for accepting the guru's view (and a second follower does not provide additional grounds for accepting a first follower's view) even if all followers are precisely as reliable as the guru himself (or as one another)—which followers must be, of course, if they believe exactly the same things as the guru (and one another) on the topics in question. Let me demonstrate this through a Bayesian analysis.

Under a simple Bayesian approach, an agent who receives new evidence should update his degree of belief in a hypothesis H by conditioning on that evidence. This means that he should use the ratio (or quotient) of two likelihoods: the likelihood of the evidence occurring if H is true and the likelihood of the evidence occurring if H is false. In the present case the evidence in question is the belief in H on the part of one or more putative experts. More precisely, we are interested in comparing (A) the result of conditioning on the evidence of a single putative expert's belief with (B) the result of conditioning on the evidence of concurring beliefs by two putative experts. Call the two putative experts X and Y, and let X(H) be X's believing H and Y(H) be Y's believing H. What we wish to compare, then, is the magnitude of the likelihood quotient expressed in (1) with the magnitude of the likelihood quotient expressed in (2).

$$\frac{P(X(H) \,/\, H)}{P(X(H) \,/\, {\sim}H)} \tag{1}$$

$$\frac{P(X(H)\&Y(H)/H)}{P(X(H)\&Y(H)\ /\sim H)} \tag{2}$$

The principle we are interested in is the principle that the likelihood ratio given in (2) is always larger than the likelihood ratio given in (1), so that an agent who learns that X and Y both believe H will always have grounds for a larger upward revision of his degree of belief in H than if he learns only that X believes H. At least this is so when X and Y are each somewhat credible (reliable). More precisely, such comparative revisions are in order if the agent is *justified* in believing these things in the different scenarios. I am going to show that such comparative revisions are not always in order. Sometimes (2) is not larger than (1); so the agent—if he knows or justifiably believes this—is not justified in making a larger upward revision from the evidence of two concurring believers than from one believer.

First let us note that according to the probability calculus, (2) is equivalent to (3).

$$\frac{P(X(H)\ /\ H)\ P(Y(H)\ /\ X(H)\ \&\ H)}{P(X(H)\ /\sim H)\ P(Y(H)\ /\ X(H)\ \&\sim H)} \tag{3}$$

While looking at (3), return to the case of blind followers. If Y is a blind follower of X, then anything believed by X (including H) will also be believed by Y. And this will hold whether or not H is true. So,

$$P(Y(H)\ /\ X(H)\ \&\ H) = 1, \tag{4}$$

and

$$P(Y(H)\ /\ X(H)\ \&\sim H) = 1. \tag{5}$$

Substituting these two values into expression (3), (3) reduces to (1). Thus, in the case of a blind follower, (2) (which is equivalent to (3)) is the same as (1), and no larger revision is warranted in the two-concurring-believers case than in the single-believer case.

Suppose that the second concurring believer, Y, is not a *blind* follower of X. Suppose he would sometimes agree with X but not in all circumstances. Under that scenario, does the addition of Y's concurring belief always provide the agent (who possesses this information) with more grounds for believing H? Again the answer is no. The appropriate question is whether Y is more likely to believe H when X believes H and H is true than when X believes H and H is false. If Y is just as likely to follow X's opinion whether H is true or false, then Y's concurring belief adds nothing to the agent's evidential grounds for H (driven by the likelihood quotient). Let us see why this is so.

If Y is just as likely to follow X's opinion when H is false as when it's true, then (6) holds:

$$P(Y(H) / X(H) \& H) = P(Y(H) / X(H) \& \sim H) \qquad (6)$$

But if (6) holds, then (3) again reduces to (1), because the right-hand sides of both numerator and denominator in (3) are equal and cancel each other out. Since (3) reduces to (1), the agent still gets no extra evidential boost from Y's agreement with X concerning H. Here it is not required that Y is certain to follow X's opinion; the likelihood of his following X might only be 0.80, or 0.40, or whatever. As long as Y is just as likely to follow X's opinion when H is true as when it's false, we get the same result.

Let us describe this last case by saying that Y is a *non-discriminating reflector* of X (with respect to H). When Y is a non-discriminating reflector of X, Y's opinion has no extra evidential worth for the agent above and beyond X's opinion. What is necessary for the novice to get an extra evidential boost from Y's belief in H is that he (the novice) be justified in believing (6'):

$$P(Y(H) / X(H) \& H) > P(Y(H) / X(H) \& \sim H) \qquad (7)$$

If (6') is satisfied, then Y's belief is at least partly *conditionally independent* of X's belief. Full conditional independence is a situation in which any dependency between X and Y's beliefs is accounted for by the dependency of each upon H. Although full conditional independence is not required to boost N's evidence, *partial* conditional independence is required.[18]

We may now identify the trouble with the (unqualified) numbers principle. The trouble is that a novice cannot automatically count on his putative experts being (even partially) conditionally independent of one another. He cannot automatically count on the truth of (6'). Y may be a non-discriminating reflector of X, or X may be a non-discriminating reflector of Y, or both may be non-discriminating reflectors of some third party or parties. The same point applies no matter how many additional putative experts share an initial expert's opinion. If they are all non-discriminating reflectors of someone whose opinion has already been taken into account, they add no further weight to the novice's evidence.

What type of evidence can the novice have to justify his acceptance of (or high level of credence in) (6')? N can have reason to believe that Y's *route* to belief in H was such that even in possible cases where X fails to recognize H's falsity (and hence believes it), Y *would* recognize its falsity. There are two types of causal routes to Y's belief of the right sort. First, Y's route to belief in H might entirely *bypass* X's route. This would be exemplified by cases in which X and Y are causally independent eyewitnesses of the occurrence or non-occurrence of H; or by cases in which X and Y base their respective beliefs on independent experiments that bear on H. In the eyewitness scenario X might falsely believe H through mis-perception of the actual event, whereas Y might perceive the event cor-rectly and avoid belief in H. A second possible route to Y's belief in H might go *partly through* X but not involve uncritical reflection of X's belief. For example, Y might listen to X's reasons for believing H, consider a variety of possible defeaters of these reasons that X never considered, but finally rebut the cogency of these defeaters and concur in accepting H. In either of these scenarios Y's partly "autonomous" causal route made him poised to avoid belief in H even though X believes it (possibly falsely). If N has reason to think that Y used one of these more-or-less autonomous causal routes to belief, rather than a causal route that guar-antees agreement with X, then N has reason to accept (6'). In this fashion, N would have good reason to rate Y's belief as increasing his evidence for H even after taking account of X's belief.

Presumably, novices could well be in such an epistemic situation vis-à-vis a group of concurring (putative) experts. Certainly in the case of con-curring *scientists*, where a novice might have reason to expect them to be critical of one another's viewpoints, a presumption of partial indepen-dence might well be in order. If so, a novice might be warranted in giving greater evidential weight to larger numbers of concurring opinion-holders. According to some theories of scientific opinion formation, however, this warrant could not be sustained. Consider the view that scientists' beliefs are produced entirely by negotiation with other scientists, and in no way reflect reality (or Nature). This view is apparently held by some social constructionists about science, e.g., Bruno Latour and Steve Woolgar (1979/1986); at least this is Kitcher's (1993: 165–66) interpretation of their view.[19] Now if the social constructionists are right, so interpreted, then nobody (at least nobody knowledgeable of this fact) would be war-ranted in believing anything like (6'). There would never be reason to think that any scientist is more likely to believe a scientific hypothesis H when it's true (and some other scientist believes it) than when it's false (and the other scientist believes it). Since causal routes to scientific belief never reflect "real" facts—they only reflect the opinions, interests, and so forth of the community of scientists—(6') will never be true. Anybody who accepts or inclines toward the indicated social-constructionist thesis would never be justified in believing (6').[20]

Setting such extreme views aside, won't a novice normally have reason to expect that different putative experts will have some causal indepen-dence or autonomy from one another in their routes to belief? If so, then if a novice is also justified in believing that each putative expert has some slight level of reliability (greater than chance), then won't he be justified in using the numbers of concurring experts to tilt toward one of two ini-tial rivals as opposed to the other? This conclusion might be right when *all* or *almost all* supplementary experts agree with one of the two initial rivals. But this is rarely the case. Vastly more common are scenarios in which the numbers are more evenly balanced, though not exactly equal. What can a novice conclude in those circumstances? Can he legitimately let the greater numbers decide the issue?

This would be unwarranted, especially if we continue to apply the Bayesian approach. The appropriate change in the novice's belief in H should be based on two sets of concurring opinions (one in favor of H and one against it), and it should depend on *how reliable* the members of each set are and on *how (conditionally) independent* of one another they are. If the members of the smaller group are more reliable and more (conditionally) independent of one another than the members of the larger group, that might imply that the evidential weight of the smaller group exceeds that of the larger one. More precisely, it depends on what the novice is *justified* in believing about these matters. Since the novice's justifiedness on these matters may be very weak, there will be many situations in which he has no distinct or robust justification for going by the relative numbers of like-minded opinion-holders.

This conclusion seems perfectly in order. Here is an example that, by my own lights, sits well with this conclusion. If scientific creationists are more numerous than evolutionary scientists, that would not incline me to say that a novice is warranted in putting more credence in the views of the former than in the views of the latter (on the core issues on which they disagree). At least I am not so inclined on the assumption that the novice has roughly comparable information as most philosophers currently have about the methods of belief formation by evolutionists and creationists respectively.[21] Certainly the numbers do not *necessarily* outweigh considerations of individual reliability and mutual conditional independence. The latter factors seem more probative, in the present case, than the weight of sheer numbers.[22]

5. EVIDENCE FROM INTERESTS AND BIASES

I turn now to the fourth source of possible evidence on our original list: evidence of distorting interests and biases that might lie behind a putative expert's claims. If N has excellent evidence for such bias in one expert and no evidence for such bias in her rival, and if N has no other basis for preferential trust, then N is justified in placing greater trust in the unbiased expert. This proposal comes directly from common sense and experience. If two people give contradictory reports, and exactly one of them has a reason to lie, the relative credibility of the latter is seriously compromised.

Lying, of course, is not the only way that interests and biases can reduce an expert's trustworthiness. Interests and biases can exert more subtle distorting influences on experts' opinions, so that their opinions are less likely to be accurate even if sincere. Someone who is regularly hired as an expert witness for the defense in certain types of civil suits has an economic interest in delivering strong testimony in any current trial, because her reputation as a defense witness depends on her present performance.

As a test of expert performance in situations of conflict of interest, consider the results of a study published in the *Journal of American Medical Association* (Friedberg et al., 1999). The study explored the relationship between published research reports on new oncology drugs that had been sponsored by pharmaceutical companies versus those that had been sponsored by nonprofit organizations. It found a statistically significant relationship between the funding source and the qualitative conclusions in the reports. Unfavorable conclusions were reached by 38% of nonprofit-sponsored studies but by only 5% of pharmaceutical company-sponsored studies.

From a practical point of view, information bearing on an expert's interests is often one of the more accessible pieces of relevant information that a novice can glean about an expert. Of course, it often transpires that *both* members of a pair of testifying experts have interests that compromise their credibility. But when there is a non-negligible difference on this dimension, it is certainly legitimate information for a novice to employ.

Pecuniary interests are familiar types of potential distorters of an individual's claims or opinions. Of greater significance, partly because of its greater opacity to the novice, is a bias that might infect a whole discipline, sub-discipline, or research group. If all or most members of a given field are infected by the same bias, the novice will have a difficult time telling the real worth of corroborating testimony from other experts and meta-experts. This makes the numbers game, discussed in the previous section, even trickier for the novice to negotiate.

One class of biases emphasized by feminist epistemologists involves the exclusion or underrepresentation of certain viewpoints or standpoints within a discipline or expert community. This might result in the failure of a community to gather or appreciate the significance of certain types of relevant evidence. A second type of community-wide bias arises from the economics or politics of a sub-discipline, or research community. To advance its funding prospects, practitioners might habitually exaggerate the probativeness of the evidence that allegedly supports their findings, especially to outsiders. In competition with neighboring sciences and research enterprises for both resources and recognition, a given research community might apply comparatively lax standards in reporting its results. Novices will have a difficult time detecting this, or weighing the merit of such an allegation by rival experts outside the field.[23]

6. USING PAST TRACK RECORDS

The final category in our list may provide the novice's best source of evidence for making credibility choices. This is the use of putative experts' past track records of cognitive success to assess the likelihoods of their having correct answers to the current question. But how can a novice assess past track records? There are several theoretical problems here, harking back to matters discussed earlier.

First, doesn't using past track records amount to using the method of (direct) "calibration" to assess a candidate expert's expertise? Using a past track record means looking at the candidate's past success rate for previous questions in the E-domain to which she offered answers. But in our earlier discussion (section 2), I said that it's in the nature of a novice that he has no opinions, or no confidence in his own opinions, about matters falling within the E-domain. So how can the novice have any (usable) beliefs about past answers in the E-domain by which to assess the candidate's expertise? In other words, how can a novice, *qua* novice, have any opinions at all about past track records of candidate experts?

A possible response to this problem is to revisit the distinction between *esoteric* and *exoteric* statements. Perhaps not every statement in the E-domain is esoteric. There may also be a body of exoteric statements in the E-domain, and they are the statements for which a novice might assess a candidate's expertise. But does this really make sense? If a statement is an exoteric statement, i.e., one that is epistemically accessible to novices, then why should it even be included in the E-domain? One would have thought that the E-domain is precisely the domain of propositions accessible only to experts.

The solution to the problem begins by sharpening our esoteric/exoteric distinction. It is natural to think that statements are categorically either esoteric or exoteric, but that is a mistake. A given (timeless) statement is esoteric or exoteric only *relative* to an epistemic standpoint or position. It might be esoteric relative to one epistemic position but exoteric relative to a different position. For example, consider the statement, "There will be an eclipse of the sun on April 22, 2130, in Santa Fe, New Mexico." Relative to the present epistemic standpoint, i.e., the standpoint of people living in the year 2000, this is an esoteric statement. Ordinary people in the year 2000 will not be able to answer this question correctly, except by guessing. On the other hand, on the very day in question, April 22, 2130, ordinary people on the street in Santa Fe, New Mexico will easily be able to answer the question correctly. In that different epistemic position, the question will be an exoteric one, not an esoteric one.[24] You won't need specialized training or knowledge to determine the answer to the question. In this way, the epistemic status of a statement can change from one time to another.

There is a significant application of this simple fact to the expert/novice problem. A novice might easily be able to determine the truth-value of a statement after it has become exoteric. He might be able to tell *then* that it is indeed true. Moreover, he might learn that at an earlier time, when the statement was esoteric for the likes of him, another individual managed to believe it and say that it is (or would be) true. Furthermore, the same individual might repeatedly display the capacity to assert statements that are esoteric at the time of assertion but become exoteric later, and she might repeatedly turn out to have been right, as determined under the subsequently exoteric circumstances. When this transpires, novices can infer that this unusual knower must possess some special manner of knowing—some distinctive expertise—that is not available to them. They presumably will not know exactly what this distinctive manner of knowing involves, but presumably it involves some proprietary fund of information and some methodology for deploying that information. In this fashion, a novice can verify somebody else's expertise in a certain domain by verifying their impressive track record within that domain. And this can be done without the novice himself somehow being transformed into an expert.

The astronomical example is just one of many, which are easily proliferated. If an automobile, an air-conditioning system, or an organic system is suffering some malfunction or impairment, untrained people will often be unable to specify any true proposition of the form, "If you apply treatment X to system Y, the system will return to proper functioning." However, there may be people who can repeatedly specify true propositions precisely of this sort.[25] Moreover, that these propositions are true can be verified by novices, because novices might be able to "watch" the treatment being applied to the malfunctioning system and see that the system returns to proper functioning (faster than untreated systems do). Although the truth of the proposition is an exoteric matter once the treatment works, it was an esoteric matter before the treatment was applied and produced its result. In such a case the expert has knowledge, and can be determined to have had knowledge, at a time when it was esoteric.[26]

It should be emphasized that many questions to which experts provide answers, at times when they are esoteric, are not merely yes/no questions that might be answered correctly by lucky guesses. Many of them are questions that admit of innumerable possible answers, sometimes indefinitely many answers. Simplifying for purposes of illustration, we might say that when a patient with an ailment sees a doctor, he is asking her the question, "Which medicine, among the tens of thousands of available medicines, will cure or alleviate this ailment?" Such a question is unlikely to be answered correctly by mere guesswork. Similarly, when rocket scientists were first trying to land a spaceship on the moon, there were indefinitely many possible answers to the question, "Which series of steps will succeed in landing this (or some) spaceship on the moon?" Choosing a correct answer from among the infinite list of possible answers is unlikely to be a lucky guess. It is feats like this, often involving technological applications, that rightly persuade novices that the people who get the correct answers have a special fund of information and a special methodology for deploying it that jointly yield a superior capacity to get right answers. In this fashion, novices can indeed determine that others are experts in a domain in which they themselves are not.

Of course, this provides no algorithm by which novices can resolve all
their two-expert problems. Only occasionally will a novice know, or be
able to determine, the track records of the putative experts that dispute
an issue before him. A juror in a civil trial has no opportunity to run out
and obtain track record information about rival expert witnesses who testify before him. Nonetheless, the fact that novices can verify track records
and use them to test a candidate's claims to expertise, at least in principle
and in some cases, goes some distance toward dispelling utter skepticism
for the novice/2-expert situation. Moreover, the possibility of "directly"
determining the expertise of a few experts makes it possible to draw plausible inferences about a much wider class of candidate experts. If certain
individuals are shown, by the methods presented above, to have substantial
expertise, and if those individuals train others, then it is a plausible inference that the trainees will themselves have comparable funds of information and methodologies, of the same sort that yielded cognitive success for
the original experts.[27] Furthermore, to the extent that the verified experts
are then consulted as "meta-experts" about the expertise of others (even if
they didn't train or credential them), the latter can again be inferred to
have comparable expertise. Thus, some of the earlier skepticism engendered by the novice/2-expert problem might be mitigated once the foundation of expert verification provided in this section has been established.

7. CONCLUSION

My story's ending is decidedly mixed, a cause for neither elation nor
gloom. Skeptical clouds loom over many a novice's epistemic horizons
when confronted with rival experts bearing competing messages. There
are a few silver linings, however. Establishing experts' track-records is not
beyond the pale of possibility, or even feasibility. This in turn can bolster
the credibility of a wider class of experts, thereby laying the foundation for
a legitimate use of numbers when trying to choose between experts. There
is no denying, however, that the epistemic situations facing novices are
often daunting. There are interesting theoretical questions in the analysis
of such situations, and they pose interesting practical challenges for "applied" social epistemology. What kinds of education, for example, could
substantially improve the ability of novices to appraise expertise, and what
kinds of communicational intermediaries might help make the novice-
expert relationship more one of justified credence than blind trust.[28]

Notes

1 Thanks to Scott LaBarge for calling Plato's treatment of this subject to my
attention.

2 In his 1991 paper, Hardwig at first says that trust must be "at least partially
blind" (p. 693). He then proceeds to talk about knowledge resting on trust and
therefore being blind (pp. 693, 699) without using the qualifier "partially".

3 However, there is some question whether Foley can consistently call the epistemic right he posits a "fundamental" one, since he also says that it rests on (A) my justified *self*-trust, and (B) the *similarity* of others to me—presumably the *evidence* I have of their similarity to me (see pp. 63–64). Another question for Foley is how the fundamentality thesis fits with his view that in cases of conflict I have more reason (prima facie) to trust myself than to trust someone else (see p. 66). If my justified trust in others is really fundamental, why does it take a back-seat to self-trust?

4 Moreover, according to Baron-Cohen, there is a separate module called the "shared attention mechanism", which seeks to determine when another person is attending to the same object as the self is attending to.

5 For one thing, it may be argued that babies' interpretations of what people say is, in the first instance, constrained by the assumption that the contents concern matters within the speakers' perceptual ken. This is not an empirical finding, it might be argued, but an a prion posit that is used to fix speakers' meanings.

6 Some theorists of testimony, Burge included, maintain that a hearer's justificational status vis-à-vis a claim received from a source depends partly on the justificational status of the source's own belief in that claim. This is a *transpersonal, preservationist,* or *transmissional* conception of justifiedness, under which a recipient is not justified in believing p unless the speaker has a justification and entitlement that he *transmits* to the hearer. For purposes of this paper, however, I shall not consider this transmissional conception of justification. First, Burge himself recognizes that there is such a thing as the recipient's "proprietary" justification for believing an interlocutor's claim, justification localized "in" the recipient, which isn't affected by the source's justification (1993: 485–486). I think it is appropriate to concentrate on this "proprietary" justification (of the recipient) for present purposes. When a hearer is trying to "choose" between the conflicting claims of rival speakers, he cannot appeal to any inaccessible justification lodged in the heads of the speakers. He can only appeal to his *own* justificational resources. (Of course, these might include things *said* by the two speakers by way of defense of their contentions, things which also are relevant to *their own* justifications.) For other types of (plausible) objections to Burge's preservationism about testimony, see Bezuidenhout (1998).

7 In posing the question of justifiedness, I mean to stay as neutral as possible between different approaches to the concept of justifiedness, e.g., between internalist versus externalist approaches to justifiedness. Notice, moreover, that I am not merely asking whether and how the novice can justifiably decide to accept one (candidate) expert's view *outright*, but whether and how he can justifiably decide to give *greater* credence to one than to the other.

8 I do not mean to be committed to the exhaustiveness of this list. The list just includes some salient categories.

9 In what follows I shall for brevity speak about two experts, but I shall normally mean two *putative* experts, because from the novice's epistemic perspective it is problematic whether each, or either, of the self-proclaimed experts really is one.

10 It might be helpful to distinguish *semanticallp* esoteric statements and *epistemically* esoteric statements. (Thanks to Carol Caraway for this suggestion.) Semantically esoteric statements are ones that a novice cannot assess because he does not even *understand* them; typically, they utilize a technical vocabulary he has not mastered. Epistemically esoteric statements are statements the novice understands but still cannot assess for truthvalue.

11 By "direct" justification I do not, of course, mean anything having to do with the basicness of the conclusion in question, in the foundationalist sense of basicness. The distinction I am after is entirely different, as will shortly emerge.

12. Edward Craig (1990: 135) similarly speaks of "indicator properties" as what an inquirer seeks to identify in an informant as a guide to his/her truth-telling ability.

13 Scott Brewer (1998) discusses many of the same issues about novices and experts canvassed here. He treats the present topic under the heading of novices' using experts' "demeanor" to assess their expertise. Demeanor is an especially un-trustworthy guide, he points out, where there is a lucrative "market" for demeanor itself—where demeanor is "traded" at high prices (1998: 1622). This practice was prominent in the days of the sophists and is a robust business in adversarial legal systems.

14. Of course, in indirect argumentative justification the novice must at least *hear* some of the expert's premisesf—or intermediate steps between "ultimate" premises and conclusion. But the novice will not share the expert's *justifiedness* in believing those premises.

15 These items fall under Kitcher's category of "unearned authority" (1993: 315).

16. Appealing to other experts to validate or underwrite a putative expert's opinion—or, more precisely, the *basis* for his opinion—has a precedent in the legal system's procedures for deciding the admissibility of scientific expert testimony. Under the governing test for admitting or excluding such testimony that was appli-cable from 1923 to 1993, the scientific principle (or methodology) on which a proffered piece of testimony is based must have "gained general acceptance in the particular field in which it belongs". (*Frye v. United States*, 292 F. 1013 D.C. Cir. (1923)). In other words, appeal was made to the scientific community's opinion to decide whether the basis of an expert's testimony is sound enough to allow that testimony into court. This test has been superseded as the uniquely appropriate test in a more recent decision of the Supreme Court (*Daubert v. Merrell Dow Pharma-ceuticals*, 509 U.S. 579 (1993)); but the latter decision also appeals to the opinions of other experts. It recommends that judges use a combination of four criteria (none of them necessary or sufficient) in deciding whether proffered scientific expert testimony is admissible. One criterion is the old general acceptance criterion and another is whether the proffered evidence has been subjected to peer review and publication. Peer review, obviously, also introduces the opinions of other experts. Of course, the admissibility of a piece of expert testimony is not the same question as how heavily a hearer—e.g., a juror—should trust such testimony if he hears it. But the two are closely intertwined, since courts make admissibility decisions on the assumption that jurors are likely to be influenced by any expert testimony they hear. Courts do not wish to admit scientific evidence unless it is quite trustworthy. Thus, the idea of ultimately going to the opinions of other experts to assess the trustworthiness of a given expert's proffered testimony is certainly a well-precedented procedure for trying to validate an expert's trustworthiness.

17. Lehrer and Wagner say (p. 20) that one should assign somebody else a positive weight if one does not regard his opinion as "worthless" on the topic in question-i.e., if one regards him as better than a random device. So it looks as if every clone of a leader should be given positive weight—arguably, the same weight as the leader himself, since their beliefs always coincide—as long as the leader receives positive weight. In the Lehrer-Wagner model, then, each clone will exert a positive force over one's own revisions of opinion just as a leader's opinion

will exert such force; and the more clones there are, the more force in the direction of their collective opinion will be exerted.

18 I am indebted here to Richard Jeffrey (1992: 109–10). He points out that it is only conditional independence that is relevant in these kinds of cases, not "simple independence" defined by the condition: $P(Y(H)/X(H)) = P(Y(H))$. If X and Y are even slightly reliable independent sources of information about H, they won't satisfy this latter condition.

19 I myself interpret Latour and Woolgar as holding a more radical view, viz., that there is no reality that could causally interact, even indirectly, with scientists' beliefs.

20 This is equally so under the more radical view that there are no truths at all (of a scientific sort) about reality or Nature.

21 More specifically, I am assuming that believers in creation science have greater (conditional) dependence on the opinion leaders of their general viewpoint than do believers in evolutionary theory.

22 John Pollock (in a personal communication) suggests a way to bolster support for the use of "the numbers". He says that if one can argue that $P(X(H)/Y(H) \& H) = P(X(H)/H)$, then one can cumulate testimony on each side of an issue by counting experts. He further suggests that, in the absence of countervailing evidence, we should believe that $P(X(H)/Y(H) \& H) = P(X(H)/H)$. He proposes a general principle of probabilistic reasoning, which he calls "the principle of nonclassical direct inference", to the effect that we are defeasibly justified in regarding additional factors about which we know nothing to be irrelevant to the probabilities. In Pollock (2000) (also see Pollock 1990) he formulates the idea as follows. If factor C is irrelevant (presumably he means *probabilistically* irrelevant) to the causal relation between properties B and A, then conjoining C to B should not affect the probability of something's being A. Thus, if we have no reason to think that C is relevant, we can assume defeasibly that $P(Ax/Bx \& Cx) = P(Ax/Bx)$. This principle can be applied, he suggests, to the case of a concurring (putative) expert. But, I ask, is it generally reasonable for us—or for a novice—to assume that the opinion of one expert is probabilistically irrelevant to another expert's holding the same view? I would argue in the negative. Even if neither expert directly influences the opinion of the other, it is extremely common for two people who work in the same intellectual domain to be influenced, directly or indirectly, by some common third expert or group of experts. Interdependence of this sort is widespread, and could be justifiably believed by novices. Thus, probabilistic irrelevance of the sort Pollock postulates as the default case is highly questionable.

23 In a devastating critique of the mental health profession, Robyn Dawes (1994) shows that the real expertise of such professionals is, scientifically, very much in doubt, despite the high level of credentialism in that professional community.

24 In the present discussion only *epistemic* esotericness, not *semantic* esotericness, is in question (see note 10).

25 They can not only recognize such propositions as true when others offer them; they can also produce such propositions on their own when asked the question, "What can be done to repair this system?"

26 I have discussed such cases in earlier writings: Goldman 1991 and Goldman 1999 (p. 269).

27 Of course, some experts may be better than others at transmitting their expertise. Some may devote more effort to it, be more skilled at it, or exercise

stricter standards in credentialing their trainees. This is why good information about training programs is certainly relevant to judgments of expertise.

28 For helpful comments on earlier drafts, I am indebted to Holly Smith, Don Fallis, Peter Graham, Patrick Rysiew, Alison Wylie, and numerous participants at the 2000 Rutgers Epistemology Conference, the philosophy of social science roundtable in St. Louis, and my 2000 NEH Summer Seminar on "Philosophical Foundations of Social Epistemology".

References

Baron-Cohen, Simon (1995). *Mindblindness*. Cambridge, MA: MIT Press.

Bezuidenhout, Anne (1998). "Is Verbal Communication a Purely Preservative Process?" *Philosophical Review* 107: 261–88.

Brewer, Scott (1998). "Scientific Expert Testimony and Intellectual Due Process," *Yale Law Journal* 107: 1535–681.

Burge, Tyler (1993). "Content Preservation," *Philosophical Review* 102: 457–88.

Coady, C. A. J. (1992). *Testimony*. Oxford: Clarendon Press.

Craig, Edward (1990). *Knowledge and the State of Nature—An Essay in Conceptual Synthesis*. Oxford: Clarendon Press.

Dawes, Robyn (1994). *House of Cards: Psychology and Psychotherapy Built on Myth*. New York: Free Press.

Foley, Richard (1994). "Egoism in Epistemology," in F. Schmitt, ed., *Socializing Epistemology*. Lanham, MD: Rowman & Littlefield.

Friedberg, Mark et al. (1999). "Evaluation of Conflict of Interest in Economic Analyses of New Drugs Used in Oncology," *Journal of the American Medical Association* 282: 1453–57.

Gentzler, J. (1995). "How to Discriminate between Experts and Frauds: Some Problems for Socratic Peirastic," *History of Philosophy Quarterly* 3: 227–46.

Goldman, Alvin (1991). "Epistemic Paternalism: Communication Control in Law and Society," *Journal of Philosophy* 88: 113–31.

Goldman, Alvin (1999). *Knowledge in a Social World*. Oxford: Clarendon Press.

Hardwig, John (1985). "Epistemic Dependence," *Journal of Philosophy* 82: 335–49.

Hardwig, John (1991). "The Role of Trust in Knowledge," *Journal of Philosophy* 88: 693–708.

Jeffrey, Richard (1992). *Probability and the Art of Judgment*. New York: Cambridge University Press.

Kitcher, Philip (1993). *The Advancement of Science*. New York: Oxford University Press.

LaBarge, Scott (1997). "Socrates and the Recognition of Experts," in M. McPherran, ed., *Wisdom, Ignorance and Virtue: New Essays in Socratic Studies*. Edmonton: Academic Printing and Publishing.

Latour, Bruno and Woolgar, Steve (1979/1986). *Laboratory Life: The Construction of Scientific Facts*. Princeton: Princeton University Press.

Lehrer, Keith and Wagner, Carl (1981). *Rational Consensus in Science and Society*. Dordrecht: Reidel.

Pollock, John (1990). *Nomic Probability and the Foundations of Induction*. New York: Oxford University Press.

Pollock, John (2000). "A Theory of Rational Action." Unpublished manuscript, University of Arizona.

III

REASONABLE PEER DISAGREEMENT

7

Reasonable Religious Disagreements

Richard Feldman

A few years ago I co-taught a course on "Rationality, Relativism, and Religion" to undergraduates majoring in either philosophy or religion. Many of the students, especially the religion majors, displayed a pleasantly tolerant attitude. Although a wide variety of different religious views were represented in the class and the students disagreed with one another about many religious issues, almost all the students had a great deal of respect for the views of the others. They "agreed to disagree" and concluded that "reasonable people can disagree" about the issues under discussion In large part, the point of this essay is to explore exactly what this respectful and tolerant attitude can sensibly amount to. The issue to be discussed is a general one, applying to disagreements in many areas other than religion. However, I will focus here on religious disagreement.

Clearly, not everyone responds to apparent disagreements with the tolerance and respectful way my students did. Sometimes people respond by being intolerant and dismissive of those with whom they disagree. Some people advocate a kind of "relativism" according to which everyone is in some sense right. I will discuss these two responses in Section I. The rest of the essay will be about "reasonable disagreements" of the sort my students had.

My own religious beliefs will not figure prominently in this essay. However, it probably is best to acknowledge the point of view I had when I began thinking carefully about the issues I will address. I have long been what might plausibly be described as a "complacent atheist." I grew up in a minimally observant Jewish family. I went to Hebrew school and Sunday school for several years, had my bar mitzvah, and soon afterward acknowledged that I did not believe in the existence of God and did not feel much attachment to the religion. In fact, I felt some disapproval of the business-like aspect of our temple, which, as I recall, refused to allow the younger brother of one of my friends to celebrate his bar mitzvah because my friend had reneged on an alleged commitment to continue attending, and paying for, classes beyond his own bar mitzvah. In college and graduate school I found the arguments about the existence of God philosophically interesting, but studying them did nothing to change my beliefs. I remain a relatively complacent atheist, though the issue discussed in this essay challenges that complacency.

I. INTOLERANCE AND RELATIVISM

A. Intolerance

Intolerance can be found on all sides of all issues. I react strongly, perhaps intolerantly, to intolerance, perhaps because it conflicts so sharply with what I have learned in the areas in philosophy that I have studied most extensively, epistemology and critical thinking. Epistemology is the abstract study of knowledge and rationality. Critical thinking, as I understand it, is a kind of applied epistemology, the underlying idea being that thinking clearly and carefully about any issue requires understanding and applying some fundamental epistemological concepts. These include the ideas of truth and rationality, the difference between good reasons and mere persuasiveness or rhetorical effectiveness, and the fundamental concepts of logic. In my view, to think critically and effectively about hard issues requires reconstructing in clear and precise terms the important arguments on the issue with the aim of discovering whether those arguments succeed in establishing or lending rational support to their conclusions. So conceived, arguments are tools for helping us figure out what it is most reasonable to believe. They are decidedly not tools with which we can clobber our "opponents."[1]

In fact, the idea that people with different views are opponents gets us off on the wrong foot. It is better to see others, as far as possible, as engaged in a collective search for the truth, with arguments being precise ways of spelling out reasons supporting a particular conclusion. Intolerant and dismissive responses fail to engage these arguments, and therefore fail to conform to the most fundamental requirements of effective thinking. To respond to someone's argument in a dismissive way has the effect, perhaps intended, of cutting off discussion. It is as if one said, "I refuse to think carefully about what you said. I will simply stick to my own beliefs about the topic." This is inconsistent with the rigorous, careful, and open-minded examination of real issues, which is the essence of critical thinking.

Although religious matters often are discussed rigorously, carefully, and open-mindedly, some discussions appealing to religious ideas constitute blatant refusals to engage in intellectually serious argument analysis. An example of the kind of thinking I have in mind can be found in a column by Cal Thomas, a widely syndicated columnist whose foolish and simplistic words regularly disgrace my local newspaper. In a column about gay marriage, Thomas writes:

Let's put it this way. If you tell me you do not believe in G-d and then say to me that I should brake for animals, or pay women equally, or help the poor, on what basis are you making such an appeal? If no standard for objective truth, law, wisdom, justice, charity, kindness, compassion and fidelity exists in the universe, then what you are asking me to accept is an idea that has taken hold in your head but that has all of the moral compulsion of a bowl of cereal. You are a sentimentalist, trying to persuade me to a point of view based on your feelings about the subject and not rooted in the fear of G-d or some other unchanging earthly standard.[2]

There is much that is troubling about this brief passage. For one thing, Thomas wrongly equates atheism with a denial of "objective" standards of truth, justice, and the rest. In addition, as anyone who has thought hard about arguments knows, there are difficult questions about when it is sensible to appeal to authority to resolve an issue. There are surely times when a sensible person does defer to authority. Many people who have looked under the hood of a malfunctioning car will understand why. To attempt to resolve a contemporary social issue by appeal to the authority of the difficult to interpret words in an ancient text is quite another matter. Furthermore, even if Thomas made his case more politely, it is hard to see the point of arguing about such an issue in a mass circulation public newspaper when you know that your premises are widely disputed among the readers. Good argument proceeds, whenever possible, by appeal to shared premises. Dismissing without argument the views of those with whom you disagree is of no intellectual value. Given all the time and energy I've put into teaching critical thinking, I react strongly to things that represent such small-minded departures from it.

It is difficult to say how, or if, we can get knowledge or justified beliefs about moral issues. Some sophisticated thinkers believe that all moral thoughts really are just "sentiments." Most disagree. But the idea that your moral thoughts are based entirely in sentiments if you do not believe in God, but have some more legitimizing force if you do believe in God is not at the forefront of enlightened thought. Let's put it this way. Cal Thomas is no insightful philosopher, and his thoughts about moral epistemology are scarcely worth more than a moment's reflection. The remarks quoted are from a column asserting that same-sex marriage should not be permitted. That is a complex issue. Judgments about what social arrangements are best for our society are difficult to establish. Well-intentioned people come to different conclusions. Religious bigotry makes no useful contribution to the discussion.

What is most irritating about Thomas's column is its bigotry. Imagine replacing the word "atheist" with names for other groups of people in the sentence, "If you are an atheist, then your moral views are not worth a bowl of cereal." Imagine what an editor would do with the column if it said this about Jews or Muslims. Or if it dismissed in the same way the views of people of some ethnic or racial group in the country. But attacking atheists in this way passes the mainstream acceptability test. Cal

Thomas may be dismissed as a lightweight, fringe thinker. But the view he expresses is a more extreme version of the altogether too common idea that atheists are somehow less than decent people. This attitude is revealed in the undeclared axiom of contemporary American politics that any remotely serious candidate for president, and for many other offices as well, must proclaim religious faith. Acknowledged atheists need not apply. A few months before I wrote this essay (in 2004), a candidate in the Democratic presidential primaries (Howard Dean), got into considerable trouble because he was forced to profess his devoutness in order to remain a viable candidate. I have no idea what his actual religious beliefs were, but it was difficult to dismiss the thought that he was not a religious man and knew that he couldn't acknowledge this fact without giving up all chances of winning the nomination. The reason he could not admit this truth – if it is in fact a truth – is the idea that he somehow he could not be a decent person or a good leader were he not religious. I have no idea how widespread this nonsense is, but it is at least prevalent enough to insert itself into the popular press from time to time. The asymmetry of this situation is notable. While it is acceptable for atheists to be treated with disrespect by the likes of Cal Thomas, it seems (at least to me) that it is widely accepted that atheists are supposed to treat theists with respect and to approach theistic views with attitudes of tolerance.

The Cal Thomas's of the world illustrate one intellectually bankrupt response to disagreement: intolerance and dismissiveness. I turn next to what may seem to be a diametrically opposed response.

B. Relativism

Relativists shy away from acknowledging that there really are disagreements. Relativists wonder why there must be just one right answer to a question and they often say that while one proposition is "true for" one person or one group of people, different and incompatible propositions are "true for" others. I think of this view as "mindless relativism." This sort of relativism is not at all unusual, and it may well be that some of my students had a response along these lines. These relativists think that somehow it can be that when you say that there is a God, you are right and when I say that there is not, I am right as well.

Appealing as it may be to some, this kind of relativism cannot be right.[3] It is true that people on different sides of a debate do have their respective beliefs. But in many cases they really do disagree. They simply cannot both be right, even if we are not in a position to know who is right. To say that the different propositions are "true for" people on the different sides of the issue is just another way to say that they believe different things. It does not make the disagreement go away.

While mindless relativists are in some ways more tolerant and respectful than those who respond in the first way described here, it is notable that they also fail to engage with the arguments of others. Since their own view is "true for them," relativists do not see their own positions as challenged by the views of others. Therefore, they need not examine with care the arguments for those dissenting views. It is as if they responded to arguments on the other side of an issue by saying, "Well, that argument may be a good one for you, but I have my own view and I will stick to it since it is true for me." In a way, this response is almost as dismissive as the intolerance displayed by Cal Thomas, but it is coupled with a difficult to interpret assertion that the other view is right also. Of course, relativists need not respond in this way. It is consistent with their relativism to take competing arguments seriously. However, it is difficult to make sense of their overall position and hard to see just what they think the arguments are supposed to accomplish.

Neither intolerance nor relativism is an acceptable response to disagreement. Advocates of both tend to fail to take seriously the arguments for views opposed to their own. I will set them aside and turn to the more subtle and sophisticated view that I think most of my students had in mind.

II. DISAGREEMENTS

Unlike relativists, most of my students saw that there were real disagreements about religious issues. Unlike Cal Thomas, they took other views seriously. They thought that reasonable people could disagree about the issues, and that this was exactly what was going on their case. But what, exactly, can this respectful and tolerant attitude really amount to? A brief discussion of disagreements generally will help to set the stage for a more detailed investigation of this question in the remainder of this essay.

A. Genuine Disagreements

The students in my class disagreed with one another about significant religious matters. Some – the atheists like me – believed that there is no God. The majority believed that God does exist. Among the theists there were notable differences about the nature of God and about God's relation to the world. The details of those differences will not matter for the discussion that follows and I will not attempt to spell them out here. It just matters that there were some such differences. As my central example, I'll use the disagreement between the atheists and the theists. But most of what I will say could just as well be applied to disagreements among the theists, or to disagreements about other topics.

In saying that there were disagreements among the students, I am saying only that there were propositions that some of them affirmed and some of them denied. When there is a disagreement, it is not possible for both sides to be right. Most obviously, if there is a God, then the atheists are mistaken no matter how sincere, well-meaning, and thoughtful they were. If there is no God, then theists are mistaken. The same goes for the other propositions about which they disagreed: What some of them believed was not simply different from what the others believed. Their beliefs were incompatible. If one side had it right, then the other had it wrong.

Some disagreements are merely apparent and not genuine. That is, there are situations in which people seem to disagree about some proposition but actually do not. For example, people arguing about such things as pornography may not have any real disagreement. Those "against" it may think that it has harmful social consequences. Those "for" it may think that it should not be made illegal. There may be no disagreement about any specific proposition. Of course, there may be real disagreements about one of these more specific propositions concerning pornography. But the example illustrates one way in which an apparent disagreement can be merely apparent.

Disagreements can also be merely apparent when people use words in different ways without realizing it. If you and I are arguing about whether John went to the bank, but you are thinking of a financial institutions and I am thinking about a riverside, then we may have no genuine disagreement. Our disagreement is merely apparent, resulting from our different interpretations of the word. The unnoticed ambiguity of the word masks our agreement about the underlying facts.

There are several differences among people of different faiths that do not amount to genuine disagreements. For example, one difference between people of different religious faiths is that they commit to following differing practices. The holidays they observe and the character of their places of worship will differ. And a variety of other customs and practices will differ. These differences are not, in their own right, disagreements about the truth of any specific propositions.

Another difference that need not involve a genuine disagreement involves the presence or absence of a "spiritual" attitude. There is a sense of wonder or awe that some people experience, and this may play a role in religious belief. Of course, atheists sometimes express feelings of awe at the size, complexity, and natural beauty of the world, and may express this as a feeling of spirituality. I do not know exactly what spirituality is, but a difference that amounts to the presence or absence of this feeling is not a disagreement over the truth of religious propositions.

One could try to reinterpret professions and denials of religious faith not as statements of beliefs about how things are but as expressions of commitment to different ways of life or as mere expressions of spiritual attitudes. But any such effort is an evasion. It is obvious that theists and atheists do not merely differ in how they live their lives. They really do disagree about the truth of the proposition that God exists. Any attempt to turn religious disagreements into mere differences in lifestyles fails to do justice to the plain facts of the case and is, perhaps, part of an effort to paper over troublesome questions. In the remainder of this essay I will assume that religious differences are not merely differences involving commitments to ways of living or differences concerning the presence or absence of feelings of spirituality. They include genuine disagreements.

It is important to emphasize the existence of genuine disagreement does not rule out significant areas of agreement. There are obviously many things about which theists and atheists can agree. And there are many things about which theists of different types can agree. It may be that the points of agreement among the theists are in some ways more important than the points of disagreement. It is no part of my goal to overstate the extent of disagreement. Rather, I begin with the fact that there is disagreement and raise questions about reasonable attitudes toward it.

B. Clarifying the Questions

My students seemed to feel uncomfortable if they were forced to acknowledge that they actually thought that those with whom they disagreed were wrong about the proposition about which they disagreed. But that, of course, is what they must think if they are to maintain their own beliefs. If you think that God exists, then, on pain of inconsistency, you must think that anyone who denies that God exists is mistaken. You must think that this person has a false belief. You must think that, with respect to the points about which you disagree with someone, that you have it right and the other person has it wrong.

Thinking someone else has a false belief is consistent with having any of a number of other favorable attitudes toward that person and that belief. You can think that the person is *reasonable*, even if mistaken. And this seems to be what my students thought: while they had their own beliefs, the others had reasonable beliefs as well. I think that the attitude that my students displayed is widespread. It is not unusual for a public discussion of a controversial issue to end with the parties to the dispute agreeing that this is a topic about which reasonable people can disagree. (Think of *The News Hour* on PBS.)

Some prominent contemporary philosophers have expressed similar views. For example, Gideon Rosen has written:

> It should be obvious that reasonable people can disagree, even when confronted with a single body of evidence. When a jury or a court is divided in a difficult case, the mere fact of disagreement does not mean that someone is being unreasonable. Paleontologists disagree about what killed the dinosaurs. And while it is possible that most of the parties to this dispute are irrational, this need not be the case. To the contrary, it would appear to be a fact of epistemic life that a careful review of the evidence does not guarantee consensus, even among thoughtful and otherwise rational investigators.[4]

But how exactly can there be reasonable disagreements? And how can there be reasonable disagreements when the parties to the disagreement have been confronted with a single body of evidence? And can they sensibly acknowledge, as I have suggested they do, that the other side is reasonable as well?

To sharpen these questions, I will introduce some terminology. Let's say that two people have a *disagreement* when one believes a proposition and the other denies (i.e., disbelieves) that proposition. Let's say that two people have a *reasonable disagreement* when they have a disagreement and each is reasonable (or justified) in his or her belief. Let's say that people are *epistemic peers* when they are roughly equal with respect to intelligence, reasoning powers, background information, etc.[5] When people have had a full discussion of a topic and have not withheld relevant information, we will say that they have *shared their evidence* about that topic.[6] There is some question about whether people can ever share *all* their evidence. This issue will arise later.

With all this in mind, I can now pose in a somewhat more precise way the questions the attitudes of my students provoked.

Q1) Can epistemic peers who have shared their evidence have reasonable disagreements?

Q2) Can epistemic peers who have shared their evidence reasonably maintain their own belief yet also think that the other party to the disagreement is also reasonable?

The point about the people being peers and sharing their evidence is crucial. No doubt people with different bodies of evidence can reasonably disagree. Suppose Early and Late both watch the 6:00 news and hear the weather forecast for rain the next day. Early goes to sleep early, but Late watches the late news and hears a revised forecast, calling for no rain. When they get up in the morning they have different beliefs about what the weather will be that day. We may assume that each is reasonable. Their differing evidence makes this easy to understand. But if they were to share the evidence, in this case by Late telling Early about the revised forecast, it would be harder to see how a reasonable disagreement would still be possible. So the puzzling case is the one in which each person knows about the other's reasons.

People who are not peers because of vastly different experiences and life histories can justifiably believe very different things. For example, the ancients may have justifiably believed that the Earth is flat, and thus "disagreed" with our view that it is approximately round. There is nothing particularly mysterious about this. But this does not help explain how there could be a reasonable disagreement in my classroom. No matter how isolated my students had been earlier in their lives, they were not isolated any more. They knew that there were all these smart kids in the room who believed very different things. And they had a good idea of why these other students believed as they did. (Q1) asks whether they could reasonably disagree under those conditions. In effect, (Q2) asks whether a party to one these disagreements can reasonably think that their disagreement is in fact a reasonable one. This is a way of asking whether a party to a disagreement can reasonably come away from that disagreement thinking "reasonable people can disagree about this." Can they think something like, "Well, my answer is correct, but your answer is a reasonable one as well"?

Affirmative answers to (Q1) and (Q2) will support the tolerant and supportive attitudes my students wanted to maintain. In most of what follows, I will emphasize (Q2), but (Q1) will enter the discussion as well. Unfortunately, I cannot see a good way to defend affirmative answers, at least when the questions are interpreted in what I take to be their most straightforward senses. As will become apparent, open and honest discussions seems to have the puzzling effect of making reasonable disagreement impossible.

C. Avoiding Misinterpretations

It will be useful to distinguish the questions I am focusing on from some others that might be expressed in similar language. The need for this clarification of the questions arises from the fact that the word "reasonable" is used in many different ways. To be clear about our questions, it is necessary to separate out the intended usage from some others.

One might describe a person who generally thinks and behaves in a reasonable way as a "reasonable person." Just as an honest person might tell an infrequent lie, a reasonable person might have an occasional unreasonable belief. When he has such a belief, the reasonable person would disagree with another reasonable person who has similar evidence but is not suffering from this lapse of rationality. The issue that puzzles me is not about whether generally reasonable people can disagree in a specific case, even when they have the same evidence. Surely they can. The issue is whether they are both reasonable in the contested case.

People sometimes use the word "reasonable" in a watered-down way, so that anyone who is not being flagrantly unreasonable counts as being reasonable. If a person holding a belief is trying to be sensible, and is not making self-evident blunders, then the belief counts as "reasonable" in this watered-down sense. This strikes me as far too lenient a standard. It counts as reasonable a variety of beliefs that rest on confusions, misunderstandings, incorrect evaluations of evidence, and the like. If this is all that is required to be reasonable, then it is easy to see that there can be reasonable disagreements among people who have shared their evidence. But this minimal concept of reasonableness is not what I have in mind, and it is surely not what my students had in mind. They did not want to say of their fellow students merely that they were not making obvious blunders. They wanted to say something more favorable than that. According to this stronger notion of being reasonable, a belief is reasonable only when it has adequate evidential support.

Sometimes a belief has enormous practical significance for a person. Consider, for example, a hostage and a neutral reporter on the scene. They may have the same evidence about the prospects for the hostage's release. However, the hostage may have a better chance of surviving his ordeal if he has the optimistic belief that he will be set free, while the reporter may have no special interest in the case. The hostage, therefore, has a motive for believing he will be released that the reporter lacks. Even if he has only a very limited amount of supporting evidence, we might say that the hostage is reasonable in so believing, given the practical value the belief has for him. The reporter would not be reasonable in that same belief. This, however, is not an evaluation of the evidential merit of the belief, but rather of its prudential or practical value. One somewhat odd way to put the point is to say that it is (prudentially or practically) reasonable for the hostage to have an (epistemically) unreasonable belief in this situation. My interest is in the epistemic, or evidential, evaluations.

This point is particularly significant in the present setting. The issue I am raising about religious beliefs, and disagreements involving them, is not about whether religious belief is beneficial. It may in fact be beneficial to some people and not others. It may be that the some or all of the theists in my class led better lives partly as a result of their theism, and it may be that the atheists are better off being atheists. Nothing that I will say here has any direct bearing on that question. My topic has to do with questions about what to make of disagreements about whether religious beliefs are true.

Finally, my questions have to do with belief, not with associated behavior. There are cases in which people with similar evidence reasonably behave differently. Suppose that we are on the way to an important meeting and we come to a fork in the road. The map shows no fork and we have no way to get more information about which way to go. We have to choose. You choose the left path and I choose the right path. Each of us may be entirely reasonable in choosing as we do. Of course, we would have been reasonable in choosing otherwise. But, as you go left and I go right, neither of us would be reasonable in believing that we've chosen the correct path. Believing differs from acting in a case like this. The reasonable attitude to take toward the proposition that, say, the left path is the correct path is suspension of judgment. Neither belief nor disbelief is supported. Each of us should suspend judgment about which path is best, while picking one since, as we envision the case, not taking either path would be the worst choice of all. As this case illustrates, acting and believing are different. Sometimes it is reasonable to act a certain way while it is not reasonable to believe that that way of acting will be successful.

It is possible that the choice about being religious or not, or the choice among the various religions, is in some ways like the fork in the road example. This is an extremely important choice we must make, and our information about the matter is limited. No one is to be criticized for making a choice. If this is right, it may show that our religious choices have a kind of practical rationality. However, it does not show that our religious beliefs are epistemically rational.

All the cases described in this section are cases in which one might plausibly say that epistemic peers who have shared their evidence about a proposition can reasonably disagree. But they are not the sorts of cases I want to examine. I take it that the students in my class wanted to say that other students with other beliefs were epistemically reasonable with respect to their specific beliefs, and not just generally reasonable folks. They were not saying merely that others were not patently unreasonable. And they weren't saying that the beliefs of the others were merely of practical value. Nor were they saying that some related behavior was reasonable. They were saying that these were genuinely reasonable disagreements with shared, or at least nearly shared, evidence. These are the core cases of apparent reasonable disagreement.

III. DEFENSES OF REASONABLE DISAGREEMENTS

In this section, I will consider four lines of thought supporting the view that my students could have been having a reasonable disagreement.

A. Drawing Different Conclusions from the Same Evidence

One might think that it is clear that people can reasonably draw different conclusions from the same evidence. A simple example seems to support that claim. I will argue, however, that reflection on the example shows that it supports the opposite conclusion.

There are situations in which one might say that a good case can be made for each of two incompatible propositions. For example, suppose a detective has strong evidence incriminating Lefty and also has strong evidence incriminating Righty of the same crime. Assume that the detective knows that only one suspect could be guilty. One might think that since a case could be made for either suspect, the detective could reasonably believe that Lefty is guilty and Righty is not, but could also reasonably believe that Righty is guilty and Lefty is not. She gets to choose. If anything like this is right, then there can be reasonable disagreements in the intended sense. If there were two detectives with this same evidence, they could reasonably disagree, one believing that Lefty is guilty and the other believing that Righty is guilty. Each could also agree that the other is reasonable in drawing the contrary conclusion.

I think, however, that this analysis of the case is seriously mistaken. It is clear that the detectives should suspend judgment in this sort of case (given only 2 possible candidates for guilt). The evidence for Lefty is evidence against Righty. Believing a particular suspect to be guilty on the basis of this combined evidence is simply not reasonable. Furthermore, it is hard to make clear sense of the thought that the other belief is reasonable. Suppose one of the detectives believes that Lefty is guilty. She can then infer that Righty is not guilty. But if she can draw this inference, she cannot also reasonably think that it is reasonable to conclude that Righty is guilty. This combination of beliefs simply does not make sense.

Thinking about the case of Lefty and Righty suggests that one cannot reasonably choose belief or disbelief in a case like this. The only reasonable option is to suspend judgment. These considerations lend support to an idea that I will call "The Uniqueness Thesis". This is the idea that a body of evidence justifies at most one proposition out of a competing set of propositions (e.g., one theory out of a bunch of exclusive alternatives) and that it justifies at most one attitude toward any particular proposition. As I think of things, our options with respect to any proposition are believing, disbelieving, and suspending judgment. The Uniqueness Thesis says that, given a body of evidence, one of these attitudes is the rationally justified one.

disorderly not continuous

If The Uniqueness Thesis is correct, then there cannot be any reasonable disagreements in cases in which two people have exactly the same evidence. That evidence uniquely determines one correct attitude, whether it be belief, disbelief, or suspension of judgment. And reflection on the case of Left and Righty lends strong support to The Uniqueness Thesis.

It is worth adding that the order in which one gets one's evidence on the topic makes no difference in cases like this. Suppose the detective first learns the evidence about Lefty, and reasonably concludes that Lefty is guilty. She then acquires the comparable evidence about Righty. The fact that she already believes that Lefty is guilty makes no difference. She still should suspend judgment. The principles of rational belief do not include a law of inertia.

B. Different Starting Points

One might think that, in addition to the evidence one brings to bear on an issue, there are some fundamental principles or starting points that affect one's conclusions. Whether these starting points amount to fundamental claims about the world or epistemological principles about how to deal with evidence, the idea is that these differences enable people with the same evidence to reasonably arrive at different conclusions.

The idea behind this thought can be developed as an objection to my analysis of the case of Lefty and Righty. It is possible that two detectives looking at the same evidence may come to different conclusions because they weigh the evidential factors differently.[7] Suppose part of the case against Lefty includes the fact Lefty has embezzled money from the firm while part of the case against Righty includes the fact he is suspected of having had an affair. One detective might think that one factor is more significant, or a better indicator of guilt, while the other weighs the other factor more heavily. Hence, they have the same evidence, yet they weigh the elements of that evidence differently and thus come to different conclusions. To make a case for reasonable disagreements out of this, it must be added that either way of weighing these factors counts as reasonable.

I think, however, that this response just pushes the question back a step. We can now ask which factor should be weighed more heavily. It could be that the detectives have reasons for weighing the factors as they do. If so, then they can discuss those reasons and come to a conclusion about which really is most significant. If not, then they should acknowledge that they do not really have good reasons for weighing them as they do and thus for coming to their preferred conclusions. To think otherwise requires thinking that, in effect, they get their preferred ways to weigh the factors for "free" — they do not need reasons for these preferences. But I see no reason at all to grant them this license.

A related idea is that people may have different fundamental principles or world views. Perhaps there are some basic ways of looking at things that people typically just take for granted. Maybe acceptance of a scientific world view is one such fundamental principle. Maybe a religious outlook is another. Or, maybe there are some more fundamental principles from which these differences emerge. A difficult project, which I will not undertake here, is to identify just what these starting points or fundamental principles might be and to explain how they might affect the sorts of disagreements under discussion. But what whatever they are, I do not think that they will help to solve the problem. Once people have engaged in a full discussion of issues, their different starting points will be apparent. And then those claims will themselves be open for discussion and evaluation. These different starting points help to support the existence of reasonable disagreements only if each side can reasonably maintain its starting point after they have been brought out into the open. And this idea can support the tolerant attitude my students wanted to maintain only if people can think that their own starting point is reasonable, but different and incompatible starting points are reasonable as well.[8] I cannot understand how that could be true. Once you see that there are these alternative starting points, you need a reason to prefer one over the other. There may be practical benefit to picking one. But it does not yield rational belief. The starting points are simply analogues of the two forks in the road, in the example considered earlier.

C. The Evidence Is Not Fully Shared

In any realistic case, the totality of one's evidence concerning a proposition will be a long and complex story, much of which may be difficult to put into words. This makes it possible that each party to a disagreement has an extra bit of evidence, evidence that has not been shared. You might think that each person's unshared evidence can justify that person's beliefs. For example, there is something about the atheist's total evidence that can justify his belief and there is something different about the theist's total evidence that can justify her belief. Of course, not all cases of disagreement need to turn out this way. But perhaps some do, and perhaps this is what the students in my class thought was going on in our class. And, more generally, perhaps this is what people generally think is going on when they conclude that reasonable people can disagree.

On this view, the apparent cases of reasonable disagreement are cases in which people have shared only a portion of their evidence. Perhaps if *all* the evidence were shared, there could not be a reasonable disagreement. This is the consequence of The Uniqueness Thesis. But, according to the present idea, there are no cases of fully shared evidence, or at least no realistic cases. If we take (Q1) and (Q2) to be about cases in which all the evidence is shared, then the answer to both questions is "No". But if we take the questions to be about cases in which the evidence is shared as fully as is realistically possible, then the answers are "Yes". We might say that the reasonable disagreements are possible in those cases in which each side has private evidence supporting its view.

It is possible that the private evidence includes the private religious (or non-religious) experiences one has. Another possible way to think about private evidence is to identify it with the clear sense one has that the body of shared evidence – the arguments – really do support one's own view. The theist's evidence is whatever is present in the arguments, plus her strong sense or intuition or "insight" that the arguments on balance support her view.[9] Similarly for the atheist. A similar idea emerges in Gideon Rosen's discussion of disagreement in ethics. He talks of the sense of "obviousness" of the proposition under discussion. He writes:

> . . . if the obviousness of the contested claim survives the encounter with . . . [another person] . . . then one still has some reason to hold it: the reason provided by the seeming. If, after reflecting on the rational tenability of an ethos that prizes cruelty, cruelty continues to strike me as self-evidently reprehensible, then my conviction that it is reprehensible has a powerful and cogent ground, despite my recognition that others who lack this ground may be fully justified in thinking otherwise.[10]

The idea, then, is that the seeming obviousness, or the intuitiveness correctness, of one's position counts as evidence. The theist and the atheist each have such private evidence for their respective beliefs. Hence, according to this line of thought, each is justified. That's how both parties to the disagreement can reasonably draw different conclusions.

This response will not do. To see why, compare a more straightforward case of regular sight, rather than insight. Suppose you and I are standing by the window looking out on the quad. We think we have comparable vision and we know each other to be honest. I seem to see what looks to me like the Dean standing out in the middle of the quad. (Assume that this is not something odd. He's out there a fair amount.) I believe that the Dean is standing on the quad. Meanwhile, you seem to see nothing of the kind there. You think that no one, and thus not the Dean, is standing in the middle of the quad. We disagree. Prior to our saying anything, each of us believes reasonably. Then I say something about the Dean being on the quad, and we find out about our situation. In my view, once that happens, each of us should suspend judgment. We each know that something weird is going on, but we have no idea which of us has the problem. Either I am "seeing things" or you are missing something. I would not be reasonable in thinking that the problem is in your head, nor would you be reasonable in thinking that the problem is in mine.

Similarly, I think, even if it is true that the theists and the atheists have private evidence, this does not get us out of the problem. Each may have his or her own special insight or sense of obviousness. But each knows about the other's insight. Each knows that this insight has evidential force. And now I see no basis for either of them justifying his own belief simply because the one insight happens to occur inside of him. A point about evidence that plays a role here is this: evidence of evidence is evidence. More carefully, evidence that there is evidence for P is evidence for P. Knowing that the other has an insight provides each with them with evidence.

Consider again the example involving the two suspects in a criminal case, Lefty and Righty. Suppose now that there are two detectives investigating the case, one who has the evidence about Lefty and one who has the evidence incriminating Righty. They each justifiably believe in their man's guilt. And then they find out that the other detective has evidence incriminating the other suspect. If things are on a par, then suspension of judgment is called for. If one detective has no reason at all to think that the other's evidence is inferior to hers, yet she continues to believe that Lefty is guilty, she would be unjustified. She is giving special status to her own evidence with no reason to do so, and this is an epistemic error, a failure to treat like cases alike. She knows that there are two bodies of equally good evidence for incompatible propositions, and she is favoring the one that happens to have been hers originally.

In each case, one has one's own evidence supporting a proposition, knows that another person has comparable evidence supporting a competing proposition, and has no reason to think that one's own reason is the non-defective one. In the example about seeing the Dean, I cannot reasonably say, "Well, it's really seeming to me like the Dean is there. So, even though you are justified in your belief, your appearance is deceptive." I need some reason to think you are the one with the problem rather than me. The detective needs a reason to think it is the other's evidence, and not her own, that is flawed. The theist and the atheist need reasons to think that their own insights or seemings are accurate rather than the other's. To think otherwise, it seems to me, is to think something like this: "You have an insight according to which ~P is true. I have one according to which P is true. It's reasonable for me to believe P in light of all this because, gosh darn it, *my* insight supports P." If one's conviction survives the "confrontation with the other," to use Rosen's phrase, this seems more a sign of tenacity and stubbornness than anything else.

Thus, even though the parties to a disagreement might not be able to share all their evidence, this does not show that they can reasonably disagree in the cases in which their evidence is shared as well as possible. Their bodies of evidence are very similar, and each has evidence about what the other's private evidence supports. It is especially clear that neither person can justifiably believe both sides are reasonable. If I think that you do have good evidence for your view, then I admit that there is this good evidence for your view, and thus my own beliefs must take this into account. I need a reason to think that you are making a mistake, and not me. The unshared evidence does not help.

D. Having a Reasonable Disagreement Without Realizing It

I have considered and found unsatisfactory three ways in which one might attempt to defend the view that the participants in a purported case of reasonable disagreement can reasonably maintain their own beliefs yet grant that those on the other side are reasonable as well. These were unsuccessful attempts to support affirmative answers to (Q1) and (Q2). In this section I will consider a view according to which people can reasonably disagree but the participants to the disagreement cannot reasonably see it that way. On this view, they will think (mistakenly) that the other side is unreasonable. This view, then, gives an affirmative answer to (Q1) but a negative answer to (Q2).

The fundamental assumption behind the view under discussion in this section is that one can reasonably weigh more heavily one's own experiences or perspective than those of another person. When confronted with a case of disagreement on the basis of shared evidence, according to this view, one can reasonably conclude that the other person is not adept at assessing the evidence or that the person is simply making a mistake in this particular case as a result of some sort of cognitive failing. One way or another, then, the conclusion drawn is that the other person does not have a reasonable or justified belief. And the idea is that *both* parties to the disagreement can reasonably draw this conclusion. Thus, both parties have a reasonable belief, yet they reasonably think that the other side is not reasonable.

Applied to our specific case of disagreement about the existence of God, this situation might work out as follows. The theists reasonably think that the atheists are assessing the evidence incorrectly or that they have a kind of cognitive defect. Thus, for example, the theists can think that in spite of their general intelligence, the atheists have a kind of cognitive blindness in this case. They are unable to see the truth in religion and they are unable to appreciate the significance of the theist's reports on their own experience. The theists, then, are justified in maintaining their own beliefs and rejecting those of the atheists as false and unjustified. The atheists, on the other hand, are justified in thinking that the theists are making some kind of mistake, perhaps because psychological needs or prior conditioning blind them to the truth. Thus, the atheists are justified in maintaining their own beliefs and rejecting those of the theists as false and unjustified.[11] A neutral observer, aware of all the facts of their respective situations, could correctly report that both sides have justified beliefs. As a result, the answer to (Q1) is "Yes," since there can be a reasonable disagreement. Yet the answer to (Q2) is "No," since the participants cannot see it that way.

Since my main goal in this essay is an examination of the tolerant and supportive view that implies an affirmative answer to (Q2), I will not pursue this response at length. I will say, however, that I think that this defense of reasonable disagreements rests on an implausible assumption. Beliefs about whether expertise or cognitive illusions are occurring in oneself or in a person with whom one disagrees depend for their justification on evidence, just like beliefs about other topics. If the atheists or the theists in our central example have any reasons for thinking that they themselves, rather than those on the other side, are the cognitive superiors in this case, then they can identify and discuss those reasons. And the result will be that the evidence shows that all should agree about who the experts are or the evidence will show that there is no good basis for determining who the experts are. If the evidence really does identify experts, then agreeing with those experts will be the reasonable response for all. If it does not, then there will no basis for anyone to prefer one view to the other and suspension of judgment will be the reasonable attitude for all. There is no way this setup can lead to reasonable a disagreement.

IV. THE REMAINING OPTIONS

In the previous section I considered and rejected some lines of thought according to which there can be reasonable disagreements. I argued that none of them succeeded. Suppose, then, that there cannot be reasonable disagreements. What can we say about people, such as my students, in the situations that are the best candidates for reasonable disagreements? What is the status of their beliefs? In this section I will examine the possibilities. There are really only two.

A. The Hard Line

You might think that the evidence must really support one side of the dispute or the other. This might lead you to think that those who take that side have reasonable beliefs and those who believe differently do not have reasonable beliefs. The answer to both (Q1) and (Q2) is "No." We can apply this idea to the dispute between the theists and the atheists in my class. Assume that they have shared their evidence to fullest extent possible. Their disagreement is not about which belief is more beneficial or morally useful or any of the other matters set aside earlier. In that case, according to the present alternative, one of them has a reasonable belief and the other does not. Of course, one of them has a *true* belief and the other does not. But that is not the current issue. The current issue is about rationality, and the hard line says that the evidence they share really must support one view or the other, and the one whose belief fits the evidence is the rational one. Either the evidence supports the existence of God or it doesn't. Either the theists or the atheists are rational, but not both. There can be no reasonable disagreements. This is the Hard Line response.

The hard line response seems clearly right with respect to some disagreements. Examples may be contentious, but here is one. Suppose two people look carefully at the available relevant evidence and one of them comes away from it thinking that astrological explanations of personality traits are correct and the other denies this. The defender of astrology is simply making a mistake. That belief is not reasonable. As Peter van Inwagen says, belief in astrology is "simply indefensible."[12] Similarly, the hard line view may be correct in Rosen's example about a person who favors an ethos prizing cruelty. That person is just missing something. It is likely that a detailed discussion of the rest of the person's beliefs will reveal enough oddities to render the whole system suspect. Such a person's moral view is simply indefensible.

However, the hard line is much harder to defend in other cases. These other cases are the ones in which any fair minded person would have to admit that intelligent, informed, and thoughtful people do disagree. In these moral, political, scientific, and religious disputes, it is implausible to think that one side is simply unreasonable in the way in which (I say) the defenders of astrology are.

The hard line response is particularly difficult to accept in cases in which people have been fully reflective and openly discussed their differing responses. In our example, once people discuss the topic and their evidence, they are forced to consider two propositions:

1. God exists.
2. Our shared evidence supports (1).

The theist says that both (1) and (2) are true. The atheist denies both (1) and (2). Notice that after their discussion their evidence includes not only the original arguments themselves and their own reactions to them, but also the fact the other person — an epistemic peer — assesses the evidence differently. So consider the theist in the dispute. To stick to his guns, he has to think as follows: "The atheist and I have shared our evidence. After looking at this evidence, it seems to me that (1) and (2) are both true. It seems to her that both are false. I am right and she is wrong." The atheist will, of course, have comparable beliefs on the other side of the issue. It is difficult to see why one of them is better justified with respect to (2) than the other. But it also is clear that for each of them, (1) and (2) sink or swim together. That is, it is hard to imagine it being the case that, say, the theist is justified in believing (1) but should suspend judgment about (2). Analogous remarks apply to the atheist. It looks like both should suspend judgment. It is difficult to maintain the Hard Line position once the parties to the dispute are reflective about their situations and their evidence includes information about the contrary views of their peers.

Admittedly, it is difficult to say with complete clarity just what differentiates the cases to which the Hard Line view is appropriate (astrology, Rosen's ethos of cruelty) from the cases to which it is not (the serious disputes). One difference, perhaps, is that an honest look at what the evidence supports in the latter cases reveals that our evidence is decidedly modest to begin with. Even if our individual reflections on these hard questions provides some justification for the beliefs that may seem correct to us, that evidence is counterbalanced when we learn that our peers disagree. This leads us to our final view about disagreements.

B. A Modest Skeptical Alternative

One reaction of a party to an apparent reasonable disagreement might go something like this:

> After examining this evidence, I find in myself an inclination, perhaps a strong inclination, to think that this evidence supports P. It may even be that I can't help but believe P. But I see that another person, every bit as sensible and serious as I, has an opposing reaction. Perhaps this person has some bit of evidence that cannot be shared or perhaps he takes the evidence differently than I do. It's difficult to know everything about his mental life and thus difficult to tell exactly why he believes as he does. One of us must be making some kind of mistake or failing to see some truth. But I have no basis for thinking that the one making the mistake is him rather than me. And the same is true of him. And in that case, the right thing for both of us to do is to suspend judgment on P.

This, it seems to me, is the truth of the matter. At least for some range of hard cases. There can be apparent reasonable disagreements, as was the case in my classroom. And when you are tempted to think that you are in one, then you should suspend judgment about the matter under dispute. If my students thought that the various students with varying beliefs were equally reasonable, then they should have concluded that suspending judgment was the right thing to do.[13]

This is a modest view, in the sense that it argues for a kind of compromise with those with whom one disagrees. It implies that one should give up one's beliefs in the light of the sort of disagreement under discussion. This is a kind of modesty in response to disagreement from one's peers. This is also a skeptical view, in the limited sense that it denies the existence of reasonable beliefs in a significant range of cases.

This may see to be a distressing conclusion. It implies that many of your deeply held convictions are not justified. Worse, it implies that many of my deeply held, well-considered beliefs are not justified. Still, I think that this is the truth of the matter. And perhaps the conclusion is not so distressing. It calls for a kind of humility in response to the hard questions about which people so often find themselves in disagreement. It requires us to admit that we really do not know what the truth is in these cases. When compared to the intolerant views with which we began, this is a refreshing outcome.

V. CONCLUSION

My conclusion, then, is that there cannot be reasonable disagreements of the sort I was investigating. That is, it cannot be that epistemic peers who have shared their evidence can reasonably come to different conclusions. Furthermore, they cannot reasonably conclude that both they and those with whom they disagree are reasonable in their beliefs. Thus, I cannot make good sense of the supportive and tolerant attitude my students displayed. It is possible, of course, that the favorable attitude toward others that they expressed really only conceded to the others one of the lesser kinds of reasonableness that I set aside in section II, part C. If this is correct, then either the hard line response applies and this is an example in which one side is reasonable and the other simply is not, or it is a case to which the more skeptical response applies. If that's the case, then suspension of judgment is the epistemically appropriate attitude. And this is a challenge to the complacent atheism with which I began.

I have not here argued for a conclusion about which category the disagreements between theists and atheists, or the various disagreements among theists, fall into. For all I've said, some of these cases may be ones in which one side simply is making a mistake and those on other side are justified in both sticking to their guns and ascribing irrationality to the other side. Others may be cases that call for suspension of judgment. To defend my atheism, I would have to be justified in accepting some hypothesis explaining away religious belief, for example the hypothesis that it arises from some fundamental psychological need. And, while I am inclined to believe some such hypothesis, the more I reflect on it, the more I realize that I am no position to make any such judgment with any confidence at all. Such psychological conjectures are, I must admit, highly speculative, at least when made by me.

This skeptical conclusion does not imply that people should stop defending the views that seem right to them. It may be that the search for the truth is most successful if people argue for the things that seem true to them. But one can do that without being epistemically justified in believing that one's view is correct.[14]

Notes

1 I develop this method of argument analysis in *Reason and Argument* 2ⁿᵈ edition (Englewood Cliffs, NJ: Prentice Hall, 1999).

2 Rochester Democrat and Chronicle, March 3, 2004.

3 This assumes that we use the word "God" in the same way. See the discussion of ambiguity in Section II.

4 "Nominalism, Naturalism, Philosophical Relativism," *Philosophical Perspectives* 15, 2001, pp. 69–91. The quotation is from pp. 71–2.

5 I borrow this term from Tom Kelly.

6 People who aren't peers can share their evidence. But the interesting case involves peers who share their evidence.

7 I thank Allen Orr for pressing me on this point.

8 It is also possible that each side is justified in maintaining its own "starting point" and rejecting the starting point of the others. This would make the present idea just like the ideas discussed in the subsection D.

9 Peter van Inwagen suggests this in "Is It Wrong Everywhere, Always, and for Anyone to Believe Anything on Insufficient Evidence?" in Jordan and Howard-Snyder, eds, *Faith Freedom and Rationality* 1996. He does not refer to the insight as evidence.

10 "Nominalism, Naturalism, Philosophical Relativism," p. 88.

11 Both sides can still regard the others as peers because of their general capacities. The difference over this case does not disqualify them as peers.

12 "Is It Wrong Everywhere, Always, and for Anyone to Believe Anything on Insufficient Evidence?"

13 There are technical puzzles here. There are many varieties of theism. If the view proposed implies that you should think that they are equally probable, then you can't also think that each of those versions of theism as probable as atheism and also think that theism is as probable as atheism. I will not attempt to deal with this here.

14 I am grateful to Louise Antony, John Bennett, Allen Orr, and Ed Wierenga for helpful comments on earlier drafts of this paper. The paper is a revised version of talks given at Ohio State University, Washington University, the University of Miami, the University of Michigan, the Inland Northwest Philosophy Conference, and the Sociedad Filosofica Ibero-American. I am grateful to the audiences on all those occasions for helpful discussion.

8

Reflection and Disagreement

Adam Elga*

ABSTRACT   *How should you take into account the opinions of an advisor? When you completely defer to the advisor's judgment (the manner in which she responds to her evidence), then you should treat the advisor as a guru. Roughly, that means you should believe what you expect she would believe, if supplied with your extra evidence. When the advisor is your own future self, the resulting principle amounts to a version of the Reflection Principle—a version amended to handle cases of information loss.*

When you count an advisor as an epistemic peer, you should give her conclusions the same weight as your own. Denying that view— call it the "equal weight view"—leads to absurdity: the absurdity that you could reasonably come to believe yourself to be an epistemic superior to an advisor simply by noting cases of disagreement with her, and taking it that she made most of the mistakes. Accepting the view seems to lead to another absurdity: that one should suspend judgment about everything that one's smart and well-informed friends disagree on, which means suspending judgment about almost everything interesting. But despite appearances, the equal weight view does not have this absurd consequence. Furthermore, the view can be generalized to handle cases involving not just epistemic peers, but also epistemic superiors and inferiors.

1. INTRODUCTION

There are experts and gurus, people to whom we should defer entirely. There are fakes and fools, who should be ignored. In between, there are friends and other advisors (including our own future and past selves), whose opinions should guide us in a less than fully authoritative way.

How, exactly, should we be guided by outside opinions?

2. EXPERTS AND GURUS

Start with the simplest case: complete deference. When it comes to the weather, I completely defer to the opinions of my local weather forecaster. My probability for rain, given that her probability for rain is 60%, is also 60%. And the corresponding constraint holds for other propositions about the weather. Using a variant of Gaifman's (1988) terminology: I treat her as an **expert** about the weather. That means: conditional on her having probability x in any weather proposition, my probability in that proposition is also x.[1]

In treating my forecaster this way, I defer to her in two respects. First, I defer to her *information*: "As far as the weather goes," I think to myself, "she's got all the information that I have—and more." Second, I defer to her *judgment*: I defer to the manner in which she forms opinions on the basis of her information.

In the above case, we may suppose, I am right to treat my forecaster as an expert. But advisors don't always deserve such respect. For example, suppose that the forecaster has plenty of meteorological information, but I can see that she is dead drunk and so isn't responding properly to that information. In that case, I shouldn't treat her as an expert. Or suppose that the forecaster responds perfectly well to her information, but I can see that I have information that she lacks. In that case too, I shouldn't treat her as an expert.

Even in such cases, I shouldn't just ignore her opinion. How should I incorporate it? If my forecaster is drunk or otherwise addled, then I should only partially defer to her judgment. I postpone discussion of such cases. For now, suppose that I do completely defer to my forecaster's judgment. Nevertheless, I think that she lacks relevant information that I possess. What then?

An example will suggest the answer. Suppose that my forecaster lacks one highly relevant tidbit: that I have been secretly seeding the clouds for rain. Suppose that I'm sure her probability for rain is low—5%, say. In this case, I shouldn't set my probability for rain to that same low value, since my cloud-seeding activities make rain much more likely. But I *should* be guided by the forecaster's opinions. Roughly: my probability for rain should be what hers would be *if she were informed that I'd been seeding the clouds*.

More precisely: when I have information that my forecaster lacks, I shouldn't defer to her unconditional opinions. For those opinions are based on an impoverished evidential base. But I *should* defer to her *conditional* opinions: her opinions conditional on all of my extra information. When an agent defers to an advisor in this way, let us say that the agent treats the advisor as a **guru**.

Formally: suppose that I have probability function P. Then I treat an advisor as an **expert** if for any proposition H and for any probability function P' that I think the advisor may have,

$$P(H \mid \text{advisor has } P') = P'(H).$$

In contrast, I treat the advisor as a **guru** if

$$P(H \mid \text{advisor has } P') = P'(H \mid X),$$

where X is my extra information, supposing that the advisor has probability function P'.[2,3]

3. REFLECTION

The above discussion concerns the manner in which one ought to take into account the opinions of others. But one should also take into account the opinions of one's own future self. How? A provocative and precise answer is given by the **Reflection Principle**[4], according to which one should treat one's future self as an expert. The Reflection Principle entails, for example, that one's current probability for rain, given that one will tomorrow have probability 25% for rain, ought also to be 25%. And it entails that the corresponding constraint should hold for all other propositions and time intervals.

But recall the weather forecaster case. To treat my forecaster as an expert is to defer to her with respect to both judgment and information. I shouldn't defer to her in this way if I have reason to doubt her on either score. And the same goes for my future self: if I expect that I won't be thinking straight next week, or if I expect that I will lose information between now and next week, then I *shouldn't* treat my next-week self as an expert (Christensen 1991, Skyrms 1987, Talbott 1991).

Reflection has been criticized on exactly these grounds. But we should distinguish two complaints. On the one hand, there is the complaint: rationality does not require that one defer to one's future *judgment*, since one may expect that one's judgment will become impaired. For example, Bob may reasonably doubt that at midnight he will be in good shape to drive, even if he expects that by midnight he'll be drunkenly confident that his driving skills are perfect (Christensen 1991). In this case, Bob is reasonable, but violates Reflection. Against this complaint, I will propose a revised version of Reflection, appropriate for situations of partial deference.[5] Hold off on that until section 6.

For now focus on a second complaint, to which there is an easy and satisfying response. The second complaint: it isn't a rational requirement that one defer to one's future self with respect to *information*, since one may expect to lose information. For example, Joe may reasonably be confident that this morning he had sushi for breakfast, even if he expects that in a year, he will have forgotten the truth of that claim (Talbott 1991). In this case, Joe is reasonable, but violates Reflection.

In response to this second complaint, it has been suggested that Reflection be limited so that it simply does not apply to cases of expected information loss.[6] Such a limited principle would avoid trouble by remaining silent about the trouble cases. But Reflection should not remain silent about such cases, since one's future opinion *should* constrain one's present opinion, even if one expects to lose information.

For a better response, think back to the previous section. Suppose that I defer to the judgment of my weather forecaster. Then, even if I have information that she lacks, her opinion *should* constrain my own. Roughly, I should believe what I think she would believe, if she were given my extra information. More precisely: I should treat my forecaster not as an expert, but a guru.

The same holds with respect to my future self. Suppose that I defer to the judgment of my future self. Then, even if I have information that I will later lack, my future opinion *should* constrain my present opinion. Roughly, I should believe what I think my future self would believe, if my future self were given my present extra information. More precisely: I should treat my future self not as an expert, but as a guru.

The moral is that expected information loss does not *break* the connection between one's future opinion and one's present opinion: it *modifies* that connection. The modified connection is expressed by the principle "Treat your future self as a guru". Formally, the proposal is that for any proposition H and for any probability function P' that one thinks one may have at a future time t,

$$P(H \mid \text{I have } P' \text{ at } t) = P'(H \mid X),$$

where X is the extra information one presently possesses, supposing that one has P' at t.[7,8]

This modified principle handles cases of information loss not by remaining silent, but by yielding reasonable verdicts. For example, recall the case of Joe, the forgetful sushi-eater. The modified principle yields the desired verdict, that Joe should be confident that he had sushi for breakfast. For though Joe expects his future self to doubt this claim, he expects his future self to be confident in it, *conditional on his current extra information* (which includes vivid memories of having recently eaten sushi).

4. LOSING TRACK OF THE TIME

There is another sort of information loss, a sort associated with losing track of who one is or what time it is. Information loss of that sort can also lead to violations of Reflection. For example[9], suppose that you are waiting for a train. You are only 50% confident that the train will ever arrive, but are sure that if it does arrive, it will arrive in exactly one hour. Since you have no watch, when fifty-five minutes have in fact elapsed you will be unsure whether an hour has elapsed. As a result, at that time you will have reduced confidence—say, only 40% confidence—that the train will ever arrive. So at the start, you can be sure that when fifty-five minutes have elapsed, your probability that the train will ever arrive will have gone down to 40%. But that doesn't show that your current probability should be 40%. So your anticipated imperfect ability to keep track of time creates a violation of Reflection. (Another example: Horgan (2004) convincingly diagnoses the Reflection-violating belief change associated with the Sleeping Beauty problem as resulting from information loss about what time it is.)

Again, the proper lesson is not that the connection between current and future beliefs is broken, but rather that it is modified. But the above proposal—that one ought to treat one's future self not as an expert but as a guru—does not suffice. An additional, completely separate fix is required.

To motivate the fix, notice that in the waiting-for-the-train case your probabilities should not match what you expect to believe in fifty-five minutes. Instead they should match what you expect to believe in fifty-five minutes *given that exactly fifty-five minutes have elapsed*. More generally, the definition of what it is to treat someone as a guru can be modified in order to "bracket off" the manner in which an agent's uncertainty about what time it is (and who she is) affects her beliefs about other matters. Applied to the case of a single person over time, the resulting principle requires that for any subject S with probability function P at time t, any proposition H, and any probability function P' that the subject thinks she might have at future time t',

$$P(H \mid \text{I have } P' \text{ at } t' \,\&\, \text{I am } S \text{ at } t) = P'(H \mid X \,\&\, \text{I am } S \text{ at } t'),$$

where X is the subject's extra information at time t, on the supposition that she has P' at t'.[10]

5.   EXPERTS AND GURUS ARE RARE

So: when one completely defers to one's future judgment, one should treat one's future self as a guru. But when should one completely defer to one's future judgment? More generally, when should one completely defer to the judgment of any advisor?

Rarely.

Only in highly idealized circumstances is it reasonable to defer to someone's opinion *absolutely whatever* that opinion might be. For example, upon finding out that my forecaster is confident that it will snow tomorrow, I will follow suit. But upon finding out that my forecaster is confident that it will rain eggplants tomorrow, I will not follow suit. I will conclude that my forecaster is crazy. The same goes for the news that I myself will believe

that it will rain eggplants tomorrow. In realistic cases, one reasonably dis-
counts opinions that fall outside an appropriate range.

In addition, not even a perfect advisor deserves absolute trust, since one
should be less than certain of one's own ability to *identify* good advisors.[11]

So: only in highly idealized cases is it appropriate to treat someone as an
expert or a guru, and so to completely defer to that person's judgment. All
the more reason to consider cases of partial deference, to which we now turn.

6. DIVIDING THE QUESTION

How should one take into account the opinions of an advisor who may
have imperfect judgment? That question factors into two parts:

1. To what degree should one defer to a given advisor's judgment?
   For example, when should one count an advisor's judgment as
   completely worthless? Or as approximately as good as one's own?
   Or as better than one's own, but still less than perfect?
2. Given one's assessment of an advisor's level of competence, how
   should one take that advisor's opinion into account?

On the first question, I have no substantive answer to offer here. My
excuse is that the question concerns a huge, difficult, and domain-specific
matter. How should one judge the epistemic abilities of weather forecasters, dentists, math professors, gossipy neighbors, and so on? This is a
question with the same sort of massive scope as the question: "When does
a batch of evidence support a given hypothesis?" Fearsome questions
both, and worthy of investigation. But leave them for another day.

Here I will focus on the second question. Assume that you defer to an
advisor's judgment to a certain degree. *Given* that rating of the advisor's
judgment, how should you take her opinions into account? We have
already settled this in the special case in which you utterly defer to the
advisor's judgment. In that case, you should treat the advisor as a guru. It
remains to consider cases in which you defer to an advisor's judgment
only partially.

Start with the simplest such case, a case that has been the subject of
considerable discussion and dispute (Christensen 2007, Feldman 2004,
Kelly 2005, Plantinga 2000, van Inwagen 1996): how should your opinion
be guided by an advisor who you count as having judgment that is as good
as your own?

7. PEER DISAGREEMENT: SETUP

Suppose that you and your friend independently evaluate the same factual claim—for example, the claim that the death penalty significantly

deterred crime in Texas in the 1980s.[12] Each of you has access to the same crime statistics, sociological reports, and so on, and has no other relevant evidence. Furthermore, you count your friend as an **epistemic peer**—as being as good as you at evaluating such claims.[13,14]

You perform your evaluation, and come to a conclusion about the claim. But then you find out that your friend has come to the opposite conclusion. How much should this news move you in the direction of her view? Should you always give your friend's assessment equal weight, and think that it is no more likely that you're right than that she is? Or can it sometimes be rational for you to stick to your guns, or at least give your own assessment *some* extra weight?

Answer: you should give the assessments equal weight.

Before refining and defending this **equal weight view**, let me attack it.

8. UNWELCOME CONSEQUENCE OF THE EQUAL WEIGHT VIEW

According to the equal weight view, one should give the same weight to one's own assessments as one gives to the assessments of those one counts as one's epistemic peers. If the view is right for the case of one peer, it surely is also right for the case of many peers.[15] But in the case of many peers, the view seems to have unwelcome consequences.

First unwelcome consequence: spinelessness. Consider an issue on which you count many of your associates as epistemic peers. If the issue is at all tricky, your peers undoubtedly take a wide spectrum of stances on it. (This is especially true if your peers are philosophers.) The equal weight view then requires you to weigh each stance equally, along with your own. But that requires you to think, of each stance, that it is very unlikely to be right. Typically, it will follow that you ought to suspend judgment on the issue. Since it seems that you are in this circumstance with respect to a great many issues, the equal weight view requires you to suspend judgment on all of these. Do you have any convictions on controversial political, philosophical, or scientific matters? The equal weight view seems to say: kiss them goodbye. It is implausible that rationality requires such spinelessness (Pettit 2005, van Inwagen 1996).

Second unwelcome consequence: lack of self-trust. Suppose that a great fraction of those you count as your epistemic peers agree with you on some issue. Then the equal weight view says: stick with your initial assessment. Great! Except that the *reason* for sticking to that assessment has very little to do with your own evaluation of the common stock of evidence, and very much to do with the fraction of your peers who agree with you. Shouldn't your own careful consideration of the issue count for more than 1/100th, even if there are 99 people you count as epistemic peers? If not, then one might just as well form views on controversial matters by simply sending out a poll (Landesman 2000). It is implausible that rationality requires you to give your own consideration of the issue such a minor role.[16]

These are unwelcome consequences of the equal weight view. One might try to mitigate the consequences by claiming that most of the disputed issues are not matters of fact, or that people rarely share their relevant evidence, or that one shouldn't count many of one's associates as peers after all.[17] Or one might try to make the consequences more palatable (Christensen 2007, Feldman 2004). I will not discuss these strategies at present. The present point is this: even if the equal weight view is right, it is not *obviously* right.

What reinforces this point is that the equal weight view stands in com petition with views that clearly avoid the unwelcome consequences. Two such views deserve special note.

9. COMPETITORS TO THE EQUAL WEIGHT VIEW

The first competing view is the **extra weight view**, according to which one should give one's own assessment more weight than the assessments of those one counts as epistemic peers.[18] For example, when you find out that your sole epistemic peer has arrived at a contrary conclusion, the extra weight view says that you should be pulled a *bit* in the peer's direction—but not half way. You should still think it more likely that you are right than that the peer is.

By granting special status to one's own assessments, the extra weight view mitigates the unwelcome consequences described in the previous section. For if your own assessment gets extra weight, you may reasonably stick to your guns to a great degree, even if a handful of your peers disagree. So the extra weight view does not require a spineless suspension of judgment on all controversial matters. Furthermore, on the extra weight view, your own assessment of the evidence has more impact on the formation of your overall view than it does on the equal weight view.

To introduce another competitor to the equal weight view, recall the guiding question: when you find out that your peer has arrived at the opposite conclusion as you, how much should you be moved?

According to the **right-reasons view**, the answer depends on how good your initial evaluation of the evidence was.[19] For example, suppose that the shared batch of evidence *in fact* strongly supports the disputed claim. You correctly apprehend this, but your peer misjudges the force of the evidence and as a result disagrees. In this case, the right-reasons view says it can be reasonable for you to stick to your (correct) evaluation.

What motivates the view is that there is an asymmetry in the above sort of dispute. Although each disputant *thinks* that he has correctly assessed the force of the evidence, at most one of the disputants has *in fact* done so (Kelly 2005, 180). A defender of the right-reasons view invites us to think of things as follows. Suppose that you have arrived at the conclusion that the evidence in fact supports—call it Conclusion C. Your peer has gotten things wrong and arrived at some other conclusion. What does rationality require? That you *stick* with Conclusion C, and that your peer *switch* to Conclusion C.[20]

The right-reasons view mitigates the problems of spinelessness and lack of self-trust. For when you have in fact assessed the evidence correctly, the view entails that you may reasonably stick to that assessment, even if a handful of your peers disagree. For the same reason, the view allows that even if you have many peers, your own assessment of the evidence need not be swamped.

To sum up: when you disagree with your peer, the situation is symmetric in the sense that your assessment seems right to you, and your peer's assessment seems right to him. What might break the symmetry? The extra weight view says: you should give your own assessment extra weight because it is *yours*. The right-reasons view says: if in fact your assessment is right, it deserves extra weight because it is *right*. Both views avoid the unwelcome consequence that your own assessments must be swamped when you have a large number of peers.

In contrast, the equal weight view says: even though your assessment is your own, and even if it is in fact correct, you shouldn't favor it even a tiny bit. It is time to defend the equal weight view.

10. FOR THE EQUAL WEIGHT VIEW: BOOTSTRAPPING

To see the correctness of the equal weight view, start with a case of perceptual disagreement.

You and a friend are to judge the same contest, a race between Horse A and Horse B. Initially, you think that your friend is as good as you at judging such races. In other words, you think that in case of disagreement about the race, the two of you are equally likely to be mistaken. The race is run, and the two of you form independent judgments. As it happens, you become confident that Horse A won, and your friend becomes equally confident that Horse B won.

When you learn of your friend's opposing judgment, you should think that the two of you are equally likely to be correct. For suppose not— suppose it were reasonable for you to be, say, 70% confident that you are correct. Then you would have gotten some evidence that you are a better judge than your friend, since you would have gotten some evidence that you judged this race correctly, while she misjudged it. But that is absurd. It is absurd that in this situation you get any evidence that you are a better judge (Christensen 2007, Section 4).

To make this absurdity more apparent, suppose that you and your friend independently judge the same long series of races. You are then allowed to compare your friend's judgments to your own. (You are given no outside information about the race outcomes.) Suppose for *reductio* that in each case of disagreement, you should be 70% confident that you are correct. It follows that over the course of many disagreements, you should end up extremely confident that you have a better track record than your friend. As a result, you should end up extremely confident that you are a better judge. But that is absurd. Without some antecedent reason to think that you are a better judge, the disagreements between you and your friend are no evidence that she has made most of the mistakes.

Furthermore, the above judgment of absurdity is independent of who *in fact* has done a better job. Even if in fact you have judged the series of races much more accurately than your friend, simply comparing judgments with your friend gives you no evidence that you have done so.

Here is the bottom line. When you find out that you and your friend have come to opposite conclusions about a race, you should think that the two of you are equally likely to be correct.

The same goes for other sorts of disagreements.

Suppose that instead of judging a race, you and your friend are to judge the truth of a claim, based on the same batch of evidence. Initially, you count your friend as an epistemic peer—you think that she is about as good as you at judging the claim. In other words, you think that, conditional on a disagreement arising, the two of you are equally likely to be mistaken.[21] Then the two of you perform your evaluations. As it happens, you become confident that the claim is true, and your friend becomes equally confident that it is false.

When you learn of your friend's opposing judgment, you should think that the two of you are equally likely to be correct. The reason is the same as before. If it were reasonable for you to give your own evaluation extra weight—if it were reasonable to be more than 50% confident that you are right—then you would have gotten some evidence that you are a better evaluator than your friend. But that is absurd.

Again, the absurdity is made more apparent if we imagine that you and your friend evaluate the same long series of claims. Suppose for *reductio* that whenever the two of you disagree, you should be, say, 70% confident that your friend is the mistaken one. It follows that over the course of many disagreements, you should end up extremely confident that you have a better track record than your friend. As a result, you should end up extremely confident that you are a better evaluator. But that is absurd. Without some antecedent reason to think that you are a better evaluator, the disagreements between you and your friend are no evidence that she has made most of the mistakes.

Again, this absurdity is independent of who has in fact evaluated the claims properly. Even if in fact you have done a much better job than your friend at evaluating the claims, simply comparing your verdicts to those of your friend gives you no evidence that this is so.

The above argument has the same form as a certain well-known objection to reliabilism (Goldman 1986, Sosa 1997). According to reliabilism, one can gain knowledge by a reliable method, even if one does not know that the method is reliable. For example, suppose that your color vision is in fact reliable. In that case—according to reliabilism—by looking at a red wall you can come to know that the wall is red, even if you don't know that your vision is reliable.[22]

Now for the objection. If reliabilism is right, then in the above case you get some evidence that your vision is reliable merely by looking at the wall. That is because you come to know that your vision has operated correctly on that occasion. By looking at many walls, you can come to know that your vision has operated correctly on many occasions, and hence can come to know that your vision is reliable. In other words, you can come to know that your vision is reliable merely by checking that the outputs of your visual system agree with . . . the outputs of your visual system. Such procedures, called "bootstrapping" (Vogel 2000, 615) or the gaining of "easy knowledge" (Cohen 2002), are clearly illegitimate. But it follows from reliabilism they can be legitimate. That is the objection.

We have seen that rivals to the equal weight view are subject to an analogous objection. For suppose that it was legitimate to give your own evaluations more weight than those of a friend who you initially count as a peer. Then it could be legitimate for you to "bootstrap"—to come to be confident that you are a better evaluator than the friend merely by noting cases of disagreement, and taking it that the friend made most of the errors.[23] But that is absurd. So it is not legitimate to give your own evaluations more weight than those who you count as peers. A similar argument shows that it is not legitimate to give your own evaluations less weight than those who you count as peers.

So the equal weight view is correct.

11. THE EQUAL WEIGHT VIEW, REFINED

This section describes two complications. They require tweaking the equal weight view, but not in a way that interferes with the above defense.

To start, recall what the equal weight view says. Suppose that before evaluating a claim, you think that you and your friend are equally likely to evaluate it correctly. When you find out that your friend disagrees with your verdict, how likely should you think it that you are correct? The equal weight view says: 50%.

But here is a complication. Suppose that while evaluating the claim, you get some relevant information about the circumstances of the disagreement. For example, suppose that the weather gets extremely hot, and you know that your friend—unlike you—can't think straight in hot weather. In that case, when you find out that your friend disagrees, you should end up fairly confident that she is the mistaken one.

In particular, suppose that before evaluating the claim, the following was true: conditional on a disagreement arising in hot weather, you were 80% confident that your friend would be the mistaken one. In that case, when a disagreement *does* arise in hot weather, you should be 80% confident that your friend is the mistaken one (Christensen 2007, Section 4). And the same goes for initial degrees of confidence other than 80%.

The point is that you should not be guided by your prior assessment of your friend's *overall* judging ability. Rather, you should be guided by your prior assessment of her judging ability *conditional on what you later learn about the judging conditions.*

Notice that the above view is more general than the equal weight view, as first stated. For at the start, the equal weight view applied only to cases in which you initially count your advisor as a peer—as equally likely to be right, on the supposition that the two of you end up disagreeing. But the modified view also applies to cases in which you initially count an advisor as an epistemic superior—as being more than 50% likely to be right, on the supposition that the two of you end up disagreeing. Likewise, the view applies to cases in which you initially count an advisor as an epistemic inferior.

Also note that one might have differing assessments of an advisor's abilities with respect to different issues. For example, one might count an advisor as a peer with respect to arithmetic, but as less than a peer with respect to disputes about euthanasia. So despite the name, the equal weight view does not in general call for simply averaging together one's probability function with that of one's advisor.

There is a second complication. The above view appeals to your prior assessment of your friend's abilities—the assessment you had before thinking through the disputed issue. But what if you thought through the disputed issue years ago, before you even met this friend? Then it won't help to consider what you believed about the friend's abilities way back then. For at that time, you had not even met the friend (and hence had no informed opinion of her abilities). So the equal weight view is useless in this case. How can it be fixed?

For an answer, notice that the whole point of considering your past beliefs was to get access to a state of opinion untainted by your detailed reasoning about the disputed issue.[24] *One* way to do that is to consider what you believed before thinking the issue through. But that is not the only way. Sometimes we may sensibly ask what a given agent believes, *bracketing* or *factoring off* or *setting aside* certain considerations. For example, suppose that your views on the trustworthiness of Jennifer Lopez derive from both tabloid reports and face-to-face interactions. In this case, we may sensibly ask what your views of Lopez are, setting aside what the tabloids say. To ask this is not to ask about your actual beliefs at some previous time. Rather, it is to ask what happens when we remove or extract tabloid-based information from your current state of belief.

Likewise, in case of disagreement between you and a friend, we may ask what you believe, setting aside your detailed reasoning (and what you know of your friend's reasoning) about the disputed issue. In particular, we may ask who you think would likely be correct, setting that reasoning aside. By construction, the resulting belief state is untainted by ("prior to") your reasoning about the disputed issue. But since *only* the disputed reasoning has been extracted, that belief state still reflects your general information about your friend's abilities. The equal weight view is best understood as invoking this non-temporal notion of prior belief.[25] Here is the resulting view:

> **Equal weight view** Upon finding out that an advisor disagrees, your probability that you are right should equal your prior conditional probability that you would be right. Prior to what? Prior to your thinking through the disputed issue, and finding out what the advisor thinks of it. Conditional on what? On whatever you have learned about the circumstances of the disagreement.[26]

Note that in applying the view, the "circumstances of a disagreement" should not include a detailed specification of the chain of reasoning that led you to your conclusion. For if they did, then making the relevant conditional probability judgment would involve thinking through the disputed issue—and hence would not be prior to your doing so.

For example, suppose that you and a friend get different answers to the same multiplication problem. In applying the equal weight view to this case, the circumstances of disagreement might include such factors as: the amount of scratch paper available to you and your friend; how much coffee each of you has recently drunk; how confident the two of you were in your respective answers (after doing the calculation, but before finding out about the disagreement); how absurd each of you finds the other's answer; and whether the calculation involves carrying many 1s (this last factor would be relevant if, for example, you know your friend often forgets to carry his 1s).

In general, circumstances of disagreement should be individuated just coarsely enough so that the relevant conditional probability judgment is genuinely prior to your reasoning about the disputed issue. (This coarseness constraint is what makes the equal weight view nontrivial. For otherwise—if the view simply required that one's new opinion should equal one's prior opinion, conditional on *all* of one's new information—the view would be tantamount to the requirement that one conditionalize on one's new information.)

Taking into account circumstances of disagreement also provides an answer to a natural objection to the equal weight view.[27] The objection is that when an advisor you treated as a peer comes up with a conclusion that you find utterly insane, you can be reasonable in thinking it more likely that you are right than that the advisor is. Christensen (2007) gives a nice example of this: you and your friend do some arithmetic to divide the bill on a modest dinner. You get an answer of $28, and your friend gets an answer of $280. It certainly seems as though you should be more confident that you are right than that your friend is. And that is incompatible with what the equal weight view seems to entail about the case.

The reply to the objection is that the equal weight view delivers the intuitively correct verdict. For according to the equal weight view, your probability that you are right should equal your prior probability that you would be right, *conditional on what you later learn about the circumstances of the disagreement*. And one circumstance of the split-the-check disagreement is that you are *extremely* confident that your advisor's answer is wrong—much more confident than you are that your answer is right. Indeed, her answer strikes you as obviously insane. So in order to apply the equal weight view, we must determine your prior probability that you would be right, conditional on these circumstances arising.

To do so, think of your state of mind before doing the calculation. We have assumed that, conditional on the two of you disagreeing, you think that your advisor is just as likely as you to be right. But it is also natural to assume that, conditional on the two of you disagreeing *and your finding her answer utterly insane*, you think that you are much more likely to be right. If so, then when that circumstance arises the equal weight view instructs you to favor your own answer. That is the intuitively correct verdict about the case.[28]

What makes the above answer work is an asymmetry in the case. You find your advisor's answer insane, but have no special information about her reaction to your answer. We might add to the case to restore the symmetry. Suppose that in addition to her answer, you also find out what your advisor thinks of your answer: that it is utterly insane, obviously out of the ballpark, and so on. In other words, you find out that she has exactly the same attitude about your answer as you have about hers.

To get the equal weight view's verdict about this case, turn again to your state of mind before doing the calculation. Conditional on the two of you disagreeing, and each of you finding the other's answer to be insane, do you think that the two of you are likely to be right? The description of the case doesn't settle this, but suppose that the answer is "yes". (Perhaps the two of you have had many such disagreements, and that upon settling them, each of you has had to sheepishly admit defeat about half of the time.) In that case, the equal weight view does entail that when the disagreement arises, you should think it just as likely that your advisor is right about the check as that you are. But with the symmetry-restoring additions to the case, that verdict independently plausible.

That completes my explanation of the equal weight view, an account of how to incorporate the opinions of an advisor to whom one only partially defers. But it does not complete my defense. For recall that the view seemed to have some unwelcome consequences.

12. THE PROBLEMS OF SPINELESSNESS AND SELF-TRUST

It is time to face the problems of spinelessness and self-trust. Start with the problem of spinelessness—the problem that an egalitarian view on how to respond to disagreement will recommend suspension of judgment on virtually all controversial issues. Let me pose the problem again, from a slightly different angle.

Views on disagreement face pressure from two directions. On the one hand, when one considers clean, pure examples of disagreement, it seems obvious that something like the equal weight view is correct. It seems obvious that when you disagree about an arithmetic problem with a friend who you previously considered to be equally good at arithmetic, you should think yourself no more likely to be correct than your friend.

On the other hand, when one considers messy examples of real-world disagreements about hard issues, the equal weight view seems to lead to absurdity. Example: your friends take a range of stances on some basic political or ethical claim. By your lights, these friends are just as thoughtful, well-informed, quick-witted, and intellectually honest as you. Still, it seems obviously wrong that you are thereby required to suspend judgment on the claim, as the equal weight view seems to entail. To require this would be to require you to suspend of judgment on almost everything.

So: with respect to the clean, pure cases, there is pressure in the direction of the equal weight view. With respect to messy real-world cases, the equal weight view seems to lead to absurdity. What gives?

The answer is that the equal weight view does not lead to absurdity, because there is a relevant difference between the two sorts of cases. The difference is that in the clean cases one is in a position to count one's associates as peers *based on reasoning that is independent of the disputed issue*. But in the messy real-world cases, one is rarely in a position to do so. That is because in the messy cases, one's reasoning about the disputed issue is tangled up with one's reasoning about many other matters (Pettit 2005). As a result, in real-world cases one tends not to count one's dissenting associates—however smart and well-informed—as epistemic peers.

Let me explain, by way of a few examples.

Suppose that you disagree with your friend about the multiplication problem "What is 5243324 × 922?". You nevertheless count your friend as a peer: setting aside your reasoning about this particular problem, you think that she is equally likely to get the right answer in case of disagreement.[29] Your evaluation may be based on such factors as your friend's mathematical track record, what sort of training she has had, and so on. It need not based on any particular view on the value of 5243324 × 922, or on the answers to similar multiplication problems.[30]

In messy real-world cases, such independent peer evaluations are often unavailable. For example, consider Ann and Beth, two friends who stand at opposite ends of the political spectrum. Consider the claim that abortion is morally permissible.[31] Does Ann consider Beth a peer with respect to this claim? That is: setting aside her own reasoning about the abortion claim (and Beth's contrary view about it), does Ann think Beth would be just as likely as her to get things right?

The answer is "no". For (let us suppose) Ann and Beth have discussed claims closely linked to the abortion claim. They have discussed, for example, whether human beings have souls, whether it is permissible to withhold treatment from certain terminally ill infants, and whether rights figure prominently in a correct ethical theory. By Ann's lights, Beth has reached wrong conclusions about most of these closely related questions. As a result, even setting aside her own reasoning about the abortion claim, Ann thinks it unlikely that Beth would be right in case the two of them disagree about abortion.

In other words, setting aside Ann's reasoning about abortion does not set aside her reasoning about allied issues. And by Ann's lights, the accuracy of an advisor's views on these allied issues indicates how accurate the advisor is likely to be, when it comes to abortion. The upshot is that Ann does not consider Beth an epistemic peer with respect to the abortion claim.

So the abortion case is quite different than the multiplication case. Furthermore, the contrast between them is representative. In the clean, pure cases of disagreement used to motivate the equal weight view, the disputed issues are relatively separable from other controversial matters.[32] As a result, the agents in those examples often count their smart friends and associates as peers about the issues under dispute. But in messy real-world cases, the disputed issues are tangled in clusters of controversy. As a result, though agents in those examples may count their associates as thoughtful, well-informed, quick-witted, and so on, they often do *not* count those associates as peers. For example, Ann does not count Beth as a peer with respect to the abortion claim.

Think of a smart and well-informed friend who has a basic political framework diametrically opposed to your own. Imagine that the two of you are both presented with an unfamiliar and tricky political claim. You haven't thought things through yet, and so have no idea what you will eventually decide about the claim. Still—don't you think that you are more likely than your friend to correctly judge the claim, supposing that the two of you end up disagreeing? If so, then however quick-witted, well-informed, intellectually honest, and thorough you think your friend is, you do not count her as an epistemic peer with respect to that claim. And if you do not count her as a peer, the equal weight view does not require you give her conclusion the same weight as your own. Indeed, if you think that your friend has been consistently enough mistaken about allied issues, then the equal weight view requires you to become *more* confident in your initial conclusion once you find out that she disagrees.

At the other extreme, think of a smart friend who has a basic political framework extremely similar to your own. Again, imagine that both of you have just been presented with an unfamiliar political claim. In this case, you may well think that in case of disagreement, your friend is just as likely as you to be correct. If so, and if you and your friend end up coming to opposite verdicts, then the equal weight view requires you to think it just as likely that she is right as that you are. But notice that friends like these—friends who agree with you on issues closely linked to the one in question—will very often agree with you on the one in question as well.

Moral: with respect to many controversial issues, the associates who one counts as peers tend to have views that are similar to one's own. That is why—contrary to initial impressions—the equal weight view does not require one to suspend judgment on everything controversial.

That is how the equal weight view escapes the problem of spinelessness.

What of the problem of self-trust? That problem arose because the equal-weight view entails that one should weigh equally the opinions of those one counts as peers, even if there are many such people. The problem is that it seems wrong that one's independent assessment should be so thoroughly swamped by sheer force of numbers. Shouldn't one's own careful consideration count for more than 1/100th, even if there are 99 people one counts as epistemic peers?

The short answer is: no. If one really has 99 associates who one counts as peers who have independently assessed a given question, then one's own assessment *should* be swamped. This is simply an instance of the sort of group reliability effect commonly attributed to Condorcet. To make this answer easier to swallow, consider a mathematical case. When you get one answer to an arithmetic problem, and 99 people you count as arithmetical peers get another answer, it is quite clear that you should become extremely confident in the answer of the majority.

The above discussion of the problem of spinelessness also is of use here. From that discussion we learned that the people one counts as peers on a given issue are (1) more rare than one would initially have thought, and (2) very often in agreement with oneself. So in messy real-world cases (involving basic political disagreement, for example), the equal weight view permits one's independent thinking on many matters to have significant weight. It also requires one's opinions to be swamped by the majority when one counts a very great many of one's advisors as peers. That is a little odd, but in this case we should follow the Condorcet reasoning where it leads: we should learn to live with the oddness.

13. OBJECTIONS

Objection. The equal weight view escapes the problem of spinelessness only by advocating an ostrich-like policy of listening only to those with whom one already agrees.

Reply. First, everything said so far is compatible with the advice: listen to opposing arguments with an open mind. Everyone agrees that one should do that. At issue is the degree to which the mere fact of disagreement should change one's position. In other words, at issue is how much one should be moved when one either doesn't know the reasoning behind an advisor's dissenting conclusion, or does know the reasoning, but doesn't find it compelling.

Second, the equal weight view often requires one to be moved a fair bit by dissenting opinion (far more than most of us in fact tend to be moved). For though controversial matters tend to be linked together in clusters, it is not as though everyone walks in lockstep with their political, scientific, or philosophical clique. For example, imagine that you and a friend are presented with a tricky claim that you have not yet thought through. You may well think that your friend is almost as likely as you to evaluate the claim correctly, even if the two of you differ a bit on allied issues. If so, and if you and your friend end up disagreeing, then the equal weight view requires you to be significantly moved.

So the equal weight view doesn't say: bury your head in the sand. It does say: defer to an advisor in proportion to your prior probability that the advisor would be correct in case of disagreement. In practice, this means deferring most to advisors whose views (on matters closely linked to the issue in question) are similar to one's own.[33]

Objection. Return to the case of Ann and Beth, friends at opposite ends of the political spectrum. Ann counts Beth as less than an epistemic peer when it comes to abortion. She does so because she judges that Beth has gone wrong on many issues linked to abortion. But that judgment rests on the assumption that Ann's views on the linked issues are correct—an assumption to which Ann is not entitled.

Rather than taking her views on the surrounding issues for granted, Ann should attend to the larger disagreement between her and Beth: disagreement about a whole cluster of issues linked to abortion. Ann should think of this whole cluster as a single compound issue, and should take into account Beth's disagreement about *that*. When she does so, she can no longer penalize Beth for going wrong on surrounding issues. So the equal weight view entails that Ann should suspend judgment about abortion, in light of Beth's disagreement. Furthermore, similar reasoning applies in many cases of real-world disagreement. So the equal weight view does after all require suspension of judgment on virtually everything controversial.

Reply. Consider the cluster of issues linked to abortion. Contrary to what the objection supposes, Ann does *not* consider Beth a peer about that cluster. In other words, setting aside her reasoning about the issues in the cluster, and setting aside Beth's opinions about those issues, Ann does not think Beth would be just as likely as her to get things right. That is because there is no fact of the matter about Ann's opinion of Beth, once so many of Ann's considerations have been set aside. Hence the equal weight view does not require Ann to suspend judgment about the cluster. That blocks the objection.

But why is there no fact of the matter about Ann's opinion, setting aside her reasoning about the cluster? To see why, return to the example in which you know Jennifer Lopez both from face-to-face interactions and tabloid reports. In that example, there is a determinate answer to the question: "What is your opinion of Lopez, setting aside what the tabloids say?" That is because there is a relatively self-contained path along which the tabloids influence your beliefs about Lopez. As a result, there is a natural way of factoring your belief state into a "prior" state, together with some additional tabloid-based information.

In contrast, there is no determinate answer to the question: "What is your opinion of Lopez, setting aside that humans have bodies and that the Earth exists?" That is because there is no unique way of factoring your belief state into a "prior" state, together with that additional information. Setting aside that humans have bodies and that the Earth exists, how confident are you that Lopez dated Ben Affleck? Or that one of Lopez's movies was recently panned by critics? Or that Hollywood even exists? These questions have no answers because the information to be set aside is enmeshed in too much of your reasoning to be cleanly factored off.

The same goes for Ann's reasoning about the cluster of issues linked to abortion. That cluster includes a wide range of issues: whether humans have souls, the age at which humans begin feeling pain, whether rights figure prominently in a correct ethical theory, and so on. To set aside Ann's reasoning about all of these issues is to set aside a large and central chunk of her ethical and political outlook. Once so much has been set aside, there is no determinate fact about what opinion of Beth remains.

Of course, Ann may have opinions about Beth's ability in other domains, such as mathematics, etiquette, and film criticism. Suppose that these opinions are independent of the cluster of issues surrounding abortion. Why don't they determine Ann's evaluation of Beth once abortion-related matters are set aside?

To see why not, note that such evaluations would depend on further opinions: opinions on the extent to which ability in other domains predicts the ability to correctly answer questions in ethics. Ann's opinions on these matters—on what sorts of abilities are predictive of good ethical reasoning—are themselves wrapped up in Ann's ethical and political views. So setting aside Ann's opinions on abortion-related matters means setting these opinions aside. As a result, once abortion-related matters have been set aside, Ann has no determinate opinion of Beth's ability to determine whether abortion is permissible.

It follows that in this case the equal weight view issues no determinate verdict about how Ann should respond to the larger disagreement between her and Beth. So the objection fails.

In the above discussion it was assumed that the disagreement between Ann and Beth goes extremely deep—so deep that there is no common ground from which Ann could sensibly assess Beth's basic political out look. What about cases of less extreme disagreement? For example, suppose that Ann and Beth agree on a significant portion of their political outlooks, and disagree only on abortion and some closely linked issues. In that case, it may well be that Ann considers Beth a peer (or almost a peer) regarding the issues in dispute between them. If so, then the equal weight view does require Ann to give Beth's view significant weight.

So in such cases—cases in which disagreement does not run so very deep—the equal weight view *does* entail suspension of judgment on controversial matters. But such cases only represent a small portion of cases of disagreement about hotly disputed matters. As a result, the equal weight view does not require an implausible across-the-board suspension of judgment. It does require much more deference to advisors than most of us in fact exhibit, but that is no embarrassment to the view.

14. PARTIAL DEFERENCE TO ONESELF

We have seen how the equal weight view applies to cases of disagreement with outside advisors. It says that one should defer to an advisor in proportion to one's prior conditional probability that the advisor would be correct. But the view also applies to cases of disagreement with one's future or past self. It constrains how one should take into account the opinions one had, or expects to have, when one has less than perfect trust in one's past or future judgment.

To see how the constraint operates, take the example of being guided by past opinion (the case of being guided by future opinion is similar). Suppose that you have just reevaluated a philosophical theory that you accepted years ago. If not for your past opinion, you would now reject the theory as false. How much should your past acceptance of the theory temper your present rejection? The answer is that you should defer to your past opinion in proportion to your prior conditional probability that your past opinion would be right. More precisely, the crucial question is: setting aside your recent rethinking of the issue, and setting aside your old conclusion about it, which self would you expect to be right in case of this sort of disagreement?

There are a number of factors that determine the answer: whether you think you've gotten sharper over the years, or have received relevant background information, or have caught what is clearly a mistake in your old reasoning. But one factor is of particular note: the degree to which your past and present selves agree on issues surrounding the disputed one.

If there is a great deal of agreement, then you will likely count your past self as a peer, or as nearly one. If so, you should give your past conclusions plenty of weight. In contrast, suppose that between then and now you have undergone a fundamental change in view. Perhaps you have experienced a spiritual revelation, or a quick deconversion. Perhaps you were exposed to a philosophical idea that dramatically reorganized your thinking about a large cluster of issues. Or perhaps you were part of an episode of scientific change that was revolutionary in the sense of Kuhn

(1970). In such cases, you should regard your past self as having many mistaken views about issues surrounding certain disputed ones. So in such cases, you should severely discount your previous dissenting opinion.

What this shows is that the equal weight view provides a graded version of Reflection—a version covering cases in which one only partially defers to the judgment of one's future or past self. The view has the effect of tying one's beliefs together over time. But note that the strength of the ties is highly variable. Across periods of ordinary (modest) belief change, the ties are strong. For across such periods, there is a great deal of background agreement. In contrast, across periods in which there is abrupt or dramatic belief change, the ties are weak. For across those periods there is little common ground between the selves at the earlier and later times.[34] In such cases it may be inevitable that one's earlier and later selves regard each other as not to be trusted.

Notes

*Thanks to Cian Dorr, Andy Egan, John Hawthorne, Agustín Rayo, David Christensen, Alan Hájek, Jim Pryor, Philip Pettit, Tom Kelly, Roger White, Sarah McGrath, the Corridor Group, and audiences at CUNY, the University of Michigan, Australian National University, the University of Sydney, the 2006 Formal Epistemology Workshop, and the 2006 Bellingham Summer Philosophy Conference.

1 See also Hájek (2003, 311), to which I owe both the above example and also the notion of subject-matter-restricted expertise. Rich Thomason has pointed out that this way of restricting expertise to a subject matter can be at most a rough approximation. For there is no limit to the sort of evidence that might be relevant to the evaluation of weather-propositions. As a result, to treat the forecaster as an expert in the above sense is to potentially defer to her on the evaluation of any sort of evidence.

2 Compare to the motivation given in Hall (1994) for the move from the Old Principal Principle to the New Principal Principle.

3 The above definition is appropriate only if countably many potential credence functions are in play, in which case it entails the following requirement: $P(H \mid$ advisor's prob for H is $x) = x$. In the more general case, a fancier reformulation is in order. Such a reformulation might invoke a conception of conditional probability that allows for probabilities conditional on probability-zero propositions (Popper 1952, Renyi 1955). Or it might invoke integrals over probability densities. I suppress such elaborations here and in subsequent discussion. Thanks here to Grant Reaber.

4 See van Fraassen (1984), van Fraassen (1995), Goldstein (1983).

5 Some defenses of the original version are explored in van Fraassen (1995).

6 Such limited principles include "Reflection Restricted", from Jeffrey (1988, 233), and "Confidence", from Hall (1999, 668).

7 Here for simplicity it is assumed that one's total evidence is the strongest proposition one believes with certainty. If that assumption is relaxed, one would have to take as basic the notion of an agent's total evidence, and modify the proposal accordingly. Thanks here to Bas van Fraassen.

8 For a similar proposal, along with criticisms of the present one, see Weisberg (2005, Section 5).

9 This example is a retelling of the "prisoner in the cell" case from Arntzenius (2003).

10 See also Schervish et al. (2004).

11 I owe this point to Peter Railton.

12 I borrow this example from van Inwagen (1996, 141).

13 I owe the term "epistemic peer" to Gutting (1982) by way of Kelly (2005), though I use it in a different way than they do. See note 21.

14 Note that in setting up the problem, the initial assumption is that you *count* your friend as your epistemic peer. That contrasts with some presentations, in which the initial assumption is that your friend *is* your epistemic peer. The former assumption is appropriate, however. For example, one sometimes is reasonable in thinking wise advisors to be foolish. Evidence, after all, can be misleading. In such cases, one is reasonable in being guided by one's *assessments* of the advisor's ability, even if those assessments are in fact incorrect.

15 Or at least: a very natural generalization of it is right for the case of many peers. The generalization would have to take into account, for example, the degree to which one judges that one's peers reached their conclusions independently. For simplicity, I suppress such complications here.

16 Furthermore, in light of such considerations, one might be tempted to avoid the hard work of thinking an issue through oneself, by simply deferring to the aggregated opinions of one's peers. This leads to the free-rider problem explored in List and Pettit (2003).

17 van Inwagen (1996) scotches many such strategies.

18 This view is described (but not endorsed) in Feldman (2004, 14). A close cousin of it—the view that "egocentric epistemic bias" is legitimate—is defended in Wedgwood (2007, Chapter 11).

19 I learned of this view from Kelly (2005, 180). Here is a representative quotation:

> The rationality of the parties engaged in [a disagreement among epistemic peers] will typically depend on who has *in fact* correctly evaluated the available evidence and who has not. If you and I have access to the same body of evidence but draw different conclusions, which one of us is being more reasonable (if either) will typically depend on which of the different conclusions (if either) is in fact better supported by that body of evidence.

20 In its most extreme form, the right-reasons view holds that when a disputant has correctly assessed the force of the evidence, rationality permits him to be *entirely unmoved* by the news of peer disagreement. A more modest version holds that when a disputant has correctly assessed the force of the evidence, rationality permits him to be moved *less than half way* in the direction of a peer's contrary assessment.

21 My use of the term "epistemic peer" is nonstandard. On my usage, you count your friend as an epistemic peer with respect to an about-to-be-judged claim if and only if you think that, conditional the two of you disagreeing about the claim, the two of you are equally likely to be mistaken. On more standard usages, an epistemic peer is defined to be an equal with respect to such factors as "intelligence, perspicacity, honesty, thoroughness, and other relevant epistemic virtues" (Gutting 1982, 83), "familiarity with the evidence and arguments which bear on [the relevant] question", and "general epistemic virtues such as intelligence,

thoughtfulness, and freedom from bias" (Kelly 2005). In defense of my use, suppose that you think that conditional on the two of you disagreeing about a claim,
your friend is more likely than you to be mistaken. Then however intelligent,
perspicacious, honest, thorough, well-informed, and unbiased you may think your
friend is, it would seem odd to count her as an epistemic peer with respect to that
claim, at least on that occasion. You think that on the supposition that there is
disagreement, she is more likely to get things wrong.

22   For ease of exposition, a simplified version of reliabilism about knowledge
is targeted here. But the guiding idea of the objection can be wielded against more
sophisticated versions.

23   Proponents of the right-reasons view are only committed to the legitimacy
of this sort of bootstrapping when the bootstrapper does in fact evaluate the evidence better than her opponent. The bootstrapping conclusion is absurd even in
this case.

24   Compare to the requirement of Christensen (2007) that explanations of a
disagreement be evaluated independently from the disputed issue.

25   This non-temporal notion of prior belief is similar to the notion of a "pre-
prior" invoked in Hanson (2006), and the equal weight view is similar to the "pre-
rationality condition" defended in that paper.

26   In talking about your conditional probability that one is "right", the above
formulation assumes that disputants arrive at all-or-nothing assessments of the
claim under dispute. That assumption is adopted only as a convenience. It is
relaxed in the following more general formulation of the view:

> Your probability in a given disputed claim should equal your prior condi-
> tional probability in that claim. Prior to what? Prior to your thinking
> through the claim, and finding out what your advisor thinks of it. Condi-
> tional on what? On whatever you have learned about the circumstances of
> how you and your advisor have evaluated the claim.

Note that this formulation governs one's response not just to cases in which your
advisor disagrees, but also to cases in which she agrees or suspends judgment.
Note also that this formulation does not presuppose any view on the "uniqueness
thesis" (Feldman 2004), according to which rational disagreements can only arise
from differences in evidence.

27   Thanks to Paolo Santorio for pressing me on this objection.

28   This is a generalization of the reply to this case in Christensen (2007).

29   Attempts to represent uncertainty about mathematics face the so-called
"problem of logical omniscience" (Stalnaker 1991). For present purposes, it
does no harm to treat arithmetical claims as logically independent contingent
claims in the manner of Garber (1983). Arithmetical reasoning will simply be
assumed to change these probabilities over time, in a way not represented in the
model.

30   The situation is different in case of disagreement about exceedingly
simple mathematical or logical problems. When a friend disagrees about
whether $1 + 1 = 2$, one may well not count her as a peer. For one's views on such
a simple problem are closely linked to one's basic reasoning. For that reason,
there may be no determinate fact about what one believes, setting aside one's
views on whether $1 + 1 = 2$. For further discussion of this point, see the reply
to the objection on p. 24.

31 If you think that moral claims such as this are not factual claims, then please substitute a clearly factual, hotly contested political claim. Unfortunately, many such claims exist.

32 Such pure cases include the savant cases from Feldman (2004) and Moller (2004), and the "split the check" case from Christensen (2007).

33 Compare to Foley (2001, 105), which argues that one has (defeasible) reason to trust the beliefs of an anonymous advisor, on the grounds that there are "broad commonalities in the intellectual equipment and environment of peoples across times and cultures".

34 For a detailed presentation of such a case, see Cook (1987).

References

Frank Arntzenius. Some problems for Conditionalization and Reflection. *Journal of Philosophy*, 100(7):356–371, 2003.

David Christensen. Clever bookies and coherent beliefs. *Philosophical Review*, pages 229–247, 1991.

David Christensen. Epistemology of disagreement: the good news. *Philosophical Review*, 116:187–217, 2007.

Stewart Cohen. Basic knowledge and the problem of easy knowledge. *Philosophy and Phenomenological Research*, 65(2):309–328, 2002.

J. Thomas Cook. Deciding to believe without self-deception. *Journal of Philosophy*, 84(8):441–446, 1987.

Richard Feldman. Reasonable religious disagreements. Manuscript, July 2004. URL http://www.ling.rochester.edu/~feldman/papers/reasonable%20religious%20disagreements.pdf.

Richard Foley. *Intellectual trust in oneself and others*. Cambridge University Press, Cambridge, 2001.

Haim Gaifman. A theory of higher-order probabilities. In Skyrms and Harper (1988).

Daniel Garber. Old evidence and logical omniscience in Bayesian confirmation theory. In John Earman, editor, *Minnesota studies in the philosophy of science*, volume 10, pages 99–131. University of Minnesota Press, 1983.

Alvin Goldman. *Epistemology and cognition*. Harvard University Press, Cambridge, MA, 1986.

Michael Goldstein. The prevision of a prevision. *Journal of the American Statistical Association*, 78(384):817–819, 1983.

Gary Gutting. *Religious Belief and Religious Skepticism*. University of Notre Dame Press, Notre Dame, 1982.

Alan Hájek. On what conditional probability could not be. *Synthese*, 137: 273–323, 2003.

Ned Hall. Correcting the guide to objective chance. *Mind*, 103:505–518, 1994.

Ned Hall. How to set a surprise exam. *Mind*, 108(432):647–703, 1999.

Robin Hanson. Uncommon priors require origin disputes. *Theory and Decision*, 61(4):318–328, 2006.

Terry Horgan. Sleeping Beauty awakened: New odds at the dawn of the new day. *Analysis*, 64(1):10–21, 2004.

R. Jeffrey. Conditioning, kinematics, and exchangeability. In Skyrms and Harper (1988).

Thomas Kelly. The epistemic significance of disagreement. In John Hawthorne and Tamar Gendler, editors, *Oxford studies in epistemology*, volume 1. Oxford University Press, Oxford, 2005.

Thomas S. Kuhn. *The structure of scientific revolutions*. University of Chicago Press, Chicago, 2nd edition, 1970.

Cliff Landesman, 2000. Personal communication.

Christian List and Philip Pettit. An epistemic free-riding problem? Technical report, RSSS, SPT, ANU, 2003. URL http://eprints.anu.edu.au/archive/00002233/.

Dan Moller. Disagreement manifesto. Discussion group notes, 2004.

Philip Pettit. When to defer to the majority—and when not. *Analysis*, 2005. Forthcoming.

Alvin Plantinga. Pluralism: a defense of religious exclusivism. In Philip L. Quinn and Kevin Meeker, editors, *The philosophical challenge of religious diversity*, pages 172–192. Oxford University Press, Oxford, 2000.

Karl R. Popper. *The Logic of Scientific Discovery*. Basic Books, New York, second edition, 1952.

A. Renyi. On a new axiomatic theory of probability. *Acta Math. Acad. Scient. Hungaricae*, 6:285–335, 1955.

M.J. Schervish, T. Seidenfeld, and J.B. Kadane. Stopping to reflect. *Journal of Philosophy*, 101(6):315–322, 2004.

B. Skyrms and William Harper, editors. *Causation, chance, and credence*. Kluwer, Dordecht, 1988.

Brian Skyrms. The value of knowledge. In C. Wade Savage, editor, *Justification, discovery, and the evolution of scientific theories*. University of Minnesota Press, Minneapolis, 1987.

Ernest Sosa. Reflective knowledge in the best circles. *Journal of Philosophy*, 94, 1997.

Robert Stalnaker. The problem of logical omniscience. *Synthese*, 89(3):425–440, 1991.

W. J. Talbott. Two principles of Bayesian epistemology. *Philosophical Studies*, pages 135–150, 1991.

Bas C. van Fraassen. Belief and the will. *Journal of Philosophy*, 81:235–256, 1984.

Bas C. van Fraassen. Belief and the problem of Ulysses and the Sirens. *Philosophical Studies*, 77:7–37, 1995.

Peter van Inwagen. It is wrong, everywhere, always, and for anyone, to believe anything upon insufficient evidence. In Jeff Jordan and Daniel Howard-Snyder, editors, *Faith, Freedom, and Rationality: Philosophy of Religion Today*, pages 137–53. Rowman and Littlefield, London, 1996.

Jonathan Vogel. Reliabilism leveled. *Journal of philosophy*, pages 602–623, 2000.

Ralph Wedgwood. *The Nature of Normativity*. Oxford University Press, 2007.

Jonathan Weisberg. Conditionalization without reflection. Manuscript, 2005.

9

Peer Disagreement and Higher Order Evidence

Thomas Kelly

1.

My aim in this article is to develop and defend a novel answer to a question that has recently generated a considerable amount of controversy. The question concerns the normative significance of *peer disagreement*. Suppose that you and I have been exposed to the same evidence and arguments that bear on some proposition: there is no relevant consideration that is available to you but not to me, or vice versa. For the sake of concreteness, we might picture

- You and I are attentive members of a jury charged with determining whether the accused is guilty. The prosecution, following the defense, has just rested its case.
- You and I are weather forecasters attempting to determine whether it will rain tomorrow. We both have access to the same meteorological data.
- You and I are professional philosophers interested in the question of whether free will is compatible with determinism. Each of us is thoroughly acquainted with all of the extant arguments, thought experiments, and intuition pumps that the literature has to offer.

Suppose further that neither of us has any particular reason to think that he or she enjoys some advantage over the other when it comes to assessing considerations of the relevant kind, or that he or she is more or less reliable about the relevant domain. Indeed, let us suppose that, to the extent that we do possess evidence about who is more reliable—evidence afforded, perhaps, by a comparison of our past track records—such evidence suggests that we are more or less equally reliable when it comes to making judgments about the domain in question.[1] Nevertheless, despite being peers in these respects, you and I arrive at different views about the question on the basis of our common evidence. For example, perhaps I find myself quite confident that the accused is guilty, or that it will rain tomorrow, or that free will and determinism are compatible, while you find yourself equally confident of the opposite. Question: once you and I learn that the other has arrived at a different conclusion despite having been exposed to the same evidence and arguments, how (if at all) should we revise our original views?

Some philosophers hold that in such circumstances, you and I are rationally required to *split the difference*. According to this line of thought, it would be unreasonable for either of us to simply retain his or her original opinion. Indeed, given the relevant symmetries, each of us should give *equal* weight to his or her opinion and to the opinion of the other in arriving at a revised view. Thus, given that I am confident that the accused is guilty while you are equally confident that he is not, both of us should retreat to a state of agnosticism in which we suspend judgment about the question. This is the equal weight view:

> In cases of peer disagreement, one should give equal weight to the opinion of a peer and to one's own opinion.

Recently, the equal weight view has been endorsed by a number of philosophers. Here, for example, is Richard Feldman:

> [C]onsider those cases in which the reasonable thing to think is that another person, every bit as sensible, serious, and careful as oneself, has reviewed the same information as oneself and has come to a contrary conclusion to one's own. . . . An honest description of the situation acknowledges its symmetry. . . . In those cases, I think, the skeptical conclusion is the reasonable one: it is not the case that both points of view are reasonable, and it is not the case that one's own point of view is somehow privileged. Rather, suspension of judgement is called for (2006, p. 235)[2]
>
> It is no surprise that the equal weight view has found sophisticated advocates; it is in many respects an appealing view. Indeed, reflection on certain kinds of cases can make it seem almost trivial or obviously true. Consider, for example, cases involving conflicting perceptual judgments such as the following:
>
> *Case 1*. You and I, two equally attentive and well-sighted individuals, stand side-by-side at the finish line of a horse race. The race is extremely close. At time t0, just as the first horses cross the finish line, it looks to me as though Horse A has won the race in virtue of finishing slightly ahead of Horse B; on the other hand, it looks to you as though Horse B has won in virtue of finishing slightly ahead of Horse A. At time 1, an instant later, we discover that we disagree about which horse has won the race. How, if at all, should we revise our original judgments on the basis of this new information?

Many find it obvious that, in such circumstances, I should abandon my original view that Horse A won the race and you should abandon your original view that Horse B won the race. For each of us, suspension of judgment is now the uniquely reasonable attitude. We should become agnostics about which horse won the race until further evidence becomes available. This, of course, is exactly what the equal weight view enjoins. But one might expect that what holds for perceptual judgments holds also for judgments of other kinds, and thus, in general.

Further evidence for the equal weight view seems to be afforded by certain natural analogies involving inanimate measuring devices. Consider for example

> *Case 2.* You and I are each attempting to determine the current temperature by consulting our own personal thermometers. In the past, the two thermometers have been equally reliable. At time t0, I consult my thermometer, find that it reads sixty-eight degrees, and so immediately take up the corresponding belief. Meanwhile, you consult your thermometer, find that it reads seventy-two degrees, and so immediately take up that belief. At time t1, you and I compare notes and discover that our thermometers have disagreed. How, if at all, should we revise our original opinions about the temperature in the light of this new information?[3]
>
> I take it as obvious that in these circumstances I should abandon my belief that it is sixty-eight degrees and you should abandon your belief that it is seventy-two degrees. In particular, it would be unreasonable for me to retain my original belief simply because this was what *my* thermometer indicated. Indeed, inasmuch as the relevant evidence available to us is exhausted by the readings of the two thermometers, neither of us should be any more confident of what his or her thermometer says than of what the other person's thermometer says. In these circumstances, we should treat the conflicting thermometer readings as equally strong pieces of evidence. But—one might naturally conclude—what holds for the conflicting readings of equally reliable thermometers holds also for the conflicting judgments of individuals who are peers in the relevant respects. The mere fact that I originally judged that the accused is guilty is no reason for me to retain that view once I learn that you originally judged that he is innocent. Just as I should retreat to a state of agnosticism about whether the temperature is sixty-eight or seventy-two degrees once I learn what your thermometer indicates, so, too, I should retreat to a state of agnosticism about whether the accused is guilty or innocent once I learn your opinion about the matter.

In view of considerations such as these and others that have been offered on its behalf, the equal weight view can seem quite compelling. Nevertheless, I believe that here appearances are misleading: the equal weight view is false. The main negative burden of what follows is to show that (and why) this is so. After offering a critique of the equal weight view, I will use that critique as a point of departure for the development of an alternative proposal about how we should respond to peer disagreement. For reasons that will emerge, I call this alternative proposal the total evidence view.

I begin with some taxonomy.

Philosophers who hold views inconsistent with the equal weight view maintain that, in at least some cases of peer disagreement, it can be reasonable to *stick to one's guns.*[4] A particularly radical alternative is this:

The *no independent weight view:* In at least some cases of peer disagreement,
it can be perfectly reasonable to give no weight at all to the opinion of the
other party.

That is, even if one retains one's original opinion with wholly undimin-
ished confidence on learning that a peer thinks otherwise, one's doing so
might be perfectly reasonable.

According to more moderate alternatives, while one is always rationally required to give at least some weight to the opinion of a peer, one is
not always required to split the difference. That is, even if one's new opinion is closer to one's own original opinion than to the original opinion of
one's peer, one's new opinion might nevertheless be perfectly reasonable.
Of course, there are many possible views of this kind. We might picture
these possibilities as constituting a spectrum: at one end of the spectrum
sits the equal weight view; at the other end the no independent weight
view; in between, the more moderate alternatives, arranged by how much
weight they would have one give to the opinion of a peer relative to one's
own. The more weight one is required to give to a peer's opinion relative
to one's own, the more the view in question will resemble the equal
weight view; the less weight one is required to give, the more it will
resemble the no independent weight view.

Among alternatives to the equal weight view, another distinction is
worth marking. Suppose that, on learning that we hold different opinions
about some issue, neither you nor I splits the difference: each of us either
simply retains his or her original opinion, or else moves to a new opinion
that is closer to that opinion than to the original opinion of the other.
Again, according to the equal weight view, both you and I are unreasonable for responding to our disagreement in this way. Among views inconsistent with the equal weight view, distinguish between those according
to which you and I might *both* be reasonable in responding in this way
and those according to which *at most one* of us is being reasonable. As an
example of the former, consider a view according to which everyone is
rationally entitled to give some special, presumptive weight to his or her
own judgment.[5] If such a view is true, then both you and I might be perfectly reasonable even though neither one of us splits the difference. As
an example of the latter kind of view, consider a view according to which
how far you and I should move in response to our disagreement depends
on whose original opinion better reflects our original evidence (Kelly
2005). Given such a view, and given certain further assumptions, it might
be that when you and I fail to split the difference, at most one of us is
being reasonable.

Taking these two distinctions together, the view most radically at odds
with the equal weight view would seem to be the following:

The *symmetrical no independent weight view:* In at least some cases of peer
disagreement, both parties to the dispute might be perfectly reasonable
even if neither gives any weight at all to the opinion of the other party.

Thus, according to *the symmetrical no independent weight view*, even if both you and I remain utterly unmoved on learning that the other holds a different opinion, it might be that neither one of us is responding unreasonably.

It is not my purpose to defend the symmetrical no independent weight view. Indeed, the view about peer disagreement that I will ultimately endorse is consistent with both it and its negation. That having been said, I am inclined to think that the symmetrical no independent weight view is true. Moreover, I also believe that, precisely because it contrasts so sharply with the equal weight view, considering it can help to illuminate the equal weight view by making plain some of the less obvious dialectical commitments incurred by proponents of the equal weight view. For these reasons, I want to briefly explore what might be said on behalf of the symmetrical no independent weight view.

2. CASES IN WHICH BOTH YOU AND I ARE PERFECTLY REASONABLE, DESPITE GIVING NO WEIGHT TO THE OTHER'S POINT OF VIEW

First, a preliminary remark about the equal weight view. It is sometimes defended in contexts in which the propositional attitude of belief is treated as an all-or-nothing matter: for any proposition one considers, one has in effect three doxastic options—one either believes the proposition, disbelieves the proposition, or suspends judgment as to its truth.[6] However, in considering the equal weight view, it is for various reasons more natural to treat belief not as an all-or-nothing matter but as a matter of degree. Indeed, it does not seem that the equal weight view can even be applied in full generality in a framework that treats belief as an all-or-nothing matter. Thus, consider a possible world that consists of two peers, one of whom is a theist and the other an atheist. When the theist and the atheist encounter one another, the response mandated by the equal weight view is clear enough: the two should split the difference and become agnostics with respect to the question of whether God exists. Suppose, however, that the two-person world consists not of a theist and an atheist but an atheist and an agnostic. How do they split the difference? (In this case, of course, agnosticism hardly represents a suitable compromise.) In general, the simple tripartite division between belief, disbelief, and suspension of judgment does not have enough structure to capture the import of the equal weight view when the relevant difference in opinion is that between belief and suspension of judgment, or between suspension of judgment and disbelief. Clearly, the natural move at this point is to employ a framework that recognizes more fine-grained psychological states. Let us then adopt the standard Bayesian convention according to which the credence one invests in a given proposition is assigned a numerical value between 0 and 1 inclusive, where 1 represents maximal confidence that the proposition is true, 0 represents maximal confidence that the proposition is false, .5 represents a state of perfect agnosticism as to the truth of the proposition, and so on. Thus, if the agnostic gives credence .5 to the proposition that God exists while the atheist gives credence .1 to the same proposition, the import of the equal weight view is clear: on learning of the other's opinion, each should give credence .3 to the proposition that God exists.

Moreover, even if one restricts one's attention to what are sometimes called "strong disagreements," that is, cases in which the relevant proposition is initially either believed or disbelieved by the parties,[7] it seems that an advocate of the equal weight view still has strong reasons to insist on a framework that treats belief as a matter of degree. For consider a world of three peers, two of whom are theists and one of whom is an atheist. The animating thought behind the equal weight view, namely that the opinion of any peer should count for no more and no less than that of any other, would seem to be clearly violated by the suggestion that the parties to the dispute should retreat to a state of agnosticism, since that would seem to give more weight to the opinion of the atheist than to the opinion of either theist. (The atheist's opinion is in effect given as much weight as the opinions of both theists taken together in determining what should ultimately be believed by the three.) On the other hand, the suggestion that theism wins simply because the atheist finds himself outnumbered would seem to give too little weight to the atheist's original opinion if it is understood to mean that all three should ultimately end up where the two theists begin. Once again, it seems that an advocate of the equal weight view should insist on a framework that treats belief as a matter of degree since only such a framework can adequately capture what is clearly in the spirit of his or her view.

Having noted this elementary point, I will now describe a possible case in which it is plausible that you and I are both perfectly reasonable despite giving zero weight to the other person's opinion:

> *Case 3.* How things stand with me: At time t0, my total evidence with respect to some hypothesis H consists of E. My credence for H stands at .7. Given evidence E, this credence is perfectly reasonable. Moreover, if I was slightly less confident that H is true, I would also be perfectly reasonable. Indeed, I recognize that this is so: if I met someone who shared my evidence but was slightly less confident that H was true, I would not consider that person unreasonable for believing as she does.
>
> How things stand with you:
>
> At time t0, your total evidence with respect to H is also E. Your credence for H is slightly lower than .7. Given evidence E, this credence is perfectly reasonable. Moreover, you recognize that, if your credence was slightly higher (say, .7), you would still be perfectly reasonable. If you met someone who shared your evidence but was slightly more confident that H was true, you would not consider that person unreasonable for believing as she does.

At time t1, we meet and compare notes. How, if at all, should we revise our opinions?

According to the equal weight view, you are rationally required to increase your credence while I am rationally required to decrease mine. But that seems wrong. After all, *ex hypothesi*, the opinion I hold about H is within the range of perfectly reasonable opinion, as is the opinion you hold. Moreover, both of us have recognized this all along. Why then would we be rationally required to change?

Someone sympathetic to the equal weight view might attempt to heroically defend the idea that you and I are rationally required to revise our original credences in these circumstances. However, a more promising line of resistance, I think, is to deny that Case 3 is possible at all. That is, an adherent of the equal weight view should endorse

> The *uniqueness thesis*: For a given body of evidence and a given proposition, there is some one level of confidence that it is uniquely rational to have in that proposition given that evidence.[8]
>
> Suppose that the uniqueness thesis is true. Then, if it is in fact reasonable for me to give credence .7 to the hypothesis, it follows that you are guilty of unreasonable diffidence for being even slightly less confident. On the other hand, if you are reasonable in being slightly less confident than I am, then I am guilty of being unreasonably overconfident. Hence, the description of Case 3 offered above is incoherent; Case 3 is not in fact a possible case.

How plausible is the uniqueness thesis? For my part, I find that its intuitive plausibility depends a great deal on how one thinks of the psychological states to which it is taken to apply. The uniqueness thesis seems most plausible when one thinks of belief in a maximally coarse-grained way, as an all-or-nothing matter.[9] On the other hand, as we think of belief in an increasingly fine-grained way, the more counterintuitive it seems. But as we have seen, the advocate of the equal weight view has strong reasons to insist on a framework that employs a fine-grained notion of belief.

Some philosophers find it pretheoretically obvious that the uniqueness thesis is false.[10] Many others accept substantive epistemological views from which its falsity follows.[11] Although the uniqueness thesis is inconsistent with many popular views in epistemology and the philosophy of science, its extreme character is perhaps best appreciated in a Bayesian framework. In Bayesian terms, the uniqueness thesis is equivalent to the suggestion that there is some single prior probability distribution that it is rational for one to have, any slight deviation from which already constitutes a departure from perfect rationality. This contrasts most strongly with so-called orthodox Bayesianism, according to which any prior probability distribution is reasonable so long as it is probabilistically coherent. Of course, many Bayesians think that orthodoxy is in this respect overly permissive. But notably, even Bayesians who are considered hard liners for holding that there are substantive constraints on rational prior probability distributions other than mere probabilistic coherence typically want nothing to do with the suggestion that there is some uniquely rational distribution. With respect to this long-running debate, then, commitment to the uniqueness thesis yields a view that would be considered by many to be beyond the pale, too hard-line even for the taste of most hard-liners themselves.

Of course, despite its radical character, the uniqueness thesis might nevertheless be true. In fact, some formidable arguments have been offered on its behalf.[12] Because I believe that the uniqueness thesis is false, I believe that the symmetrical no independent weight view is true, and (therefore) that the equal weight view is false. However, especially in light of the fact that here I will neither address the arguments for the uniqueness thesis nor argue against it more directly, I will not appeal to the possibility of so-called reasonable disagreements in arguing against the equal weight view. Indeed, because I am convinced that we should reject the equal weight view in any case, I will proceed in what follows as though (what I take to be) the fiction of uniqueness is true. My dialectical purpose in emphasizing the apparent link between the uniqueness thesis and the equal weight view is a relatively modest one. As noted, the equal weight view can sometimes seem to be almost *obviously* or *trivially* true, as though its truth can be established by quick and easy generalization from a few simple examples or analogies. However, if I am correct in thinking that commitment to the equal weight view carries with it a commitment to the uniqueness thesis, then this is one possibility that can be safely ruled out. Even if turns out to be true, the uniqueness thesis is an extremely strong and unobvious claim. Inasmuch as the ultimate tenability of the equal weight view is bound up with its ultimate tenability, the equal weight view is similarly an extremely strong and unobvious claim.

I turn next to some arguments against the equal weight view.

3. WHY WE SHOULD REJECT THE EQUAL WEIGHT VIEW

Let us suppose for the sake of argument, then, that the uniqueness thesis is correct: for a given batch of evidence, there is some one way of responding to that evidence that is the maximally rational way. Consider

> *Case 4.* Despite having access to the same substantial body of evidence E, you and I arrive at very different opinions about some hypothesis H: while I am quite confident that H is true, you are quite confident that it is false. Indeed, at time t0, immediately before encountering one another, my credence for H stands at .8 while your credence stands at .2. At time t1, you and I meet and compare notes. How, if at all, should we revise our respective opinions?

According to the equal weight view, you and I should split the difference between our original opinions and each give credence .5 to H. This is the reasonable level of confidence for both of us to have at time t1. As a general prescription, this strikes me as wrongheaded, for the following reason. Notice that, in the case as it has been described thus far, nothing whatsoever has been said about the relationship between E and H, and in particular, about the extent to which E supports or fails to support H. But it is implausible that how confident you and I should be that H is true at time t1 is wholly independent of this fact. For example, here is a way of filling in the details of the case that makes it implausible to suppose that you are rationally required to split the difference with me:

> *Case 4, continued*. In fact, hypothesis H is quite unlikely on evidence E. Your giving credence .2 to H is the reasonable response to that evidence. Moreover, you respond in this way precisely because you recognize that H is quite unlikely on E. On the other hand, my giving credence .8 to H is an unreasonable response and reflects the fact that I have significantly overestimated the probative force of E with respect to H.

At time t0, then, prior to encountering the other person, things stand as follows: you hold a reasonable opinion about H on the basis of your total evidence, while I hold an unreasonable opinion about H on the basis of the same total evidence. (Again, the difference in the normative statuses of our respective opinions is due to the fact that your opinion is justified by our common evidence while mine is not.) If one were to ask which one of us should revise his or her view at *this* point, the answer is clear and uncontroversial: while it is reasonable for you to retain your current level of confidence, I should significantly reduce mine, since, *ex hypothesi*, this is what a correct appreciation of my evidence would lead me to do.

For an advocate of the equal weight view, this seemingly important asymmetry completely washes out once we become aware of our disagreement. Each of us should split the difference between his or her original view (regardless of whether that view was reasonable or unreasonable) and the original view of the other (regardless of its status).

I take this to be an extremely dubious consequence of the equal weight view.[13] We should be clear, however, about exactly which consequences of the equal weight view warrant suspicion and which do not. According to the equal weight view, after you and I meet, I should be significantly less confident that the hypothesis is true. That much is surely correct. (After all, I should have been significantly less confident even before we met.) The equal weight view also implies that, after we meet, you should be more confident that the hypothesis is true, despite having responded correctly to our original evidence. While less obvious, this is also—for reasons that I explore below—not implausible. What *is* quite implausible, I think, is the suggestion that you and I are rationally required to make *equally* extensive revisions in our original opinions, given that your original opinion was, while mine was not, a reasonable response to our original evidence. After all, what it is reasonable for us to believe after we meet at time t1 presumably depends on the total evidence we possess at that point. Let's call the total evidence we possess at time t1 E*. What does E* include? Presumably the following:

> Our original body of evidence E
> The fact that I responded to E by believing H to degree .8
> The fact that you responded to E by believing H to degree .2

Notice that, on the equal weight view, the bearing of E on H turns out to be completely irrelevant to the bearing of E* on H. In effect, what it is reasonable for you and I to believe about H at time t1 supervenes on how you and I respond to E at time t0. With respect to playing a role in determining what is reasonable for us to believe at time t1, E gets completely swamped by purely psychological facts about what you and I believe.

I find this consequence a strange one. Of course, others might not share my sense of strangeness, and even those who do might very well be prepared to live with this consequence, given that other considerations might seem to tell strongly in favor of the equal weight view. For this reason, I want to press the point by offering four additional arguments. I offer the first two arguments in the spirit of plausibility considerations, designed to further bring out what I take to be the counterintuitiveness of the suggestion that the original evidence gets completely swamped by psychological facts about how we respond to it. The third and fourth arguments are considerably more ambitious, inasmuch as they purport to show that there is something approaching absurdity in this idea.

3.1. A Comparison: Interpersonal and Intrapersonal Conflicts

Compare the question of how it is rational to respond to interpersonal conflicts between the beliefs of different individuals with the question of how it is rational to respond to intrapersonal conflicts among one's own beliefs. Suppose that one suddenly realizes that two beliefs one holds about some domain are inconsistent with one another. In such circumstances, one has a reason to revise one's beliefs. But how should one revise them? We can imagine a possible view according to which whenever one is in such circumstances, one is rationally required to abandon *both* beliefs. This view about how to resolve intrapersonal conflicts is the closest analogue to the equal weight view. But such a view has little to recommend it. In some cases of intrapersonal conflict, the reasonable thing to do might be to abandon both beliefs until further evidence comes in. But in other cases, it might be perfectly reasonable to resolve the conflict by dropping one of the two beliefs and retaining the other. What would be a case of the latter kind? Paradigmatically, a case in which one of the two beliefs is well supported by one's total evidence but the other is not. A normative view about how it is reasonable to resolve inconsistencies among one's beliefs that completely abstracts away from facts about which beliefs are better supported by one's evidence, and that would have one treat one's prior beliefs on a par, regardless of how well or ill supported they are by one's total evidence, would not be an attractive one. But the features that make such a view unattractive are shared by the equal weight view.

3.2. Implausibly Easy Bootstrapping.[14]

Consider

> *Case 5.* You and I both accept the equal weight view as a matter of theory. Moreover, we scrupulously follow it as a matter of practice. At time t0, each of us has access to a substantial, fairly complicated body of evidence. On the whole this evidence tells against hypothesis H: given our evidence, the uniquely rational credence for us to have in H is .3. However, as it happens, both of us badly mistake the import of this evidence: you give credence .7 to H while I give it .9. At time t1, we meet and compare notes. Because we both accept the equal weight view, we converge on credence .8.

On the equal weight view, our high level of confidence that H is true at time t1 is the attitude it is reasonable for us to take, despite the poor job each of us has done in evaluating our original evidence. (Indeed, it would be unreasonable for us to be any less confident than we are at that point.) However, it is dubious that rational belief is so easy to come by.

Can the equal weight view be interpreted in such a way that it does not allow for such bootstrapping? A proponent might suggest the following: in response to peer disagreement, one is *rationally required* to split the difference, but it does not follow that the opinion at which one arrives by doing so is reasonable. Rather, splitting the difference is a *necessary but insufficient condition* for the reasonableness of the opinion at which one arrives. In order for that opinion to be reasonable, one must not only have arrived at it by splitting the difference, but one must have correctly responded to the original evidence as well. Thus, peers who scrupulously adhere to the equal weight view will wind up with reasonable opinions if they begin from reasonable opinions, but not if they begin from unreasonable opinions. In this way, the current bootstrapping objection is apparently blocked.

However, this proposed interpretation runs into serious problems elsewhere. Consider again Case 4, in which you but not I respond to the original evidence E in a reasonable manner. At time t1, we discover our disagreement and split the difference, converging on a credence of .5. On the present proposal, your credence of .5 is perfectly reasonable, since you have responded to the evidence correctly at every stage. On the other hand, my credence of .5 is *not* reasonable, since I misjudged the original evidence; the mere fact that I respond appropriately to your opinion by splitting the difference is not sufficient to render the opinion at which I thereby arrive reasonable. But here something seems to have gone wrong. After all: notice that at time t1, you and I have exactly the same evidence that bears on H (viz. E, plus our knowledge of how each of us originally responded to that evidence), and we invest exactly the same credence in H on the basis of that evidence (viz. .5), yet your credence is reasonable on the evidence while mine is not. That seems wrong.[15] Thus, although this interpretation of the equal weight view manages to avoid the charge of bootstrapping, it is untenable on other grounds. I therefore set it aside.

3.3. Even Easier, and More Implausible, Bootstrapping: Single Person Cases

On the equal weight view, the evidence that determines what it is reasonable for us to believe in cases of peer disagreement consists in facts about the distribution of opinion among the peers. Let us call such evidence psychological evidence. Let us call the original evidence on which the peers base their opinions nonpsychological evidence.[16] There is at least one special case in which—as the advocate of the equal weight view would have it—it is highly plausible that what it is reasonable to believe is entirely fixed by the psychological evidence, namely a case in which the psychological evidence is all the evidence one has to go on. When one is aware of nothing relevant to some issue other than facts about the distribution of opinion, it is unsurprising that such facts suffice to fix what it is reasonable for one to believe about that question. In the even more special case in which one is aware of nothing relevant other than the distribution of opinion among a group of one's peers, one should give equal weight to each of their opinions. (Crucially, these thoughts are not the exclusive property of the equal weight view, a point to which I will return below.)

At one end of the spectrum, then, are cases in which one's evidence is exhausted by psychological evidence concerning facts about the distribution of opinion (i.e., cases in which one's nonpsychological evidence has dwindled to nothing). At the other end of the spectrum are cases in which all of one's evidence is nonpsychological (i.e., cases in which one's psychological evidence has dwindled to nothing). Consider a case of the latter kind: at time t0, one possesses a body of nonpsychological evidence E that bears on some question, but one is completely ignorant of what anyone else thinks about that question, nor has one yet formed an opinion about the issue oneself. Presumably, at this point a proponent of the equal weight view will agree that what it is reasonable for one to believe is wholly fixed by the nonpsychological evidence (to the extent that what is reasonable to believe is fixed by the evidence at all). At time t1, one first forms an opinion about the hypothesis on the basis of this nonpsychological evidence; let us suppose that one gives credence .7 to the hypothesis on the basis of the evidence. Assuming that one has access to facts about one's own confidence via introspection, one thus acquires one's first piece of psychological evidence that bears on the question. For one can now adopt a third person perspective on one's own opinion and treat the fact that one believes as one does as evidence that bears on the truth of the hypothesis. At time t1, then, one's total evidence consists of one's original body of nonpsychological evidence E, plus a single piece of psychological evidence, namely the fact that one believes as one does. Call this new body of total evidence E+:

> E+ (one's evidence at time t1)
> The original body of nonpsychological evidence E
> The fact that one believes the hypothesis to degree .7

Suppose that at time t2 one gains an additional piece of psychological evidence: one learns the opinion of a peer. Suppose that the peer gives credence .3 to the hypothesis. At time t2, then, one's total evidence—call it E++—consists of the following:

> E++ (one's evidence at time t2)
> The original nonpsychological evidence E
> The fact that one believes the hypothesis to degree .7
> The fact that one's peer believes the hypothesis to degree .3

According to the equal weight view, one should split the difference with one's peer and believe the hypothesis to degree .5 at time t2. I have criticized the view on the grounds that it implausibly suggests that the psychological evidence swamps the nonpsychological evidence in these circumstances. At present, however, I want to inquire about what a proponent of the equal weight view should say about what one is rationally required to believe back at time t1, when one knows one's own opinion about the hypothesis but no one else's. Does the psychological evidence swamp the nonpsychological evidence *even then?* It would seem that the only principled answer for the proponent of the equal weight view to give to this question is yes. For the proponent of the equal weight view will insist that, at time t2, what one is rationally required to believe is entirely determined by the original opinions of the two peers; moreover, if, at an even later time t3, one becomes aware of the opinion of a third peer, then what one is rationally required to believe will be entirely determined by the original opinions of the three peers; and if, at some still later time t4, one becomes aware of the opinion of a fourth peer . . . and so on. In general, for any time tn, a proponent of the equal weight view will hold that what one is rationally required to believe is entirely fixed by the opinions of the n peers. Why then should things be any different back at time t1, when the number of peers is 1? It seems as though the only principled, not ad hoc stand for the proponent of the equal weight view to take is to hold that the psychological evidence swamps the nonpsychological evidence even when the psychological evidence is exhausted by what you yourself believe. On this view, before one forms some opinion about the hypothesis, how confident one should be that the hypothesis is true is determined by the nonpsychological evidence; after one arrives at some level of confidence—in the present example, a degree of belief of .7—how confident one should be given the evidence that one then possesses is—.7. Of course, if one had responded to the original evidence in some alternative way—say, by giving credence .6 or .8 to the hypothesis—then the rationally required credence would be .6 or .8. On the picture of evidence suggested by the equal weight view, the distinction between believing and believing rationally seems to collapse in cases in which one is aware of what one believes but unaware of what others believe.

Here I note an interesting general feature of the equal weight view and how it makes for trouble in the present case. On the operative conception of peerhood, peers resemble each other in possessing a similar general competence for assessing relevant evidence and arguments. If you regard someone as incompetent compared to yourself with respect to his or her ability to assess relevant considerations, then you do not regard that person as your peer. (As a relatively extreme case, we might think here of the relationship in which the qualified teacher of philosophy stands to those of her students who have not yet developed any sophistication in evaluating arguments.) Of course, in order to respond correctly to one's evidence on a given occasion, it is not sufficient that one is competent to do so; one must actually manifest one's competence. Even against a general background of competence, one might still overestimate or underestimate one's evidence on a given occasion: one commits a performance error, as it were. Notice that it is characteristic of the equal weight view to credit the views of others in proportion to their general competence while abstracting away from facts about actual performance. What it is reasonable to believe in cases of peer disagreement is determined by giving equal weight to the opinions of the peers; crucially, in this calculation, the opinions that have been arrived at via the commission of performance errors will count for just as much as those opinions that are appropriate responses to the shared evidence.[17] Bare truths about who has in fact manifested his or her underlying competence and who has not make no difference in cases of peer disagreement. However, once facts about general competence are privileged in this way in multiperson cases, it seems arbitrary and unmotivated to continue to maintain that actual performance makes a significant difference in single-person cases (i.e., cases in which a single individual arrives at an opinion on the basis of the nonpsychological evidence he or she possesses). Rather, on the suggested picture, if I am generally competent in the way I respond to evidence (and I know that I am), then this should be enough to guarantee that I am reasonable in responding to my evidence in whatever way I do. But this contradicts our initial assumption, namely that one way of ending up with an unreasonable belief is to respond incorrectly to one's evidence, despite possessing the ability to respond to that evidence correctly.

3.4. The Litmus Paper Objection

Let us set aside, for the moment, the special case of disagreement among peers, and reflect on a much more general question: in what circumstances does it make sense for me to treat the fact that someone else believes as she does as evidence for the truth of that which she believes? A true (although perhaps not especially informative) answer: exactly when I take her belief to be a reliable indication of how things stand in the relevant part of reality. Thus, suppose that I know, on the basis of extensive past experience, that when my weather forecaster judges that it will rain the next day, it tends to rain 80 percent of the time. In that case, I will treat her judgments to the effect that it will rain as evidence that it will rain, inasmuch as I take there to be a positive correlation between the two. Notice that, in this respect, there is absolutely nothing special about the way the judgments of another person come to count as evidence. Compare: I treat the fact that the litmus paper turns red as evidence that the liquid in which it is immersed is an acid because, on the theories I accept, the former is a reliable indication of the latter. This seems perfectly parallel to the reason why I treat the fact that my weather forecaster expects it to rain tomorrow as evidence that it will rain tomorrow. In general, the way the judgments of some other mind come to play the role of evidence does not differ from the way other states of the world do.

I believe that this observation, while elementary, is already enough to cast significant doubt on the equal weight view. For consider your perspective, as one attempting to determine what to believe about some proposition. You carefully survey what you take to be your evidence: various states of the world, the obtaining of which you take to provide clues as to whether the proposition is true or false. Some of these states of the world are bits of psychological reality, the beliefs of others—that Smith is highly confident that the proposition is true, that Jones is less so, and so on. Others of these states of the world are bits of nonpsychological reality—for example, the fact that the litmus paper turned a given color in such-and-such circumstances. Insofar as you think it relatively unlikely that some part of psychological reality would be as it is unless the proposition were true, you regard the fact that things are arranged thus and so as evidence that speaks in favor of the proposition. But by the same token, insofar as you think it relatively unlikely that some piece of nonpsychological reality would be as it is unless the proposition were true, you regard the fact that things are arranged that way as evidence that speaks in favor of the proposition. Now consider the special case in which you possess a considerable amount of nonpsychological evidence, but where your psychological evidence is exhausted by the fact that (1) you yourself are confident that the proposition is true, and (2) some peer is equally confident that the proposition is false. Again, on the equal weight view, you should split the difference with your peer and retreat to a state of agnosticism; in effect, one ought to give no weight to the non-psychological evidence in the presence of the psychological evidence. But what could be the rationale for such a policy of invidious discrimination? Why should the psychological evidence count for everything, and the nonpsychological evidence for nothing, *given that the way the two kinds of evidence qualify as such is exactly the same?*

4. THE TOTAL EVIDENCE VIEW

Recall from above

> The *no independent weight view:* In some cases of peer disagreement, one might be perfectly reasonable even if one gives no weight at all to the opinion of one's peer.

and

> The *symmetrical no independent weight view:* In some cases of peer disagreement, both parties to the dispute might be perfectly reasonable even if neither gives any weight at all to the opinion of the other party.

Assuming that the uniqueness thesis is true, the symmetrical no independent weight view is false. However, even if the symmetrical no independent weight view is false, the no independent weight view might still be true. For even if it cannot be reasonable for both you and I to give no weight to the other's opinion, perhaps it is nevertheless reasonable for you to give no weight to my opinion if you have evaluated the evidence correctly and I have not. As formulated above, the no independent weight view states that it might be perfectly reasonable to give no weight to the opinion of one's peer "in some cases." We have now arrived at a proposal for what the relevant class of cases is, namely, the class of cases in which one's original opinion correctly reflects the evidence that one shares with one's peer but his opinion does not. Consider then

> The asymmetrical no independent weight view: In cases of peer disagreement, it is reasonable to give no weight to the opinion of a peer as long as one's own opinion is the reasonable response to the original evidence.

On this view, if either of the two peers engaged in a disagreement has in fact evaluated their shared evidence correctly, then that peer should stick to his or her guns, and the other peer should convert, since the opinion in question is the one that is in fact best supported by their evidence.

However, the asymmetrical no independent weight view is false. Even if one responds to the original evidence in an impeccable manner and one's peer does not, the fact that one's peer responds as he does will typically make it rationally incumbent upon one to move at least some way in his direction. First let us satisfy ourselves that this is so; we will then inquire as to why it is so.

Consider

> Case 6. You are a professional mathematician. Within the mathematics community, there is substantial and longstanding interest in a certain mathematical

conjecture. (Call it The Conjecture.) If forced to guess, some members of the community would guess that The Conjecture is true, others that it is false; all agree that there is no basis that would justify a firm opinion one way or the other. Then, one day, the unexpected happens: alone in your study, you succeed in proving The Conjecture. On the basis of your proof, you become extremely confident, indeed practically certain, that The Conjecture is true. Because your high degree of confidence is based on a genuine proof that you correctly recognize as such, it is fully justified. Later, you show the proof to a colleague whose judgment you respect. Much to your surprise, the colleague, after examining the proof with great care, declares that it is unsound. Subsequently, you show the proof to another colleague, and then to a third, and then to a fourth. You approach the colleagues independently and take pains to ensure that they are not influenced by one another in arriving at their judgments about the status of your proof. In each case, however, the judgment is the same: the proof is unsound. Ultimately, your proof convinces no one: the entire mathematical community is united in its conviction that it is unsound, and thus, that the status of The Conjecture remains very much an open question.

In the face of this consensus, it would be unreasonable for you to remain practically certain that The Conjecture is true. You should be less confident of The Conjecture after your proof has been deemed unsound by the mathematical community than you were immediately after you first proved The Conjecture, back when you were alone in your study. Of course, because the proof is in fact sound, the judgment of the community to the contrary is misleading evidence, evidence that points in the wrong direction. But misleading evidence is evidence nonetheless, and the acquisition of such evidence will typically make a difference to what it is reasonable for one to believe. Moreover, if you are rationally required to be less confident after *all* of your peers have disagreed with you, then it would seem that you are also required to be at least somewhat less confident after even *one* of your peers disagrees with you. For suppose that it was rationally permissible to give zero weight to the opinion of the first colleague. In that case, you could have left her office as rationally confident as when you entered, in which case you would have been in the same state of practical certainty on entering the office of the second colleague you consulted. Indeed, in that case it seems that you might as well simply forget about the fact that the whole unpleasant business with the first colleague occurred at all before visiting the second colleague, in which case you would be in more or less exactly the same position on entering the office of the second colleague. And if it is rationally permissible to give zero weight to *his* opinion . . . and so on.

Moral: the fact that a peer believes differently can make it rationally incumbent on you to change what you currently believe, even if, had the peer responded to the evidence in a reasonable manner, he, too, would believe exactly as you believe. One should give some weight to one's peer's opinion even when from the God's-eye point of view one has evaluated the evidence correctly and he has not. But why? Exactly because one does not occupy the God's-eye point of view with respect to the question of who has evaluated the evidence correctly and who has not.[18] Typically, when one responds reasonably to a body of evidence, one is not utterly blind to the fact that one has done so; on the other hand, such facts are not perfectly transparent either. Even if one has in fact responded to the evidence impeccably on a given occasion, one might still have reason to doubt that one's performance was impeccable. Such a reason is provided when a peer responds to the same evidence differently. To give no weight to the fact that a peer responds to the evidence differently is in effect to treat it as certain that one's peer is the one who has misjudged the evidence. But it would be unreasonable to be certain of this, even when it is true.[19]

Rationality consists in responding appropriately to one's evidence. But one's evidence includes evidence to the effect that one does not always respond appropriately to one's evidence (i.e., evidence to the effect that one is fallible in responding appropriately to one's evidence), as well as evidence to the effect that one is more likely to have responded inappropriately when one finds oneself in certain circumstances. When one possesses higher order evidence to the effect that one is currently in circumstances in which one is more likely than usual to have made a mistake in responding to one's first order evidence, one has a reason to temper one's confidence— even if that confidence is in fact an impeccable response to the first order evidence.

When one finds oneself in the position of a minority of one in the way one has responded to the evidence, one should temper one's confidence, for one now possesses higher order evidence that suggests that the bearing of the original, first order evidence is something other than what one initially took it to be. Moreover, this is so even if the higher order evidence is misleading, as when one has in fact responded appropriately to the first order evidence and one's peers have not.

On the present view, cases in which one in fact responds impeccably to one's evidence but one's peer responds inappropriately are much like cases in which one engages in a flawless piece of practical reasoning despite being inebriated. The fact that a peer has responded to the evidence differently should lead one to temper one's confidence in one's own response, just as the fact that one is inebriated should lead one to temper one's confidence in one's practical reasoning. In both cases, it is the fact that the status of one's performance is not perfectly transparent that opens the door for higher order considerations to make a difference.

Of course, to acknowledge that higher order considerations make *some* difference is not to fall back into the mistake of thinking that they make *all* the difference. After all, even when one's current level of inebriation makes it significantly more likely that one will over- or underestimate the strength of one's practical reasons (and one knows that this is so), one can still make more or less rational decisions, and the status of a given decision

will typically depend a great deal on the overall disposition of those practical reasons. Similarly for the theoretical case: although you should be
somewhat less confident that The Conjecture is true on finding that a
colleague remains unconvinced despite having been presented with your
proof, it is a mistake to think that at that point the only evidence that
makes a difference are the respective psychological reactions of you and
your colleague. When one possesses what is in fact a genuine proof that
one correctly recognizes as such, one possesses an extremely strong piece
of evidence. (Indeed, it would perhaps be difficult to imagine a stronger
single piece of evidence for anything.) The justification afforded by such a
piece of evidence has a certain robustness in the face of challenge: it is not
easily washed away by the fact that another mistakenly fails to appreciate
it on a given occasion. Of course, your colleague might feel just as confident that your proof is unsound as you feel that it is sound. Indeed, all of
the psychological accompaniments of the two judgments might be the
same. But in any case, we have independent reason to be skeptical of the
idea that phenomenology is that on which epistemic status supervenes. In
general, when one reasons badly, one's phenomenology might be indistin-
guishable from one's phenomenology when one reasons impeccably (in
both cases, one has the same feelings of subjective certainty, and so on).
We should not thereby be driven to the conclusion that the deliverances
of good reasoning and bad reasoning have the same epistemic status.[20]

Where does this leave us?

In section 3, I argued that, in cases of peer disagreement, getting the
original, first order evidence right typically counts for *something* (pace the
equal weight view). In this section, I have argued that doing so does not
count for *everything* (pace the no independent weight view). Indeed, from
the present perspective, there is a sense in which the equal weight view
and the no independent weight view both suffer from the same fault: they
embody overly simple models of how one's first order evidence and one's
higher order evidence interact in determining facts about what it is
reasonable to believe all things considered. On the equal weight view,
what it is reasonable to believe in cases of peer disagreement in effect
supervenes on facts about the distribution of peer opinion. On the no
independent weight view, what it is reasonable to believe in such cases
supervenes on facts about the first order evidence possessed by the peers.
On the present view, both of these supervenience claims are false: neither
class of facts suffices on its own to fix the facts about what it is reasonable
to believe. Rather, what it is reasonable to believe depends on both the
original, first order evidence as well as on the higher order evidence that
is afforded by the fact that one's peers believe as they do. For this reason,
it seems appropriate to call the view on offer the total evidence view.

Even if both the equal weight view and the no independent weight
view are unsatisfactory, we might still wonder: which is closer to the
truth? Granted that on the total evidence view both the first order
evidence and the higher order evidence count for something, which kind

of evidence plays a greater role in fixing facts about what it is reasonable to believe?

It is a mistake, I believe, to think that there is some general answer to this question. In some cases, the first order evidence might be extremely substantial compared to the higher order evidence; in such cases, the former tends to swamp the latter. In other cases, the first order evidence might be quite insubstantial compared to the higher order evidence; in such cases, the latter tends to swamp the former. (We will consider plausible examples of each of these types of case below.) In still other cases, the two kinds of evidence might play a more or less equal role in fixing facts about what it is reasonable to believe. So the question of which counts for *more*—peer opinion, or the evidence on which the peers base their opinion?—is not, I think, a good question when it is posed at such a high level of abstraction.

Nevertheless, we can offer some general observations that bear on this issue here. Consider again the kind of case I have employed in attempting to undermine the equal weight view: initially, you and I have access to the same substantial body of evidence E, evidence that in fact strongly favors H over not-H; you respond reasonably and so are quite confident that H is true; I on the other hand respond unreasonably and am equally confident that H is false. Once we compare notes, our new total evidence consists of E*:

(1) Our original evidence E
(2) The fact that you are quite confident that H is true
(3) The fact that I am quite confident that H is false

What is it reasonable for us to believe about H on total evidence E*? Given that you and I are peers, it is plausible to suppose that the two pieces of higher order psychological evidence ((2) and (3)) are more or less equally strong pieces of evidence that point in opposite directions. All else being equal, then, one would expect E* to favor H over not-H inasmuch as it is composed of a substantial body of evidence that strongly favors H over not-H, supplemented by two additional pieces of evidence of approximately equal strength, one that tends to confirm H, another that tends to disconfirm H.

Indeed, it is tempting to think that, if in fact our respective psychological reactions count as more or less equally strong pieces of evidence that point in opposite directions, then they in effect cancel each other out and leave what it is reasonable for us to believe unchanged. According to this line of thought, what it is reasonable for us to believe about H on E* is identical to whatever it was reasonable for us to believe about H on E, inasmuch as the net effect of adding the two new pieces of evidence comes to zero. Here the asymmetrical no independent weight view threatens to return via the back door, at least in a special class of cases, namely those in which peer opinion is evenly divided. For in such cases, the evidence afforded by peer opinion is perfectly counterbalanced.

However, this tempting line of thought is mistaken. The addition of the counterbalanced psychological evidence *does* make a difference to what it is reasonable for us to believe. For once the counterbalanced evidence is added to our original evidence, a greater proportion of our total evidence supports an attitude of agnosticism than was previously the case; the evidence available to us now is on the whole less supportive of H than before. The addition of (2) and (3) thus has a moderating impact and tends to push what it is reasonable for us to believe about the hypothesis in the direction of agnosticism. Therefore, given that E is a substantial body of evidence that strongly favors H over not-H, we would expect that E* will also favor H over not-H, although not to as great a degree as E does. (That is, all else being equal, the reasonable level of confidence to have in hypothesis H on evidence E* will be greater than .5 but less than whatever it was reasonable to have on evidence E.)

Significantly, the point generalizes beyond the two-person case. As more and more peers weigh in on a given issue, the proportion of the total evidence that consists of higher order psychological evidence increases, and the proportion of the total evidence that consists of first order evidence decreases. As the number of peers increases, peer opinion counts for progressively more in determining what it is reasonable for the peers to believe, and first order considerations count for less and less. At some point, when the number of peers grows large enough, the higher order psychological evidence will swamp the first order evidence into virtual insignificance. In such cases, the total evidence view becomes more or less extensionally equivalent to the equal weight view with respect to what it requires the peers to believe. Moreover, this holds regardless of the particular way opinion is distributed among the peers. That is, it holds for cases in which peer opinion is evenly divided and for cases in which peer opinion is unanimous, as well as for intermediate cases.

Imagine an infinite number of peers confronted with a finite amount of evidence that bears on some issue. Each of the peers inspects the evidence and independently arrives at a view. When the peers compare notes, they find that opinion among them is perfectly divided: every peer on one side of the issue has one and only one counterpart on the other side. In these circumstances, the peers should suspend judgment about the issue, even if that response is not the most rational response to the original, first order evidence. With respect to this case, the equal weight view returns the correct verdict from the perspective of one who holds the total evidence view. This is so *not* because the higher order evidence trumps the first order evidence in general, as the proponent of the equal weight view maintains. Rather, it is because in sufficiently extreme cases, the higher order psychological evidence might be so substantial compared to the first order nonpsychological evidence that the former in effect swamps the latter into virtual insignificance.

The same holds true for cases in which the peers find that they agree. Earlier, we looked askance at the idea that two peers, both of whom irrationally hold some view that is not in fact supported by their evidence, might bootstrap their way into rationally holding that view simply by encountering one another and comparing notes. Indeed, we took the fact that the equal weight view licenses such two-person bootstrapping as a consideration that counts against it (see section 3.2). However, as the number of generally reliable peers who independently respond to their evidence in the same mistaken manner increases, such bootstrapping seems less and less objectionable. At some point, it becomes, I believe, unobjectionable. If I hold some belief on the basis of fallacious reasoning, then it will typically not be reasonable for me to hold that belief. However, in the unlikely but possible situation in which a large number of generally reliable peers mistakenly arrive at the same conclusion by independently committing the same fallacy, it will typically be reasonable for them to believe that conclusion on comparing notes, even if there is no legitimate first order reasoning by which they could have arrived at the conclusion. Again, in this case the equal weight view yields the correct verdict from the perspective of the total evidence view. As before, this is not due to some general tendency of higher order evidence to trump first order evidence. Rather, it is due to the fact that in this case, the higher order evidence that has been amassed is sufficiently substantial compared to the first order evidence that it effectively determines the bearing of the overall evidence.

Does this in effect give the game away to someone who takes the diversity of opinion with respect to various controversial issues to mandate an attitude of agnosticism about those issues? That is, even if the equal weight view is false and the total evidence view is true, won't all of the interesting/threatening/radical consequences that seemed to follow from the equal weight view still be true, at least if one is sufficiently generous in attributing the status of "peer" to other people? Isn't agnosticism the only reasonable stance to take toward all of those controversial issues on which peer opinion is heavily divided, as the proponent of the equal weight view has insisted all along?

Consider also those philosophical questions with respect to which there is consensus, or near consensus. Suppose, plausibly, that there are very few if any genuine skeptics about other minds: informed philosophical opinion is (close to) unanimous in holding that one is typically in a position to know that there are minds other than one's own. In Kelly (2005a), I took a dim view of the suggestion that this fact would suffice to make it unreasonable to embrace skepticism about other minds: rather, whether it is reasonable or unreasonable to embrace skepticism about other minds is primarily a matter of the quality of the first order arguments for and against such skepticism, arguments that do not make reference to empirical, sociological facts about the number of skeptics and nonskeptics. However, in light of the present view, a reversal of this judgment might seem to be in order. Could it really be that the unreasonableness of skepticism about other minds consists in the *unpopularity* of such skepticism among the relevant class of people?

Before acquiescing in this line of thought, we should note an important element of idealization in our discussion to this point, an element that looms large in the present context. Throughout, we have been concerned with the probative force of peer opinion in cases in which the peers arrive at their opinions *independently* of one another. This assumption of independence tends to maximize the probative force of peer opinion relative to the probative force of first order evidence. Impressive evidence that a given answer to a question is the correct answer is afforded when a large number of generally reliable peers independently converge on that answer. On the other hand, the less their convergence is an independent matter, the less weight such convergence possesses as evidence.[21] Similarly, evidence that strongly favored agnosticism with respect to some question would be a more or less even distribution of opinion among a substantial number of peers, where each of the peers has arrived at his or her own opinion independently of the others. Again, the less such independence is present, the weaker the higher order evidence will be relative to the first order evidence.

Consider, as an especially extreme illustration of the importance of independence, the venerable "common consent" argument for the existence of God. In its simplest and most straightforward form, the argument runs as follows:

(Premise) Everyone believes that God exists.
(Conclusion) Therefore, God exists.

(In a slightly less crude form, the premise of the argument is that *almost* everyone, or the great majority of humankind, believes that God exists.)[22]

As arguments go, the common consent argument for the existence of God is not exactly an overwhelming one, possessing as it does the twin defects of transparent invalidity and the having of an obviously false claim as its sole premise. Nevertheless, even though *God exists* does not follow from *Everyone believes that God exists*, we can ask: if it were true that everyone, or almost everyone, believed that God exists, how much support would that lend (if any) to the proposition that God exists?

This is a complicated question about which much could be said; here I note the following. Whatever evidence is afforded for a given claim by the fact that several billion people confidently believe that that claim is true, that evidence is less impressive to the extent that the individuals in question have not arrived at that belief independently. That is, the evidence provided by the fact that a large number of individuals hold a belief in common is weaker to the extent that the individuals who share that belief do so because they have influenced one another, or because they have been influenced by common sources. (I assume that both of these conditions play a large role in the case of religious belief.) In principle, the fact that a small handful of people arrive at the same belief independently of one another might be better evidence that that belief is true than if many millions of people arrive at the same belief nonindependently. The intellectual case for Islam would not be any stronger today if birthrates in Muslim countries had been twice as high in past decades as they actually were; nor would the case be any weaker if such birthrates had been significantly lower.

The same holds for cases in which there is widespread disagreement but the members of the contending factions have not arrived at their opinions independently. In an interesting recent essay, G. A. Cohen (2000) notes that the Oxford-trained philosophers of his generation are almost unanimously of the opinion that there is a philosophically important distinction between analytic and synthetic truths. But on the other hand,

> people of my generation who studied philosophy at Harvard rather than at Oxford for the most part *reject* the analytic/synthetic distinction. And I can't believe that this is an accident. That is, I can't believe that Harvard just *happened* to be a place where both its leading thinker rejected that distinction and its graduate students, for independent reasons—merely, for example, in the independent light of reason itself—also came to reject it. And vice versa, of course, for Oxford. I believe, rather, that in each case students were especially impressed by the reasons respectively for and against believing in the distinction, because in each case the reasons came with all the added persuasiveness of personal presentation, personal relationship, and so forth. (18, emphases in original)

Consider Cohen's position as one attempting to determine what to believe about this issue. On the one hand, there are the first order considerations that have been offered for and against the existence of a philosophically significant analytic-synthetic distinction. In addition, Cohen is also aware of the views of other individuals who are similarly acquainted with those first order considerations and whom he regards as his peers in other relevant respects. In weighing evidence of the latter kind, Cohen should sharply discount for the fact that (as he sees it) many individuals on both sides of the issue hold the views that they do because those views were held by their teachers. That is, in the counterfactual situation in which the distribution of peer opinion is exactly as it is, but in which each of the peers arrived at his or her view in response to "the independent light of reason itself," the higher order evidence possessed by Cohen would be much more substantial than it is as things actually stand. The point is not that individuals who believe what their teachers believe are less reliable than they would be if they made up their own minds. Indeed, as a general matter, this is not even true. (If your teacher is better at assessing the arguments than you are, then you will be more reliable if you simply believe as she does than if you arrive at a view on the basis of your own assessment of the arguments.) The point, rather, is that insofar as one believes as one does because this is what one's teacher believes, the fact that one believes as one does is not an *additional* piece of psychological evidence, over and above the psychological evidence afforded by the teacher's belief.

The general moral: even in cases in which opinion is sharply divided among a large number of generally reliable individuals, it would be a mistake to be impressed by the sheer number of such individuals on both sides of the issue. For numbers mean little in the absence of independence. If one uncritically assumes that the members of the contending factions have arrived at their views independently, then one will tend to overestimate the importance of other people's opinions as evidence and underestimate the importance of the first order evidence and arguments. One will be too quick to conclude that agnosticism is the reasonable stance in cases in which opinion is sharply divided, and too quick to conclude that deference to the majority is the reasonable course in cases in which opinion is not sharply divided.[23]

Nevertheless, it is true that on the total evidence view, there will be possible cases in which the higher order evidence is sufficiently substantial compared to the first order evidence that the latter counts for (almost) nothing. By the same token, however, there will be possible cases in which the opposite is true. What is a case in which peer opinion effectively counts for nothing in virtue of being overwhelmed by the first order considerations? Consider a case discussed by both Christensen (2007, pp. 199–203) and Elga (2007, pp. 490–91). You and I go to dinner with several friends; at the end of the meal we independently calculate what an individual share of the total bill comes to (imagine that the group has agreed to split the bill evenly among its members). You judge that an individual share is $43 per person, a perfectly plausible (and, let us suppose, correct) answer to the question of what each of us owes. I, however, arrive at an absurd answer of $450, an amount that significantly surpasses the total bill. Both Christensen and Elga think that, in *these* circumstances, you are *not* required to treat my answer and your answer with equal respect; indeed they think that you are entitled to more or less dismiss my answer entirely. The difficulty is how to account for this on a picture according to which splitting the difference is typically the appropriate response to peer disagreement. In general, it is at least a prima facie embarrassment for the equal weight view that the following is possible: a person for whom one has arbitrarily strong evidence that he or she is a peer might nevertheless give a patently absurd answer on a given occasion. For it seems incredible that, in such circumstances, one would be unreasonable if one failed to treat the peer's patently absurd answer and one's own nonabsurd answer evenhandedly.

Unsurprisingly, both Christensen and Elga have interesting and detailed stories to tell about why, in these but not in otherwise similar cases, one need not give any weight to the view of one's peer.[24] I will not pause to evaluate the specifics of their respective proposals; here I note only how the total evidence view offers an extremely straightforward and compelling explanation of why you are entitled to effectively discount my absurd opinion. Quite simply: given the totality of considerations available to you that bear on the question at issue (e.g., your knowledge that the total bill is n, a number that is less than $450), it would be completely unreasonable for you to give any significant credence to the proposition that a share of the total bill is $450, despite the fact that this is what I, your peer, believe. In this case, it is the nonpsychological considerations that swamp the psychological considerations into epistemic insignificance.

5. CONSIDERATIONS THAT SEEM TO FAVOR THE EQUAL WEIGHT VIEW

5.1. Perceptual Judgments

As mentioned above, I believe that much of the appeal of the equal weight view derives from reflection on certain kinds of examples. In particular, the equal weight view can seem almost obviously or trivially correct when one reflects on examples involving the conflicting perceptual judgments of individuals equally well suited to make those judgments. Recall Case 1: you and I, two equally attentive and well-sighted individuals, watch the horses cross the finish line from equally good vantage points. It looks to me as though Horse A finishes slightly ahead of Horse B, while it looks to you as though Horse B finishes slightly ahead of Horse A. The intuitive verdict: once we find that our initial judgments conflict, the uniquely reasonable course is for us to split the difference and retreat to a state of agnosticism about which of the two horses actually won the race.

I do not contest the intuitive verdict; indeed, I take it to be correct. What I do contest is the idea that the intuitive verdict has any tendency to support the equal weight view over the total evidence view. For when the total evidence view is correctly applied to Case 1, it, too, returns the intuitively correct verdict that you and I should abandon our original opinions and retreat to a state of agnosticism.

First, note that there are at least some cases in which the total evidence view will rationally require two individuals who began with conflicting opinions to adopt a new opinion that is perfectly intermediate between their original opinions. Here is one such case:

> Case 7. At time t0, you and I possess different evidence that bears on some hypothesis H. Your evidence suggests that H is true; my evidence suggests that it is false. Moreover, each of us responds to his or her evidence in a reasonable manner: you believe that H is true while I believe that it is false. At time t1, we encounter one another and pool our evidence. After doing so, our new total evidence does not favor H over not-H; nor does it favor not-H over H.

Given that the total evidence available to us at time t1 favors neither alternative over the other, an advocate of the total evidence view will maintain that we should suspend judgment. You should abandon your belief that the hypothesis is true, while I should abandon my belief that it is false. In the light of our new total evidence, we should converge on the point that is intermediate between our original opinions. With respect to Case 7 then, the total evidence view will require us to respond in a way that is extensionally equivalent to the way that we would respond if we were both following a norm of "split the difference."

Notice, however, that Case 7 is simply Case 1, abstractly described. As you and I watch the horses cross the finish line, it appears to me as though Horse A finishes just ahead of Horse B. To the extent that I have evidence for my judgment that Horse A finished ahead of Horse B, that evidence consists of my perceptual evidence: the fact that it *looks* or *appears* to me that Horse A finishes ahead, or that my visual experience represents Horse A as having finished ahead. In the absence of other evidence that bears on the question, it is at that point reasonable for me to believe that Horse A finished ahead of Horse B, since this is what my total evidence supports. Similarly, your initial judgment that Horse B finished just ahead of Horse A is a reasonable response to the evidence that you possess at time t0, namely the fact that it looked or seemed to you as though Horse B finished just ahead of Horse A. At time t1, we compare notes: you learn that I think that Horse A won because that is how it looked to me; I learn that you think that Horse B won because that is how it looked to you. At this point, the total evidence that is available to each of us has changed in a rather dramatic way: I have gained evidence that suggests that Horse B won, while you have gained evidence that Horse A won. Moreover, given the relevant background assumptions and symmetries, it is natural to think that the total evidence that we now share favors neither the proposition that Horse A finished ahead of Horse B nor the proposition that Horse B finished ahead of Horse A. Thus, given our new total evidence, you and I should abandon our initial opinions about which horse won the race. The total evidence view, no less than the equal weight view, requires us to suspend judgment and retreat to a state of agnosticism in Case 1 and in cases of relevantly similar structure. Thus, it is a mistake to think that such cases favor the equal weight view over the total evidence view.[25]

5.2. A (No) Bootstrapping Argument for the Equal Weight View?

Elga argues as follows:

> Suppose that . . . you and your friend are to judge the truth of a claim, based on the same batch of evidence. Initially, you count your friend as an epistemic peer—you think that she is about as good as you at judging the claim. In other words, you think that, conditional on a disagreement arising, the two of you are equally likely to be mistaken. Then the two of you perform your evaluations. As it happens, you become confident that the claim is true, and your friend becomes equally confident that it is false.
>
> When you learn of your friend's opposing judgment, you should think that the two of you are equally likely to be correct. The reason is [this]. If it

were reasonable for you to give your own evaluation extra weight—if it were reasonable to be more than 50% confident that you are right—then you would have gotten some evidence that you are a better evaluator than your friend. But that is absurd.

[T]he absurdity is made more apparent if we imagine that you and your friend evaluate the same long series of claims. Suppose for *reductio* that whenever the two of you disagree, you should be, say, 70% confident that your friend is the mistaken one. It follows that over the course of many disagreements, you should end up extremely confident that you have a better track record than your friend. As a result, you should end up extremely confident that you are a better evaluator. But that is absurd. Without some antecedent reason to think that you are a better evaluator, the disagreements between you and your friend are no evidence that she has made most of the mistakes. (2007, p. 487)

Elga takes the argument of this passage to successfully undermine any alternative to the equal weight view. In particular, he takes the argument offered here to undermine both "the extra weight view"—according to which each party to the dispute is permitted to give some special, presumptive weight to his or her own judgment—as well as views akin to the total evidence view, on which it matters which of the parties has in fact done a better job evaluating the evidence.[26] However, I believe that while Elga's bootstrapping argument has considerable force against the extra weight view, it has little to none against the total evidence view.

In order to see this, let us focus our attention directly on the situation in which Elga claims the absurdity of any alternative to the equal weight view is most apparent, namely the situation in which you and your friend each evaluates a long series of claims. Elga formulates the argument as a reductio ad absurdum. The supposition from which the absurd consequences are alleged to follow is this:

Whenever you and your friend disagree, you should be, say, 70 percent confident that your friend is the mistaken one.

Crucially, however, this supposition is *not* something to which the proponent of the total evidence view is committed. That is, the proponent of the total evidence view is not committed to the idea that, whenever you and your friend disagree, you should be n percent confident that your friend is the one who has made the mistake (where n is some number greater than 50). Indeed, on the contrary: the proponent of the total evidence view will stand with Elga in rejecting any such general policy as an unreasonable one. On the total evidence view, it is not true, in general, that you should be more confident that your friend has made the mistake whenever the two of you disagree. In *some* cases, it might be reasonable for you to be more confident that your friend is the one who has made the mistake. But in other cases, it might be reasonable, given the total evidence available to you, to be more confident that *you* are the one who has made the mistake. On the total evidence view, it is not true that there is some general answer to the question of how confident you should be that it is your friend who has made the mistake (as there is on both the extra weight view and on the equal weight view). And this is because how confident it is reasonable to be that your friend has made a mistake is not something that floats entirely free of the evidence on which he bases his opinion. Thus, since the proponent of the total evidence view would not accept the supposition from which Elga derives the absurd consequence, the reductio ad absurdum on offer cannot show that her view is false.

Consider another view rejected by Elga, the extra weight view. As interpreted by Elga, the extra weight view would license you in being extremely confident that you are a better evaluator than your friend simply by noting the many cases in which the two of you disagree. In a parallel manner, the extra weight view would license your friend in being extremely confident that *he* is the better evaluator by appeal to the very same disagreements. This seems odd (to say the least): exactly the same events are legitimately treated by you as confirming evidence for the claim that you are a better evaluator than your friend and by your friend as confirming evidence that he is a better evaluator than you. Moreover, even if you are in fact the inferior evaluator, and you consistently do a worse job evaluating the evidence on particular occasions, it will nevertheless be reasonable for you to conclude that you are superior to your friend *on the basis of those very cases*. (That is, it will be reasonable for you to conclude that you are a better evaluator of evidence on the basis of disagreements whose existence is underwritten by the fact that you have done a *worse* job than your friend has with respect to evaluating the evidence.) Here I agree with Elga: such a view makes it absurdly easy to arrive at evidence that one is a better evaluator. However, no similar absurdity follows from the total evidence view. It is true that the proponent of the total evidence view is committed to the following possibility: over time, you reasonably become quite confident that someone who you initially regarded as your peer is not your peer, on the basis of a large number of cases in which the two of you disagree. Consider, for example

> Case 8. At the outset you regard your friend as your peer. Subsequently, however, many disagreements emerge. With respect to the vast majority of these disagreements, the position that you hold is in fact better supported by the available evidence than the position held by your friend. In these cases, your conviction that your friend's position is not adequately supported by his evidence is based on your own appreciation of that evidence, an appreciation that is more accurate than his. Over time, you thus become increasingly confident that you are a better evaluator of the evidence than your friend. You thus cease to regard your friend as your peer and conclude that your initial judgment to that effect was mistaken.

As Elga would have it, the proponent of the total evidence view is indeed committed to the possibility that such a change in view is reasonable in the envisaged circumstances. However, there is no absurdity here.

Elga's bootstrapping argument purports to establish that any view other than the equal weight view makes it too easy to reasonably conclude that you are a better evaluator than your friend. The danger in question is a real one: some views (e.g., the extra weight view) do fall victim to it. However, there is also the opposite danger: that a given view will make it *too difficult* to reasonably conclude that another person is not, contrary to what one initially thought, one's peer. Indeed, the line of argument offered by Elga seems to suggest something like the following. Once you come to regard your friend as a peer about a given set of questions, it is not reasonable for you to demote him from the ranks of those to whom you accord that status on the basis of subsequent disagreements about those questions (rather, one would need to have independent evidence that you are a better evaluator than he is, evidence that is independent of the disputed issues themselves). But that seems too strong: to the extent that the argument purports to show this, the argument proves too much. For in some cases, it might very well be rational for you to conclude that your friend is not your peer after all, where your only basis for so concluding is the lack of judgment that he displays in subsequent cases in which the two of you disagree. The possibility of rationally downgrading someone from the status of peer in this way will be especially apparent in cases in which one's initial judgment that the other person is a peer was itself based on relatively insubstantial evidence. Consider for example

> *Case 9.* At the first meeting of our seminar, I strike you as a perfectly reasonable and sensible person. For the most part, we find the same arguments and considerations persuasive. Even on those few occasions when we express different views, my view seems to you to be well within the bounds of reasonable opinion, no less than your own (suppose here that you do *not* accept the uniqueness thesis). On the basis of this first meeting, then, you form the opinion that I am your peer.
>
> In subsequent meetings of the seminar, however, you and I disagree often. Moreover, when we disagree, my views often seem to you to be based on relatively flimsy arguments; when I attempt to parry objections, what I say strikes you as weak and unresponsive, and so on. (Needless to say, I would dispute such assessments.) By the end of the semester, you no longer regard me as your peer.[27]

Here, your revised estimate of my competence is based on your negative assessment of my performance in judging issues that are disputed between us. Moreover, the disputed issues are the very sorts of questions with respect to which you once reasonably took me to be a peer. Does this guarantee that it is unreasonable for you to demote me from the ranks of those to whom you accord such status? There is no such guarantee. On the other hand, there is also no guarantee that your demoting me *is* reasonable in the circumstances, given only the description of Case 9 offered above. Whether your demoting me is reasonable will typically depend on such things as whether my best attempts to parry objections are weak and unresponsive, as you take them to be, or whether your conviction that they are weak and unresponsive is due to (e.g.) your being so dogmatically committed to the opposite conclusions that you fail to appreciate the merits of what I say. The more the former is the case, the more reasonable it will be for you to revise your estimate of my competence in a downward direction; the more the latter is the case, the less reasonable such revision is. Of course, from your perspective, it might be very difficult to tell which of these is the case. From the inside, a case in which you fail to appreciate the genuine merits of what I say on behalf of my view because of dogmatic commitment on your part might seem just like a case in which my defense is indeed without merit. But the fact that it might be difficult to tell which of these is the case does not mean that it makes no difference whether your revised estimate of my competence is based on your having recognized genuine shortcomings on my part or is instead an artifact of your own shortcomings. Here as elsewhere, there is no escape from the fact that one's judgment is fallible and subject to corruption in ways that tend to elude detection.

According to Elga, (1) the relevant kind of bootstrapping is never rationally permissible, (2) the equal weight view proscribes such bootstrapping, and (3) no other plausible view does so. He thus concludes that the equal weight view is true. I hold that, on the contrary, because there are at least some possible cases in which such bootstrapping clearly *is* permissible, no view that generally proscribes it can be correct. Hence, on the assumption that Elga is correct in thinking that the equal weight view generally proscribes such bootstrapping, we have arrived at another good reason for thinking that it is false.

Notes

This essay is something of a sequel to Kelly (2005a). While in many respects it is faithful to the position advanced there, it departs in others; significant departures are noted along the way. Earlier versions of this essay were presented at New York University, MIT, Rutgers University, Brown University, Princeton University, and the University of California at Irvine; I am grateful to the audiences present on those occasions. In addition, I would like to thank Aaron Bronfman, David Christensen, Adam Elga, Hartry Field, Allan Gibbard, Margaret Gilbert, Daniel Greco, Aaron James, Jim Joyce, Sarah McGrath, Philip Pettit, Jim Pryor, Walter Sinnott-Armstrong, Roy Sorensen, and Ernest Sosa for helpful conversations on the topic.

*Editorial note: this essay is a significantly abridged version of one by the same title published in *Disagreement*, edited by Richard Feldman and Ted Warfield Oxford: Oxford University Press (2010).

1 Of course, the kind of uncontroversial "track record" evidence that bears most directly on questions of comparative reliability will be much easier to come by in some domains than in others. (In this respect, contrast reliability in accurately forecasting the weather with reliability in accurately answering metaphysical questions.)

2 Compare Feldman (2003): after reviewing a number of examples of the kind at issue here, Feldman draws the conclusion: "In the situations most plausibly thought to be cases of reasonable disagreement, suspension of judgment is the reasonable attitude to take toward the disputed proposition" (p. 189). The equal weight view is explicitly embraced by Adam Elga (2007), whose views I consider at some length below; David Christensen (2007) exhibits considerable sympathy for a policy of "splitting the difference" throughout his own discussion of the topic. Although the view I will put forth differs from theirs, I have learned much from each of these authors.

3 A case of this general form was put to me by Roy Sorensen in conversation. Compare Christensen's (2007, p. 196) "Acme watch" example and Feldman (2006, p. 234).

4 Notable here are van Inwagen (1996), Plantinga (2000a, 2000b), and Rosen (2001); another is Kelly (2005a).

5 Compare "the Extra Weight View" discussed by Elga (2007), who argues against it.

6 See, for example, Feldman (2003, 2006).

7 Again, this is characteristic of Feldman's work on the topic.

8 "The Uniqueness Thesis" is Feldman's (2007) label; compare Christensen's (2007) "Rational Uniqueness." Feldman both argues for and endorses the thesis; Christensen exhibits some sympathy for it and offers some considerations for thinking that it is true. White (2005) argues for it at length but stops short of endorsing it.

9 Most plausible, but still not especially plausible, I think. Again, it comes under pressure from marginal cases. Suppose that the evidence available to me is just barely sufficient to justify my belief that it will rain tomorrow: if the evidence was even slightly weaker than it is, then I would be unjustified in thinking that it will rain. Suppose further that you have the same evidence but are slightly more cautious than I am, and so do not yet believe that it will rain tomorrow. It is not that you are dogmatically averse to concluding that it will rain; indeed, we can suppose that if the evidence for rain gets even slightly stronger, then you, too, will take up the relevant belief. Is there some guarantee, given what has been said so far, that you are being less reasonable than I am?—I doubt it.

10 Here, for example, is Gideon Rosen:

> It should be obvious that reasonable people can disagree, even when con-
> fronted with a single body of evidence. When a jury or a court is divided in
> a difficult case, the mere fact of disagreement does not mean that someone
> is being unreasonable. (2001, p. 71)

11 See, e.g., the brief survey in White (2005, pp. 445–46).

12 I take the most formidable case to have been made by White (2005), although he himself does not endorse the thesis. I respond to some, though not all, of White's arguments in Kelly (2005b).

13 Is there some way of interpreting the equal weight view so that it does not have the consequence in question? On this possibility, see section 3.2.

14 The objection raised in this section is due to Aaron Bronfman. I utilize it here with his permission.

15 In any case, I take it that it is not an acceptable consequence for an eviden-tialist like Feldman, who explicitly maintains that what one is justified in believing

at any given time supervenes on what evidence one possesses at that time. See Conee and Feldman (2004), especially essay 4 and the introduction.

16 Some might find this terminology suboptimal on the grounds that *all* of one's evidence is ultimately psychological inasmuch as it consists of one's own psychological states. I think that this complaint rests on a mistaken view about the ontology of evidence, but no matter: one who thinks that all of our evidence ultimately consists of psychological states might read "psychological evidence" and "nonpsychological evidence" as "doxastic evidence" and "nondoxastic evidence" in what follows.

17 At least, so long as one has no *independent* grounds for attributing such performance errors. Of course, it is open to a proponent of the equal weight view to say that, even if you and I possess similar general competence, it is permissible for you to discount my opinion when (e.g.) you notice that I was distracted while surveying the evidence in a way that you were not, or that I did so while under the influence of some temporarily mind-numbing drug, or so on. What the proponent of the equal weight view will *not* allow is that my actually having committed a performance error can make a difference when your only grounds for attributing such an error to me consists in the fact that I have arrived at (what you take to be) an incorrect answer to the question about which we disagree. It is this feature of the equal weight view that distinguishes it from the alternative view that I will offer and leaves it vulnerable to the current objection.

18 See the lucid and illuminating discussions of this point in Christensen (2007, 2008).

19 In Kelly (2005a), I suggested that we should regard the views of a generally reasonable person as in effect providing *higher order evidence*: that is, evidence about the normative upshot of the evidence to which she has been exposed. (See especially the discussion at 185–90). So, for example, the fact that a generally reasonable person S believes p is (defeasible) evidence in favor of the epistemic proposition that *it is reasonable to believe p given S's evidence*. I emphasized that higher order evidence of this sort bears most directly on epistemic propositions and that acquiring such evidence will often make a straightforward difference to what it is reasonable for one to believe *about* particular bodies of evidence. On the other hand, I expressed considerable skepticism about the idea that the higher order evidence provided by the fact that a generally reasonable person believes a given proposition will also make a difference to what it is reasonable for one to believe about that proposition in a case in which one knows that one already possesses all of the evidence on which the person bases her belief. (Foremost among my reasons for skepticism: the "double-counting" argument rehearsed at 187–88.) What I say here constitutes a departure from the earlier skeptical attitude: on this view, higher order evidence about the bearing of one's first order evidence *is* typically relevant to what it is reasonable to believe on the basis of that evidence.

20 Recent—and to my mind, compelling—critiques of the idea that there is any interesting and important epistemic status that supervenes on phenomenology are provided by Timothy Williamson (2000) and Ernest Sosa (1999, 2002, 2007).

21 On the importance and nature of independence, see especially the illuminating discussion in Goldman (2001, pp. 150–56). In that essay Goldman is specifically concerned with the interesting question of how a nonexpert should respond to disagreement among the experts, but the analysis of independence he offers would seem to be highly relevant to a host of other important issues in social epistemology as well.

22 Perhaps unsurprisingly, the common consent argument is not taken very seriously any more, even in those circles in which arguments for the existence of God are still taken seriously. It is, for example, rarely if ever included among the usual rogue's gallery of arguments for the existence of God (the ontological argument, the cosmological argument, etc.) in anthologies or course syllabi devoted to the philosophy of religion. Historically, however, it was taken *quite* seriously. A list of prominent thinkers who endorsed some recognizable variant of it would include Cicero, Seneca, the Cambridge Platonists, Gassendi, and Grotius; in addition, it was discussed critically by (among many others) both Locke and Mill. For an overview, see the useful survey in Edwards (1967).

23 Indeed, as Hartry Field pointed out to me, the need to discount the numbers is not limited to cases in which there is causal dependence present, as in the examples considered above. If I know that two individuals will respond to given evidence in the same manner, then I should treat their having arrived at some particular answer as *one* piece of evidence, and not two pieces of evidence, in favor of that answer (even if their both having arrived at that answer is in no way underwritten by some causal link).

24 See Christensen (2007, pp. 200–203) and Elga (2007, p. 491).

25 In general, it is important to distinguish between (1) cases in which multiple individuals have equally strong but different bodies of evidence, and (2) cases in which multiple individuals have equally strong bodies of evidence in virtue of sharing the same evidence. Splitting the difference will often be the reasonable response in the former kind of case, but this in itself has no tendency to show that the same is true in cases of the latter kind. Of course, a commitment to certain views about the nature of evidence might make it difficult, if not impossible, to consistently observe the distinction between (1) and (2). For example, on a view of evidence according to which one's evidence ultimately consists of one's own private mental states, one never literally shares one's evidence with a peer; at best, one's evidence is similar in various salient respects to the evidence one's peer possesses. Because this is the closest surrogate for genuinely sharing evidence in the literal sense, it becomes easy to conflate (1) and (2). But such conflation should be resisted.

26 Elga makes the last point explicit on the same page:

> Again, this absurdity is independent of who has in fact evaluated the claims properly. Even if in fact you have done a much better job than your friend at evaluating the claims, simply comparing your verdicts to those of your friend gives you no evidence that this is so. (2007, p. 487)

27 This case was inspired by a similar example devised by Daniel Greco.

References

Christensen, David (2007). "Epistemology of Disagreement: The Good News." *Philosophical Review* 116, no. 2, 187–217.

Christensen, David (2008). "Does Murphy's Law Apply in Epistemology? Self-doubt and Rational Ideals." In *Oxford Studies in Epistemology*, vol. 2. Oxford: Oxford University Press, pp. 3–31.

Cohen, G. A. (2000). *If You're an Egalitarian, How Come You're So Rich?* (Cambridge, MA: Harvard University Press).

Conee, Earl, and Feldman, Richard (2004). *Evidentialism*. Oxford: Oxford University Press.

Edwards, Paul (1967). "Common Consent Arguments for the Existence of God." In Paul Edwards (ed.), *The Encyclopedia of Philosophy*, vol. 2 New York: Macmillan, pp. 147–55.

Elga, Adam (2007). "Reflection and Disagreement." *Nous* 41, no. 3, 478.

Feldman, Richard (2003). *Epistemology*. Upper Saddle River, N.J.: Prentice Hall.

Feldman, Richard (2005). "Respecting the Evidence." In *Philosophical Perspectives, vol.19, Epistemology*. Oxford: Blackwell, pp. 95–119.

Feldman, Richard (2006). "Epistemological Puzzles about Disagreement." In Stephen Hetherington (ed.), *Epistemology Futures*. Oxford: Oxford University Press, pp. 216–36.

Feldman, Richard (2007). "Reasonable Religious Disagreements." In Louise Antony (ed.), *Philosophers without Gods: Meditations on Atheism and the Secular Life* (Oxford: Oxford University Press), pp. 194–214.

Goldman, Alvin (2001). "Experts: Which Ones Should You Trust?" *Philosophy and Phenomenological Research* 63: 85–110.

Greco, Daniel (2006). "Disagreement and the Equal Weight View." Senior thesis, Princeton University.

Kelly, Thomas (2005a). "The Epistemic Significance of Disagreement." In Tamar Szabo Gendler and John Hawthorne (eds.), *Oxford Studies in Epistemology*, vol. 1. Oxford: Oxford University Press, pp. 167–96.

Kelly, Thomas (2005b). "Comments on White, 'Epistemic Permissiveness.'" Remarks delivered at the annual meeting of the Eastern Division of the American Philosophical Association. Available at www.princeton.edu/~tkelly/.

Plantinga, Alvin (2000a). "Pluralism: A Defense of Religious Exclusivism." In Philip L. Quinn and Kevin Meeker (eds.), *The Philosophical Challenge of Religious Diversity*. Oxford: Oxford University Press, pp. 172–92.

Plantinga, Alvin (2000b). *Warranted Christian Belief*. Oxford: Oxford University Press.

Rosen, Gideon (2001). "Nominalism, Naturalism, Epistemic Relativism." *Philosophical Perspectives* 15, 69–91.

Sosa, Ernest (1999). "Skepticism and the Internal/External Divide." In John Greco and Ernest Sosa (eds.), *The Blackwell Guide to Epistemology.*, MA: Blackwell.

Sosa, Ernest (2002). "Privileged Access." In Quentin Smith and A. Jokcik (eds.), *Consciousness: New Philosophical Essays*. Oxford: Oxford University Press, pp. 273–95.

Sosa, Ernest (2007). *A Virtue Epistemology*. Oxford: Oxford University Press.

van Inwagen, Peter (1996). "It Is Wrong, Everywhere, Always, and for Anyone, to Believe Anything upon Insufficient Evidence." In Jeff Jordan and Daniel Howard-Snyder (eds.), *Faith, Freedom, and Rationality: Philosophy of Religion Today*. London: Rowman and Littlefield, pp. 137–53.

Wedgwood, Ralph (2007). *The Nature of Normativity*. Oxford: Oxford University Press.

White, Roger (2005). "Epistemic Permissiveness." In *Philosophical Perspectives, vol. 19, Epistemology*. Oxford: Blackwell, pp. 445–59.

Williamson, Timothy (2000). *Knowledge and Its Limits*. Oxford: Oxford University Press.

Williamson, Timothy (2007) *The Philosophy of Philosophy*. Oxford: Blackwell.

IV

JUDGMENT AGGREGATION

10

Group Knowledge and Group Rationality: A Judgment Aggregation Perspective

Christian List[1]

In this paper, I introduce the emerging theory of judgment aggregation as a framework for studying institutional design in social epistemology. When a group or collective organization is given an epistemic task, its performance may depend on its 'aggregation procedure', i.e. its mechanism for aggregating the group members' individual beliefs or judgments into corresponding collective beliefs or judgments endorsed by the group as a whole. I argue that a group's aggregation procedure plays an important role in determining whether the group can meet two challenges: the 'rationality challenge' and the 'knowledge challenge'. The rationality challenge arises when a group is required to endorse consistent beliefs or judgments; the knowledge challenge arises when the group's beliefs or judgments are required to track certain truths. My discussion seeks to identify those properties of an aggregation procedure that affect a group's success at meeting each of the two challenges.

1. INTRODUCTION

Institutional design has received much attention in the social sciences. Many different institutional structures of societies, organizations or social groups have been investigated with respect to their effects on social decision making. Examples of such institutional structures are constitutions, electoral systems, legislative and judicial procedures, forms of government and other organizational forms. A widely accepted conclusion is that institutions matter. Different institutional structures may lead to different social outcomes even if everything else remains fixed. Some institutional structures may lead to more optimal, stable or rational outcomes than others (for an overview, see Goodin 1996).

Questions about institutional design arise in social epistemology too. Many epistemic tasks are performed not by individuals, but by multi-member groups such as expert panels, committees and organizations.

How is the epistemic performance of such groups affected by their institutional structure? The failure of the US intelligence services to draw certain inferences from available information before 9/11, for example, has often been attributed to flaws in their institutional structure, and various institutional reforms have been proposed in response to 9/11 (Goldman 2004). Some institutional structures may facilitate the integration of information held by different individuals, others not.

In this paper, I suggest a formal approach to thinking about institutions in social epistemology, drawing on the newly emerging theory of judgment aggregation. I argue that institutions matter here too. I focus on particular institutional structures that affect a group's epistemic performance: 'aggregation procedures', as defined in the theory of judgment aggregation (e.g. List and Pettit 2002, 2004; Pauly and van Hees 2005; Dietrich 2005; List 2005a,b). Aggregation procedures are mechanisms a multi-member group can use to combine ('aggregate') the individual beliefs or judgments held by the group members into collective beliefs or judgments endorsed by the group as a whole.

I argue that in designing an aggregation procedure for a group, we are faced with two challenges. Inspired by Goldman (2004), I call these the 'rationality challenge' and the 'knowledge challenge'. The rationality challenge arises when the group's collectively endorsed beliefs or judgments have to be consistent. The knowledge challenge arises when those beliefs or judgments have to track certain truths.

But while Goldman has associated these challenges with two different approaches to social epistemology, I argue that they can be studied within a single approach, namely within the theory of judgment aggregation. I argue that whether a group can meet each of the two challenges depends on the group's aggregation procedure, and I investigate the ways in which aggregation procedures matter.

The paper is structured as follows. I begin with some introductory remarks about social epistemology in section 2 and introduce the concept of an aggregation procedure in section 3. The core of my discussion consists of sections 4 and 5, in which I address the rationality and knowledge challenges, respectively. In section 6, I draw some conclusions.

2. EPISTEMOLOGY: INDIVIDUAL AND SOCIAL

Epistemology is the study of the processes by which beliefs and knowledge are acquired and justified. In traditional epistemology, the agents acquiring beliefs or knowledge are individuals, and the relevant processes usually involve only a single individual. Examples of such processes are perception, memory or reasoning (Goldman 2004).

Social epistemology comes in less and more radical forms. In social epistemology of the less radical form, the epistemic agents are still individuals, but the focus is on processes of belief or knowledge acquisition involving social interaction. Examples of such processes are testimony, discourses and information transmission in social networks (Goldman 1999). Social epistemology of this form is an extension of traditional epistemology, distinguished primarily by its recognition that individuals often acquire their beliefs or knowledge not in isolation, but in interaction with others.

In social epistemology of the more radical form, by contrast, certain multi-member groups themselves are taken to be epistemic agents capable of acquiring beliefs or knowledge. As Goldman (2004, p. 12) has noted, "[i]n common parlance . . . organizations are treated as subjects for knowledge attribution", such as in discussions about what the FBI did or did not know before 9/11. My discussion in this paper concerns social epistemology of this more radical form.

To pursue social epistemology of this form, one has to be prepared to consider groups as epistemic agents over and above their individual members. Many philosophers and individualistically minded social scientists are reluctant to treat groups as agents on a par with individuals. Others may be prepared to treat certain groups as agents, provided some stringent conditions are met (Rovane 1998; Pettit 2003; List and Pettit 2005a,b). In particular, to be an agent, a group must exhibit patterns of behaviour vis-à-vis the outside world that robustly satisfy certain rationality conditions. Many groups fail to exhibit such rational integration in their behaviour. For example, a group of people who happen to be at London's Leicester Square at the same time lacks the required level of integration. On the other hand, a well organized committee or organization with clearly established decision-making procedures might well qualify as sufficiently integrated.

Here I set aside the broader question of whether groups can be fully fledged agents, and focus instead on the narrower question of how they perform as *epistemic* agents, i.e. how they perform at acquiring beliefs or knowledge. Of course, not all groups are capable of forming collectively endorsed beliefs, let alone knowledge. Whether or not they are capable of forming such beliefs depends on their (formal or informal) institutional structure. An example of a group incapable of forming collective beliefs is once again the random crowd at Leicester Square. But if a group's institutional structure allows the group to make certain public declarations, then that group may well count as an epistemic agent capable of acquiring beliefs or even knowledge. An example might be an expert panel or research group that publishes a joint report on some scientific matter, the monetary policy committee of a central bank that makes an economic forecast, or a court that publicly announces its factual judgments relevant to some case.

In short, a necessary condition for epistemic agency in a group is an institutional structure (formal or informal) that allows the group to endorse certain beliefs or judgments as collective ones; and the group's performance as an epistemic agent depends on the details of that institutional structure.

3. THE CONCEPT OF AN AGGREGATION PROCEDURE

How can we think about a group's institutional structure? Let me introduce the concept of an 'aggregation procedure' to represent (a key part of) a group's institutional structure. As defined in the theory of judgment aggregation (List and Pettit 2002, 2004; List 2005a), an aggregation procedure is a mechanism by which a group can generate collectively endorsed beliefs or judgments on the basis of the group members' individual beliefs or judgments (illustrated in Figure 10.1). A simple example is '(propositionwise) majority voting', whereby a group judges a given proposition to be true whenever a majority of group members judges it to be true. Below I discuss several other aggregation procedures.

Of course, an aggregation procedure captures only part of a group's institutional structure (which may be quite complex), and there are also multiple ways (both formal and informal ones) in which a group might implement such a procedure.

Nonetheless, as argued below, aggregation procedures are important factors in determining a group's epistemic performance.

In the next section, I ask what properties a group's aggregation procedure must have for the group to meet the rationality challenge, i.e. to generate consistent collective judgments, and in the subsequent section, I ask what properties it must have for the group to meet the knowledge challenge, i.e. to track the truth in its judgments. Both discussions illustrate that a group's performance as an epistemic agent depends on its aggregation procedure.

4. THE RATIONALITY CHALLENGE

Suppose a group has to form collectively endorsed beliefs or judgments on certain propositions. Can it ensure the consistency of these judgments?

Input
individual beliefs or judgments

Aggregation
procedure

Output
collective beliefs or judgments   **Figure 10.1.** An aggregation procedure

4.1. A 'discursive dilemma'

Consider an expert committee that has to prepare a report on the health consequences of air pollution in a big city, especially pollution by particles smaller than 10 microns in diameter. This is an issue on which there has recently been much debate in Europe. The experts have to make judgments on the following propositions:

p: The average particle pollution level exceeds $50\mu gm^{-3}$ (micrograms per cubic meter air).

p→q: If the average particle pollution level exceeds $50\mu gm^{-3}$, then residents have a significantly increased risk of respiratory disease.

q: Residents have a significantly increased risk of respiratory disease.

All three propositions are complex factual propositions on which the experts may disagree.[2] Suppose the experts use majority voting as their aggregation procedure, i.e. the collective judgment on each proposition is the majority judgment on that proposition, as defined above. Now suppose the experts' individual judgments are as shown in Figure 10.2.

Then a majority of experts judges p to be true, a majority judges p→q to be true, and yet a majority judges q to be false, an inconsistent collective set of judgments. The expert committee fails to meet the rationality challenge in this case. This problem – sometimes called a 'discursive dilemma' – illustrates that, under the initially plausible aggregation procedure of majority voting, a group may not achieve consistent collective judgments even when all group members hold individually consistent judgments (Pettit 2001; List and Pettit 2002, 2004; List 2005a).

Is the present example just an isolated artefact, or can we learn something more general from it?

4.2. An impossibility theorem

Consider again any group of two or more individuals that has to make judgments on a set of non-trivially interconnected propositions, as in the expert committee example.[3] Suppose that each individual holds

	p	p → q	q
Individual 1	True	True	True
Individual 2	True	False	False
Individual 3	False	True	False
Majority	True	True	False

Figure 10.2. A 'discursive dilemma'

complete and consistent judgments on these propositions, and that the group judgments are also required to be complete and consistent.[4] One can then prove the following impossibility result.

Theorem (List and Pettit 2002). There exists no aggregation procedure generating complete and consistent collective judgments that satisfies the following three conditions simultaneously:

Universal domain. The procedure accepts as admissible input any logically possible combinations of complete and consistent individual judgments on the propositions.

Anonymity. The judgments of all individuals have equal weight in determining the collective judgments.

Systematicity. The collective judgment on each proposition depends only on the individual judgments on that proposition, and the same pattern of dependence holds for all propositions.

In short, majority voting is not the only aggregation procedure that runs into problems like the one illustrated in Figure 10.2 above. Any procedure satisfying universal domain, anonymity and systematicity does so. If these conditions are regarded as indispensable requirements on an aggregation procedure, then one has to conclude that a multi-member group cannot meet the rationality challenge in forming its collective judgments. But this conclusion would be too quick. The impossibility theorem should be seen as characterizing the logical space of aggregation procedures (List and Pettit 2002; List 2005a). In particular, we can characterize different aggregation procedures in terms of which conditions they meet and which they violate.

To find an aggregation procedure that allows a group to meet the rationality challenge, we have to relax at least one of the conditions of the theorem.

4.3. First solution: giving up universal domain

If the amount of disagreement in a particular group is limited or if the group has mechanisms in place for reducing disagreement – such as mechanisms of group deliberation – the group might opt for an aggregation procedure that violates universal domain. For example, a deliberating group that successfully avoids combinations of individual judgments of the kind in figure 10.2 might use majority voting as its aggregation procedure and yet meet the rationality challenge.

But this solution does not work in general. Even in an expert committee whose task is to make judgments on factual matters without conflicts of interest, disagreement may still be significant and pervasive. Although one can study conditions that make the occurrence of judgment combinations of the kind in figure 10.2 less likely (Dryzek and List 2003; List 2002), I here set this issue aside and assume that groups involved in epistemic tasks should normally use aggregation procedures satisfying universal domain.

4.4. Second solution: giving up anonymity

It can be shown that, if we give up anonymity but insist on the other two conditions, the only possible aggregation procedure is a 'dictatorial procedure', whereby the collective judgments are always those of some antecedently fixed group member (the 'dictator') (Pauly and van Hees 2005). Some groups might be prepared to put one individual – say a committee chair – in charge of forming its collective judgments. But this solution conflicts with the idea of a democratically organized group or committee. Moreover, as discussed below, a group organized in this dictatorial way loses out on the epistemic advantages of a democratic structure. (But I also suggest that some groups' epistemic performance may benefit from using an aggregation procedure that gives up anonymity together with systematicity, so as to implement a division of epistemic labour among several individuals.)

4.5. Third solution: giving up systematicity

A potentially promising solution lies in giving up systematicity, i.e. treating different propositions differently in the process of forming collective judgments. In particular, a group may designate some propositions as 'premises' and others as 'conclusions' and assign epistemic priority either to the premises or to the conclusions (for a more extensive discussion of this process, see List 2005a).

If the group assigns priority to the premises, it may use the so-called 'premise-based procedure', whereby the group first makes a collective judgment on each premise by taking a majority vote on that premise and then derives its collective judgments on the conclusions from these collective judgments on the premises. In the expert committee example, propositions p and p→q might be designated as premises (perhaps on the grounds that p and p→q are more basic than q), and proposition q might be designated as a conclusion. The committee might then take majority votes on p and p→q and derive its judgment on q from its judgments on p and p→q.[5]

Alternatively, if the group assigns priority to the conclusions, it may use the so-called 'conclusion-based procedure', whereby the group takes a majority vote only on each conclusion and makes no collective judgments on the premises. In addition to violating systematicity, this aggregation procedure fails to produce complete collective judgments. But sometimes a group is required to make judgments only on conclusions, but not on premises, and in such cases incompleteness in the collective judgments on the premises may be defensible.

The premise- and conclusion-based procedures are not the only aggregation procedures violating systematicity. Further interesting possibilities arise when the group is willing to give up both systematicity and anonymity. The group can then adopt an aggregation procedure that not only assigns priority to the premises, but also implements a division of epistemic labour. Specifically, the group may use the so-called 'distributed premise-based procedure'. Here different individuals specialize on different premises and give their individual judgments only on these premises. Now the group makes a collective judgment on each premise by taking a majority vote on that premise among the relevant 'specialists', and then the group derives its collective judgments on the conclusions from these collective judgments on the premises. This procedure is discussed in greater detail below.

For many epistemic tasks performed by groups, giving up systematicity and using a (regular or distributed) premise-based or conclusion-based procedure may be an attractive way to avoid the impossibility result explained above. Each of these procedures allows a group to meet the rationality challenge. Arguably, a premise-based or distributed premise-based procedure makes the pursuit of epistemic agency at the group level particularly visible. A group using such a procedure may seem to act like a reason-driven agent when it derives its collective judgments on conclusions from its collective judgments on relevant premises.

However, giving up systematicity comes with a price. Aggregation procedures that violate systematicity may be vulnerable to manipulation by prioritizing propositions strategically. For example, in the case of a regular premise-based procedure, the collective judgments may be sensitive to the choice of premises. In the example of figure 10.2, if p and $p{\to}q$ are designated as premises, then all three propositions, p, $p{\to}q$ and q, are collectively judged to be true; if p and q are designated as premises, then p is judged to be true and both q and $p{\to}q$ are judged to be false; finally, if q and $p{\to}q$ are designated as premises, then $p{\to}q$ is judged to be true, and both p and q are judged to be false. Although there seems to be a natural choice of premises in the present example, namely p and $p{\to}q$, this may not generally be the case, and the outcome of a premise-based procedure may therefore depend as much on the choice of premises as it depends on the individual judgments to be aggregated. In the case of a distributed premise-based procedure, an additional sensitivity to the choice of 'specialists' on each premise arises. Likewise, in the case of the conclusion-based procedure, the choice of conclusions obviously matters, since the group makes collective judgments only on these conclusions and on no other propositions.[6]

4.6. FOURTH SOLUTION: PERMITTING INCOMPLETE COLLECTIVE JUDGMENTS

The first three solutions to the rationality challenge have required giving up one of the three minimal conditions on how individual judgments are aggregated into collective judgments. The present solution preserves these minimal conditions, but weakens the requirements on the collective judgments themselves by permitting incompleteness in these judgments (see also List 2005a).

If a group is prepared to refrain from making a collective judgment on some propositions – namely on those on which there is too much disagreement between the group members – then it may use an aggregation procedure such as the 'unanimity procedure', whereby the group makes a judgment on a proposition if and only if the group members unanimously endorse that judgment. Propositions judged to be true by all members are collectively judged to be true; and ones judged to be false by all members are collectively judged to be false; no collective judgment is made on any other propositions. (Instead of the unanimity procedure, the group might also use 'supermajority voting' with a sufficiently large supermajority threshold.)

Groups operating in a strongly consensual manner may well opt for this solution, but in many cases making no judgment on some propositions is simply not an option. For example, when an expert committee is asked to give advice on a particular issue, it is usually expected to take a determinate stance on that issue.

4.7. Lessons to be drawn

I have shown that aggregation procedures matter with respect to the rationality challenge: a group of individuals that seeks to make collective judgments on a set of non-trivially interconnected propositions can meet the rationality challenge only if it is willing to adopt a procedure that violates one of universal domain, anonymity or systematicity or that produces incomplete collective judgments. Moreover, different aggregation

	p	$p{\to}q$	q
Majority voting*	True	True	False
Premise-based procedure with p, p→q as premises	True	True	True
Conclusion-based procedure with q as conclusion	No judgment	No judgment	False
Distributed premise-based procedure with individual 1 specializing on p and individual 2 specializing on p→q	True	False	False
Unanimity procedure	No judgment	No judgment	No judgment
Dictatorship of individual 3	False	True	False

* inconsistent

Figure 10.3. Different aggregation procedures applied to the individual judgments in Figure 10.2

procedures may lead to different collective judgments for the same combination of individual judgments. As an illustration, figure 10.3 shows
the collective judgments for the individual judgments in figure 10.2
under different aggregation procedures.

If we were to assess a group's epistemic performance solely on the basis
of whether the group meets the rationality challenge, this would give us
insufficient grounds for selecting a unique aggregation procedure. As I
have illustrated, many different aggregation procedures generate consistent collective judgments, and even if we require completeness in addition
to consistency, several possible aggregation procedures remain. To recommend a suitable aggregation procedure that a group can employ for a given
epistemic task, the question of whether the group meets the rationality
challenge alone is not a sufficient criterion. Goldman (2004) has noted
this point in his critique of a pure rationality-based approach to social
epistemology.

5. THE KNOWLEDGE CHALLENGE

Can a group's collective beliefs or judgments constitute knowledge?
Following Nozick (1981), an agent knows that p if four conditions are
met. First, p is true. Second, the agent believes that p. Third, if p were true,
the agent would believe that p. Fourth, if p were not true, the agent would
not believe that p. These conditions can be applied to any epistemic agent,
individual or collective. In particular, if a group's instutitional structure
allows the group to form collectively endorsed beliefs or judgments,
then one can ask whether these beliefs or judgments satisfy Nozick's
conditions. (Readers who prefer a different account of knowledge may
substitute their preferred account.)

As a simple reliabilist measure of how well an agent satisfies Nozick's
third and fourth conditions, I use two conditional probabilities (List
2005a): the probability that the agent believes p to be true given that p is
true, and the probability that the agent does not believe p to be true given
that p is false. Call these two conditional probabilities the agent's 'positive' and 'negative reliability' on p, respectively.

By considering a group's positive and negative reliability on various propositions under diffferent aggregation procedures and different scenarios, I
now show that it is possible for a group to meet the knowledge challenge,
but that, once again, the aggregation procedure affects a group's success.

5.1. The first scenario and its lesson: epistemic gains from democratization

Suppose that a group has to make a collective judgment on a single factual proposition, such as proposition p in the expert committee example

above. As a baseline scenario (e.g. Grofman, Owen and Feld 1983), suppose that the group members hold individual judgments on proposition p, where two conditions are met. First, each group member has the same positive and negative reliability r on proposition p, where $1 > r > 1/2$ (the 'competence' condition); so individual judgments are noisy but biased towards the truth. Second, the judgments of different group members are mutually independent (the 'independence' condition). (Obviously, it is also important to study scenarios where these conditions are violated, and below I consider some such scenarios.[7])

The group must use an aggregation procedure to make its collective judgment on p based on the group members' individual judgments on p. What is the group's positive and negative reliability on p under different aggregation procedures?

Let me compare three different procedures: first, a dictatorial procedure, where the collective judgment is always determined by the same fixed group member; second, the unanimity procedure, where agreement among all group members is necessary for reaching a collective judgment; and third, majority voting, which perhaps best implements the idea of democratic judgment aggregation (at least in the case of a single proposition).

Under a dictatorial procedure, the group's positive and negative reliability on p equals that of the dictator, which is r by assumption.

Under the unanimity procedure, the group's positive reliability on p equals r^n, which approaches 0 as the group size increases, but its negative reliability on p equals $1-(1-r)^n$, which approaches 1 as the group size increases. This means that the unanimity procedure is good at avoiding false positive judgments, but bad at reaching true positive ones. A determinate collective judgment on p is reached only if all individuals agree on the truth-value of p; if they don't agree, no collective judgment on p is made.

Finally, under majority voting, the group's positive and negative reliability on p approaches 1 as the group size increases. Why does this result hold? Each individual has a probability $r > 0.5$ of making a correct judgment on p; by the law of large numbers, the proportion of individuals who make a correct judgment on p approaches $r > 0.5$ as the group size increases and thus constitutes a majority with a probability approaching 1. Informally, majority voting allows the group to extract the signal from the group members' judgments, while filtering out the noise. This is the famous 'Condorcet jury theorem'. Figure 10.4 shows the group's positive and negative reliability on p under majority voting and under a dictatorial procedure, and figures 10.5 and 10.6 show, respectively, the group's positive and negative reliability on p under a dictatorial procedure and under the unanimity procedure. In each case, individual group members are assumed to have a positive and negative reliability of $r = 0.54$ on p. In all tables, the group size is on the horizontal axis and the group's reliability on the vertical axis.[8]

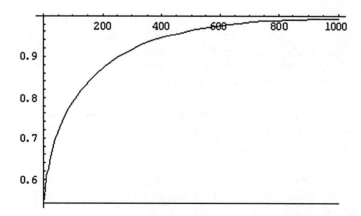

Figure 10.4. The group's positive and negative reliability on p majority voting (top curve); dictatorship (bottom curve) (setting r = 0.54 as an illustration)

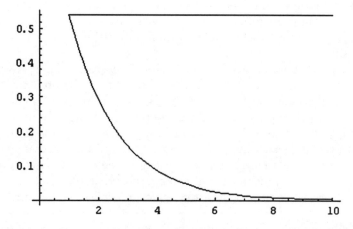

Figure 10.5. The group's positive reliability on p: dictatorship (top curve); unanimity procedure (bottom curve) (setting r = 0.54 as an illustration)

What lessons can be drawn from this first scenario? If individuals are independent, fallible, but biased towards the truth, majority voting outperforms both dictatorial and unanimity procedures in terms of maximizing the group's positive and negative reliability on p. The unanimity procedure is attractive only in those special cases where the group seeks to minimize the risk of making false positive judgments (such as in some jury decisions); a dictatorial procedure fails to pool the information held by different individuals.

Hence, when a group seeks to meet the knowledge challenge, there may be 'epistemic gains from democratization', i.e. from making a collective judgment on a given proposition democratically by using majority voting. More generally, even when individual reliability differs between

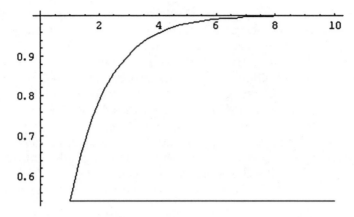

Figure 10.6. The group's negative reliability on p: unanimity procedure (top curve); dictatorship (bottom curve) (setting r = 0.54 as an illustration)

individuals, a weighted form of majority voting still outperforms a dictatorship by the most reliable individual: each individual's vote simply needs to have a weight proportional to $\log(r/(1\text{-}r))$, where r is the individual's reliability on the proposition in question (Ben-Yashar and Nitzan 1997).

5.2. The second scenario and its lesson: epistemic gains from disaggregation

Suppose now that a group has to make a collective judgment not only on a single factual proposition, but on a set of interconnected factual propositions. As an illustration, suppose that there are $k > 1$ premises $p_1, \ldots, p_k$ and a conclusion q, where q is true if and only if the conjunction of $p_1, \ldots, p_k$ is true. (This structure also allows representing a variant of the expert committee example above. For extensive discussions of the present scenario and other related scenarios, see Bovens and Rabinowicz 2005 and List 2005a,b. Analogous points apply to the case where q is true if and only if the disjunction of $p_1, \ldots, p_k$ is true.)

In this case of multiple interconnected propositions, individuals cannot generally have the same reliability on all propositions. Suppose, as an illustration, that each individual has the same positive and negative reliability r on each premise $p_1, \ldots, p_k$ and makes independent judgments on different premises. Then each individual's positive reliability on the conclusion q is r^k, which is below r and often below 0.5 (whenever $r < \sqrt[k]{0.5}$), while his or her negative reliability on q is above r. Here individuals are much worse at detecting the truth of the conclusion than the truth of each premise, but much better at detecting the falsehood of the conclusion than the falsehood of each premise. In the expert committee example, it might be easier to make correct judgments on propositions p and p→q than on proposition q. Of course, other scenarios can also be constructed, but the point remains that individuals typically have different levels of reliability on different propositions (List 2005a).

What is the group's positive and negative reliability on the various propositions under different aggregation procedures? As before, suppose the judgments of different group members are mutually independent.

Majority voting performs well only on those propositions on which individuals have a positive and negative reliability above 0.5. As just argued, individuals may not meet this condition on all propositions. Moreover, majority voting does not generally produce consistent collective judgments (on the probability of majority inconsistencies, see List 2005b). Let me now compare dictatorial, conclusion-based and premise-based procedures.

Under a dictatorial procedure, the group's positive and negative reliability on each proposition equals that of the dictator; in particular, the probability that *all* propositions are judged correctly is r^k, which may be very low, especially when the number of premises k is large.

Under the conclusion-based procedure, unless individuals have a high reliability on each premise, namely $r > {}^k\!\sqrt{0.5}$ (e.g. 0.71 when k = 2, or 0.79 when k = 3), the group's positive reliability on the conclusion q approaches 0 as the group size increases. Its negative reliability on q approaches 1. Like the unanimity procedure in the single-proposition case, the conclusion-based procedure is good at avoiding false positive judgments on the conclusion, but (typically) bad at reaching true positive ones.

Under the premise-based procedure, the group's positive and negative reliability on every proposition approaches 1 as the group size increases. This result holds because, by the Condorcet jury theorem as stated above, the group's positive and negative reliability on each premise $p_1, \ldots, p_k$ approaches 1 with increasing group size, and therefore the probability that the group derives a correct judgment on the conclusion also approaches 1 with increasing group size.

As illustration, suppose that there are k = 2 premises and individuals have a positive and negative reliability of r = 0.54 on each premise. Figure 10.7 shows the group's probability of judging *all* propositions correctly under the premise-based procedure and under a dictatorial procedure. Figures 10.8 and 10.9 show, respectively, the group's positive and negative reliability on the conclusion q under a dictatorial procedure and under the conclusion-based procedure.

What lessons can be drawn from this second scenario? Under the present assumptions, the premise-based procedure outperforms both dictatorial and conclusion-based procedures in terms of simultaneously maximizing the group's positive and negative reliability on every proposition. Like the unanimity procedure before, the conclusion-based procedure is attractive only when the group seeks to minimize the risk of making false positive judgments on the conclusion; again, a dictatorial procedure is bad at information pooling.

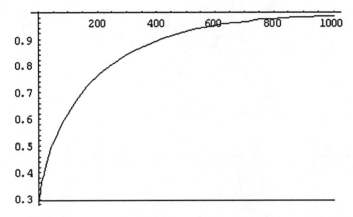

Figure 10.7. The group's probability of judging all propositions correctly: premise-based procedure (top curve); dictatorship (bottom curve) (setting r = 0.54 as an illustration)

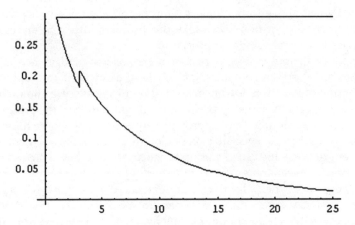

Figure 10.8. The group's positive reliability on the conclusion q dictatorship (top curve); conclusion-based procedure (bottom curve) (setting r = 0.54 as an illustration)

Hence, if a larger epistemic task such as making a judgment on some conclusion can be disaggregated into several smaller epistemic tasks such as making judgments on relevant premises, then there may be 'epistemic gains from disaggregation', i.e. from making collective judgments on that conclusion on the basis of separate collective judgments on those premises. (For a discussion of different scenarios, see List 2005a.)

5.3. The third scenario and its lesson: epistemic gains from distribution

When an epistemic task is complex in that it requires making judgments on several propositions, different individuals may have different levels of

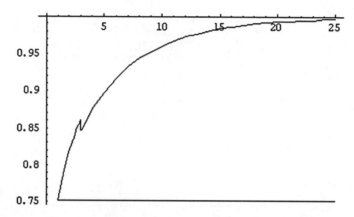

Figure 10.9. The group's negative reliability on the conclusion q conclusion-based procedure (top curve); dictatorship (bottom curve) (setting r = 0.54 as an illustration)

expertise on different propositions. An individual may lack the temporal, computational and informational resources to become sufficiently reliable on every proposition. If we take this problem into account, can we improve on the premise-based procedure?

Suppose, as before, that a group has to make collective judgments on $k > 1$ premises $p_1, \ldots, p_k$ and a conclusion q, where q is true if and only if the conjunction of $p_1, \ldots, p_k$ is true. Instead of requiring every group member to make a judgment on every premise, we might partition the group into k subgroups (for simplicity, of approximately equal size), where the members of each subgroup specialize on one premise and make a judgment on that premise alone. Instead of a using a regular premise-based procedure as in the previous scenario, the group might now use a distributed premise-based procedure: the collective judgment on each premise is made by taking a majority vote within the subgroup specializing on that premise, and the collective judgment on the conclusion is then derived from these collective judgments on the premises.

When does the distributed premise-based procedure outperform the regular premise-based procedure at maximizing the group's probability of making correct judgments on the propositions?

Intuitively, there are two effects here that pull in opposite directions. First, there may be 'epistemic gains from specialization': individuals may become more reliable on the proposition on which they specialize. But, second, there may also be 'epistemic losses from lower numbers': each subgroup voting on a particular proposition is smaller than the original group (it is only approximately 1/k the size of original group when there are k premises), which may reduce the benefits from majoritarian judgment aggregation on that proposition.

Whether or not the distributed premise-based procedure outperforms the regular premise-based procedure depends on which of these two opposite effects is stronger. Obviously, if there were no epistemic gains from specialization, then the distributed premise-based procedure would suffer only from losses from lower numbers on each premise and would therefore perform worse than the regular premise-based procedure. On the other hand, if the epistemic losses from lower numbers were relatively small compared to the epistemic gains from specialization, then the distributed premise-based procedure would outperform the regular one. The following result holds:

Theorem (List 2003). For any group size n (divisible by k), there exists an individual (positive and negative) reliability level $r^* > r$ such that the following holds: if, by specializing on some proposition p, individuals achieve a reliability above r^* on p, then the majority judgment on p in a subgroup of n/k specialists (each with reliability r^* on p) is more reliable than the majority judgment on p in the original group of n non-specialists (each with reliability r on p).

Hence, if by specializing on one premise, individuals achieve a reliability above r^* on that premise, then the distributed premise-based procedure outperforms the regular premise-based procedure. How great must the reliability increase from r to r^* be to have this effect? Strikingly, a small reliability increase typically suffices. Figure 10.10 shows some sample calculations. For example, when there are k = 2 premises, if the original individual reliability was r = 0.52, then a reliability above $r^* = 0.5281$ after specialization suffices; it it was r = 0.6, then a reliability above $r^* = 0.6393$ after specialization suffices.

Figure 10.11 shows the group's probability of judging *all* propositions correctly under regular and distributed premise-based procedures, where are k = 2 premises and where individuals have positive and negative reliabilities of r = 0.54 and $r^* = 0.58$ before and after specialization, respectively.

What lessons can be drawn from this third scenario? Even when there are only relatively modest gains from specialization, the distributed premise-based procedure and distributed premise-based procedures, may outperform the regular premise-based procedure in terms of maximizing the group's positive and negative reliability on every proposition.

Hence there may be 'epistemic gains from distribution': if a group has to perform a complex epistemic task, the group may benefit from subdividing the task into several smaller tasks and distributing these smaller tasks across multiple subgroups.

	k = 2, n = 50			k = 3, n = 51			k = 4, n = 52		
r =	0.52	0.6	0.75	0.52	0.6	0.75	0.52	0.6	0.75
r^* =	0.5281	0.6393	0.8315	0.5343	0.6682	0.8776	0.5394	0.6915	0.9098

Figure 10.10. Reliability increase from r to r^* required to outweigh the loss from lower numbers

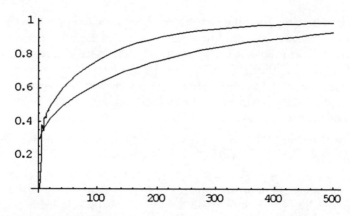

Figure 10.11. The group's probability of judging all propositions correctly: distributed (top curve) and regular premise-based procedure (bottom curve) (setting r = 0.54 and r* = 0.58 as an illustration)

Such division of epistemic labour is also the mechanism underlying the successes of 'collectively distributed cognition', as recently discussed in the philosophy of science. For example, Knorr Cetina (1999) provides a case study of distributed cognition in science. Investigating the research practices in high-energy physics at the European Center for Nuclear Research (CERN), Knorr Cetina observes that experiments, which lead to research reports and papers, involve many researchers and technicians, using complex technical devices, with a substantial division of labour, expertise, and authority (for a critical discussion, see also Giere 2002).[9] Such research practices rely on mechanisms similar to those represented, in a stylized form, by the distributed premise-based procedure.

In conclusion, when a group is faced with a complex epistemic task, it is possible for the group to meet the knowledge challenge, but the group's aggregation procedure plays an important role in determining its success.

6. CONCLUDING REMARKS

I have explained several key concepts and results from the theory of judgment aggregation in order to suggest a formal approach to thinking about institutions in social epistemology. Within this framework, I have discussed the rationality and knowledge challenges that groups as epistemic agents face. I have argued that, rather than pointing towards two different approaches to social epistemology, the two challenges should be seen as two important problems that can be addressed within a single approach. In relation to both challenges, a group's aggregation procedure, and thus its institutional structure, matters.

With regard to the rationality challenge, I have discussed an impossibility theorem, which allows us to characterize the logical space of aggregation procedures under which a group can meet the rationality challenge. No aggregation procedure generating complete and consistent collective judgments can simultaneously satisfy universal domain, anonymity and systematicity. To find an aggregation procedure that allows a group to meet the rationality challenge, it is therefore necessary to relax one of universal domain, anonymity or systematicity, or to permit incomplete collective judgments. Which relaxation is most defensible depends on the group and epistemic task in question.

With regard to the knowledge challenge, I have identified three effects that are relevant to the design of a good aggregation procedure: there may be epistemic gains from democratization, disaggregation and distribution. Again, the applicability and magnitude of each effect depends on the group and epistemic task in question, and there may not exist a 'one size fits all' aggregation procedure which is best for all groups and all epistemic tasks. But the fact that a group may sometimes benefit from the identified effects reinforces the importance of institutional design in social epistemology.

Overall, the present results give a fairly optimistic picture of a group's capacity to perform as an epistemic agent. Yet there is also an abundance of work in philosophy and economics that focuses on failures of collective agency. (Consider, for example, the large literature on the impossibility results in social choice theory.) Clearly, the details of my results depend on various assumptions and may change with changes in these assumptions. But my aim has not primarily been to defend a particular set of results on how groups perform as epistemic agents; rather, it has been to illustrate the usefulness of the theory of judgment aggregation as a framework for studying institutional design in social epistemology.

Notes

1   C. List, Department of Government, London School of Economics and Political Science, London WC2A 2AE, UK, c.list@lse.ac.uk. I am grateful to Alvin Goldman, Leslie Marsh, Philip Pettit, Miriam Solomon and the participants of the 2005 EPISTEME Conference at the University of Massachusetts at Amherst for helpful comments and discussion.

2   Propositions p and p→q can be seen as 'premises' for the 'conclusion' q. Determining whether p is true requires an evaluation of air quality measurements; determining whether p→q is true requires an understanding of causal processes in human physiology; finally, determining whether q is true requires a combination of the judgments on p and p→q.

3   A set of propositions is 'non-trivially interrelated' if it is of one of the following forms (or a superset thereof): (i) it includes $k > 1$ propositions $p1, \ldots, pk$ and either their conjunction 'p1 and . . . and pk' or their disjunction 'p1 or p2 or . . . or pk' or both (and the negations of all these propositions); (ii) it includes $k > 1$ propositions $p1, \ldots, pk$, another proposition q and either the proposition 'q if and

only if (p1 and . . . and pk)' or the proposition 'q if and only if (p1 or p2 or . . . or pk)' or both (and negations); (iii) it includes propositions p, q and p→q (and negations). This definition is given in List (2005).

4 An agent's judgments are 'complete' if, for each proposition-negation pair, the agent judges either the proposition or its negation to be true; they are 'consistent' if the set of propositions judged to be true by the agent is a consistent set in the standard sense of propositional logic. This is a slightly stronger consistency notion than the one in List and Pettit (2002). But when the present consistency notion is used, no additional deductive closure requirement is needed (unlike in List and Pettit 2002).

5 In the present example, the truth-value of q is not always settled by the truth-values of p and p→q; so the group may need to stengthen its premises in order to make them sufficient to determine its judgment on the conclusion.

6 It can be shown that in some important respects, the premise-based procedure is more vulnerable to strategic manipulation than the conclusion-based procedure. See Dietrich and List (2005).

7 Cases where different individuals have different levels of reliability are discussed, for example, in Grofman, Owen and Feld (1983) and Borland (1989). Cases where there are dependencies between different individuals' judgments are discussed, for example, in Ladha (1992), Estlund (1994) and Dietrich and List (2004). Cases where individuals express their judgments strategically rather than truthfully are discussed in Austen-Smith and Banks (1996).

8 The present curves are the result of averaging between two separate curves for even- and oddnumbered group sizes. (When the group size is an even number, the group's reliability may be lower because of the possibility of majority ties.)

9 Knorr Cetina also investigates research practices in molecular biology, but argues that, in that field, research is more individualized than in high energy physics and individual researchers remain the relevant epistemic agents here.

References

Austen-Smith, David, and Banks, Jeffrey (1996). Information Aggregation, Rationality and the Condorcet Jury Theorem. *American Political Science Review* 90: 34–45.

Ben-Yashar, Ruth, and Nitzan, Shmuel (1997). The optimal decision rule for fixed-size committees in dichotomous choice situations: the general result. *International Economic Review* 38: 175–186.

Borland, Philip (1989). Majority systems and the Condorcet jury theorem. *Statistician* 38: 181–189.

Bovens, Luc, and Rabinowicz, Wlodek (2005). Democratic Answers to Complex Questions: an Epistemic Perspective. *Synthese*, forthcoming.

Dietrich, Franz (2005). Judgment aggregation: (im)possibility theorems. *Journal of Economic Theory*, forthcoming.

Dietrich, Franz, and List, Christian (2004). A model of jury decisions where all jurors have the same evidence. *Synthese* 142: 175–202.

Dietrich, Franz, and List, Christian (2005). Strategy-proof judgment aggregation. Working paper, LSE.

Dryzek, John, and List, Christian (2003). Social Choice Theory and Deliberative Democracy: A Reconciliation. British Journal of Political Science 33(1): 1–28.

Estlund, David (1994). Opinion leaders, independence and Condorcet's jury theorem. *Theory and Decision* 36: 131–162.
Giere, Ronald (2002). Distributed Cognition in Epistemic Cultures. *Philosophy of Science* 69: 637–644.
Goldman, Alvin (1999). *Knowledge in a Social World*. Oxford: Oxford University Press.
Goldman, Alvin (2004). Group Knowledge versus Group Rationality: Two Approaches to Social Epistemology. *Episteme, A Journal of Social Epistemology* 1: 11–22.
Goodin, Robert E. (ed.) (1996). *The Theory of Institutional Design*. Cambridge:Cambridge University Press.
Grofman, Bernard, Owen, Guillermo, and Feld, Scott (1983). Thirteen theorems in search of the truth. *Theory and Decision* 15: 261–278.
Knorr Cetina, Karin (1999). Epistemic Cultures: *How the Sciences Make Knowledge*. Cambridge/MA: Harvard University Press.
Ladha, Krishna (1992). The Condorcet jury theorem, free speech and correlated votes. *American Journal of Political Science* 36: 617–634.
List, Christian (2002). Two Concepts of Agreement. *The Good Society* 11(1): 72–79.
List, Christian (2003). Distributed Cognition: A Perspective from Social Choice Theory. Presentation, Australian National University, London School of Economics, University of Liverpool.
List, Christian (2005a). The Discursive Dilemma and Public Reason. *Ethics*, forthcoming.
List, Christian (2005b). The Probability of Inconsistencies in Complex Collective Decisions. *Social Choice and Welfare* 24(1): 3–32.
List, Christian, and Pettit, Philip (2002). Aggregating Sets of Judgments: An Impossibility Result. *Economics and Philosophy* 18: 89–110.
List, Christian, and Pettit, Philip (2004). Aggregating Sets of Judgments: Two Impossibility Results Compared. *Synthese* 140(1–2): 207–235.
List, Christian, and Pettit, Philip (2005a). On the Many as One. *Philosophy and Public Affairs*, forthcoming.
List, Christian, and Pettit, Philip (2005b). Group Agency and Supervenience. Working paper, LSE.
Nozick, Robert (1981). *Philosophical Explanations*. Cambridge/MA: Harvard University Press.
Pauly, Marc, and van Hees, Martin (2005). Logical Constraints on Judgment Aggregation. *Journal of Philosophical Logic*, forthcoming.
Pettit, Philip (2001) Deliberative Democracy and the Discursive Dilemma. *Philosophical Issues* (supplement to *Nous*) 11: 268–99.
Pettit, Philip (2003). Groups with Minds of their Own. In Fred Schmitt (ed.). *Socializing Metaphysics*. New York: Rowan and Littlefield.
Rovane, Carol (1998). *The Bounds of Agency*: An essay in Revisionary Metaphysics. Princeton: Princeton University Press.

11

Groups with Minds of Their Own

Philip Pettit

There is a type of organization found in certain collectivities that makes them into subjects in their own right, giving them a way of being minded that is starkly discontinuous with the mentality of their members. This claim in social ontology is strong enough to ground talk of such collectivities as entities that are psychologically autonomous and that constitute institutional persons. Yet unlike some traditional doctrines (Runciman 1997), it does not spring from a rejection of common sense. This chapter shows that the claim is supported by the implications of a distinctive social paradox—the discursive dilemma—and is consistent with a denial that our minds are subsumed in a higher form of *Geist* or in any variety of collective consciousness. Although the chapter generates a rich, metaphysical brew, the ingredients it deploys all come from austere and sober analysis.

The chapter is in six sections. In the first I introduce the doctrinal paradox, a predicament recently identified in jurisprudence, and in the second I explain how it generalizes to constitute the discursive dilemma. In the third section I show that that dilemma is going to arise for any group or grouping—henceforth I shall just say, group—that espouses or avows purposes, and that such purposive collectivities are bound to resolve it by imposing the discipline of reason at the collective rather than the individual level. In the fourth and fifth sections I argue that groups of this kind—social integrates, as I call them— will constitute intentional and personal subjects. And then in the sixth section I look briefly at how we should think of the relationship between institutional persons of this kind and the natural persons who sustain them.

THE DOCTRINAL PARADOX

The discursive dilemma is a generalized version of the doctrinal paradox that has recently been identified in jurisprudence by Lewis Kornhauser and Lawrence Sager (Kornhauser and Sager 1993; Kornhauser 1996). This paradox arises when a multimember court has to make a decision on the basis of received doctrine as to the considerations that ought to determine the resolution of a case: that is, on the basis of a conceptual sequencing of the matters to be decided (Chapman 1998). It consists in the fact that the standard practice whereby judges make their individual decisions on the case, and then aggregate their votes, can lead to a different result from that which would have ensued had they voted instead on whether the relevant considerations obtained and let those votes dictate how the case should be resolved.

A good example of the doctrinal paradox is provided by this simple case where a three-judge court has to decide on a tort case. Under relevant legal doctrine let us suppose that the court has to judge the defendant liable if and only if it finds, first, that the defendant's negligence was causally responsible for the injury to the plaintiff and, second, that the defendant had a duty of care toward the plaintiff. Now imagine that the three judges, A, B, and C, vote as follows on those issues and on the doctrinally related matter of whether the defendant is indeed liable.

	Cause of harm?	Duty of care?	Liable?
A.	Yes	No	No
B.	No	Yes	No
C.	Yes	Yes	Yes

Matrix 1

There are two salient ways in which the court might in principle make its decision in a case like this. Let us suppose that each judge votes on each premise and on the conclusion and does so in a perfectly rational manner. The judges might aggregate their votes in respect of the conclusion—the liability issue—and let the majority view on that issue determine their collective finding. Call this the conclusion-centered procedure. Under such a procedure, the defendant would go free, because there are two votes against liability. Or the judges might aggregate their votes on the individual premises—the causation and duty issues; let the majority view on each premise determine whether or not it is collectively endorsed; and let the conclusion be accepted—that the defendant is liable—if and only if both premises are collectively endorsed. Call this the premise-centered procedure. Since each premise commands majority support, the defendant would be found liable under this procedure. The doctrinal paradox, as presented in the jurisprudential literature, consists in the fact that the two procedures described yield different outcomes.

Another simple example from the jurisprudential area is provided by a case where a three-judge court has to decide on whether a defendant is liable under a charge of breach of contract (Kornhauser and Sager 1993, p. 11). According to legal doctrine, the court should find against the defendant if and only if it finds, first that a valid contract was in place, and second that the defendant's behavior was such as to breach the sort of contract that was allegedly in place. Now imagine that the three judges, A, B, and C, vote as follows on those issues and on the doctrinally related matter of whether the defendant is indeed liable.

	Contract?	Breach?	Liable?
A.	Yes	No	No
B.	No	Yes	No
C.	Yes	Yes	Yes

Matrix 2

In this case, as in the previous example, the judges might each conduct their own reasoning and then decide the case in a conclusion-centered way, by reference to the votes in the final column. Or they might decide the case in a premise-centered way by looking to the majority opinions in each of the first two columns and then letting those opinions decide the issue of liability. If they adopted the conclusion-centered approach, they would find for the defendant; if they took the premise-centered approach, then they would find against.

The paradox illustrated will arise wherever a majority in the group supports each of the premises, different majorities support different premises, and the intersection or overlap of those majorities is not itself a majority in the group. The fact that those in that overlap are not themselves a majority—in the cases considered there is only one judge, C, in the intersection—explains why there is only a minority in favor of the conclusion.[1]

The doctrinal paradox is not confined to cases where a court has to make a decision by reference to a conjunction of premises. It can also arise in cases where the court has to make its decision by reference to a disjunction of considerations; that is, in cases where the support required for a positive conclusion is only that one or more of the premises be endorsed. This is unsurprising, of course, given that a disjunction of premises, p or q, is equivalent to the negation of a conjunction: not-(not-p and not-q). Still, it may be worth illustrating the possibility.

Imagine that three judges have to make a decision on whether or not someone should be given a retrial; that a retrial is required either in the event of inadmissible evidence having been used previously or in the event of the appellant's having been forced to confess; and that the voting goes as follows among the judges (Kornhauser and Sager 1993, p. 40):

	Inadmissible evidence?	Forced confession?	Retrial?
A.	Yes	No	Yes
B.	No	Yes	Yes
C.	No	No	No

Matrix 3

This case also illustrates a doctrinal paradox, because the conclusion-centered procedure will lead to giving the defendant a retrial and a premise-centered procedure will not: at least not, so long as majority voting is all that is required for the group to reject one of the premises (see Pettit 2001).

THE DISCURSIVE DILEMMA

It should be clear that the doctrinal paradox will generalize in a number of dimensions, representing a possibility that may materialize with any number of decision makers greater than two and with any number of premises greater than one, whether those premises be conjunctively or disjunctively organized. But there are other, perhaps less obvious ways in which it can be generalized also and I now look at three of these. These give us reason, as we shall see later, to speak of a discursive dilemma. I describe them respectively as the social generalization, the diachronic generalization, and the *modus tollens* generalization.

The Social Generalization

A paradox of the sort illustrated will arise not just when legal doctrine dictates that certain considerations are conceptually or epistemically prior to a certain issue—an issue on which a conclusion has to be reached—and that judgments on those considerations ought to dictate the judgment on the conclusion. It will arise whenever a group of people discourse together with a view to forming an opinion on a certain matter that rationally connects, by the lights of all concerned, with other issues.

Consider an issue that might arise in a workplace, among the employees of a company: for simplicity, as we may assume, a company owned by the employees. The issue is whether to forgo a pay-raise in order to spend the money thereby saved on introducing a set of workplace safety measures: say, measures to guard against electrocution. Let us suppose for convenience that the employees are to make the decision—perhaps because of prior resolution—on the basis of considering three separable issues: first, how serious the danger is; second, how effective the safety measure that a pay-sacrifice would buy is likely to be; and third, whether the pay-sacrifice is bearable for members individually. If an employee thinks that the danger is sufficiently serious, the safety measure sufficiently effective, and the pay-sacrifice sufficiently bear able, he or she will vote for the sacrifice; otherwise he or she will vote against. And so each will have to consider the three issues and then look to what should be concluded about the pay-sacrifice.

Imagine now that after appropriate dialogue and deliberation the employees are disposed to vote on the relevant premises and conclusion in the pattern illustrated by the following matrix for a group of three workers. The letters *A*, *B*, and *C* represent the three employees and the "Yes" or "No" on any row represents the disposition of the relevant employee to admit or reject the corresponding judgment premise or conclusion.

	Serious danger?	Effective measure?	Bearable loss?	Pay-sacrifice?
A.	Yes	No	Yes	No
B.	No	Yes	Yes	No
C.	Yes	Yes	No	No

Matrix 4

If this is the pattern in which the employees vote, then a different decision will be made, depending on whether the group judgment is driven by how members judge on the premises or by how they judge on the conclusion. Looking at the matrix, we can see that though everyone individually rejects the pay-sacrifice, a majority supports each of the premises. If we think that the views of the employees on the conclusion should determine the group-decision, then we will say that the group-conclusion should be to reject the pay-sacrifice: there are only "No"s in the final column. But if we think that the views of the employees on the premises should determine the group- decision, then we will say that the group conclusion should be to accept the pay-sacrifice: there are more "Yes"s than "No"s in each of the premise columns.

There are familiar practices of group deliberation and decision making corresponding to the conclusion-centered and premise-centered options. Thus the group would go the conclusion-centered way if members entered into deliberation and dialogue and then each cast their personal vote on whether to endorse the pay-sacrifice or not; in that case the decision would be against the pay-sacrifice. The group would go the premise-centered way, on the other hand, if there was a chairperson who took a vote on each of the premises—say, a show of hands—and then let logic decide the outcome; in this case the decision would be in favor of the pay-sacrifice.

This example is stylized but should serve to indicate that the paradox is not confined to the domain in which legal doctrine dictates that certain judgments are to be made by reference to certain considerations. There are many social groups that have to make judgments on various issues and that routinely do so by reference to considerations that are privileged within the group.

One set of examples will be provided by the groups that are charged by an external authority with making certain decisions on the basis of designated considerations, and on that basis only. Instances of the category will be appointment and promotions committees; committees charged with deciding who is to win a certain prize or contract; trusts that have to make judgments on the basis of a trustees' instructions; associations or the executives of associations that have to justify their actions by reference to the group's charter; corporations that have to comply with policies endorsed by their shareholders; public bodies, be they bureaucratic committees or appointed boards, that have to discharge specific briefs; and governments that are more or less bound to party programs and principles. With all such groups there is likely to be a problem as to whether the group should make its judgment on a certain issue in a premise-centered or conclusion-centered way; it will always be possible that those procedures will lead in different directions.

For a second set of examples consider those groups where it is a matter of internal aspiration that members find common grounds by which to justify whatever line they collectively take. Think of the political movement that has to work out a policy program; or the association that has to decide on the terms of its constitution; or the church that has to give an account of itself in the public forum; or the learned academy that seeks a voice in the larger world of politics and journalism. In such cases members of the group may not have access to an antecedently agreed set of considerations on the basis of which to justify particular judgments. But their identification with one another will support a wish to reach agreement on such a set of reasons. To the extent that that wish gets to be satisfied, they will have to face the issue, sooner or later, as to whether they should make their decisions in a premise- centered or conclusion-centered way.

The Diachronic Generalization

For all that has been said, however, the paradox may still seem unlikely to figure much in ordinary social life. The reason is that whereas the judges in a courtroom routinely have to make their judgments by reference to shared considerations, people in other social groups will often reach collective decisions on an incompletely theorized basis (Sunstein 1999). There will be a majority, perhaps even a consensus, in favor of a certain line on some issue but there will be no agreement among the parties to that majority or consensus on the reasons that support the line. The parties will each vote that line for reasons of their own—reasons related to their own interests or their own judgments of the common interest—and there will only be a partial overlap between the different considerations they each take into account. Thus there will be no possibility of their resorting to a premise-centered procedure, let alone any prospect of that procedure yielding a different result from the conclusion-centered alternative.

But sound as this consideration is, social groups will still have to deal routinely with the choice between these two procedures. In all of the examples so far considered, the premises and the conclusion are up for synchronic determination, whether at the individual or the collective level. Under the conclusion-centered procedure, each person has to make up their own mind on the reasons they are considering in premise position—assuming they do judge by reasons—and at the same time on the conclusion that those reasons support. Under the premise-centered procedure the group has to make up its mind on the reasons that are relevant by everyone's lights and at the same time on the conclusion that is to be derived from those premise-judgments. But the problem of choosing between such procedures may arise for a group in a diachronic as distinct from a synchronic way and is likely to arise much more generally on this basis.

Suppose that over a period of time a group makes a judgment on each of a set of issues, deciding them all by majority vote and perhaps deciding them on incompletely theorized grounds: different members of the group are moved by different considerations. Sooner or later such a group is bound to face an issue such that how it should judge on that issue is determined by the judgments it previously endorsed on other issues. And in such an event the group will face the old choice between adopting a conclusion-centered procedure and adopting a premise-centered one. The members may take a majority vote on the new issue facing them, running the risk of adopting a view that is inconsistent with the views that they previously espoused as a collectivity. Or they may allow the previously espoused views to dictate the view that they should take on this new issue.

The courts will often face diachronic examples of the problem illustrated as well as the synchronic examples that we considered; this will happen when previous judgments of the court dictate the judgment that it ought to make on an issue currently before it. But, more important for our purposes, even social groups that differ from the courts in routinely securing only incompletely theorized agreements will have to confront diachronic examples of the problem. They may escape the synchronic problem through not being capable of agreeing on common considerations by which different issues are to be judged. But that is no guarantee that they will be able to escape the problem as it arises in diachronic form.

The *Modus Tollens* Generalization

The third and last point to note in generalization of the doctrinal paradox is that the options that we have been describing as the conclusion-centered procedure and the premise-centered procedure are not exhaustive of the alternatives available. The problem involved in the doctrinal paradox, even as it arises in legal and synchronic contexts, has a more general cast than the jurisprudential literature suggests.

The best way to see that the options are not exhaustive is to consider what a group may do if it finds that, relying on majority vote, it endorses each of a given set of premises while rejecting a conclusion that they support: say, deductively support. One grand option is for the collectivity to let the majority vote stand on each issue, thereby reflecting the views of its members on the different issues, while allowing the collective views to be inconsistent with one another. This approach, in effect, would vindicate the conclusion-centered procedure. But what now are the alternatives?

One possibility is for the group to ignore the majority vote on the conclusion, as in the premise-centered procedure, and to let the majority votes on the premises dictate the collective view on the conclusion. But another equally salient possibility, neglected as irrelevant in the legal context, is to ignore the majority vote on one of the premises, letting the majority votes on the other premises together with the majority vote on the conclusion dictate the collective view to be taken on that premise. The first possibility involves the collectivity practicing *modus ponens*, the second has it practice *modus tollens* instead. These two options can be seen as different forms of a single grand option that stands exhaustively opposed to the first alternative described above. Where that alternative would have the collectivity reflect the individual views of its members on each issue, this second option would have the group ensure that the views collectively espoused across those issues are mutually consistent.

It should now be clear why I speak of a discursive dilemma rather than a doctrinal paradox. The problem arises because of the requirements of discourse as such, not just because of the demands of legal doctrine. And the problem represents a hard choice or dilemma, not anything that strictly deserves to be called a paradox. The hard choice that a group in this dilemma faces is whether to let the views of the collectivity on any issue be fully responsive to the individual views of members, thereby running the risk of collective inconsistency; or whether to ensure that the views of the group are collectively rational, even where that means compromising responsiveness to the views of individual members on one or another issue. You can have individual responsiveness or collective rationality but you cannot have both—or at least you cannot have both for sure.

In arguing that the discursive dilemma presents groups with a hard choice, of course, I am assuming that they will not be happy to avoid that choice by insisting on voting by unanimity rather than majority, for example, since that would make them unable to come to agreement on many pressing questions. And equally I am assuming that collectivities will not simply refuse to draw out the implications of their views, avoiding inconsistency by avoiding deductive closure. But I say no more here on the general possibilities that arise in this area. Christian List and I have argued elsewhere for a relevant impossibility theorem (List and Pettit 2002a, 2002b).[2]

RESOLVING THE DILEMMA BY COLLECTIVIZING REASON

Any groups that seek to make deliberative, reasoned judgments, then, face a dilemma. They may maximize responsiveness to individual views, running the risk of collectively endorsing inconsistent sets of propositions. Or they may impose the discipline of reason at the collective level, running the risk of collectively endorsing a conclusion that a majority of them— perhaps even all of them—individually reject. I show in this section that many groups respond to the dilemma by adopting the second alternative—by collectivizing reason—and I go on to argue in the following two sections that groups that collectivize reason deserve ontological recognition as intentional and personal subjects.

Groups come in many different shapes and sizes (French 1984). Some are just unorganized collocations like the set of pedestrians on a given street or the people who live in the same postal area. Some are sets related in other arbitrary ways, like those who have even telephone numbers or those who are first born to their mothers. And some are classes of people who share a common feature—say, accent or mannerism—that affects how others treat them but not necessarily how they behave themselves. Yet other groups are united by a commonality, due to nature or artifice, that does affect how they behave themselves. It may affect how they behave toward one another, without leading them to do anything in common, as with linguistic groups, Internet chat groups, and other enduring or episodic networks. Or it may also affect how they behave, as we say, to a shared purpose.

Purposive groups come themselves in a number of varieties (Stoljar 1973). They include organizations that have a specific function to discharge, such as museums, libraries, trusts, and states, as well as more episodic entities like the appointments committee or the jury or the commission of inquiry. And they also include groups that do not have any one specific function but that are associated with a characteristic goal, involving the outside world or the group's own members or perhaps a mix of both. Examples would include the political party, the trade union, and the business corporation, as well as the small group of colleagues involved in collaborative research and the set of friends arranging a joint holiday.

I argue in this section that purposive groups will almost inevitably confront examples of the discursive dilemma and that, short of resorting to deception, they will be under enormous pressure to collectivize reason: usually, though not inevitably, to collectivize reason by practicing *modus ponens*—as in the premise-centered procedure—rather than *modus tollens*. In mounting this argument I shall speak as if every member of a purposive group participates equally with others in voting on what the group should do. I return to that assumption in the last section, where I try to show that the argument can survive variations in such detail.

My argument is in three parts. I argue first that a purposive collectivity will inevitably confront discursive dilemmas; second, that it will be under enormous pressure to collectivize reason in those dilemmas; and third, that in the general run of cases it will collectivize reason by following the premise-centered procedure.

The first part of the argument can be formulated in these steps.

1. Any collection of individuals who coordinate their actions around the pursuit of a common purpose—more on what this involves in the next section—will have to endorse judgments that dictate how they are to act; these will bear on the opportunities available for action, the best available means of furthering their purpose, and so on.

2. The pursuit of such a common purpose will usually require explicit discussion and deliberation about the judgments the collectivity ought to endorse—it will not be like the activity of a tug-of-war team—so that over time the group will generate a history of judgments that it is on record as making.

3. Those past judgments will inevitably constrain the judgment that the group ought to make in various new cases; only one particular judgment in this or that case will be consistent—or coherent in some looser way—with the past judgments.

4. And so the group will find itself confronted with discursive dilemmas; it will be faced across time with sets of rationally connected issues such that it will have to choose between maximizing responsiveness to the views of individual members and ensuring collective rationality.

This argument shows that discursive dilemmas of a diachronic sort are going to be more or less unavoidable for purposive groups but it is consistent, of course, with such groups also having to face synchronic dilemmas; I abstract from that possibility here. The second part of the argument goes on to show that any group of the kind envisaged will be pressured to impose the discipline of reason at the collective level. It involves a further three steps.

5. The group will not be an effective or credible promoter of its assumed purpose if it tolerates inconsistency or incoherence in its judgments across time; not all the actions shaped by those discordant judgments can advance, or be represented as advancing, one and the same purpose.

6. Every such group will need to be an effective promoter of its assumed purpose and will need to be able to present itself as an effective promoter of that purpose; it will lose any hold on members, or any respect among outsiders, if cannot do this.

7. And so every purposive group is bound to try to collectivize reason, achieving and acting on collective judgments that pass reason-related tests like consistency.

How will a purposive group be disposed to collectivize reason? We do not need to answer this question for purposes of the present argument.

But it is worth noting that two plausible, further steps argue that such a group will generally, though not of course inevitably, have to follow something like the premise-driven procedure illustrated in our earlier examples.

8. The group will be unable to present itself as an effective promoter of its purpose if it invariably seeks to establish consistency and coherence in the cases envisaged by renouncing one or other of its past commitments: if it never allows its present judgment to be dictated by past judgments; there will be no possibility of taking such a routinely in constant entity seriously.

9. Thus, any such purposive collectivity must avoid automatic recourse to the revision of past commitments; it must show that those commitments are sufficiently robust for us to be able to expect that the group will frequently be guided by them in its future judgments.

The force of this three-part line of argument can be readily illustrated. Suppose that a political party announces in March, say on the basis of majority vote among its members, that it will not increase taxes if it gets into government. Suppose that it announces in June, again on the basis of majority vote, that it will increase defense spending. And now imagine that it faces the issue in September as to whether it will increase government spending in other areas of policy or organization. Should it allow a majority vote on that issue too?

If the party does allow a majority vote, then we know that even in the event of individual members being perfectly consistent across time, the vote may favor increasing government spending in other areas. Thus the party will face the hard choice between being responsive to the views of its individual members and ensuring the collective rationality of the views it endorses. The members may vote in the pattern of members A to C in the following matrix.

	Increase taxes?	Increase defense spending?	Increase other spending?
A.	No	Yes	No (reduce)
B.	No	No (reduce)	Yes
C.	Yes	Yes	Yes

Matrix 5

But the party cannot tolerate collective inconsistency, because that would make it a laughing-stock among its followers and in the electorate at large; it could no longer claim to be seriously committed to its alleged purpose. And so it must not allow its judgments to be made in such a way that the discipline of reason is imposed only at the individual level; it has to ensure that that discipline is imposed at the collective level. In the ordinary run of things, the party will make its judgments after a premise-driven pattern, using a *modus ponens* pattern. It may occasionally revoke earlier judgments in order to be able in consistency to sustain a judgment that is supported by a majority. But it cannot make a general practice of this, on pain of again becoming a laughing-stock. It must frequently allow past judgments to serve as endorsed premises that dictate later commitments.

This argument with the political party is going to apply, quite obviously, to a large range of enduring and episodic collectivities. The argument does not rule out the possibility that those groups will occasionally adopt another course. They may choose to reject an earlier commitment in this or that case, for example, rather than revise their spontaneous judgment on the issue currently before them. Or they may even choose to live, overtly or covertly, with an inconsistency. But it is hard to see how they could generally fail in these regards and constitute effective or credible agents.

Instead of speaking of groups that collectivize reason in the manner of these collectivities I shall talk from now on of integrations of people, of integrated collectivities, and of social integrates. This way of speaking sounds a contrast with those groups that do not reason at all or that do not impose the discipline of reason at the collective level. These we naturally describe as aggregations of people, as aggregated collectivities or just as aggregates. I go on in the next two sections to argue that in an intuitive and important sense social integrates are going to be intentional and personal subjects. I continue to assume in this argument that members of social integrates all take an equal part in voting on what those collectivities should do; I come back to that assumption in the final section of the paper.

SOCIAL INTEGRATES ARE INTENTIONAL SUBJECTS

Are integrations of people likely to constitute intentional subjects, displaying intentional states like beliefs and desires, judgments and intentions, and performing the actions that such states rationalize? In particular, are integrations of people likely to constitute intentional subjects in their own right? Are we going to have to itemize them, side by side with their members—if you like, over and beyond their members—in any serious inventory of intentional subjects?

In a well-known discussion, Anthony Quinton (1975–76) maintains not. He argues that to ascribe judgments, intentions, and the like to social groups is just a way of ascribing them, in a summative way, to individuals in those groups.

> We do, of course, speak freely of the mental properties and acts of a group in the way we do of individual people. Groups are said to have beliefs, emotions, and attitudes and to take decisions and make promises. But these ways of speaking are plainly metaphorical. To ascribe mental predicates to a group is always an indirect way of ascribing such predicates to its members.

With such mental states as beliefs and attitudes, the ascriptions are of what I have called a summative kind. To say that the industrial working class is determined to resist anti-trade union laws is to say that all or most industrial workers are so minded. (p. 17)

The position adopted here by Quinton amounts to a straightforward eliminativism about collective intentional subjects. It suggests that only singular entities can constitute intentional subjects—for this reason it might also be called "singularism" (Gilbert 1989, p. 12)—and that collectivities can be described as subjects "only by figment, and for the sake of brevity of discussion" (Austin 1875, p. 364).

One reason why the position described amounts to eliminativism is this. If a collectivity can be said to form a certain belief or desire, a certain judgment or intention, so far as all or most of its members do, then it would be misleading to say that it constituted an intentional subject over and beyond its members. Asked to say how many such subjects were present in a certain domain it would be quite arbitrary to count the individuals there, and then to count the collectivity also. We might as well count as subjects, not just the total set of people there, but also every subset in which majority or unanimous attitudes give us a basis on which to ascribe corresponding attitudes to that collection of people.

This criticism suggests that Quinton tells too simple a story about the attitudes that we expect to find on the part of individuals of whom we say that they collectively judge or intend something. More recent work on the conditions that might lead us to ascribe such joint attitudes, and to posit collective subjects, has stressed the fact that we usually expect a complex web of mutual awareness on the part of individuals involved (Gilbert 1989; Searle 1995; Tuomela 1995; Bratman 1999a). Thus, Michael Bratman (1999a) argues that you and I will have a shared intention to do something just in case (1) you intend that we do it and I intend that we do it; (2) we each intend that we do it because (1) holds; and (3) those clauses are matters of which we are each aware, each aware that we are each aware, and so on in the usual hierarchy of mutual knowledge.

Suppose we complicate the Quinton story in some such pattern, adopting one of these mutual-awareness analyses. Will that undercut his eliminativism, giving us reason to think that apart from singular subjects there are also collective ones? It will certainly evade the criticism just made, for it will make it much harder than Quinton does for a collection of individuals to deserve to be described as having certain mental properties. But it will not avoid another problem. It will not ensure that a collectivity displays the sort of rationality that we expect in the performance of any system we would describe as an intentional subject. So at any rate I shall argue.

What sort of rationality do we expect in an intentional subject? By a line of argument that has been widely endorsed in recent philosophical thought, a system will count as an intentional subject only if it preserves intentional attitudes over time and forms, unforms, and acts on those attitudes—at least within intuitively feasible limits and under intuitively favorable conditions— in a rationally permissible manner: in a phrase, only if it displays a certain rational unity (Pettit 1992, ch.1). If the system believes that p and comes across evidence that not-p, it must tend to unform that belief. If the system believes that p and learns that if p then q, it must come to form the belief that q or to unform one of the other beliefs. If the system desires that p, believes that by X-ing it can bring it about that p, and believes that other things are equal, then it must tend to X. And so on.

Even if we introduce the sort of complexity postulated in mutual-awareness stories about collective subjects, that will not guarantee that those subjects have the rational unity associated with intentionality. Those stories are all consistent with the collectivity's acting by conventions that allow rational disunity. The convention established in the mutual awareness of members may ordain, for example, that the collectivity shall be deemed to judge or intend whatever a majority of members vote for its judging or intending at that time. And we know from discussion of the discursive dilemma that if such a convention obtains—if the attitudes of the collectivity are required to be continuous in that majoritarian way with the current votes of members—then the collectivity may be guilty of grievous irrationality over time. It may be as wayward in the postures it assumes as the most casual aggregate of individuals; it may fail to materialize as anything that deserves to be taken as an intentional subject in its own right.

In order for a collectivity to count as an intentional subject, not only must there be a basis in the behavior of participating members for ascribing judgments and intentions and such attitudes to the collective; that is the point on which the mutual-awareness literature rightly insists. There must also be a basis for thinking of the collectivity as a subject that is rationally unified in such a way that, within feasible limits and under favorable conditions, we can expect it to live up to the constraints of rationality; we can expect it to enter and exit states of belief and desire, judgment and intention, in a way that makes rational sense and we can expect it to perform in action as those states require. Indeed, were there a basis for ascribing such states to a collectivity, and a basis for expecting this sort of rational unity, then it is hard to see any reason why we should deny that the collectivity was an intentional subject in its own right.

How to secure the dual basis that is necessary for a collectivity to be an intentional subject? The argument of the last section suggests a salient recipe. By ensuring that the collectivity represents an integration of individuals, not just a casual aggregate. Specifically, by ensuring, first, that the collectivity has a shared purpose and forms the judgments and intentions associated with pursuit of that purpose; and second, that it collectivizes reason in forming those judgments and intentions.

I said and say nothing on what it is for a collectivity to form and have a shared purpose, or to form and have certain judgments and intentions. Presumably that can be analyzed on something like the lines explored in the mutual-awareness approach; it has to do, plausibly, with the conventions, and the associated structures of common knowledge, that prevail in the collectivity. Assuming that there is an established, conventional sense in which a collectivity has a shared purpose, and forms associated judgments and intentions, the fact that it collectivizes reason in the course of that enterprise—the fact that it is a social integrate—means that it will display precisely the sort of rational unity required of an intentional subject. Let the collectivity have made certain judgments and formed certain intentions in the past. And now imagine that it faces a theoretical or practical issue where those judgments and intentions rationally require a particular response. We can rely on the integrated collectivity to respond as those intentional states rationally require, or to make rationally permissible adjustments that undercut the requirements. Or at least we can rely on it to do this under intuitively favorable conditions and within intuitively feasible limits.

The integrated collectivity has common purposes and forms associated judgments and intentions, unlike the collections envisaged in Quinton's account. And the integrated collectivity can be relied upon to achieve a rational unity in the judgments and intentions endorsed, unlike the group that meets only the mutual-awareness conditions for forming collective attitudes. It satisfies the dual basis that is necessary for a collectivity to count as an intentional subject. But is the satisfaction of these two conditions sufficient as well as necessary for the integrated collectivity to count as an intentional subject, in particular an intentional subject that is distinct from the individual subjects who make it up?

If we are to recognize the integrated collectivity as an intentional subject, then we must admit of course that it is a subject of an unusual kind. It does not have its own faculties of perception or memory, for example, though it may be able to register and endorse facts perceived or remembered by others: in particular, by its own members. Under our characterization it is incapable of forming degrees of belief and desire in the ordinary fashion of animal subjects; its beliefs are recorded as on-off judgments, its desires as on-off intentions. And the judgments and intentions that it forms are typically restricted to the narrow domain engaged by the particular purposes that its members share. Notwithstanding these features, however, I think that it is reasonable, even compulsory, to think of the integrated collectivity as an intentional subject.

The basis for this claim is that the integrated collectivity, as characterized, is going to display all the functional marks of an intentional subject and that there is no reason to discount those marks as mere appearances. Within relevant domains it will generally act in a manner that is rationalized by independently discernible representations and goals; and within relevant domains it will generally form and uniform those representations in a manner that is rationalized by the evidence that we take to be at its disposal. In particular, it will manifest this sort of functional organization, not just at a time, but over time; it will display the degree of constancy as well as the degree of coherence that we expect in any intentional subject. But given that the integrated collectivity functions in these ways like an intentional subject, the question is whether that functional appearance is proof that it really is an intentional subject.

Why might someone deny that an entity that displays the functional marks of an intentional subject, as the integrated collectivity does, is not really an intentional subject? One ground might be that intentionality requires not just a certain form of organization, but also the realization of that form in inherently mental material, whatever that is thought to be. Few would endorse this consideration among contemporary thinkers, however, because there appears to be nothing inherently mental about the biological material out of which our individual minds are fashioned (but see Searle 1983). Another ground for the denial might be that the functional marks of intentional subjectivity have to come about as a result of the subject's internal organization, and not in virtue of some form of remote control or advance rigging (Jackson 1992). But this is hardly relevant to the integrated collectivity, because its judgments and intentions are clearly formed in the required, internal fashion. Still another sort of ground for denying that functional organization is sufficient for being an intentional subject is that something more is required—say, natural selection or individual training (Millikan 1984; Papineau 1987; Dretske 1988)—for the attitudes of the subject to have determinate contents. This is not relevant in the case of the integrated collectivity, however, because the contents of its judgments and intentions will inherit determinacy from the presumptively determinate words that are used by its members to express those contents.

The usual grounds for driving a wedge between functionally behaving like an intentional subject and actually being an intentional subject are unlikely, as this quick survey shows, to cause a problem with the integrated collectivity. If further grounds for making such a separation between appearance and reality are lacking, therefore, we have every reason to treat the integrated collectivity as an intentional subject. And such grounds, so far as I can see, are indeed lacking. I can think of only one other consideration that might be invoked against counting integrated collectivities as intentional subjects and it does not raise a serious problem.

The consideration is that if we treat integrated collectivities as intentional subjects, then we may be involved in a sort of double-counting. We will be counting the individual members of the collectivity as intentional subjects. And then we will be going on to say that apart from those members, there is a further subject present too: the collectivity that they compose. But I do not think that this makes for an objection. The integrated collectivity will not be distinct from its individual members, in the sense that it will not be capable of existing in the absence of such members. But it will be distinct in the sense of being a centre for the formation of attitudes that are capable of being quite discontinuous from the attitudes of the members. This is one of the lessons of the discursive dilemma.

Consider the case of the worker-owners who have to decide on whether to forgo a pay-raise in order to purchase a device for guarding against the danger of electrocution. Imagine that they cast their votes after the pattern illustrated in Matrix 4 and that they follow the premise-centered procedure in determining what to think about the issue. In such a case the group will form a judgment on the question of the pay-sacrifice that is directly in conflict with the unanimous vote of its members. It will form a judgment that is in the starkest possible discontinuity with the corresponding judgments of its members.

As the point applies to judgment, so it naturally extends to intention. The collectivity of workers that makes a judgment in favor of the pay-sacrifice will be firmly disposed to act accordingly, under the procedure it adopts, and in that sense it will form a corresponding intention. Thus the chairperson will be entitled by the premise-driven procedure to announce on the basis of the premise-votes: "Colleagues, our intention is fixed: we will forego the pay- raise." But at the moment where the intention of the integrated group is thereby fixed, no one member will intend that the group act in that way, or that he or she play their part in the group's acting in that way. Such individual intentions will follow on the formation of the group intention, of course, since the group can only act through the actions of its members. But they are not the stuff out of which the group intention is constructed; on the contrary, they are effects that the formation of the group intention plays a role in bringing about.

These discontinuities between collective judgments and intentions, on the one hand, and the judgments and intentions of members, on the other, make vivid the sense in which a social integrate is an intentional subject that is distinct from its members. They represent the cost that must be paid if a collectivity is to achieve the rational unity that we expect in any intentional subject. Rational unity is a constraint that binds the attitudes of the collectivity at any time and across different times, and the satisfaction of that constraint means that those attitudes cannot be smoothly continuous with the corresponding attitudes of members.

In arguing that a social integrate is an intentional subject that is distinct from its members—that exists over and beyond its members—I hasten to add that I am not postulating any ontological mystery. The argument is consistent with the supervenience claim that if we replicate how things are with and between individuals in a collectivity—in particular, replicate their individual judgments and their individual dispositions to accept a certain procedure—then we will replicate all the collective judgments and intentions that the group makes. Collective judgments and intentions may be discontinuous with what happens at the individual level but they cannot vary independently of what happens there; they do not constitute an ontologically emergent realm.[3]

SOCIAL INTEGRATES ARE INSTITUTIONAL PERSONS

This discontinuity between an integrated collectivity and its members, and the fact that such a collectivity can constitute a distinct intentional subject, is quite surprising. But there is more to come. For it turns out that the way in which the judgments and intentions of social integrates are formed and policed forces us to think of those collectivities as institutional persons. It leads us to see that like individual human beings, and unlike nonhuman animals, they display everything that is strictly necessary in personal as distinct from just intentional subjects.

What distinguishes personal from merely intentional subjects? As I assumed in the previous discussion that intentional subjects have to display a certain rational unity, so I make a parallel assumption in discussing this question. I assume that whereas intentional subjects must have intentional states and perform associated actions in a way that satisfies rational unity—whether or not they are aware of doing so—persons must be capable of being held to that ideal; they must be such that they can be held responsible for failures to unify their intentional states and actions in a rational way (Rovane 1997; Pettit 2001, ch. 4). Rational unity is a constraint that intentional systems must be designed to fulfill, if only at subpersonal, unconscious levels. Rational unification is a project for which persons must be taken to assume responsibility, at least on a case-by-case basis.

The commitment that persons make to rational unification, according to this account, means that persons don't just possess intentional states and perform corresponding actions. They also avow those states and actions, acknowledging them as their own. And, avowing them, they hold themselves open to criticism in the event of not proving to live up to them: not proving to satisfy rational unity in their regard. Let a person avow a belief that p and a belief that if p then q, for example, and we can expect them to form and avow the belief that q. Or if they fail to do so, then we can expect them to have a justification or an excuse to offer. The justification may be that they had a change of mind in respect of "p" or "if p then q," the excuse that the conditions under which they were operating made it difficult to think straight.

The assumption that persons are marked off from ordinary intentional subjects—say, nonhuman animals—by the commitment to rational unification makes for a rich conception of personhood. But for that very reason it will hardly be contested in the present context, for the richness of the account should make it harder rather than easier to argue that integrations of people count as persons. In any case I say nothing more in its defense here. I shall take as persons those intentional agents who can avow their intentional states and the actions they perform in words—or in signs of some other sort—and who can then be held to the associated expectations. We may describe as persons those human beings who do not yet have this capacity, who no longer have it, or who do not have it at all.

But that usage is readily seen as an extension based on the fact that they are of a kind—that is, of a species—with creatures who are persons in that strict sense.

Assuming that persons are intentional agents who make and can be held to avowals, what are we to say of integrated groups? I have no hesitation in arguing that this means that they are institutional persons, not just institutional subjects or agents (Rovane 1997 argues a similar line). Integrated collectivities bind themselves to the discipline of reason at the collective level, and that means that they are open to criticism in the event of not achieving rational unity in relevant regards. They avow judgments, intentions, and actions and prove able to be held responsible for failures to achieve consistency and other such ideals in their associated performance. They are subjects that can be treated as properly conversable interlocutors (Pettit and Smith 1996).

Social integrates contrast in this respect with any groups that do not impose the discipline of reason at the collective level. Collectivities of this aggregate kind will not be answerable in the same way to words previously authorized or deeds previously performed. And that will be so, no matter how tight we make the mutual-awareness constraints on when they can be said to authorize words or perform deeds. It will always be possible for such an aggregate to vote in favor of a judgment or an intention or an action that is out of kilter with earlier commitments, and to do so without being exposed to legitimate criticism. Opinion poll research may tell us that the populace as a whole supports cutting taxes, increasing defense expenditure, and also increasing other expenditure. Since all the individuals involved may hold consistent views, that finding that will not give us reason to criticize the populace for holding such opinions, as we might criticize a political party for doing so. For even if it is taken as an intentional subject, the populace cannot be expected to police itself for the rational unity of the things it believes and then be held to that expectation. It does not constitute a person in the relevant sense and it contrasts in that regard with the political party.

Whenever we speak of persons we think it is appropriate to speak of selves. We expect that persons will think of themselves in the first person and be able to self-ascribe beliefs and desires and actions by the use of an indexical expression like "I" or "my," "me" or "mine." This association between being a person and thinking in self-ascriptive terms is borne out under the characterization of persons adopted here. If a person is to avow certain states and actions, and assume responsibility for achieving rational unity in their regard, then those states and actions are bound to have a distinctive salience in their experience. Individual subjects are bound to see them—by contrast with the states and actions of others—as matters of what *I* believe, what *I* desire, what *I* do, and so on (Pettit 2001, ch. 4).

Why must the personal point of view have this indexical, first-personal character? Why must I as a conversable subject be aware of myself in this indexical way, rather than just under a name, say as PP? A well-known line of argument provides the answer (Perry 1979; Burge 1998). Were I to conceive of myself under a name, as PP, then there would always be a deliberative gap between my thinking that PP believes both that p and that "p" entails "q" and my actually adjusting beliefs—say, in response to conversational challenge—by coming to believe that q or by giving up one of the other beliefs. For why should my beliefs about PP's beliefs have any reason-mediated effect on what I believe and assert, short of my believing that I am PP? And if I can think that I am PP, of course, then I do think of myself in the first person, not just under a name.

So far as integrated collectivities operate on the same lines as individual persons, they will also have this capacity to think in first-person terms. From the standpoint of those in an integrated collectivity the words defended in the past, for example, will stand out from any words emanating from elsewhere as words that bind and commit them. Specifically, they will stand out for those of us in the collectivity as words that "we" as a plural subject maintain. The argument in the singular case for why I as a person must conceive of my attitudes as matters of what I think applies in the plural case too, showing that we, the members of an integrated collectivity, must think of the group's attitudes as matters of what *we* think.

The members of a social integrate, S, will face the same deliberative gap as that which appeared in the singular case, if they conceive of the existing commitments of the group just as those that hold. Suppose that we in that group recognize both that p and that the truth of "p" entails the truth of "q." That will not lead us as a group to judge that q, unless we make the extra judgment that we are S. And if we do make that judgment then of course we do think of ourselves in the first person plural. As members of the integrated group, we are possessed of a personal point of view and it is marked out by this indexical usage.

The emphasis on the importance of "we" connects with the insistence by writers like Margaret Gilbert (1989), John Searle (1995), and Annette Baier (1997a) that there is no possibility of analyzing we-talk in I-talk, or indeed in impersonal talk of what named individuals do (see too Tuomela 1995, p.183). The obstacle to reducing talk of "we" to talk of "I" will be just the obstacle that stands in the way of reducing indexical talk of what I think and do to nonindexical talk of what PP thinks and does. As there is a personal perspective that is available only with talk of "I," so there is a personal perspective that becomes available only with talk of "we."

The autonomy of "we" talk that has to obtain under our account of what it is for a collectivity to be integrated nicely emphasizes the significance of the claim that such collectivities are personal as well as intentional agents. Not only do social integrates have a rational unity that constrains their performance over time and that makes them distinct from their own members. The rational unity they display is one that they themselves police and implement in the fashion of creatures whom we can hold responsible: creatures who count as persons (McGeer and Pettit 2001). They are rationally unifying as well as rationally unified subjects and the enterprise of unification in which they are involved forces them to think in the manner of a self. It makes it natural and indispensable for members to resort to a distinctively proprietary use of "we," "us," and "ours."

Once again, I should say, there is no ontological mystery in any of this: no suggestion of reality sundering into distinct realms, for example, indexical and non-indexical. If we fix the way the world is in impersonal, nonindexical terms, then we will have fixed all the indexical truths—in particular all the I-truths and all the we-truths—as well. Indexical truths supervene on nonindexical, because the same indexical sentences will be true at the same locations of utterance in impersonally indiscernible worlds (Jackson 1998; Pettit 2000). But this sort of fixing—this ontological reducibility—is quite consistent with the perspective of non-indexical talk failing to register things in the way required for singular conversability and indeed with the perspective of I-talk failing to register things in the way required for plural conversability. Such idioms may fail to be intertranslatable, and yet not direct us to independent realms of reality.

NATURAL AND INSTITUTIONAL PERSONS

The claim just defended is that social integrates have to be regarded as persons, on a par with individual human beings. But it is consistent, of course, with acknowledging that such institutional persons differ from natural persons in as many ways as they resemble them. As we saw earlier, institutional persons are not centers of perception or memory or sentience, or even of degrees of belief and desire. Institutional persons form their collective minds only on a restricted range of matters, to do with whatever purpose they are organized to advance. And institutional persons are artificial creatures whose responses may be governed by reason, not in the spontaneous manner that is characteristic of individual human beings, but only in a painstaking fashion. Their reasoning may be as tortuous as that of the impaired human being who has to work out reflectively, case by case, that in virtue of believing that p and that if p then q, he or she ought also believe that q. Integrated collectivities are persons in virtue of being conversable and responsible centers of judgment, intention, and action. But they are persons of a bloodless, bounded, and crudely robotic variety.

Even granted this, however, there are still important questions as to how institutional and natural persons relate to one another; in particular, how institutional persons and the members who constitute them relate to one an other. I address two such questions in this section.

First Question

The first is a more or less straightforward question as to the institutional profiles that members have to assume so far as they constitute a single collective person. Throughout this chapter I have been assuming that even if just one individual has to act on behalf of a collective, the members are all equal participants in the formation of the collective's judgments and intentions, having equal voting power with others. But this is unrealistic as an assumption about most real-world collectives, and the first question is how far membership is consistent with the absence of such voting power.

There are two ways in which individuals may be said to endorse a collective procedure or outcome. First, by actively voting in its favor; and second, by having a capacity for exit or contestation or something of the kind—this, as a matter of common awareness—but not exercising that power. Although active voting is the most obvious mode of endorsement, it must also be possible for people to endorse a collective pattern in the second, virtual mode. The members of a collectivity cannot vote on every procedure that they are to follow, on pain of infinite regress; the problem is akin to that which would be involved in trying to endorse as an explicit premise every principle of inference deployed in an argument (Carroll 1895). If regress is to be avoided, therefore, then some of the procedures followed by the members of a collectivity must be followed without the endorsement of an explicit vote and just on the basis that is how things are done among members, and done without contestation.

But if all the members of a group must endorse some procedures in a virtual way—that is, by not exercising a power of exit or contestation or whatever—then it is clearly possible that on many matters of procedure, and on many outcomes, some members will play an active voting part—they may even serve as plenipotentiaries for resolving various irrationalities (List and Pettit 2002a)—while others are involved only in that virtual manner. And this is how it is, obviously, with most integrated collectivities. Such collectivities sometimes involve all of their members in deliberation on every decision. But more often they stage their decisions so that the full assembly only votes on general matters, delegating others to smaller bodies and to officers of the group. Or they may involve a membership that is largely passive, with most being involved in official decisions only to the extent of needing to be pacified. Or they may be articulated into subunits that are each passive in relation to one another. And so on: the details need not concern us.

Second Question

The second question raised by our discussion bears on how natural and institutional persons relate to one another within the psychology of a given member. Suppose that someone is faced with a decision on which they as a natural person tend to go one way, while an institutional person of which they are a member—perhaps the relevant, executive member—would tend to go another. What is to happen in such a case? For all that we have said, it might be that the psychology of the individual is taken over, willy nilly, either by the natural person associated with it or by the institutional person. Or it might be that which person is to be present in that psychology is determined, at least ideally, by considerations that the two persons can debate— debate within the same head, as it were—and reach agreement on. Or it might be that the natural person is always primary and has the task of deciding whether to act in their own name—in their own interests, perhaps, or according to their own values—or in the name of the collective. The first model is clearly crazy, suggesting that persons take over psychologies in the way demons are said to assume possession of souls. But which of the other two models is the more plausible?

My own inclination is to go for the last alternative, giving priority to natural persons. I reject the picture according to which persons, natural and institutional, are of more or less the same standing and have equal presumptive claims in the sort of case envisaged on the resources of the member's psychology (Rovane 1997 supports this image). I hold that natural persons have an inescapable priority and that in this kind of case it will be up to the natural person to decide whether or not to cede place to the institutional, acting in furtherance of the collective goal and in neglect of his or her own priorities.

There are a couple of reasons why I hold by this image rather than the other. One is that it fits well with the intentional manner in which, as it seems, natural persons go about constituting and enacting institutional agents. Natural persons are in intentional control of whether they enter or exit most of the collectives to which they belong. And when they act on be-half of a collective they are reinforced in their identity as natural persons, and the intentional control they have as natural persons, by the way others relate to them; others call on Jones to do what the collective requires of them, others congratulate Jones for doing his or her bit, and so on.

Another reason for preferring my model is that there are cases where it is going to be quite misleading to think of two persons, one natural and the other institutional, debating within a single head as to who should be the one to prevail. That model may apply when the reasons that they take into account are agent-neutral considerations to do with what is for the best overall but it will be unrealistic where each person has an agent-relative reason—say, one to do with personal prospects or commitments or allegiances—for wanting to go their preferred way. When ordinary people diverge in that way, then reason runs out and they may have to compete in some nondeliberative manner—or toss a coin—to determine who wins. We cannot envisage a natural and an institutional person competing in that way within the same head.[4]

It is sometimes said that before we know what it is rational for a human being to do, we need to be told which identity that agent is enacting; in particular we need to be told whether they are acting in their own name or the name of a collectivity (Hurley 1989). Thus Elizabeth Anderson (2001, p. 30) defends "The Priority of Identity to Rational Principle: what principle of choice it is rational to act on depends on a prior determination of personal identity, of who one is." The line just taken suggests that this is not so. The natural person is the ultimate center of action and if it is rational for a human being to act in the name of a collectivity—that is, rational in the sense of maximizing relevant preferences—then it is rational in terms of the natural person's preferences.

CONCLUSION

In maintaining points of the kind defended in this chapter, we make contact with the tradition that the nineteenth-century German historian Otto von Gierke sought to track and to revitalize: the tradition of emphasizing the institutional personality of many groups and the significance of such personality for legal, political and social theory (Hager 1989; Runciman 1997; McLean 1999). This tradition is deeply organicist in its imagery and led adherents to speak for example of "the pulsation of a common purpose which surges, as it were, from above, into the mind and behaviour of members of any true group" (Gierke, Troeltsch, and Barker 1950, p. 61). But the organic, often overblown metaphors should not be allowed to discredit the tradition. The points they were designed to emphasize are perfectly sensible observations of the kind that our analysis of integrated groups supports.

I have argued elsewhere that consistently with being individualistic about the relation between human beings and the social regularities under which they operate—consistently with thinking that social regularities do not compromise individual agency—we may oppose the atomism that insists on the coherence of the solitary thinker; we may argue that individuals depend noncausally on one another for having the capacity to think (Pettit 1993). What we have seen in this chapter is that consistently with being individualistic we may also oppose the singularism that insists on the primacy of the isolated agent and claims that we can describe collectivities as persons only in a secondary sense.

Individualism insists on the supervenience claim that if we replicate how things are with and between individuals, then we will replicate all the social realities that obtain in their midst: there are no social properties or powers that will be left out (Macdonald and Pettit 1981; Currie 1984; Pettit 1993). But this insistence on the supervenience of the social in relation to the individual is quite consistent with emphasizing that the entities that individuals compose can assume a life of their own, deserving the attribution of discontinuous judgments and intentions and displaying all the qualities expected in personal agents.

The world of living organisms did not cease to be interesting when scientists dismissed the conceit of a *vis vitalis*. And neither should the world of social groups cease to be interesting just because we choose to exorcise the specter of a *vis socialis*. On the contrary, the recognition that the realm of collectivities is an artifact of human hands should excite the sociological, the political, and the historical imagination. The sociological, because we badly need general models of how collectivities can be created and sustained (Coleman 1974). The political, because we need to develop criteria for assessing the performance of collectivities and proposals for containing their power (Hager 1989). And the historical, because we have only the sketchiest understanding of how the most important collectivities in our lives emerged and stabilized as integrated agents (Skinner 1989).

ACKNOWLEDGMENTS

I was greatly helped in developing this chapter by conversations with John Ferejohn, Chandran Kukathas, Christian List, and Victoria McGeer. I am indebted to the discussion it received at a number of venues: the Summer Institute on "Social Ontology after *The Common Mind*," held in Erasmus University, Rotterdam, July 2000, where my commentators were Ron Mallon and Rafal Wierzschoslawski; and during seminars at Columbia and Yale. I am also grateful for a useful set of comments from Elizabeth Anderson and for discussions of the priority of identity principle with Akeel Bilgrami and Carol Rovane.

Notes

1 The structure involved is this:

1. there is a conclusion to be decided among the judges by reference to a conjunction of independent or separable premises—the conclusion will be endorsed if relevant premises are endorsed, and otherwise it will be rejected;
2. each judge forms a judgment on each of the premises and a corresponding judgment on the conclusion;
3. each of the premises is supported by a majority of judges but those majorities do not coincide with one another;
4. the intersection of those majorities will support the conclusion, and the others reject it, in view of 1.; and
5. the intersection of the majorities is not itself a majority; in our examples only one judge out of the three is in that intersection.

2 Let the views of certain individuals on a rationally connected set of issues be rationally satisfactory in the sense of being consistent, complete, and deductively closed. The impossibility theorem shows that any procedure whereby an equally satisfactory set of views may be derived from the individual views must fail in one

of the following regards. It must be incapable of working with some profiles of individual view. Or it must fail to treat some individual or some issue even-handedly: roughly, it must let some individual or individuals be treated as less important than another—at the limit, the other may be given the status of a dictator—or it must downgrade some issue in the sense of letting the collective view on that issue be determined, not by majority vote, by the collective views on other issues.

3   There are other ontological questions that I do not address here. One is the issue of whether a group at any time is constituted in some sense by the individuals involved or is identical with the fusion of those individuals. This parallels the familiar 192 *Philip Pettit* sort of question raised about whether a statue is constituted by the body of clay used in its manufacture or whether it is identical with that body of clay. Different positions may be taken on this question, consistently with the claims made in the text.

4   This line of thought might be blocked by a consequentialist argument to the effect that all such divergences have to be judged ultimately by reference to agentneutral considerations. But it would be strange to tie one's view of the relationship between natural and institutional persons to a consequentialist commitment. And in any case it is possible for consequentialists to argue that it is often best for people—best in agent-neutral terms—to think and even compete in agent-relative ways.

References

Anderson, Elizabeth. 2001. "Unstrapping the Straightjacket of 'Preference': A Comment on Amartya Sen's Contributions to Philosophy and Economics." *Economics and Philosophy* 17: 21–38.

Austin, John. 1875. *Lectures on Jurisprudence, or the Philosophy of Positive Law.* London: J. Murray.

Baier, Annette. 1997a. *The Commons of the Mind.* Chicago: Open Court.

Bratman, Michael. 1999a. *Faces of Intention: Selected Essays on Intention and Agency.* Cambridge: Cambridge University Press.

Burge, Tyler. 1998. "Reason and the First Person." In *Knowing Our Own Mind*, edited by Crispin Wright, Barry C. Smith, and Cynthia Macdonald. Oxford: Clarendon.

Campbell, Keith, John Bacon, and L. Reinhart, eds. 1992. *Ontology, Causality, and Mind: Essays on the Philosophy of David Armstrong.* Cambridge: Cambridge University Press.

Carroll, Lewis. 1895. "What the Tortoise Said to Achilles." *Mind* 4: 278–80.

Chapman, B. 1998. "More Easily Done Than Said: Rules, Reason, and Rational Social Choice." *Oxford Journal of Legal Studies* 18: 293–329.

Coleman, Jules. 1974. *Power and the Structure of Society.* New York: Norton.

Currie, G. 1984. "Individualism and Global Supervenience." *British Journal for the Philosophy of Science* 35: 345–58.

Dretske, Fred. 1988. *Explaining Behavior.* Cambridge: MIT Press.

French, Peter. 1984. Collective and Corporate Responsibility. New York: Columbia University Press.

Gierke, Otto von, Ernst Troeltsch, and Ernest Barker 1950. *Natural Law and the Theory of Society, 1500–1800.* Cambridge: Cambridge University Press.

Gilbert, Margaret. 1989. *On Social Facts.* London: Routledge. Reprinted 1992, Princeton, N.J.: Princeton University Press.

Judgment Aggregation

Hager, M.M. 1989. "Bodies Politic: The Progressive History of Organizational 'Real Entity' Theory." *University of Pittsburgh Law Review* 50: 575–654.

Hurley, S. 1989. *Natural Reasons*. New York: Oxford University Press.

Jackson, Frank. 1992. "Block's Challenge." In Campbell, Bacon, and Rhinehart (1992).

Jackson, Frank. 1998. *From Metaphysics to Ethics: A Defense of Conceptual Analysis*. Oxford: Oxford University Press.

Kornhauser, Lewis A. 1996. "Conceptions of Social Rule." In *Social Rules: Origin; Character; Logic; Change*, edited by David Braybrooke, Boulder, Colo: Westview.

Kornhauser, Lewis A. and L.G. Sager. 1993. "The One and The Many: Adjudication in Collegial Courts." *California Law Review* 81: 1–59.

List, Christian and Philip Pettit. 2002a. "Aggregating Sets of Judgements: Two Impossibility Results Compared." *Synthese* 140: 207–235.

List, Christian and Philip Pettit. 2002b. "Aggregating Sets of Judgements: An Impossibility Result." *Economics and Philosophy* 18: 89–110.

Macdonald, G. and P. Pettit. 1981. *Semantics and Social Science*. London: Routledge and Kegan Paul.

McGreer, Victoria and Philip Pettit. 2001. "The Self-Regulating Mind." *Language and Communication* 22: 281–99.

McLean, J. 1999. "Personality and Public Law Doctrine." *University of Toronto Law Journal* 49: 123–49.

Millikan, Ruth Garrett. 1984. *Language, Thought, and Other Biological Categories*. Cambridge, Mass.: MIT Press.

Papineau, Daivd. 1987. *Reality and Representation*. Oxford: Blackwell.

Perry, John. 1979. "The Essential Indexical." *Nous* 13: 3–21.

Pettit, Philip. 1993. *The Common Mind: An Essay on Psychology, Society and Politics*. Oxford: Oxford University Press.

Pettit, Philip. 2000. "A Sensible Perspectivism." In *Dealing with Diversity*, edited by M. Baghramian and A. Dunlop. London: Routledge.

Pettit, Philip. 2001. *A Theory of Freedom: From the Psychology to the Politics of Agency*. Cambridge: Polity.

Pettit, Philip and Michael Smith. 1996. "Freedom in Belief and Desire." *The Journal of Philosophy* 93: 429–49.

Quinton, Anthony. 1975–76. "Social Objects." *Proceedings of the Aristotelian Society* 75: 1–27.

Rovane, Carol. 1997. *The Bounds of Agency: An Essay on Revisionary Metaphysics*. Princeton, NJ: Princeton University Press.

Runciman, D. 1997. *Pluralism and the Personality of the State*. Cambridge: Cambridge University Press.

Searle, John. 1983. *Intentionality*. Cambridge: Cambridge University Press.

Searle, John. 1995. *The Construction of Social Reality*. New York: Free Press.

Skinner, Q. 1989. "The State." In *Political Innovation and Conceptual Change*, edited by T. Ball, J. Farr, and R. Hansen. Cambridge: Cambridge University Press.

Stoljar, S.J. 1973. *Groups and Entities: An Inquiry Into Corporate Theory*. Canberra: Australian National University Press.

Sunstein, Cass. 1999. *One Case at a Time*. Cambridge, Mass.: Harvard University Press.

Toumela, Raimo. 1995. *The Importance of Us: A Philosophical Study of Basic Social Notions*. Stanford: Stanford University Press.

V

SYSTEMS DESIGN

12

Thinking about Error in the Law

Larry Laudan

> We need hardly say that we have no wish to lessen the fairness
> of criminal trials. But it must be clear what fairness means in this
> connection. It means, or ought to mean, that the law should be
> such as will secure as far as possible that the result of the trial is
> the right one.
>
> —Criminal Law Revision Committee[1]

> Underlying the question of guilt or innocence is an objective
> truth: the defendant, in fact, did or did not commit the acts con-
> stituting the crime charged. From the time an accused is first
> suspected to the time the decision on guilt or innocence is made,
> our criminal justice system is designed to enable the trier of fact
> to discover the truth according to law.
>
> —Justice Lewis Powell[2]

A ROAD MAP

If we look closely at the criminal justice system in the United States (or
almost anywhere else for that matter), it soon becomes evident that there
are three distinct families of basic aims or values driving such systems.
One of these core aims is to find out the truth about a crime and thus
avoid false verdicts, what I will call the goal of *error reduction.* A second is
premised on the recognition that, however much one tries to avoid them,
errors will occur from time to time. This goal addresses the question of
which sort of error, a false acquittal or a false conviction, is more serious,
and thus more earnestly to be avoided. In short, the worry here is with
how the errors distribute themselves. Since virtually everyone agrees that
convicting an innocent person is a more costly mistake than acquitting a
guilty one, a whole body of doctrine and practices has grown up in the
common law about how to conduct trials so as to make it more likely that,

when an error does occur, it will be a false acquittal rather than a false conviction. For obvious reasons, I will say that this set of issues directs itself to the question of *error distribution*. The third set of values driving any legal system is a more miscellaneous grab bag of concerns that do not explicitly address trial error but focus instead on other issues important to the criminal justice system. At stake here are questions about the efficient use of resources, the protection of the rights of those accused of a crime, and various other social goods, such as the sanctity of marriage (spouses cannot be made to testify against one another) or preserving good relations with other nations (diplomats cannot generally be convicted of crimes, however inculpatory the evidence). I will call these *nonepistemic policy values*. Such concerns will figure here because, although not grounded in the truthseeking project, their implementation frequently conflicts with the search for the truth.

Judges and legal scholars have insisted repeatedly and emphatically that the most fundamental of these values is the first: that of finding out whether an alleged crime actually occurred and, if so, who committed it. The U.S. Supreme Court put the point concisely in 1966: "The basic purpose of a trial is the determination of the truth."[3] Without ascertaining the facts about a crime, it is impossible to achieve justice, since a just resolution crucially depends on correctly figuring out who did what to whom. Truth, while no guarantee of justice, is an essential precondition for it. Public legitimacy, as much as justice, demands accuracy in verdicts. A criminal justice system that was frequently seen to convict the innocent and to acquit the guilty would fail to win the respect of, and obedience from, those it governed. It thus seems fair to say that, whatever else it is, a criminal trial is first and foremost an *epistemic* engine, a tool for ferreting out the truth from what will often initially be a confusing array of clues and indicators. To say that we are committed to error reduction in trials is just another way of saying that we are earnest about seeking the truth. If that is so, then it is entirely fitting to ask whether the procedures and rules that govern a trial are genuinely truth-conducive.

The effort to answer that question constitutes what, in the subtitle of this book, I have called "legal epistemology." Applied epistemology in general is the study of whether systems of investigation that purport to be seeking the truth are well engineered to lead to true beliefs about the world. Theorists of knowledge, as epistemologists are sometimes known, routinely examine truthseeking practices like science and mathematics to find out whether they are capable of delivering the goods they seek.

Legal epistemology, by contrast, scarcely exists as a recognized area of inquiry. Despite the nearly universal acceptance of the premise that a criminal trial is a search for the truth about a crime, considerable uncertainty and confusion reign about whether the multiple rules of proof, evidence, and legal procedure that encumber a trial enhance or thwart the discovery of the truth. Worse, there has been precious little systematic study into the question of whether existing rules could be changed to enhance the likelihood that true verdicts would ensue. legal epistemology, properly conceived, involves both a) the *descriptive* project of determining which existing rules promote and which thwart truth seeking and b) the *normative* one of proposing changes in existing rules to eliminate or modify those rules that turn out to be serious obstacles to finding the truth.

The realization of a legal epistemology is made vastly more difficult because, as just noted, nonepistemic values are prominently in play as well as epistemic ones. In many but not all cases, these nonepistemic values clash with epistemic ones. Consider a vivid example. If we were serious about error reduction, and if we likewise recognized that juries sometimes reach wrong verdicts, then the obvious remedy would be to put in place a system of judicial review permitting appeals of both acquittals and convictions. We have the latter, of course, but not the former. *Every* erroneous acquittal eludes detection because it escapes review. The absence of a mechanism for appealing acquittals is patently not driven by a concern to find the truth; on the contrary, such an asymmetry guarantees far more errors than are necessary. The justification for disallowing appeal of acquittals hinges on a policy value. Double jeopardy, as it is known, guarantees that no citizen can be tried twice for the same crime. Permitting the appeal of an acquittal, with the possibility that the appeal would be reversed and a new trial ordered, runs afoul of the right not to be tried more than once. So, we reach a crossroads, seemingly faced with having to choose between reducing errors and respecting traditional rights of defendants. How might we think through the resolution of conflicts between values as basic as these two are? Need we assume that rights always trump the search for the truth, or vice versa? Or, is there some mechanism for accommodating both sorts of concerns? Such questions, too, must form a core part of the agenda of legal epistemology.

This book is a first stab at laying out such an agenda. In this chapter, I formulate as clearly as I can what it means to speak of legal errors. Absent a grasp of what those errors are, we obviously cannot begin to think about strategies for their reduction. In Chapters 2 through 4, we examine in detail a host of important questions about error distribution. Chapters 5 through 8 focus on existing rules of evidence and procedure that appear to pose serious obstacles to truth seeking. Those chapters include both critiques of existing rules and numerous suggestions for fixing such flaws as I can identify. The final chapter assays some possible solutions to the vexatious problems generated by the tensions between epistemic values and nonepistemic ones.

A BOOK AS THOUGHT EXPERIMENT

The two passages in the epigraph to this chapter from Supreme Court Justice Lewis Powell and England's Criminal Law Revision Committee articulate a fine and noble aspiration: finding out the truth about the guilt or innocence of those suspected of committing crimes. Yet, if read as a *description* of the current state of American justice, they remain more an aspiration than a reality. In saying this, I do not mean simply that injustices, false verdicts, occur from time to time. Occasional mistakes are inevitable, and thus tolerable, in any form of human inquiry. I mean, rather, that many of the rules and procedures regulating criminal trials in the United States – rules for the most part purportedly designed to aid the truth-finding process – are themselves the *cause* of many incorrect verdicts. I mean, too, that the standard of proof relevant to criminal cases, beyond reasonable doubt, is abysmally unclear to all those – jurors, judges, and attorneys – whose task is to see that those standards are honored. In the chapters that follow, I will show that the criminal justice system now in place in the United States is not a system that anyone concerned principally with finding the truth would have deliberately designed.[4]

A natural way to test that hypothesis would be to examine these rules, one by one, to single out those that thwart truth seeking. And, in the chapters to follow, I will be doing a fair share of precisely that. But, as we will discover, it is often harder than it might seem to figure out whether a given evidential practice or procedure is truth promoting or truth thwarting. In short, we need some guide lines or rules of thumb for deciding whether any given legal procedure furthers or hinders epistemic ends. Moreover, for purposes of analysis, we need to be able to leave temporarily to one side questions about the role of nonepistemic values in the administration of justice. We will have to act as if truth finding were the predominant concern in any criminal proceeding. In real life, of course, that is doubtful.

As I noted at the outset, criminal trials are driven by a host of extra-epistemic values, ranging from concerns about the rights of the defendant to questions of efficiency and timeliness. (Not for nothing do we insist that justice delayed is justice denied.) The prevailing tendency among legal writers is to consider all these values – epistemic and nonepistemic – as bundled together. This, I think, can produce nothing but confusion. Instead of the familiar form of analysis, which juggles all these values in midair at the same time, I am going to propose a thought experiment. I will suggest that we focus initially entirely on questions of truth seeking and error avoidance. I will try to figure out what sorts of rules of evidence and procedure we might put in place to meet those ends and will identify when existing rules fail to promote epistemic ends. Then, with that analysis in hand, we can turn to compare the current system of evidence rules and procedures with a system that is, as it were, epistemically optimal. When we note, as we will repeatedly, discrepancies between the kind of rules we would have if truth seeking were really the basic value and those rules we find actually in place, we will be able then to ask ourselves whether these epistemically shaky rules conduce to values other than truthseeking and, if they do, when and whether those other values should prevail over more epistemically robust ones. Although I ignore such values in the first stage of the analysis, I do not mean for a moment to suggest that they are unimportant or that they can be ignored in the *final* analysis. But if we are to get a handle on the core epistemic issues that are at stake in a criminal trial, it is best – at the outset – to set them to one side temporarily.

If it seems madcap to try to understand the legal system by ignoring what everyone concedes to be some of its key values, I remind you that this method of conceptual abstraction and oversimplification has proved its value in other areas of intellectual activity, despite the fact that every oversimplification is a falsification of the complexities of the real world. Consider what is perhaps the best-known example of the power of this way of proceeding: During the early days of what came to be known as the scientific revolution, Galileo set out to solve a conundrum that had troubled natural philosophers for almost two millennia, to wit, how heavy bodies fall. Everyone vaguely understood that the velocity of fall was the result of several factors. The shape of a body makes a difference: A flat piece of paper falls more slowly than one wadded into a ball. The medium through which a body is falling likewise makes a crucial difference: Heavy bodies fall much faster through air than they do through water or oil. Earlier theories of free fall had identified this resistance of the medium as the key causal factor in determining the velocity of fall. Galileo's strategy was to turn that natural assumption on its head. Let us, he reasoned, ignore the shapes of bodies *and* their weights *and* the properties of the media through which they fall – obvious facts all. Assume, he suggested, that the only relevant thing to know is how powerfully bodies are drawn to the earth by virtue of what we would now call the gravitational field in which they find themselves. By making this stark simplification of the situation, Galileo was able to develop the first coherent account of fall, still known to high school students as Galileo's Law. Having formulated a model of how bodies would fall if the resistance of the medium were negligible (which it is not) and the shape of the body were irrelevant (which it likewise is not), and the weight of a body were irrelevant (which it is), Galileo proceeded to reinsert these factors back into the story in order to explain real-world phenomena – something that would have been impossible had he not initially ignored these real-world constraints. The power of a model of this sort is not that it gets things right the first time around, but that, having established how things would go under limited and well-defined conditions, we can then introduce further complexities as necessary, without abandoning the core insights offered by the initial abstraction.

I have a similar thought experiment in mind for the law. Taking the Supreme Court at its word when it says that the principal function of a criminal trial is to find out the truth, I want to figure out how we might conduct criminal trials supposing that their *predominant* aim were to find out the truth about a crime. Where we find discrepancies between real-world criminal procedures and epistemically ideal ones (and they will be legion), we will need to ask ourselves whether the epistemic costs exacted by current real-world procedures are sufficiently outweighed by benefits of efficiency or the protection of defendant rights to justify the continuation of current practices.

Those will not be easy issues to resolve, involving as they do a weighing of values often considered incommensurable. But such questions cannot even be properly posed, let alone resolved, until we have become much clearer than we now are about which features of the current legal regime pose obstacles to truth seeking and which do not. Because current American jurisprudence tends to the view that rights almost invariably trump questions of finding out the truth (when those two concerns are in conflict), there has been far less discussion than is healthy about whether certain common legal practices – whether mandated by common law traditions or by the U.S. Constitution or devised as court-designed remedies for police abuses – are intrinsically truth thwarting.

My object in designing this thought experiment is to open up conceptual space for candidly discussing such questions without immediately butting up against the purported argument stopper: "but X is a right" or "X is required (or prohibited) by the Constitution." Just as Galileo insisted that he wouldn't talk about the resistance of the air until he had understood how bodies would fall absent resistance, I will try – until we have on the table a model of what a disinterested pursuit of the truth in criminal affairs would look like – to adhere to the view that the less said about rights, legal traditions, and constitutional law, the better.

I said that this thought experiment will involve figuring out how criminal trials could be conducted, supposing that true verdicts were the principal aim of such proceedings. This might suggest to the wary reader that I intend to lay out a full set of rules and procedures for conducting trials, starting from epistemic scratch, as it were. That is not quite the project I have in mind here, since it is clear that there is a multiplicity of different and divergent ways of searching for the truth, which (I hasten to add) is not the same thing as saying that there are multiple, divergent truths to be found. Consider one among many questions that might face us: If our aim is to maximize the likelihood of finding the truth, should we have trial by judge or trial by jury? I do not believe that there is a correct answer to that question since it is perfectly conceivable that we could design sets of procedures that would enable either a judge *or* a jury to reach verdicts that were true most of the time. English speakers have a fondness for trial by jury, whereas Roman law countries prefer trial by judge or by a mixed panel of judges and jurors. For my part, I can see no overwhelming epistemic rationale for a preference for one model over the other. If we Anglo-Saxons have any rational basis, besides familiarity, for preferring trial by jury, it has more to do with the political and social virtues of a trial by one's peers rather than with any hard evidence that juries' verdicts are more likely to be correct than judges' verdicts are.

To begin with, I intend to propose a series of guidelines that will tell us what we should look for in deciding whether any particular arrangement of rules of evidence and procedure is epistemically desirable. This way of proceeding does not directly generate a structure of rules and procedures for conducting trials. What it will do is tell us how to evaluate bits and pieces of any proposed structure with respect to their epistemic bona fides. It will set hurdles or standards for judging any acceptable rule of evidence or procedure. If you want an analogy, think of how the rules of proof in mathematics work. Those rules do not generally *generate* proofs by some sort of formal algorithm; bright mathematicians must do that for themselves. What the rules of proof do (except in very special circumstances) is enable mathematicians to figure out whether a purported proof is a real proof. In effect, what I will be suggesting is a set of *meta-rules* or meta-principles that will function as yardsticks for figuring out whether any given procedure or evidence-admitting or evidence-excluding practice does, in fact, further epistemic ends or whether it thwarts them.

What I am proposing, then, is, in part, a *meta-epistemology* of the criminal law, that is, a body of principles that will enable us to decide whether any given legal procedure or rule is likely to be truth-conducive and error reducing. The thought experiment I have been describing will involve submitting both real and hypothetical procedures to the scrutiny that these meta-principles can provide. When we discover rules currently in place that fail to serve epistemic ends, we will want to ask ourselves whether they cannot be replaced by rules more conducive to finding the truth and minimizing error. If we can find a more truth-conducive counterpart for truth-thwarting rules, we will then need to decide whether the values that the original rules serve (for instance, protecting certain rights of the accused) are sufficiently fundamental that they should be allowed to prevail over truth seeking.

If, as Justice Powell says in the epigraph, the system "is designed" to discover the truth, you might reasonably have expected that we already know a great deal about the relation of each of its component parts to that grand ambition. The harsh reality is that we know much less than we sometimes think we do. Many legal experts and appellate judges, as we will see on numerous occasions in later chapters, continue to act and write as if certain portions of the justice system that actually thwart truth seeking have an epistemic rationale. Still worse, some jurists and legal scholars attribute error-reducing power to rules and doctrines that, viewed dispassionately, produce abundant false verdicts in their own right. Like Powell, they pay lip service to the mantra that the central goal of the system is to get at the truth, all the while endorsing old rules, or putting in place new ones, that hobble the capacity of that system to generate correct verdicts. So long as jurists believe, as many now do, that certain judicial rules (for instance, the suppression of "coerced" confessions[5]) promote truth finding – when in fact they do the opposite – there can be nothing but confusion concerning when and if truth seeking is being furthered.

One important reason that we know so much less than we should is that the courts in particular, but also the justice system in general, tend to discourage the sort of empirical research that would enable us to settle such questions definitively. In philosophy, my biases lean in the direction of naturalism. That means that I believe that most philosophical issues ultimately hinge on finding out what the facts are. I believe, further, that our methods of inquiry must be constantly reviewed empirically to see whether they are achieving what we expect of them. In writing this book, I have been constantly frustrated by the paucity of empirical information that would allow us to reach clear conclusions about how well or badly our legal methods are working. Where there are reliable empirical studies with a bearing on the issues addressed here, I will make use of them. Unfortunately, given the dearth of hard evidence, the analysis in this book will fall back on armchair hunches about the likely effects of various rules and procedures far more often than I would have liked. My defense for doing so is simply that one must fight one's battles with the weapons that one has at hand.

I should stress, as well, that I approach these questions as a philosopher, looking at the law from the outside, rather than as an attorney, working within the system. Although I have thought seriously about these issues over several years, I cannot possibly bring to them the competences and sensibilities of a working trial lawyer.[6] What interests me about the law is the way in which it functions, or malfunctions, theoretically, as a system for finding truth and avoiding error. In this role, I am less concerned than a civil libertarian or defense attorney might be with the rights of the accused and more concerned with how effectively the criminal justice system produces true verdicts. The analysis offered in this book does not purport to tell juries and judges how to decide a case; such dreadful decisions must depend on the case's special circumstances and its nuances. Its aim, rather, is the more prophylactic one of pointing out some errors that these fact finders should avoid in the always difficult quest for a true and just verdict.

There will be readers who expect any avowedly philosophical treatment of the law to center on issues of morality and rights or on questions about the authority and essence of the law. Such are the themes that have dominated the philosophy of law in the last half-century. The most influential philosopher of law in the English-speaking world in the twentieth century, H. L. A. Hart, managed to write a lengthy, splendid book on the philosophy of law (*The Concept of Law*, 1961) that says virtually nothing about what I am calling legal epistemology. His eminent continental counterpart, Hans Kelsen, did virtually the same thing a generation earlier in his *Pure Theory of Law* (1934). Readers expecting a similar agenda from me will be sorely disappointed. To them in particular, I say this: If it is legitimate and fruitful for *moral* philosophers, such as Gerald Dworkin or

John Rawls, to focus on the law principally as an exercise in ethics and morality, while largely ignoring the importance of truth seeking in the law (which they famously do), it is surely just as appropriate to look at the law through the lenses of epistemology and the theory of knowledge. Although one is not apt to learn so by looking at the existing philosophical literature on the subject, it is indisputable that the aims of the law, particularly the criminal law, are tied to epistemic concerns at least as profoundly as they are to moral and political ones. This book is a deliberate shot across the bow of the juggernaut that supposes that all or most of the interesting philosophical puzzles about the law concern its moral foundations or the sources of its authority.

PRINCIPAL TYPES OF ERROR

In this initial chapter, I will to begin to lay out some of the analytic tools that we will need in order to grapple with some thorny problems in the theory and practice of the criminal law. As its title already makes clear, this book is largely about legal errors. Since treating the law as an exercise in epistemology inevitably means that we will be involved in diagnosing the causes of error, we need to be clear from the outset about what kinds of errors can occur in a criminal proceeding.

Since our concern will be with purely epistemic errors, I should say straight away that I am *not* using the term "error" as appellate courts are apt to use it. For them, an "error" occurs in a trial just in case some rule of evidence or procedure has been violated, misinterpreted, or misapplied. Thus, a higher court may determine that an error occurred when a trial judge permitted the introduction of evidence that the prevailing rules should have excluded or when some constitutional right of the defendant was violated. Courts will find that an error occurred if a judge, in his instructions to the jury about the law, made some serious mistake or other, in the sense of characterizing the relevant law in a way that higher courts find misleading or incorrect. Very occasionally, they will decide that an error occurred if the jury convicted someone when the case against the defendant failed to meet the standard of proof beyond a reasonable doubt.[7]

By contrast, I will be using the term "error" in a more strictly logical and epistemic sense. When I say that an error has occurred, I will mean either a) that, in a case that has reached the trial stage and gone to a verdict, the verdict is false, or b) that, in a case that does not progress that far, a guilty party has escaped trial or an innocent person has pleaded guilty and the courts have accepted that plea. In short, for the purposes of our discussion, *an error occurs when an innocent person is deemed guilty or when a guilty person fails to be found guilty*. For obvious reasons, I will call the first sort of error a *false inculpatory finding* and the second a *false exculpatory finding*.

There are two important points to note about the way in which I am defining legal errors:

First, errors, in my sense, have nothing to do with whether the system followed the rules (the sense of "error" relevant for appellate courts) and everything to do with whether judicial outcomes convict the guilty and free the innocent. Even if no errors of the procedural sort that worries appellate courts have occurred, an outcome may be erroneous if it ends up freeing the guilty or convicting the innocent. The fact that a trial has scrupulously followed the letter of the current rules governing the admissibility of evidence and procedures – and thus avoids being slapped down by appellate courts for breaking the rules – is no guarantee of a correct outcome. To the contrary, given that many of the current rules (as we will see in detail in later chapters) are actually *conducive* to mistaken verdicts, it may well happen that trials that follow the rules are more apt to produce erroneous verdicts than trials that break some of them. Accordingly, our judgment that an error has occurred in a criminal case will have nothing to do with whether the judicial system followed its own rules and everything to do with whether the truly guilty and the truly innocent were correctly identified.

Second, standard discussions of error in the law – even from those authors who, like me, emphasize truth and falsity rather than rule following or rule breaking – tend to define errors only for those cases that reach trial and issue in a verdict. Such authors, naturally enough, distinguish between true and false verdicts. That is surely a legitimate, and an important, distinction, but it is neither the most general nor the most useful way of distinguishing errors. As my definition of "error" has already indicated, I claim that errors occur whenever the innocent are condemned by the system and whenever the guilty fail to be condemned. Obviously, one way in which these mistakes can happen is with a false conviction or a false acquittal. But what are we to say of the guilty person who has been arrested and charged with a crime that he truly committed but against whom charges were subsequently dropped by the prosecutor or dismissed by the judge? These are mistakes just as surely as a false acquittal is. Likewise, if an innocent person – faced with a powerfully inculpatory case – decides to accept a plea bargain and plead guilty, this is an error of the system just as much as a false conviction is, even though the case against the accused is never heard and a jury never renders a verdict.

Clearly, this analysis rests on being able to speak about the truly guilty and the truly innocent. Much nonsense has been creeping of late into several discussions, both popular and academic, of the law. For instance, one often hears it said (in a gross misconstrual of the famous principle of the presumption of innocence) that the accused "*is* innocent until proven guilty," as if the pronouncing of the verdict somehow created the facts of the crime. If it were correct that only a guilty verdict or guilty plea could render someone guilty, then there could be no false acquittals, for it would make no sense to say, as the phrase "false acquittal" implies, that a jury

acquitted someone who is actually guilty. Since such locutions make perfect sense, we must reject the notion that a verdict somehow *creates* guilt
and innocence.

A second obstacle to talking clearheadedly about guilt and innocence
arises from the novel but fashionable tendency to suppose that whether
someone is guilty or innocent of a crime simply depends on whether the
evidence offered at trial is sufficient to persuade a rational person that
the defendant is guilty. The confusion here is more subtle than the former
one. It is rooted in the obvious fact that the decision about guilt or innocence made by a reasonable trier of fact will necessarily depend on what
he or she comes to learn about the alleged crime. On this view, a verdict
is correct so long as it squares with the evidence presented at trial, without making reference to anything that happened in the real world outside
the courtroom. One legal scholar, Henry Chambers, has claimed that
"what is true is what the [trial] evidence indicates is true."[8] Contrary to
Chambers, I claim that nothing that a judge or jury later determines to be
the case changes any facts about the crime. Likewise, I claim that, while
what is presented in evidence surely shapes the jury's verdict, that
evidence does not define what is true and false about the crime. Unless
this were so, it would again make no sense to talk of a true or a false verdict, so long as that verdict represented a reasonable inference from the
evidence. Yet, sometimes we come to the conclusion that the evidence
presented at trial was deeply unrepresentative of the true facts of the
crime. Sometimes, truly innocent people are wrongly convicted and truly
guilty people are wrongly acquitted, even though the jury drew the
conclusions that were appropriate from the evidence available to them.
(Basically, Chambers confuses what I will be calling the *validity* of a verdict with its truth.)

I will be adamant in insisting that the presumption of innocence, properly understood, does not make a guilty person innocent nor an acquittal
of such a person into a nonerror. Likewise, I will argue that verdicts don't
make the facts and neither does the evidence presented at trial; they only
give official sanction to a particular hypothesis about those facts. Strictly
speaking, the only people innocent are those who did not commit the
crime, whatever a jury may conclude about their guilt and regardless of
what the available evidence seems to show. Likewise, the truly guilty
(those who committed the crime) are guilty even if a jury rationally
acquits them. "Being found guilty" and "being guilty" are manifestly not
the same thing; neither are "being presumed innocent" and "being innocent." The naive argument to the effect that what we *mean* when we say
that Jones committed the crime is that a jury would find him guilty utterly
confuses questions about what is really the case with questions about
judgments issued in the idiosyncratic circumstances that we call criminal
trials. There are false acquittals and false convictions, and the existence of
each entails that verdicts are not analytically true or self-authenticating.
Because they are not, we can speak of verdicts as being erroneous, even

when they result from trials that were scrupulously fair, in the sense of being in strict compliance with the rules governing such proceedings. By the same token, we can speak of outcomes or verdicts being true, even when they resulted from trials that made a mockery of the existing rules.

For future reference, it will prove useful to make explicit the moral of this discussion. In brief, it is legitimate, and in some contexts essential, to distinguish between the assertion that "Jones is guilty," in the sense that he committed the crime, and the assertion that "Jones is guilty," in the sense that the legal system has condemned him. I propose to call the first sense *material guilt* (hereinafter, guilt$_m$) and the second *probatory guilt* (guilt$_p$). Clearly, guilt$_m$ does not imply guilt$_p$, nor vice versa.

Similarly, we can distinguish between Jones's *material innocence* (innocence$_m$), meaning he did not commit the crime, and his *probatory innocence* (innocence$_p$), meaning he was acquitted or otherwise released from judicial scrutiny. Again, neither judgment implies the other. With these four simple distinctions in hand, we can combine them in various useful ways. For instance, Jones can be guilty$_m$ but innocent$_p$; again, he can be innocent$_m$ but guilty$_p$. Either of these situations would represent an error by the system.

OTHER RELEVANT DISTINCTIONS AMONG ERROR TYPES

The most basic distinction we need has already been mentioned: that between false inculpatory and false exculpatory findings. These two types of findings are just what one would expect: A false exculpatory finding occurs when the legal system fails to convict a truly guilty felon. A false inculpatory finding is a conviction of an innocent person.

Still, we need to add a couple of other important distinctions to the tool kit of error types. One involves separating valid from invalid verdicts. A verdict of guilty will be valid, as I propose to use that term, provided that the evidence presented at trial establishes, to the relevant standard of proof, that the accused person committed the crime in question. Otherwise, a guilty verdict is invalid. Naturally enough, an acquittal will be valid as long as the conditions for a valid conviction are not satisfied and invalid otherwise. The notion of validity aims to capture something important about the quality of the inferences made by the trier of fact, whether judge or jury. Invalid verdicts can occur in one or both of two ways: a) The trier of fact may give more or less weight to an item of evidence than it genuinely merits, or b) she may misconceive the height of the standard of proof. In either case, the verdict is inferentially flawed.

It is crucial to see that the valid/invalid distinction does *not* map neatly onto the true/false verdict dichotomy. We settle the truth of a verdict (or what I am calling a finding) by comparing it with the facts. That is, Jones's conviction is true just in case Jones committed the crime. By contrast, we

[margin annotation: in the sense of "legitimate" inference not equally valid]

settle the validity of a verdict by comparing it with the evidence presented at trial, asking whether that evidence meets the applicable standard of proof. Just as a deductive inference can be valid even when its conclusion is false (all horses can fly; all stallions are horses; therefore, all stallions can fly), so a verdict can be simultaneously valid and false. Using the terminology of the previous section, it can be a valid verdict that Jones is guilty$_p$, even while it is true that Jones is innocent$_m$. By the same token, a verdict of not guilty may be valid even if Jones is guilty$_m$.

Happily, it sometimes turns out that true verdicts are likewise valid ones and that false verdicts are invalid. But neither of these connections is solid. Sometimes, perhaps often, a jury will produce a valid verdict that is false, that is to say, a verdict that reflects an appropriate inference from the evidence presented at trial but that is factually false. This can occur when the evidence admitted at trial, skewed for whatever reasons, invites a conclusion at odds with what actually happened. But even when the evidence is not skewed or unrepresentative of the crime, there is still plenty of scope for a verdict that is valid but not true. Indeed, the standard of proof guarantees as much. Suppose, for the sake of argument, that the standard of proof is something like 95 percent confidence in guilt. A jury hears a case and concludes that it is 80 percent likely that the accused committed the crime. Now, the jury, if it acquits, will be producing a valid verdict, for the rules of proof demand acquittal even when the likelihood of guilt is as high as 80 percent. But that valid verdict is likely to be a false acquittal since, by hypothesis, the likelihood that the defendant committed the crime is quite high.

Likewise, it is easy to conceive how a jury might produce an invalid verdict that was nonetheless true, although these are apt to be less frequent than cases of valid verdicts that are false. What one hopes to achieve, obviously, is a verdict that is both true and valid. We want jurors to convict and acquit the right people and to do so for the right reasons. Both lack of truth and lack of validity will, as I am using the term "error," represent serious errors of the system, even though they point to quite different ways in which the system has failed. In our efforts to identify the principal sources of error in the legal system, we will be examining rules of evidence and procedure with a view to asking how such rules threaten either the truth *or* the validity of verdicts.

If the outcome of a criminal proceeding is erroneous in either of these respects – that is to say, if it is either false or invalid (or both) – the system has failed. If one or the other or both types of failure happen frequently, it may be time to change those parts of the system responsible for such errors. In later chapters, we will see that certain practices entrenched in our rules of evidence and procedure tend to produce invalid convictions and acquittals, that is to say, verdicts at odds with what a reasonable person – not bound by those rules – would conclude from the evidence available. Other features of the system, by restricting what can count as legal evidence, tend to produce verdicts that, even if valid, are false. The true/false and valid/invalid distinctions reflect the two primary ways in which a trial verdict may go awry: an inadequate (in the sense of unrepresentative) evidence base or faulty inferences from that base.

There is a third dichotomy that will prove helpful in thinking about sources of error. It distinguishes those erroneous decisions that are *reversible* from those that are *irreversible*. For instance, when Schwartz is convicted of a crime, he can appeal the verdict and may persuade a higher court to set that verdict aside. Epistemically, such a review mechanism is invaluable as a way of increasing the likelihood that the final result is correct. By contrast, if Schwartz is acquitted, the verdict cannot be appealed, however flawed may have been the reasoning that led the jury to acquit. Other things being equal, irreversible decisions are more troubling sources of error than reversible ones for the obvious reason that there is no machinery for catching and correcting the former while the latter can, in principle, be discovered and rectified. In due course, we will inquire into the rationale for creating a category of decisions, including verdicts themselves, that is wholly immunized from further review and correction.

Thus far, our focus on error has been principally with the *terminal* stage, that is, with erroneous verdicts. But many criminal investigations never get as far as this. Sometimes, police investigations simply run out of steam because of lack of clues or bad investigative practices. Although these are errors just as surely as a false acquittal is, they will not be our focus. What will command our attention are those felons who slip through the system, not for lack of incriminating clues known to the police, but who escape trial because of the ways in which the rules of evidence and procedure impede further pursuit of the case against them. These errors will be as revealing a topic of study as false verdicts are.

We need to remind ourselves that a vast number of criminal investigations (probably the overwhelming majority of police inquiries) never reach the trial stage because, although the police have identified a suspect to their own satisfaction, someone or other in authority concludes that the case against him is too weak to take to trial. It may be the police themselves who make this determination or it may be the prosecutor. It can be a grand jury that issues a "no bill," precluding trial. Or it may be an arraigning judge who dismisses the case. At each of these stages, where a decision must be made whether to proceed along the route to trial or not, the participants are bound by an elaborate body of rules of evidence and procedure. Prosecutors who have in hand a confession know that it may be tossed out if there are doubts about its provenance. Similar questions may arise about much of the other evidence seized by police. Even when prosecutors have powerful evidence of a suspect's guilt, their decision to proceed to trial must be informed by a calculation on their part as to which parts of the evidence they now have in hand will actually be allowed to go before a jury. If there are rules of admissibility that exclude relevant evidence (and much of this book will address itself to rules of precisely this sort), then those rules will exert a weighty influence not only during the trial itself but on all the preliminary decisions about whether to proceed to trial. Even if we leave aside problems generated by the rules of evidence, the standard of proof likewise works to ensure that many parties who are probably guilty never go to trial. Specifically, prosecutors may believe that the evidence against a suspect strongly suggests that he is guilty but that such evidence would probably be insufficient to persuade a jury of his guilt beyond a reasonable doubt. Short on both financial and human resources, prosecutors are unlikely to proceed with such a case. Judge Richard Posner has put the point succinctly:

> Tight [prosecutorial] screening implies that some, perhaps many, guilty people are not prosecuted and that most people who are prosecuted and acquitted are actually guilty.[9]

It puts the importance of this class of problems into vivid perspective if we remind ourselves that there are far more dismissals than acquittals in the criminal justice system. In federal courts in 1999, for instance, there were about eight judge-ordered dismissals for every acquittal.[10] Those writers who focus on the problem of error as if it principally arose in the process of a jury trial itself ignore such numbers at their peril.

This is another way of saying that every year hundreds of thousands of suspects are de facto "acquitted" by prosecutors, judges, and grand juries – without ever going to trial. That is as it should be, since many suspects are surely innocent. Dismissal of charges against an innocent person is not a failure of the system but a success. A failure occurs, in this context, when a *guilty* suspect has the case against him dropped prior to trial because relevant evidence of his guilt, although in hand, is thought likely not to be admissible if trial were to ensue. Of the three hundred thousand persons suspected of felonies each year – against whom charges are dropped or dismissed before trial – there is every reason to suspect that a certain proportion of these people are guilty. How large that proportion of failures is cannot be ascertained with confidence since the relevant data are inaccessible; instead, our analysis in this book will attempt to determine weak points in the system that *may* make such false, pretrial "acquittals" much more common than they need be.

A different, more diachronic, way of thinking about the various ways in which failures can occur emerges from imagining a series of filters that mediate between the crime, at the one extreme, and the jury's verdict, at the other. There is, to begin with, the crime itself. Jones, let us suppose, mugged Smith and stole his wallet. That event is now past. What survive are traces or remnants of the crime. These include memories of the participants and eyewitnesses and physical evidence of the crime (Jones's fingerprints on Smith's wallet, contusions on Jones's face, and so on). The police will come to find some, but rarely all, of these traces. If they and the prosecutor decide that they have a solid case against Jones, they will next have to persuade a judge or a grand jury that the case is strong enough to go forward. Supposing that all these hurdles have been leapt, the prosecutor will now choose from among the traces known to the police a subset that he intends to enter as evidence at the trial. Jones's attorney will make a similar decision. At Jones's pretrial evidentiary hearing, a judge will decide which of these submitted traces can be revealed to the jury. Once the evidence questions are settled, the judge may wrongly decide to dismiss the charges against the accused. Once the trial begins, if it gets that far, the now heavily filtered evidence will be presented and subjected to cross-examination. Once both sides have had their say, the judge will instruct the jury about the relevant law that Jones is alleged to have broken and on the threshold of proof that they should use in deciding whether to convict Jones.

There is, obviously, ample scope for error at each of these stages. Important evidence, either inculpatory or exculpatory, may elude the best efforts of prosecution and defense to find it. The prosecution may find exculpatory evidence but suppress it, and the defense may be aware of inculpatory evidence that it "forgets" to mention. The judge's rulings on the admissibility of evidence submitted for trial may end up including evidence that is likely to mislead the jury or excluding evidence that the jury should hear. The grand jury may err in their decision to indict. The defendant may refuse to testify or subpoenaed witnesses with important information may disappear. Witnesses with relevant evidence might not be called because both prosecution and defense fear that their testimony would undermine their respective cases. The judge may misinstruct the jury with respect to the relevant law or botch the instructions about the standard of proof – which occurs more often than you might imagine. (For details, see the next chapter.) Even if all else goes properly, the jury may draw inappropriate inferences about guilt or innocence from the evidence before them or they may misunderstand the level of proof required for a conviction. Even once the verdict is pronounced, the room for error has not disappeared. If the jury voted to convict, the accused may file an appeal. Appellate courts may refuse to hear it, even when the defendant is innocent. Or, they may take the appeal but reverse it when the verdict is sound or endorse the verdict when it is false. If the defendant is acquitted, double jeopardy precludes further appeal, even if the trial was riddled with acquittal-enhancing errors.

Eliminating all these possible sources of error (and I have mentioned only the more obvious) is clearly impossible. The aim of the justice system, realistically construed, should be to attempt to reduce them as far as possible. Current evidential practice in the criminal law, as we will see, often fails to do that. Worse, it frequently increases the likelihood of error deliberately by adopting rules and procedures that prevent the jury from learning highly important things about the crime.

RELEVANCE VERSUS ADMISSIBILITY

The charge that I have just made can be put in slightly more technical terms, and it will probably be useful to do so. In all reasoning about human affairs (and other contingent events), there are two key concepts regarding evidence that must be grasped. One is called *credibility* or sometimes (as in the law) *reliability*. As the term suggests, a piece of evidence or testimony is credible when there is reason to believe it to be true or at least plausible. The other pertinent concept is known, in both the law and in common sense, as evidential *relevance*. The core idea is that a piece of information is relevant to the evaluation of a hypothesis just in case, if credible, it makes that hypothesis more or less probable than it was before. If a certain bit of information, even when credible, would not alter our confidence in a hypothesis one way or the other, we deem it irrelevant to that hypothesis. In the criminal law, there are always two key hypotheses in play: a) A crime was committed and b) the defendant committed it. Any testimony or physical evidence that would make a reasonable person either more inclined or less inclined to accept either of these hypotheses is relevant. Everything else is irrelevant.

Both credibility and relevance are crucial to qualify something as germane evidence. Jurors, above all others, must assess both the credibility and the relevance of the evidence they see and hear. For reasons having roots very deep in the common law, however, the judge in a criminal trial is generally not supposed to let judgments of credibility enter into his or her decision about the acceptability of proffered evidence. This is because the jury, rather than the judge, is by tradition charged with determining the "facts" of the case. Deciding whether eyewitness testimony or physical evidence is credible would, in effect, imply a decision about its facticity. Since that is the province of the jury rather than the judge, the usual pattern is for judges to rule on relevance but not on reliability. This means that when judges make decisions about relevance, they are obliged to think hypothetically; that is, they must ask themselves, "if this evidence *were* credible, would it have a bearing on the case?" This is why, when a judge admits evidence as relevant, nothing is implied with respect to its credibility. (A significant exception to this principle occurs in decisions about the admission of expert testimony, where the judge is specifically charged to determine whether the basis for the testimony of the avowed expert is "reliable."[11])

American courts at every level of jurisdiction accept this notion of relevance. One of the important and legitimate gate-keeping functions of a judge is to see to it that the jury hears all and only relevant evidence. If American judges stuck resolutely to this principle, they could not be faulted on epistemic grounds since virtually all forms of sophisticated hypothesis evaluation (in science, medicine, and technology, for instance) work with this same notion of relevance.

Unfortunately, however, legal texts and the practices of courts routinely flout the relevance-only principle. This is because judges have a second criterion they use, alongside the demand for relevant evidence. It is often known as the admissibility requirement. To be admissible, evidence must not only be relevant; it must also meet a variety of other demands. For instance, the evidence cannot have been acquired by a violation of the rights of the accused. The evidence cannot arise from privileged relations that the accused has had with various professionals or his spouse. The evidence generally cannot have been obtained illegally, even if its being seized violated none of the rights of the accused. The evidence cannot be such that it might inflame the passions of the jurors or unfairly cast the defendant in an unfavorable light. The evidence cannot inform the jury that the defendant withdrew a confession of guilt, nor can it refer to admissions of guilt made by the defendant during negotiations about copping a plea. The evidence generally cannot come from a witness whose testimony would be self-incriminating. The jury cannot be informed when key witnesses escaped giving testimony by claiming their Fifth Amendment rights. The jury cannot be told whether the accused cooperated with the police in their inquiries. If the accused does not offer testimony on his own behalf, the judge explicitly instructs the jury to ignore that relevant fact, rather than supposing that the accused may have something to hide.

Virtually no one disputes that information of all these sorts is relevant in the technical sense, for it indubitably bears on the probability of the hypothesis that the defendant is guilty. In most jurisdictions, however, these and many other examples of admittedly relevant evidence will not be admitted during the trial. Subsequent chapters will describe many of these exclusionary principles in detail. What we should note here is that *every* rule that leads to the exclusion of *relevant* evidence is epistemically suspect.[12]

It is universally agreed, outside the law courts, that decision makers can make the best and most informed decisions only if they are made aware of as much relevant evidence as possible. Excluding relevant but nonredundant evidence, for whatever reasons, decreases the likelihood that rational decision makers will reach a correct conclusion. Accordingly, we will want to examine these exclusionary principles carefully to see whether the damage they inflict on our truthseeking interests are suitably balanced by gains of other sorts.

The Case of "Unfairly Prejudicial" Evidence

It might be instructive to include here one example of this distinction between relevance and admissibility in order to put some flesh on the skeleton of abstractions with which we have been working. A paradigmatic example of the problems we will be facing throughout the rest of the book is provided by the law's unimpressive efforts to distinguish between evidence that is "unfairly prejudicial" and evidence that is not.

At the preliminary hearing preceding a trial, both sides describe the evidence they intend to present at trial and argue about its admissibility. Despite the rule to the effect that the judge should generally admit relevant evidence, the law gives her enormous discretion to exclude evidence, however relevant and however inculpatory, if in her judgment that evidence is of such a sensational or inflammatory nature that ordinary jurors would be unable to assign it its true weight. Specifically, the judge is supposed to conduct a balancing test that ultimately comes down to this question: Is the probative power of this evidence sufficient to offset its prejudicial effects in warping the judgment of jurors? If the answer to that question is affirmative, it should be admitted; otherwise, by law it is to be excluded. To be precise, federal evidence law says:

> Although relevant, evidence may be excluded if its probative value is substantially outweighed by the danger of unfair prejudice, confusion of the issues, or misleading the jury, or by considerations of undue delay, waste of time, or needless presentation of cumulative evidence.[13]

Key here is the notion of "unfair prejudice." There are a great many things that courts have held to be apt to prejudice a jury unfairly. They include evidence that the defendant has a bad or violent character, especially vivid and gruesome depictions of the crime, and evidence of the defendant's association with causes or persons likely to evoke hostility or antipathy from jurors. The same doctrine has been used to justify excluding the confession of a nontestifying codefendant that mentions the defendant's participation in a crime,[14] graphic photos of the corpse of a homicide victim,[15] and samples of bloodstained clothing of the victim of an assault.[16]

The problem, of course, is that information of this kind is often powerful evidence of the defendant's guilt. Excluding it can weaken the case against the defendant substantially while, if it is really prejudicial, admitting it makes it more likely that jurors may make their decision on purely visceral grounds. Put in slightly more technical language, the judge is required to make a ruling about evidence that, if admitted, may lead to a false conviction while, if suppressed, may lead to a false acquittal. As we have seen, the judge is supposed to balance these two concerns against one another and decide about admissibility accordingly.

It may help to describe the problem a little more abstractly. In cases of this sort, the judge is called on to decide which of two quantities is greater: the probability of inferential error by the jury if the contested evidence is admitted (which I shall symbolize as "prob [error with e]") versus the probability of inferential error if the contested evidence is excluded (prob [error excluding e]). The first sort of error represents a potential false conviction; the second, a potential false acquittal. In making her decision about admitting or excluding e, the judge must perform an incredibly difficult task: She must decide on the relative likelihood of the two errors that may arise – that is, she must assign rough-and-ready values to prob (error with e) and to prob (error excluding e).

It seems doubtful whether this decision can be made objectively. To decide on the values of prob (error with e) and prob (error excluding e), a judge needs much more data than we currently have in hand about the likelihood that particular pieces of evidence (such as vivid, gory photos of

the crime scene) will distort a jury's ability to give such evidence its legitimate weight. Well-designed empirical studies on the prejudicial effects of
various sorts of evidence are extremely scarce. Even worse, collecting such
information would be inherently difficult since researchers would have to
be able to distinguish the emotional impact of a bit of evidence from its
rational probative weight. No one has proposed a design for an empirical
test subtle enough to make that distinction.

I do not mean to convey the impression that this decision about admitting relevant but potentially inflammatory evidence is always insoluble.
Sometimes, the problem admits of an easy solution. For instance, the
prosecution may have other types of evidence, apparently less unfairly
prejudicial, that will permit the state to make its point, in which case the
exclusion is no big deal (since the prejudicial evidence here is clearly
redundant, and redundancy is always a legitimate ground for exclusion).
But what is a judge to do when a *principal* part of the prosecution's case
involves evidence that, while highly inculpatory, may also appear "unfairly
prejudicial" and where no other evidence will do?

Consider a hypothetical example: Smith is charged with being a member of a gang that entered a busy restaurant at midday, tossing grenades,
firing weapons, and generally creating mayhem. By chance, one patron of
the restaurant took photographs during the assault, before he was himself
gunned down. One photo in particular is at issue. It shows Smith lobbing
a grenade into one corner of the restaurant and also shows, in vivid color,
mangled body parts and blood galore and is generally a horribly graphic
depiction of the crime scene. The photo obviously passes the relevancy
test. It apparently depicts the accused committing the crime with which
he is charged. It is not merely relevant but highly relevant. If we suppose
that no witnesses survived the mayhem, it is uniquely powerful in placing
Smith at the center of things.

Unfortunately, however, the judge also considers the photograph to be
so vivid and awful that it invites a purely visceral reaction from the jurors.
Seeing blood and gore depicted in this manner may, she fears, incline the
jurors to rush to judgment rather than considering objectively the other
evidence in the case, some of which may be exculpatory. Without the
photo, the jury may well acquit Smith since there were no eyewitnesses.
With the photo, reckons the judge, they will surely convict. Should the
judge admit the photograph into evidence? Currently, that decision is left
entirely up to her, with precious little assistance from the law. The guiding
legal principle, as we have seen, is that the evidence should be excluded if
it is more "unfairly prejudicial" than it is probative. Curiously, the law of
evidence includes no canonical definition of when a sample of evidence is
"*unfairly* prejudicial," apart from this gem of unclarity in Rule 403: "'Unfair
prejudice' within its context means an undue tendency to suggest decision
on an improper basis, commonly, though not necessarily, an emotional
one." Like pornography, unfair prejudice seems to be the sort of thing
that, while it eludes definition, one can recognize when one sees it. But

this won't do. As Victor Gold has noted: "Absent a coherent theory of unfair prejudice, trial courts cannot meaningfully evaluate evidence on or off the record for the presence of unfair prejudice, nor can they conduct the required balancing test."[17] How, in such circumstances, is a judge supposed to do this "balancing" to decide whether "its probative value is substantially outweighed by the danger of unfair prejudice"?

One might argue that this particular rule of evidence is not really so offensive epistemologically since in practice it should lead only to the exclusion of inflammatory evidence that is relatively nonprobative. After all, the rule itself seems to concede that, if the evidence is of very high probative value, it could be excluded only in those circumstances where its unfairly prejudicial character was even greater than its probativeness. But there are plenty of actual cases that give one some pause as to how often the weight of highly relevant evidence really is allowed to trump its being even mildly prejudicial.

Consider two real examples of the kind of balancing that goes on when trial and appellate judges try to assess unfair prejudice. In a 1994 case in south Texas, Ramón Garcia was accused of burgling Charles Webster's house. Garcia was seen in the house at the time of the burglary by a police officer who had been called to the scene by a neighbor. Taking flight, Garcia was subsequently caught. Police found no contraband on Garcia himself when he was apprehended, but several items stolen from Webster were found on the ground near the site of his arrest. By way of showing intent to commit burglary, the prosecutor introduced evidence that Garcia had arrived at the scene of the crime on a bicycle that he had stolen from a neighboring house two days earlier. The boy whose bicycle was stolen by Garcia testified that he was its owner. Garcia was convicted. His attorney appealed, arguing that the evidence of the stolen bicycle unfairly prejudiced the jury against his client. The appellate court, siding with Garcia, did not deny that the evidence of the stolen bicycle was relevant to the question of whether Garcia intended to rob the Websters but held that its relevance was outweighed by its unfairly prejudicial nature, "particularly so when the State chose to offer the evidence through the child rather than his parents."[18]

The logic of the appellate ruling is a bit tortuous, but here is what seems to be going on: Besides conceding the relevance of the fact that the defendant arrived at the scene of a burglary on a stolen bicycle to the question of Garcia's intention to rob the Websters, the superior court even seems to grant that evidence concerning the theft of the bicycle might not have been unfairly prejudicial *if* the testimony about its theft had been offered by an adult. But for a *child* to testify that his bicycle had been stolen seems to have the court in a tizzy for fear, I suppose, that the jury will conclude that anyone who would steal a bicycle from a young boy must be very bad indeed and deserves to be sent to jail, whether he robbed the Websters or not. Are we then to conclude that whenever children have inculpatory evidence to offer, the specter of unfair prejudice is

raised and that their evidence should be excluded? I doubt that is the
intended moral, but the example certainly suggests how subjective the
determination of unfair prejudice can sometimes be.

Consider briefly a second case, also from Texas, where the balancing
test seems to have gone awry. In 1992, Kenneth Nolen was accused of
aggravated possession of methamphetamine. Acting on a warrant, police
found Nolen asleep in the bedroom of a friend's house. Smelling a strong
odor, they opened the bathroom door, next to which Nolan was sleeping,
and discovered a laboratory for making amphetamine. Nolen's prints
were found on the lab equipment. To convict someone in Texas of aggravated possession, the state must show that the accused was aware of the
fact that the drug in his possession was an illegal substance. Nolen's
attorney suggested that, although his client had indeed been making
amphetamines, he did not know that such activity was illegal. To counter
that suggestion, the prosecutor sought to introduce evidence that Nolen
had been convicted three years earlier of breaking into the evidence
room of the local sheriff's office to steal laboratory equipment suitable
for making amphetamines. The prosecutor argued, and the trial judge
agreed, that the earlier theft of such equipment was highly relevant to
the question whether Nolen knew enough about amphetamines to
realize that they were illegal. In the prosecutor's closing arguments, he
insisted that "it's a reasonable deduction from the evidence that [if] that
man is so daring [as] to take lab equipment from the Hood County Sheriff, he certainly knows about am[p]hetamine and the equipment used to
produce amphetamine."[19]

The jury convicted Nolen. On appeal, a higher court reversed the verdict, insisting that "it was an abuse of [the judge's] discretion to determine
that the extraneous evidence of burglarizing the sheriffs evidence shelter
was not substantially outweighed by the danger of unfair prejudice to
Nolen, confusion of the issues, and misleading the jury."[20] How precisely
is it unfairly prejudicial to Nolen – facing a charge of knowingly making
illicit drugs and with his prints all over the equipment in question – to
show that he had previously stolen such equipment from the sheriff's
office? Since what was in dispute was whether Nolen knew that making
methamphetamine was illegal, we would seem to have here evidence
highly germane to the hypothesis that Nolen was knowledgeable about
drug making. Not so, says the appellate court, since it is not "deductively
certain" that "a man who steals glassware certainly knows the characteristics of a particular chemical compound that may be produced with that
type of glassware."[21] Well, yes. It is (just about) conceivable that Nolen
stole equipment for making amphetamines from the evidence room of
the sheriffs department without knowing what such equipment was used
for and without knowing that making such stuff was illegal. But we should
not be looking for deductive truths in the law. The question is whether
Nolen's previous conviction for theft of equipment for making amphetamines has a powerful evidential bearing on the question of whether he

knew three years later, while making amphetamines, that what he was doing was against the law. For a court to hold that such evidence is more likely to be unfairly prejudicial than relevant strikes me as extraordinarily obtuse. (I am not claiming that cases such as these two are the norm, but, at a minimum, they suggest that the balancing test demanded by the unfair prejudice rule is, at best, problematic.)

Surely, a preferable alternative would be to admit *all* evidence that is genuinely relevant, accompanied, where appropriate, by an explicit reminder from judge to jury to bring their critical faculties to bear in evaluating the relation of the evidence to the crime and in keeping their emotional reactions to the evidence firmly in check. Of course, we do not know how earnestly juries could or would follow such an instruction. But, for that matter, neither do we really know which kinds of evidence unfairly warp jurors' judgment and which do not. Since the judge has no robust empirical information about the latter issue, her decision about which potentially prejudicial evidence to include and which to exclude is likely to be every bit as suspect as an emotionally driven verdict from the jury.

It is not only the judge who has a role to play here in encouraging the jury to stay on the straight and narrow. One of the functions of the adversarial system is to give each side a shot at undermining or otherwise calling into question the case presented by the other. If there is evidence that the defense regards as misleading or that it suspects may otherwise steer a jury in the wrong direction, it is the job of defense counsel to seek to fit that evidence into a context favorable to the defendant, if that is possible. Failing that, it falls to defense counsel to persuade the jury not to attach more weight to any specimen of inculpatory evidence than it duly deserves. Like the judge, counsel may fail in this task from time to time. Jurors may conceivably rush to judgment for all sorts of inappropriate reasons, despite having been warned of the dangers of doing so.

That conceded, if we cannot generally trust jurors to keep their emotions in check, then we should abandon trial by jury altogether. The very idea of trial by jury depends on the presumed fairness and common sense of twelve peers of the accused. If jurors cannot generally give vivid but relevant evidence its appropriate weight – having been warned by the judge to do so and having heard counsel for each side make its pitch about the meaning of the evidence – then the system is rotten to the core. Paternalistically coddling jurors by shielding them from evidence that some judge intuits to be beyond their powers to reason about coherently is not a promising recipe for finding out the truth.

I use the term "paternalism" deliberately. Recall that, in a bench trial, the same judge who decides on the admissibility of evidence usually acts as the trier of fact. In short, the system trusts judges to be able to see inflammatory and unfairly prejudicial evidence and then to be able to put it into perspective, not allowing it to warp their judgment. By permitting judges in bench trials to see evidence that we would not permit juries to see, we are saying that juries are less reasonable, less objective, or less mature than judges. That may be so; as far as I know, the issue is unsettled. But, settled or not, this is not what judges are for in an adversarial system. Their job, apart from generally maintaining order in the court, is to explain to jurors what the law means. That is what they are trained to do, and there is nothing paternal about that role. It becomes paternal when, out of a systemic distrust of the good sense of jurors, we cast the judge in the role of arbiter on both empirical and policy questions that should not be hers to settle.

Put in grander terms, it will be the recurring theme of this book that, leaving redundancy aside, the only factor that should determine the admissibility or inadmissibility of a bit of evidence is its relevance to the hypothesis that a crime occurred and that the defendant committed it. The exclusion of admittedly relevant evidence on the grounds of its unfairly prejudicial character is motivated by commendable epistemic instincts. But the rule itself requires judges both to have empirical knowledge that they lack and to make policy determinations (for instance, about the relative seriousness of false acquittals and false convictions) that are beyond their ken.

As we have seen, my proposal is squarely at odds with existing practice. In American courts, "mere" relevance, even powerful relevance, does not ensure admissibility. As the U.S. Supreme Court argued in a famous case, *Michelson* v. *U.S.*:

> The State may not show defendant's prior trouble with the law, specific criminal acts, or ill name among his neighbors, even though such facts might logically be persuasive that he is by propensity a probable perpetrator of the crime. The inquiry is not rejected because character is irrelevant; on the contrary, it is said to weigh too much with the jury and to so overpersuade them as to prejudge one with a bad general record and deny him a fair opportunity to defend against a particular charge. The overriding policy of excluding such evidence, despite its admitted probative value, is the practical experience that its disallowance tends to prevent confusion of issues, unfair surprise and undue prejudice.[22]

This token of conventional folk wisdom may be grounded in the "practical experience" of the judiciary. But precious few well-designed empirical studies bear out the claim that properly instructed jurors, exposed to the confrontations typical of the adversary system, are incapable of giving inflammatory or prejudicial but relevant evidence the weight it rationally deserves. Since that is so, rules of admissibility that trump relevance cannot be shown to further epistemic ends, not even when those rules (such as the one against unfairly prejudicial evidence) are couched in epistemic terms ("preventing a jury's verdict from being shaped by prejudice rather than the facts"). On the contrary, they almost invariably thwart those ends by keeping obviously relevant evidence out of the courtroom. The proof of that thesis is the thrust of much of the rest of this book.

Notes

1 Criminal Law Revision Committee, Eleventh Report, Evidence (General) 1972, Cmnd. 4991. at §§62–4.

2 From Powell's dissent in *Bullington v. Missouri*, 451 U.S. 430 (1981).

3 *Tehan v. U.S.*, 383 U.S. 406, at 416 (1966).

4 Lest you take my remarks about the lack of a coherent design in the rules of trials as casting aspersions on the founding fathers, I hasten to add that the system now in place is one that *they* would scarcely recognize, if they recognized it at all. Many of the features of American criminal justice that work against the interests of finding truth and avoiding error-features that we will discuss in detail later on – were additions, supplements, or sometimes patent transformations of American criminal practice as it existed at the beginning of the nineteenth century. Congress or state legislatures imposed some of these changes; judges themselves created the vast majority as remedies for serious problems posed by the common law or abusive police practices. A few date from the late-nineteenth century; most, from the twentieth.

5 To see the point of the scare quotes, consult Chapter 7, where we will observe that the majority of "coerced" confessions are not coerced in the lay sense of that term.

6 Accordingly, I ask those readers who know the fine points of the practice of the law far better than I do to overlook the occasional acts of ignorance on my part, of which there are doubtless several, unless they actually impinge upon the cogency of the argument that I am making.

7 Courts typically distinguish between errors that, while acknowledged as errors, did not decisively affect the outcome of a trial (called "harmless errors") and more serious errors, which call for retrial or reversal of a conviction.

8 Henry Chambers, Reasonable Certainty and Reasonable Doubt, 81 MARQ. L. REV. 655, at 668 (1998).

9 Richard Posner, An Economic Approach to the Law of Evidence, 51 STAN. L. REV. 1477, at 1506 (1999).

10 See the Department of Justice, SOURCEBOOK OF CRIMINAL JUSTICE STATISTICS FOR 1999, Table 5.16. For a thorough discussion of this issue, see Samuel R. Gross, The Risks of Death: Why Erroneous Convictions Are Common in Capital Cases, 44 Buffalo L. REV. 469 (1996).

11 The Supreme Court has held that "the trial judge must ensure that any and all scientific testimony or evidence admitted is not only relevant, but reliable" *(Daubert v. Merrell Dow Pharms.*, 113 S. Ct. 2786, at 2795 [U.S. 1993]).

12 The only time when it is obviously appropriate to exclude relevant evidence is when it is redundant with respect to evidence already admitted. Testimony from two hundred witnesses asserting X is scarcely better than that from two or three credible ones asserting X, unless X happens to be a very bizarre event.

13 Federal Rules of Evidence, Rule 403.

14 *Bruton v. U.S.*, 391 U.S. 123 (1968).

15 *State v. Lafferty*, 749 P.2d 1239 (Utah 1988).

16 *State v. White*, 880 P.2d 18 (Utah 1994).

17   Victor Gold, Observations on the Nature of Unfairly Prejudicial Evidence, 58 WASH. L. REV. 497, at 502 (1983).

18   *Garcia v. State*, 893 S.W.2d 17, at 22 (Tex. App. 1994).

19   *Nolen v. State*, 872 S.W.2d 807, at 813 (Tex. App. 1994).

20   Ibid., at 814.

21   Ibid., at 813.

22   *Michelson v. U.S.*, 335 U.S., at 475–6 (1948).

13

Wikipistemology

Don Fallis

Somebody who reads Wikipedia is "rather in the position of a
visitor to a public restroom," says Mr. McHenry, Britannica's
former editor. "It may be obviously dirty, so that he knows to
exercise great care, or it may seem fairly clean, so that he may be
lulled into a false sense of security. What he certainly does not
know is who has used the facilities before him." One wonders
whether people like Mr. McHenry would prefer there to be no
public lavatories at all.

—*Economist*

Wikipedia is the best thing ever. Anyone in the world can write
anything they want about any subject. So you know that you are
getting the best possible information.

—Michael Scott (*The Office*)

Mass collaboration is one of the newest trends in the creation and dissemination of knowledge and information. Several people working together
to produce knowledge is nothing new, of course. But until recently, such
projects have been limited in the number of collaborators who can participate and in the distance between them. It is now possible for millions of
people separated by thousands of miles to collaborate on a single project.
Wikis, which are Web sites that anyone with Internet access can edit,
provide a popular medium for this sort of collaboration.

Such mass collaboration has often been extremely successful. A popular example is the development of open source software, such as the
Linux operating system. However, it is not a foregone conclusion that
such mass collaboration will be successful in all instances. For example, it
seems unlikely that a million people working together would write a very
good novel. But are a million people working together likely to compile a
good *encyclopedia*? This essay will investigate the success of a notable
example of mass collaboration on the Internet: the "free online encyclopedia
that anyone can edit," Wikipedia.

AN EPISTEMIC EVALUATION OF WIKIPEDIA

There are actually a number of different ways a project like Wikipedia might (or might not) be successful. It might be successful at building a good encyclopedia. But it might also be successful at simply building an online community. And it is not completely clear which of these goals has priority. In fact, one of the founders of Wikipedia, Jimmy Wales, has said that "the goal of Wikipedia is *fun* for the contributors" (quoted in Poe 2006, emphasis added).

Even if the contributors to Wikipedia ultimately just want to have fun, however, building a good encyclopedia is still an important goal of this project. Similarly, even if the owners of *Encyclopedia Britannica* ultimately just want to make money, building a good encyclopedia is still an important goal that they have. And this goal is clearly *epistemic*. A good encyclopedia is a place where people can "acquire knowledge" and sometimes "share knowledge" (). And, according to Alvin Goldman (1999), a primary task for the social epistemologist is to evaluate social institutions, such as Wikipedia, in terms of their epistemic consequences.[2]

Wikipedia certainly has the potential to have great epistemic benefits. By allowing anyone with Internet access to create and edit content (i.e., by taking advantage of what Chris Anderson calls "crowdsourcing"; 2006, 219), Wikipedia now includes millions of entries in many different languages.[3] Because all of this material is freely and easily accessible by anyone with Internet access, Wikipedia is now one of the top ten Internet domains in terms of Internet traffic along with Google, Yahoo, YouTube, and MySpace.[4] It essentially serves as an aggregation point for encyclopedic information in much the same way that the online auction Web site Ebay serves as an aggregation point for other goods (89).

The idea of Wikipedia is reminiscent of the World Encyclopedia or World Brain envisioned by the science fiction writer H. G. Wells (1971 [1938]). The World Encyclopedia was to be a compendium of all human knowledge, compiled by a decentralized network of contributors, and accessible to all people. And it is worth noting that the creation and dissemination of knowledge in general is very often such a collective activity.[5] For example, libraries, publishing companies, universities, search engine companies, and even dictionaries are typically large-scale collective endeavors. While early lexicographers, such as Samuel Johnson, worked largely on their own, subsequent dictionaries have always been produced by large teams. In fact, in its early days, the *Oxford English Dictionary*, in a strategy very similar to Wikipedia, solicited help from the general public (Winchester 1998, 101–14).

Serious concerns have been raised, however, about the quality (accuracy, completeness, comprehensibility, etc.) of the information on Wikipedia. Entries in traditional encyclopedias are often written by people with expertise on the topic in question. In addition, these entries are checked for accuracy by experienced editors before they are published. However, because Wikipedia allows anyone with Internet access to create and modify content, Wikipedia lacks these sorts of quality control mechanisms. In fact, "no one stands officially behind the authenticity and accuracy of any information in [Wikipedia]" (Denning et al. 2005). As a result, it has been suggested that "it's the blind leading the blind—infinite monkeys providing infinite information for infinite readers, perpetuating the cycle of misinformation and ignorance" (Keen 2007, 4).

In this essay, I discuss the various concerns that have been raised about the quality of the information on Wikipedia. Despite these concerns, I will argue, the epistemic consequences of people using Wikipedia as a source of information are actually likely to be quite good.

EPISTEMIC CONCERNS ABOUT WIKIPEDIA

Several different epistemic concerns have been raised about Wikipedia. For example, it has been pointed out that Wikipedia entries are often badly written and that important topics are not always covered.[6] It is clear that such failings can adversely affect people's ability to acquire knowledge from Wikipedia.

However, *inaccurate* information can easily lead people to acquire false beliefs. In other words, inaccurate information can make people epistemically worse off instead of just failing to make them epistemically better off. And epistemologists (e.g., Hume 1977 [1748], 111, Descartes 1996 [1641], 12) typically consider falling into *error* to be the most adverse epistemic consequence. Thus, the principal epistemic concern that has been raised about Wikipedia is whether people are likely to get *accurate* information from it. In other words, is Wikipedia a reliable source of information? (An information source is *reliable* if most of the information that it contains is accurate.)

As noted, more and more people are using Wikipedia as a source of information. It has even been cited in court cases (Cohen 2007). But concerns about its reliability in particular have led many people to suggest that Wikipedia should not be used as a source of information. In fact, the history department at Middlebury College has forbidden its students to cite Wikipedia (Read 2007).

Concerns about Reliability

Wikipedia differs from many other collaborative projects in that it does not directly bump up against reality. For example, in order for software to be added to the Linux operating system, the software actually has to work. By contrast, information can be added to Wikipedia and remain on Wikipedia indefinitely regardless of whether or not it is accurate.

There are several reasons to think that a significant amount of information on Wikipedia will be inaccurate. First, since anyone can contribute to Wikipedia, many of these contributors will not have much expertise in the topics they write about. As a result, they may inadvertently add inaccurate information to Wikipedia.[7] In addition, they may inadvertently remove accurate information. Thus, there will be some amount of *misinformation* on Wikipedia.

And the problem is not just that Wikipedia allows people who lack expertise to contribute. It has been suggested that Wikipedia exhibits *anti-intellectualism* and actively deters people with expertise from contributing. For example, experts rarely receive any deference from other contributors to Wikipedia as a result of their expertise.[8] Since they cannot simply appeal to their authority, experts have to fight it out just like anyone else to get their views to stick in the encyclopedia. Many experts are understandably unwilling to put in the effort to create content that might simply be removed by an unqualified individual with an axe to grind.[9] Furthermore, academics and other experts who create information and knowledge typically want to get credit for their work. But since Wikipedia entries are the creation of multiple (often anonymous) authors and editors, no one person can claim credit for the result.

Second, since anyone can contribute to Wikipedia, some of these contributors may try to deceive the readers of Wikipedia.[10] For example, the entry on the journalist John Siegenthaler was famously modified to falsely claim that he was involved in the Kennedy assassinations.[11] And this inaccurate information was on the Web site for over four months. In another case, University of Minnesota professor Taner Akcam was detained at the Canadian border because his Wikipedia entry had been changed to say that he was a terrorist (Fisk, 2007).). Thus, there will be some amount of *disinformation* on Wikipedia.

Whenever someone has an interest in convincing other people to believe something even if it is not true, there is reason to worry about the accuracy of the information she provides. For example, it is worrying when prominent individuals (e.g., members of Congress) and large organizations have been caught changing their own Wikipedia entries (Borland 2007). And even if someone is not engaged in outright deception, there is still potential for inaccurate information to be introduced as a result of unintentional bias.

Finally, there is a third category of inaccurate information that may be found on Wikipedia. Since we can all edit Wikipedia, Stephen Colbert (host of the television news satire *The Colbert Report*) has suggested that we should just construct the reality we collectively want. For example, since we are all concerned with the survival of endangered species, Colbert encouraged his viewers to edit the entry on African elephants to say that their numbers had tripled in the last six months (). This type of inaccurate information is arguably distinct from both disinformation and misinformation. Unlike someone who intends to deceive or who makes an honest mistake, the television host Colbert (or the character he is pretending to be) shows no concern for the *truth* of this Wikipedia entry. (Someone who intends to deceive not only shows no concern but is *concerned to avoid* the truth.) Several philosophers (e.g., Black 1983, Cohen 2002, Frankfurt 2005) have offered analyses of *humbug* or *bullshit*. And, according to Harry Frankfurt (2005, 33–34), it is "this lack of connection to a concern with truth—this indifference to how things really are—that I regard as of the essence of bullshit." Thus, there may also be some amount of bullshit on Wikipedia.[17]

Concerns about Verifiability

The main reason that the reliability of Wikipedia is a concern is that people can be misled by inaccurate information. And being misled can often lead to serious harm. But inaccurate information is not so serious a problem if it is possible for people to determine that this information is (or is very likely to be) inaccurate. In other words, if people are in a position to verify the accuracy of information, they are less likely to be misled by inaccurate information. Thus, we need to consider the verifiability as well as the reliability of an information source.[13] (An information source is *verifiable* if people can easily determine whether the information it contains is accurate.)

Furthermore, it is important to note that people can avoid the potential epistemic costs of inaccurate information even if they are not able to determine with absolute certainty that a particular piece of information is inaccurate. It is often sufficient for people to have a reasonable estimate of the reliability of the source of the information.[14] As Goldman (1999, 121) has established, if we have the right amount of faith in them, even fairly unreliable sources can be useful. For example, we might simply raise our degree of confidence in claims made by such sources without fully accepting that these claims are true.

However, P. D. Magnus (2006) has raised concerns about the verifiability of Wikipedia entries. He points out that we can try to verify the accuracy of a particular claim (that we are uncertain about) by considering both the *presentation* and the *content* of the information. For example, if an author makes numerous spelling and grammatical mistakes or makes other claims that are clearly false, then we have reason to be cautious about the accuracy of this particular claim. However, these are just the sorts of features that contributors to Wikipedia typically remove when they edit entries that other people have written. That is, they quickly remove spelling mistakes, grammatical mistakes, and clearly implausible claims. Thus, these features will no longer be available to someone trying to estimate the reliability of these entries. To use Mr. McHenry's analogy, the concern is that people cannot tell how dirty a restroom really is because others have come through ahead of them, picked up the trash, and wiped off the counters.

We can also try to verify the accuracy of a piece of information by considering the identity of the source of that information. For example, does this source have any *conflict of interest* that might lead her to intentionally disseminate inaccurate information on this topic? In addition, is this source sufficiently *qualified* (or does she have a good enough *track record*) on this topic that she would be unlikely to unintentionally disseminate inaccurate information? But, in the case of Wikipedia, it is somewhat difficult to determine exactly who the source of a particular piece of information is. Any given entry may have been edited by several different contributors and Wikipedia allows these contributors to remain anonymous if they wish.

WIKIPEDIA IS NOT ALL THAT BAD

Wikipedia Is Not All That Unreliable

But despite legitimate concerns about its reliability, empirical evidence actually suggests that Wikipedia is not all that unreliable. For instance, researchers have tested Wikipedia by inserting plausible errors and seeing how long it takes for the errors to be corrected (Read 2006). Such vandalism is typically corrected in just a few minutes. In addition, blind comparisons by experts of Wikipedia entries and entries in a traditional encyclopedia have been carried out. For example, a study by the journal *Nature* (Giles 2005) found that Wikipedia was only slightly less reliable than *Encyclopedia Britannica*.[15]

To be fair, it should be noted that the *Nature* study focused specifically on entries on scientific topics. Results have been more mixed when it comes to other topics. For example, in a blind comparison of Wikipedia and *Britannica* with respect to a small selection of entries on *philosophical* topics, Magnus (2006) found that "Wikipedia entries vary widely in quality." George Bragues (2009), who evaluated the Wikipedia entries on seven great philosophers using authoritative reference works on these philosophers, reached the same conclusion. Nevertheless, even on such nonscientific topics, the *reliability* of Wikipedia still seems to be comparable to that of *Britannica*. For example, Magnus found that, while Wikipedia had more "major errors," *Britannica* had many more "minor errors and infelicities." And, in fact, Bragues was "unable to uncover any outright errors [in Wikipedia]. The sins of Wikipedia are more of omission than commission."

While these empirical studies suggest that Wikipedia *is* fairly reliable, we might reasonably wonder *why* it is as reliable as it is. As Chris Anderson (2006, 71) puts it, "the true miracle of Wikipedia is that this open system of amateur user contributions and edits doesn't simply collapse into anarchy." In particular, why do contributors make Wikipedia better more often than they make it worse? One popular suggestion is that

Wikipedia is an example of the so-called Wisdom of Crowds (see Surowiecki 2004). *Large* and *decentralized* groups made up of *diverse* and *independent* members seem to be very good at getting the right answer to
many questions.[16]

But whatever the explanation for it might be, the evidence does indicate that Wikipedia is fairly reliable. Several investigators have established
this simply by rating the quality of the information on Wikipedia as
Bragues has done (by consulting authorities or authoritative sources).
However, as Goldman (1999, 92–93) points out, it is often more appro
priate to carry out a *relative* rather than an *absolute* epistemic evaluation
of some institution. That is, rather than simply determining exactly how
reliable an information source is, we should determine how reliable it is
compared to the available alternatives.

Thus, instead of comparing Wikipedia to *Britannica*, we should really
be comparing the reliability of Wikipedia against the reliability of the
information sources that people would likely be using if Wikipedia were
not available: namely, the freely available Web sites on their topic of
interest returned by their favorite search engine (Meyer 2006). It is this
comparison that will tell us whether it is, as a matter of fact, epistemically
better that people have access to Wikipedia. And, if the reliability of Wikipedia is comparable to the reliability of traditional encyclopedias, then it
presumably compares even more favorably to the reliability of randomly
chosen Web sites. Empirical studies (e.g., Fallis and Frické 2002) have
found significant amounts of inaccurate information on the Internet. And
Web sites in general are not checked as quickly (or by as many people) as
is Wikipedia.

In addition, it is important to note that the degree of reliability we
demand of an information source often depends on the circumstances.[17]
For example, when we are seeking information out of pure curiosity, it
may not be a big deal if some of this information turns out to be inaccurate. But when we are seeking information in order to decide on a medical treatment or a large investment, we would like to be sure that the
information is accurate. And if reliability is sufficiently important, we
should probably double check the information (e.g., by consulting an
independent source of information). It is often suggested that encyclopedias should be a starting point rather than an ending point for research
(Anderson 2006, 69).

Of course, people will not always double check information even when
the stakes are reasonably high. In other words, people are subject to the
so-called principle of least effort. As Thomas Mann (1993, 91) reports,
empirical studies have found that "most researchers (even "serious"
scholars) will tend to choose easily available information sources, even
when they are objectively of low quality." As a result, the easy availability
of low-quality information sources can certainly have bad epistemic consequences in actual practice. But it is also important to note that people
do not just have *epistemic* interests. And given that people have many

nonepistemic interests (e.g., they want to save time and money), it may sometimes be rational not to seek more knowledge or greater justification (Hardin 2003).[18]

Wikipedia Is Not All That Unverifiable

People may not always verify the accuracy of information on Wikipedia when they ought to. But it is not clear that Magnus is correct that the tools that they need to do so are not available. First of all, empirical studies (e.g., Fallis and Frické 2002) indicate that spelling and grammatical mistakes are not correlated with inaccuracy. So when such mistakes are removed from a Wikipedia entry, it is not clear that people have been deprived of a useful indicator of accuracy. With regard to the removal of implausible claims, some people probably are being deprived of a useful indicator of accuracy. However, claims that are clearly implausible to one person may not be clearly implausible to another. Thus, we have to weigh the epistemic cost of a loss of verifiability for some people against the epistemic benefit of removing information that will be misleading to other people.[19]

It is certainly not easy to determine the real-life identity of the author of a specific Wikipedia entry. But it is not clear that this seriously impedes our ability to verify the accuracy of the entry. First, it should be noted that it is also not very easy to determine the real-life identity of the author of a specific entry in a traditional encyclopedia.[20] Second, unlike a traditional encyclopedia, readers of Wikipedia can easily look at all the contributions a particular author has made and can evaluate the quality of these contributions. In any event, even if we could easily determine the real-life identity of an author, it would still be much too time-consuming to research her qualifications and potential biases. We typically trust a particular encyclopedia entry not because we trust its author but because we trust the process by which the entries in the encyclopedia are produced. And the process by which entries in Wikipedia are produced seems to be fairly reliable.

Admittedly, the process may not be as reliable as the process used by traditional encyclopedias. But Wikipedia warns readers about the fact that it may contain inaccurate information (Wikipedia 2010a).[21] And most people seem to be aware of this fact. By contrast, traditional encyclopedias often insist on their high level of accuracy. But the empirical studies discussed above suggest that there are many errors in traditional encyclopedias as well as in Wikipedia. As a result, there is reason to think that people are more likely to overestimate the reliability of traditional encyclopedias than the reliability of Wikipedia. As Eli Guinnee (2007) puts it, "an inaccuracy in Britannica is (mis)taken as fact, an inaccuracy in Wikipedia is taken with a grain of salt, easily confirmed or proved wrong."

Finally, in many respects, Wikipedia is actually more verifiable than most other information sources. For example, in addition to general disclaimers, "warnings" are placed at the top of Wikipedia entries whose accuracy or neutrality has been disputed. In addition, unlike traditional encyclopedias, Wikipedia is not a black box. Readers of Wikipedia have easy access to the entire editing history of every entry. In addition, readers have access to the *talk pages* that contributors use to discuss how entries should be changed. Admittedly, most readers are only going to consult the current entry itself. But if someone is particularly interested in a topic, the editing history and the talk pages can be invaluable resources. For example, one can look to see if there were any dissenting opinions, what these different viewpoints were, and what arguments have ultimately carried the day. This is right in line with John Stuart Mill's claim (1978 [1859]) that exposure to different viewpoints is the best way to learn the truth about a topic.

New technologies are also being developed that have the potential to increase the verifiability of Wikipedia. For example, Virgil Griffith has created a searchable database (Wikiscanner) that allows readers to connect specific contributions to Wikipedia with the organization that owns the Internet provider addresses from which those contributions originated (Borland 2007). So, for example, readers can easily find out if employees of the Diebold Corporation have been editing the Wikipedia entry on it.[22]

Wikipedia Has Many Other Epistemic Virtues

Concerns about Wikipedia usually focus on its reliability (or lack thereof). But there are many other epistemic virtues beyond reliability. For example, in addition to reliability, Goldman has discussed the epistemic values of *power*, *speed*, and *fecundity* (Goldman 1987, Thagard 1997). That is, we are also concerned with *how much* knowledge can be acquired from an information source, *how fast* that knowledge can be acquired, and *how many* people can acquire it. In fact, as noted, fecundity is of particular importance for an encyclopedia.

Wikipedia seems to do pretty well with regard to these other epistemic values. Because it has a huge amount of free labor working around the clock, it is likely to be very powerful.[23] Because there is no delay for new content to go through an editorial filter and because the content can be accessed quickly over the Internet, acquisition of knowledge via Wikipedia is likely to be very speedy. And because it is free to anyone with Internet access, it is likely to be very fecund.[24]

Thus, Wikipedia provides a nice example of how epistemic values can come into conflict. In particular, while Wikipedia may be slightly less reliable than *Britannica*, it is arguably much more powerful, speedy, and fecund. When there is such a conflict, we need to determine what the appropriate trade-off is.[25] And just as when reliability comes into conflict with nonepistemic interests, the relative importance of different epistemic values will often depend on the circumstances. For example, speed

p.s. It's fast quality work, not just speedy work that is important

is often extremely important in our fast-paced world. It is sufficiently important to physicists that many of them use preprint archives that provide quick access to unpublished articles that have not been checked for accuracy by anyone other than the author (Thagard 1997). Furthermore, William James (1979 [1896], 31–32) famously claimed that the value of power can sometimes outweigh the value of reliability. According to James, "a rule of thinking which would absolutely prevent me from acknowledging certain kinds of truth if those kinds of truth were really there, would be an irrational rule." Thus, in many circumstances, the epistemic benefits of Wikipedia (in terms of greater power, speed, fecundity, and even verifiability) may very well outweigh the epistemic costs (in terms of somewhat less reliability).

Finally, as any user of Wikipedia knows (and as the empirical studies cited above suggest), it is not just a mass of misinformation and disinformation. Wikipedia contains quite a lot of accurate, high-quality information. So this is not simply a case of disseminating low quality information faster and to more people. Thus, despite legitimate concerns about its reliability, it probably is *epistemically* better that people have access to this information source.

HOW WIKIPEDIA CAN BE IMPROVED

In any event, Wikipedia seems to be here to stay. Given that fact, what epistemologists can do is try to figure out how to *improve* Wikipedia. For instance, as noted, there are new projects (e.g., Wikiscanner) that have the potential to increase the reliability and verifiability of Wikipedia.[26] Such projects fall under the so-called *ameliorative* project in epistemology, which focuses on how we can modify our institutions and practices to better achieve our epistemic goals (Kitcher 1992, 64).

In addition to improving Wikipedia, epistemologists can also try to figure out how to improve *on* Wikipedia. For example, Larry Sanger is working to create a more reliable alternative to Wikipedia (Citizendium 2010).[27] Citizendium.org welcomes experts to contribute as authors and as editors, and entries that meet certain standards of quality are officially "approved" by such qualified editors. And contributors to Citizendium are not allowed to remain anonymous. In addition, Veropedia.com is an attempt to create a more reliable extension of Wikipedia. This Web site will host stable versions of Wikipedia entries that have been approved by experts in the relevant subject areas.

However, it is important to keep in mind that any proposed changes to Wikipedia are likely to have epistemic costs as well as benefits. For example, if we try to improve its reliability by giving experts more editorial control, we might end up decreasing its power since other people might be deterred from contributing.[28] In addition, if we try to improve its reliability by only including entries approved by experts, we might end up decreasing its speed since it will take longer to add and update entries.[29] So, in order to evaluate any proposed changes, we need to be clear about exactly what our epistemic values are and what the appropriate trade-offs are when there are conflicts.[30] *but will these decrease enough to matter?*

CONCLUSION

Like the Internet itself, Wikipedia is having a huge impact on how a great many people gather information about the world. So it is important for epistemologists to ask what the epistemic consequences are of people having access to this information source. While there are legitimate concerns about its reliability (since anyone can edit it), the empirical evidence suggests that Wikipedia is fairly reliable (especially compared to those information sources that are as easily accessible). In addition, it has a number of other epistemic virtues (e.g., power, speed, and fecundity) that arguably outweigh any deficiency in terms of reliability. Even so, epistemologists should be trying to identify changes (or alternatives) to Wikipedia that will bring about even better epistemic consequences. In order to do that, we need to know what our epistemic values are, and we need a better understanding of why Wikipedia works as well as it does.

Notes

This essay is a significantly abridged and revised version of my "Toward an Epistemology of *Wikipedia*," *Journal of the American Society for Information Science and Technology*, © 2008 Wiley Periodicals, Inc. I would like to thank Julia Annas, Tony Doyle, Martin Frické, Bruce Fulton, Alvin Goldman, Rachana Kamtekar, Peter Lewis, P. D. Magnus, Kay Mathiesen, Marc Meola, Larry Sanger, Heshan Sun, Dennis Whitcomb, K. Brad Wray, and the students in my course on social epistemology and information science at the University of Arizona for their feedback.

1 Encyclopedias are intended to disseminate existing knowledge rather than to produce new knowledge. Thus, the epistemology of encyclopedias falls within the scope of the *epistemology of testimony*. See Lackey and Sosa (2006) for recent work on the epistemology of testimony.

2 Goldman (2008) has recently evaluated the epistemic consequences of *blogging* (as compared to the epistemic consequences of the conventional news media).

3 See Broughton (2008) or Wikipedia (2010b) for further details about how Wikipedia works.

4 Over a third of Internet users in the United States have consulted Wikipedia, and almost 10 percent consult it every day; see Rainie and Tancer (2007).

5 Philosophical work on how people come together to collaboratively create information and knowledge goes back to Aristotle (Waldron 1995). But there has been renewed interest in this topic over the last few years (see, e.g., Smith 2002,

Wray 2002, Mathiesen 2006, Tollefsen 2007, and the journal issue "The Epistemology of Mass Collaboration" (2009).

6 Not everybody criticizes the coverage of Wikipedia. Stephen Colbert, for
example, thinks that "any site that's got a longer entry on truthiness than on
Lutherans has its priorities straight." All joking aside, I think that he has a point.

7 Simson Garfinkel (2008) has criticized Wikipedia by pointing to a case
where the subject of an article was not able to correct a statement about himself
that he very well knew to be false. His attempts to correct the inaccuracy would
quickly be reversed because he could not cite a published source that supported
his position. Although this may sound problematic on the face of it, it is not clear
that this is really a serious problem or that it is unique to Wikipedia. Most encyclopedias stick to published sources, and are arguably more reliable for doing so.
But published sources will not always have the most current or most accurate
information in particular cases.

8 In fact, people who claim expertise are sometimes greeted quite rudely. For
example, the noted philosopher of mind David Chalmers had some trouble getting
some mistakes corrected in the Wikipedia entry "Consciousness" (Healy, 2007).

9 A scholar recently revised the Wikipedia entry on the noted political
philosopher Martha Nussbaum, only to have the work immediately undone by an
anonymous administrator; see Leiter (2007).

10 In addition to people who intentionally add inaccurate or misleading information, there are people who intentionally remove content and/or replace it with
obscenities (Wikipedia 2010c). If it removes *true* content, such vandalism also
reduces the reliability of Wikipedia.

11 In a similar vein, a *Penny Arcade* comic strip shows Skeletor changing the
He-Man entry, which originally read "He-Man is the most powerful man in the
universe" to read "He-Man is actually a tremendous jackass and not all that powerful" (Krahulik and Holkins 2005). In another recent case, a college student
inserted a fake quote into the Wikipedia entry for the composer Maurice Jarre,
who had just died. Wikipedia editors quickly removed the quote because no
source was cited. However, several journalists had already found the quote, and it
appeared in obituaries of Jarre in several newspapers (Cohen 2009).

12 Of course, some bullshit might turn out to be true. In fact, some information that is intended to be false might accidentally turn out to be true. And if it is
true, then there is not much of an epistemic cost to having it in Wikipedia. However, it seems safe to say that any given instance of bullshit or disinformation is
unlikely to true. For example, it seems rather unlikely that the number of African
elephants has recently tripled.

13 Fallis (2004b) discusses how people can verify that the accuracy of information and how information can be made easier to verify.

14 There can certainly be bad epistemic consequences if one's estimate of the
reliability of a source does not match its actual reliability. For example, relevant
evidence is often withheld from juries when it is thought that they are likely to
overestimate its probative value (Goldman 1999, 294–95).

15 Encyclopedia Britannica has criticized the methodology of this study, but
Nature has defended its methodology (*Nature* 2006). The bottom line is that
there is no reason to think that any methodological failings of the study would
favor Wikipedia over *Britannica* (Magnus 2006). See Wikipedia (2010d) for an
extensive survey of empirical studies and expert opinions on the reliability of
Wikipedia.

16 This explanation is not completely satisfying. For example, it is not clear how many contributors work on any particular Wikipedia entry or how diverse these contributors are (Wilson 2008).

17 Fallis (2006) discusses how nonepistemic interests can influence one's epistemic interests.

18 While it may be rational *all things considered* not to seek more knowledge in such cases, it is not necessarily *epistemically* rational (Kelly 2003).

19 In addition, contributors to Wikipedia do not just remove the *blatantly* implausible claims. They remove any claims that they know to be false and that other people might not recognize as being false.

20 With the exception of those encyclopedias that focus on a particular subject area, such as the *Routledge Encyclopedia of Philosophy*, traditional encyclopedias rarely list the authors of each entry.

21 Traditional encyclopedias often do have similar disclaimers. But they are rarely displayed as prominently as those in Wikipedia.

22 Wikiscanner may also increase the reliability of Wikipedia by deterring people from editing entries when they have an obvious conflict of interest. However, it should be noted that there are some epistemic benefits to anonymity that we might lose as a result of tools like Wikiscanner. In particular, if people cannot disseminate information anonymously, they may be deterred from disseminating valuable information. For example, suppose that I have something critical to say about a person or an organization. If the target of my criticism can find out that I am the source (and might come after me), I may very well decide that I am better off not saying anything (Kronick 1988, 225).

23 Timothy Noah (2007) has suggested that Wikipedia could be even more powerful than it currently is. At the moment, only topics that are sufficiently *notable* are allowed to have their own entries (Wikipedia 2010e). This sort of notability constraint makes perfect sense in the context of traditional print encyclopedias, which have limited space in which to print entries and limited staff to write entries. After all, people usually prefer to acquire *significant* knowledge rather than *trivial* knowledge (Fallis 2006, 180–81; Goldman 1999, 88–89; Paterson 1979, 95). However, since Wikipedia is not limited in terms of space or staff, it is not immediately clear why its scope should be constrained in this way. It may be difficult to find authoritative and verifiable sources to cite in an entry on a fairly trivial subject, such as your next-door neighbor's dog. But entries that fail to cite authoritative and verifiable sources are already proscribed by another Wikipedia policy (Wikipedia 2010f). Without a notability constraint, it may be slightly more difficult for readers to find the entry on, for example, *the* Jack Nicholson. But an effective search tool can easily ameliorate that difficulty. Finally, the fact that a topic is covered in a traditional print encyclopedia can be a useful indicator to people that the topic is significant. But it is probably better to come up with new ways of indicating importance in our new information environment rather than unnecessarily imposing constraints on ourselves. (This final point applies to indicators of accuracy and authority as well as to indicators of importance and significance.)

24 In addition to Wikipedia being freely accessible, anyone is allowed to make copies of its content for free, and many websites do. This further increases the fecundity of Wikipedia.

25 Fallis (2004a) discusses how epistemic values can come into conflict and how such conflicts can be resolved.

26   At least one peer reviewed journal is now requiring authors of accepted articles to submit summaries of their articles to Wikipedia (Butler 2008). This strategy has the potential to increase the reliability of Wikipedia by encouraging the participation of experts.

27   It should be noted that whereas several online encyclopedias are trying to provide an alternative to Wikipedia, it is not clear that they are all trying to provide a more reliable alternative. For example, according to Andy Schlafly, founder of Conservapedia.com, "we have certain principles we adhere to . . . beyond that we welcome the facts."

28   In fact, even if contributors to Citizendium have greater expertise, Citizendium might turn out to be less reliable than Wikipedia because it has fewer contributors to look for and correct errors.

29   In order to increase the reliability of Wikipedia, users will no longer be able to make immediate changes to entries about living people. Changes to such entries will only show up in the encyclopedia after being vetted by experienced editors (Cohen 2009). Critics of this policy worry that it will drastically slow the pace at which the encyclopedia is updated.

30   With respect to information on philosophical topics, another notable alternative to Wikipedia is the *Stanford Encyclopedia of Philosophy*, an online only publication (http://plato.stanford.edu). Because its editorial policies are similar to those of traditional encyclopedias, it is probably more reliable than Wikipedia, but it is also less speedy and less powerful. However, because it is freely available over the Internet, it may be just as fecund.

References

Anderson, Chris. 2006. *The Long Tail*. New York: Hyperion.

Black, Max. 1983. *The Prevalence of Humbug and Other Essays*. Ithaca: Cornell University Press.

Borland, John. 2007. "See Who's Editing Wikipedia: Diebold, the CIA, a Campaign." *Wired*. www.wired.com/politics/onlinerights/news/2007/08/wiki_tracker.

Bragues, George. 2009. "Wiki-philosophizing in a Marketplace of Ideas: Evaluating Wikipedia's Entries on Seven Great Minds." *MediaTropes* 2: 117–58.

Broughton, John. 2008. *Wikipedia*: The Missing Manual. Sebastopol, Calif.: O'Reilly Media.

Butler, Declan. 2008. "Publish in Wikipedia or Perish." *Nature*. www.nature.com/news/2008/081216/full/news.2008.1312.html.

Citizendium (2010). "CZ: About." Retrieved August 23, 2010 from http://en/citizendium.org/wiki/CZ:About.

Cohen, G. A. 2002. "Deeper into Bullshit." In *Contours of Agency*, ed. Sarah Buss and Lee Overton. Cambridge, MA: MIT Press, 321–39.

Cohen, Noam. 2007, January 29. "Courts Turn to Wikipedia, but Selectively." *New York Times*. www.nytimes.com/2007/01/29/technology/29wikipedia.html.

———. 2009, August 24. "Wikipedia to Limit Changes to Articles on People." *New York Times*. www.nytimes.com/2009/08/25/technology/internet/25wikipedia.html.

Denning, Peter, Jim Horning, David Parnas, and Lauren Weinstein. 2005. "Wikipedia Risks." *Communications of the Association for Computing Machinery* 48: 152.

Descartes, René. 1996 [1641]. *Meditations on First Philosophy*. Ed. John Cotting-ham. Cambridge: Cambridge University Press.

"The Epistemology of Mass Collaboration." *Episteme*, Vol. 6, no. 1, 2009.

Fallis, Don. 2004a. "Epistemic Value Theory and Information Ethics." *Minds and Machines* 14: 101–7.

———. 2004b. "On Verifying the Accuracy of Information: Philosophical Perspec-tives." *Library Trends* 52: 463–87.

———. 2006. "Epistemic Value Theory and Social Epistemology." *Episteme* 2: 177–88.

Fallis, Don, and Martin Frické. 2002. "Indicators of Accuracy of Consumer Health Information on the Internet." *Journal of the American Medical Informatics Asso-ciation* 9: 73–79.

Fisk, Robert (2007). "Caught in the Deadly Web of the Internet," *The Independent*, April 21, 2007. Retrieved August 23, 2010 from http://www.independent.co.uk/news/fisk/robert-fisk-caught-in-the-deadly-web-of-the-internet-445561.html.

Frankfurt, Harry G. 2005. *On Bullshit*. Princeton: Princeton University Press.

Garfinkel, Simson L. 2008. "Wikipedia and the Meaning of Truth." *Technology Review* 3, 6: 84–86.

Giles, Jim. 2005. "Internet Encyclopaedias Go Head to Head." *Nature* 438: 900–901.

Goldman, Alvin I. 1987. "Foundations of Social Epistemics." *Synthese* 73: 109–144.

———. 1999. *Knowledge in a Social World*. New York: Oxford University Press.

———. 2008. "The Social Epistemology of Blogging." In *Information Technology and Moral Philosophy*, ed. Jeroen van den Hoven and John Weckert. Cam-bridge: Cambridge University Press, 111–22.

Guinnee, Eli. 2007. "A New Context for Knowledge Creation." *Library Student Journal*. www.librarystudentjournal.org/index.php/lsj/article/view/18/44.

Hardin, Russell. 2003. "If It Rained Knowledge." *Philosophy of the Social Sciences* 33: 3–24.

Healy, K. February 4, 2007. "Wikipedia Follies." Retrieved August 23, 2010 from http://crookedtimber.org/2007/02/04/wikipedia/.

Hume, David. 1977 [1748]. *An Enquiry Concerning Human Understanding*. Ed. Eric Steinberg. Indianapolis: Hackett.

James, William. 1979 [1896]. *The Will to Believe and Other Essays in Popular Philosophy*. Cambridge, MA: Harvard University Press.

Keen, Andrew. 2007. *Cult of the Amateur*. New York: Doubleday.

Kelly, Thomas. 2003. "Epistemic Rationality as Instrumental Rationality: A Critique." *Philosophy and Phenomenological Research* 66: 612–40.

Kitcher, Philip. 1992. "The Naturalists Return." *Philosophical Review* 101: 53–114.

Krahulik, M and Holkins, J. 2005. "I Have the Power." Retrieved August 23, 2010 from http://www.penny-arcade.com/comic/2005/12/16.

Kronick, David A. 1988. "Anonymity and Identity: Editorial Policy in the Early Scientific Journal." *Library Quarterly* 58: 221–37.

Lackey, Jennifer, and Ernest Sosa, eds. 2006. *The Epistemology of Testimony*. Oxford: Oxford University Press.

Leiter, B. June 17, 2007. "Martha Nussbaum and Wikipedia: A Case Study in the Unreliability of Information on the Internet." Retrieved August 23, 2010 from http://leiterreports.typepad.com/blog/2007/06/martha_nussbaum.html.

Magnus, P. D. 2006. "Epistemology and the Wikipedia." Paper presented at *North American Computing and Philosophy Conference*, Troy, New York. http://hdl. handle.net/1951/42589.

Mann, Thomas. 1993. *Library Research Models*. New York: Oxford University Press.

Mathiesen, Kay. 2006. "The Epistemic Features of Group Belief." *Episteme* 2: 161–75.

Meyer, Bertrand. 2006. "Defense and Illustration of Wikipedia." http://se.inf.ethz. ch/~meyer/publications/wikipedia/wikipedia.pdf.

Mill, John S. 1978 [1859]. *On Liberty*. ed. Elizabeth Rapaport. Indianapolis: Hackett.

Nature 2006. *"Nature's* Response to Encyclopaedia Britannica." Retrieved August 23, 2010 from http://www.nature.com/nature/britannica/.

Noah, Timothy. February 24, 2007. "Evicted from Wikipedia." *Slate*. www.slate. com/id/2160222/.

Paterson, R. W. K. 1979. "Towards an Axiology of Knowledge." *Journal of Philosophy of Education* 13: 91–100.

Poe, Marshall. September, 2006. "The Hive." *Atlantic Monthly*. www.theatlantic. com/doc/200609/wikipedia.

Rainie, L. and Tancer, B. April 24, 2007. "Wikipedia Users." Retrieved August 23, 2010 from http://www.pewinternet.org/Reports/2007/Wikipedia-users. aspx.

Read, Brock. 2006. "Can Wikipedia Ever Make the Grade?" *Chronicle of Higher Education* 53(10): A31.

———. 2007. "Middlebury College History Department Limits Students' Use of Wikipedia." *Chronicle of Higher Education* 53(24): A39.

Smith, Christopher. 2002. "Social Epistemology, Contextualism and the Division of Labor." *Social Epistemology* 16: 65–81.

Surowiecki, James. 2004. *The Wisdom of Crowds*. New York: Doubleday.

Thagard, Paul. 2001. "Internet Epistemology: Contributions of New Information Technologies to Scientific Research." In *Designing for Science: Implications for Professional, Instructional, and Everyday Science*. Ed. K. Crowley, C.D. Schunn, and T. Okada. Mawah, N.J.: Erlbaum, 465–485.

Tollefsen, Deborah. 2007. "Group Testimony." *Social Epistemology* 21: 299–311.

Waldron, Jeremy. 1995. "The Wisdom of the Multitude: Some Reflections on Book 3, Chapter 11 of Aristotle's *Politics*." *Political Theory* 23: 563–84.

Wells, Herbert G. 1971 [1938]. *World Brain*. Freeport, N.Y.: Books for Libraries Press.

Wikipedia 2010a. "General Disclaimer". Retrieved August 23, 2010 from http:// en.wikipedia.org/wiki/Wikipedia:General_disclaimer.

Wikipedia 2010b. "Wikipedia: About." Retrieved August 23, 2010 from http:// enwikipedia.org/wiki/Wikipedia:About.

Wikipedia 2010c. "Wikipedia: Vandalism." Retrieved August 23, 2010 from http:// en.wikipedia.org/wiki/Wikipedia:Vandalism.

Wikipedia 2010d. "Reliability_of_Wikipedia." Retrieved August 23, 2010 from http://enwikipedia.org/wiki/Reliability_of_Wikipedia.

Wikipedia 2010e. "Wikipedia: Notability." Retrieved August 23, 2010 from http:// enwikipedia.org/wiki/Wikipedia:Notability.

Wikipedia 2010f. "Wikipedia: Verifiability." Retrieved August 23, 2010 from http://en/wikipedia.org/wiki/Wikipedia:Verifiability.

Wilson, Chris. February 22, 2008. "The Wisdom of the Chaperones." *Slate*. www.slate.com/id/2184487/.

Winchester, Simon. 1998. *The Professor and the Madman*. New York: Harper-Collins.

Wray, K. B. 2002. "The Epistemic Significance of Collaborative Research." *Philosophy of Science* 69: 150–68.

14

Deliberating Groups versus Prediction Markets (or Hayek's Challenge to Habermas)

Cass R. Sunstein

ABSTRACT   *For multiple reasons, deliberating groups often converge on falsehood rather than truth. Individual errors may be amplified rather than cured. Group members may fall victim to a bad cascade, either informational or reputational. Deliberators may emphasize shared information at the expense of uniquely held information. Finally, group polarization may lead even rational people to unjustified extremism. By contrast, prediction markets often produce accurate results, because they create strong incentives for revelation of privately held knowledge and succeed in aggregating widely dispersed information. The success of prediction markets offers a set of lessons for increasing the likelihood that groups can obtain the information that their members have.*

Many institutions, both public and private, make their decisions through deliberation. But why, exactly, is deliberation important or even desirable? A central answer must be that deliberation will result in wiser judgments and better outcomes. But does deliberation actually have this effect ? The answer is by no means clear. Group members may impose pressures on one another, leading to a consensus on falsehood rather than truth. A group of like-minded people, with similar predilections, is particularly vulnerable to this problem. The idea of "groupthink," coined and elaborated by Irving Janis, suggests the possibility that groups will tend toward uniformity and censorship, thus failing to combine information and enlarge the range of arguments.[1] Without structural protections, both private and public groups are likely to err, not in spite of deliberation but because of it.

My aim here is to compare deliberation with an intriguing social innovation – prediction markets – and to explore the advantages of the latter over the former in aggregating information. One of my goals is to see how the successes of prediction markets might inform the practice of deliberation. To explain why deliberation often fails, I investigate two sets of influences on members of deliberating groups.[2] The first consists of informational influences, by which group members fail to disclose what they know out of deference to the information publicly announced by others. The second involves social pressures, which lead people to silence themselves in order not to face reputational sanctions, such as the disapproval of relevant others. As a result of these problems, groups often amplify rather than correct individual errors; emphasize shared information at the expense of unshared information; fall victim to cascade effects; and tend to end up in more extreme positions in line with the predeliberation tendencies of their members. In the United States, even federal judges are vulnerable to the relevant pressures, as both Republican and Democratic appointees show especially ideological voting when they are sitting with other judges appointed by presidents of the same political party.[3]

Because of these pressures, deliberative processes often fail to achieve their minimal goal of aggregating the information actually held by the deliberators. Indeed, such processes often fail to aggregate information even as they decrease variance, and increase confidence, among their members. A confident, cohesive, error-prone group is nothing to celebrate. On the contrary, it might be extremely dangerous, both to itself and to others.[4]

As we shall see, prediction markets often outperform deliberating groups, simply because they are so effective at pooling dispersed information among diverse people. Indeed, prediction markets realign private incentives in a way that makes them exceptionally well-designed to reduce the problems that infect deliberating groups. Such markets are worth investigating, in part because they provide an illuminating route by which to explore some characteristic defects in deliberative processes— and by which to obtain insights about how they might work better. In addition, such markets are worth investigating in their own right, if only because they promise to provide a supplement to deliberation that might well improve social decisions.

DELIBERATING GROUPS

If deliberating groups do well, we can imagine three principal reasons:

- *Groups are equivalent to their best members.* One or more group members will often know the right answer, and other members might well become convinced of this fact. For this reason, groups might perform toward or at the level of their best members. If some or many members suffer from ignorance or from a form of bias that leads to error, others might correct them. Deliberation might correct individual errors rather than propagate them, in a way that allows convergence on the judgment of the most accurate group member.

- *The whole is the sum of the parts: aggregating information.* Deliberation could aggregate existing information in a way that leads the group as a whole to know more than any individual member does. Suppose that the group contains no experts on the question at issue, but that relevant information is dispersed among members so that the group is potentially expert even if its members are not. Or suppose that the group contains a number of experts, but that each member is puzzled about how to solve a particular problem. Deliberation might elicit the relevant information and allow the group to make a sensible judgment. In this process, the whole is equal to the sum of the parts – and the sum of the parts is what is sought.
- *Improving on majority rule.* Suppose that in advance of deliberation, each group member is more than 50 percent likely to be right. The Condorcet Jury Theorem shows that the likelihood that the group's majority will be right expands to 100 percent as the size of the group increases. Perhaps deliberating groups will do better than would the majority of their individual members without deliberation – whatever the initial distribution of correct answers within those groups.
- *The whole goes beyond the sum of the parts: synergy.* The give and take of group discussion might sift information and perspectives in a way that leads the group to a good solution to a problem, one in which the whole is actually more than the sum of its parts. In such cases, deliberation is, at the very least, an ambitious form of information aggregation, one in which the exchange of views leads to a creative answer or solution.

To what extent do these mechanisms work in practice? Two points are entirely clear. First, deliberation usually reduces variance.[5] After talking together, group members tend to come into accord with one another.[6] Second, group members tend to become far more confident of their judgments after they speak with one another.[7] A significant effect of group interactions is a greater sense that one's postdeliberation conclusion is correct – whether it actually is or not. Corroboration by others increases confidence in one's judgments.[8] It follows that members of deliberating groups will usually converge on a position on which members have a great deal of confidence. This is not disturbing if that position is also likely to be correct – but if it is not, then many group members will end up sharing a view in which they firmly believe, but which turns out to be wrong (a most unfortunate and sometimes quite dangerous situation).

Unfortunately, there is no systematic evidence that deliberating groups will usually succeed in aggregating the information held by their members. With respect to questions with definite answers, deliberating groups tend to do about as well as or slightly better than their average members, but not as well as their best members.[9] Hence, it is false to say that group members usually end up deferring to their internal specialists. Truth does not win out; the most that can be said is that under some conditions, the group will converge on the truth if the truth begins with "at least some initial support" within the group when the task has "a demonstrably correct answer."[10] Note here that when a group outperforms most of its individual members, it is generally because the issue is one on which a particular answer can be shown, to the satisfaction of all or most, to be right; and that even in that condition, the group might not do well if the demonstrably correct solution lacks significant support at the outset.

In general, simple majority schemes do fairly well at predicting group judgments for many decision tasks. It follows that if the majority is wrong, the group will be wrong as well.[11] With experts, the same general conclusion holds. Thus a "structured approach for combining independent forecasts is invariably more accurate" than "traditional group meetings," which do "not use information efficiently."[12]

SOURCES OF DELIBERATIVE FAILURE

For two reasons, exposure to the views of others might lead people to silence themselves. The first involves the informational signals provided by the acts and views of other people. If most group members believe that X is true, there is reason to believe that X is in fact true, and that reason might outweigh the purely private reason a particular group member has to believe that X is false. If other group members share a particular belief, isolated or minority members might not speak out, deferring to the informational signal given by the statements of others. Not surprisingly, the strength of the signal will depend on the number and nature of the people who are giving it. People are particularly averse to being sole dissenters.[13] If all but one person in a deliberating group has said that X is true, then the remaining member is likely to agree X is true, even to the point of ignoring the evidence of his own senses. And if the group contains one or more people who are well-known to be authorities, then other group members are likely to defer to them.

The second reason that group members might silence themselves involves social influences. Their silence might stem not from a belief that they are wrong, as in the case of informational pressure, but instead from the risk of social sanctions of various sorts. In the most extreme cases, those sanctions will take the form of criminal punishment or complete exclusion from the group. In less severe cases, those who defy the dominant position within the group will incur a form of disapproval that will lead them to be less trusted, liked, and respected in the future. Here, too, people are inevitably affected by the number and nature of those with the majority position. A large majority will impose more social pressure than a small one. If certain group members are leaders or authorities willing and able to impose social sanctions of various sorts, others will be unlikely to defy them publicly.

Participation in deliberative processes, and the effects of informational and social influences, can be put into a more general framework. Suppose that group members are deliberating about some factual question; suppose, too, that each member has some information that bears on the answer to that question. Will members disclose what they know ?

For each person, the answer may well depend on the individual benefits and the individual costs of disclosure. In many situations, and entirely apart from informational and social influences, the individual benefits of disclosure will be far less than the social benefits. In this sense, participants in deliberation often face a collective action problem, in which each person, following his rational self-interest, will tell the group less than it needs to know. At least, this is so if each member receives only a small portion of the benefits that come to the group from a good outcome – a plausible view about the situation facing many institutions, including, for example, labor unions, religious organizations, student and faculty groups, corporate boards, and government agencies.

If the statements of others suggest that privately held information is wrong or unhelpful, then the private benefit of disclosure is reduced much more. In that event, the group member has reason to believe that disclosure will not improve the group's decision at all. Things are even worse if those who speak against the apparent consensus suffer reputational injury (or more). In that event, the private calculus is straightforward: Silence is golden.

Both informational pressure and social influences help explain the finding that in a deliberating group, those in a minority position often silence themselves or otherwise have disproportionately little weight. There is a more particular finding: Members of low-status groups – less-educated people, African-Americans, sometimes women – speak less and carry less influence within deliberating groups than their higher-status peers.[14] Both informational influence and social pressures, likely to be especially strong for low-status members, contribute to this result. The unfortunate consequence can be a loss of information to the group as a whole, in a way that ensures that deliberating groups do far less well than they would if only they could aggregate the information held by group members.

More generally, a comprehensive study has demonstrated that majority pressures can be powerful even for factual questions to which some people know the right answers.[15] The study involved twelve hundred people, forming groups of six, five, and four members. Individuals were asked true-false questions involving art, poetry, public opinion, geography, economics, and politics. They were then asked to assemble into groups, which discussed the questions and produced answers. The majority played a substantial role in determining each group's answers. The truth played a role, too, but a lesser one. If a majority of individuals in the group gave the right answer, the group's decision moved toward the majority in 79 percent of the cases. If a majority of individuals in the group gave the wrong answer, the group's decision nonetheless moved toward the majority in 56 percent of the cases. Hence, the truth did have an influence – 79 percent is higher than 56 percent – but the majority's judgment was the dominant one. And because the majority was influential even when wrong, the average group decision was right only slightly more often than the average individual decision (66 percent versus 62 percent). What is most important is that groups did not perform as well as they would have if they had properly aggregated the information that group members had.

HABERMAS VS. HAYEK

Do these points amount to a challenge to deliberation as an ideal, or to deliberative conceptions of democracy? Many of those interested in deliberation have attempted to specify its preconditions in a way that is intended to ensure against predictable problems that infect real-world processes. Jürgen Habermas, for example, stresses norms and practices designed to allow victory by "the better argument":

> Rational discourse is supposed to be public and inclusive, to grant equal communication rights for participants, to require sincerity and to diffuse any kind of force other than the forceless force of the better argument. This communicative structure is expected to create a deliberative space for the mobilization of the best available contributions for the most relevant topics.[16]

In Habermas's "ideal speech situation," all participants attempt to seek the truth; they do not behave strategically or attempt to decide; they accept a norm of equality.[17] Other advocates of deliberative democracy have spoken similarly about what appropriate deliberation entails.[18] On this view, deliberation, properly understood, does not simply involve the exchange of words and opinions. It imposes its own requirements and preconditions. Indeed, deliberation has its own internal morality, one that operates as a corrective to some of the effects of deliberative processes in the real world.

Unfortunately, preconditions of the sort identified by Habermas will cure few of the problems that I shall be outlining here. Those preconditions will do little to affect the key failures on the part of deliberating groups. Each of the failures is likely to arise even if discourse is public and inclusive, even if participants are sincere, and even if everyone has equal communication rights. We might therefore take the argument here as a Hayekian challenge to Habermas - a challenge that stresses (with Friedrich Hayek) the diffusion of information in society and the difficulty of aggregating that information through deliberation (as opposed to the price signal, which Hayek championed).[19]

Consider four sets of deliberative failures.

DELIBERATIVE FAILURE 1: AMPLIFICATION OF COGNITIVE ERRORS

It is well known that individuals do not always process information well. They use heuristics that lead them to predictable errors; they are also subject to identifiable biases, which produce further errors.[20] For example, most people follow the representativeness heuristic, in accordance with which judgments of probability are influenced by assessments of resemblance (the extent to which A "looks like" B).[21] The representativeness heuristic helps explain what Paul Rozin and Carol Nemeroff have called "sympathetic magical thinking," including the beliefs that some objects have contagious properties, and that causes resemble their effects.[22] The representativeness heuristic often works well, but it can also lead to severe blunders.

People often err because they use the availability heuristic to answer difficult questions about probability. When people use the availability heuristic, they answer a question of probability by asking whether examples come readily to mind.[23] Consider, for example, the question whether we should fear a hurricane, a nuclear power accident, or a terrorist attack. If it is easy to think of a case in which one of these hazards created serious harm, the assessment of probability will be greatly affected. Of course, use of the availability heuristic is not irrational, but it, too, can produce both excessive and insufficient fear.

For purposes of assessing deliberation, a central question is whether groups avoid the errors of the individuals who comprise them. There is no clear evidence that they do, and often they do not – a vivid illustration of the principle, "garbage in, garbage out," in a way that mocks the aspiration to collective correction of individual blunders. In fact, individual errors are not merely replicated but actually amplified in group decisions – a process of "some garbage in, much garbage out."

Consider some key findings. If individual jurors are biased because of pretrial publicity that misleadingly implicates the defendant, or even because of the defendant's unappealing physical appearance, juries are likely to amplify rather than correct those biases.[24] Groups have been found to amplify, rather than to attenuate, reliance on the representativeness heuristic;[25] to reflect even larger framing effects than individuals;[26] to show more overconfidence than group members;[27] to be more affected by the biasing effect of spurious arguments from lawyers;[28] to be more susceptible to the "sunk cost fallacy";[29] and to be more subject to choice-rank preference reversals.[30] In an especially revealing finding, groups have been found to make more, rather than fewer, conjunction errors than individuals when individual error rates are high – though fewer when individual error rates are low.[31] In addition, groups demonstrate essentially the same level of reliance on the availability heuristic, even when use of that heuristic leads to clear errors.[32]

DELIBERATIVE FAILURE 2: HIDDEN PROFILES AND COMMON KNOWLEDGE

Suppose that group members have a great deal of information – enough to produce the unambiguously right outcome if that information is properly aggregated. Even if this is so, an obvious problem is that groups will not perform well if they emphasize shared information and slight information that is held by one or a few members. Unfortunately, countless studies demonstrate that this regrettable result is highly likely.[33] "Hidden profiles" is the term for accurate understandings that groups could but do not obtain. Hidden profiles are, in turn, a product of the *common-knowledge effect*, through which information held by all group members has more influence on group judgments than information held by only a few members.[34] The most obvious explanation of the effect is the simple fact that as a statistical matter, common knowledge is more likely to be communicated to the group; but social influences play a role as well.

Hidden Profiles. Consider a study of serious errors within working groups, both face-to-face and online.[35] The purpose of the study was to see how groups might collaborate to make personnel decisions. Resumes for three candidates applying for a marketing manager position were placed before group members. The attributes of the candidates were rigged by the experimenters so that one applicant was clearly the best for the job described. Packets of information were given to subjects, each containing a subset of information from the resumes, so that each group member had only part of the relevant information. The groups consisted of three people, some operating face-to-face, some operating online. Almost none of the deliberating groups made what was conspicuously the right choice. The reason is simple: They failed to share information in a way that would permit the group to make that choice. Members tended to share positive information about the winning candidate and negative information about the losers. They suppressed negative information about the winner and positive information about the losers. Hence, their statements served to "reinforce the march toward group consensus rather than add complications and fuel debate."[36]

Or consider a simulation of political elections, in which information was parceled out to individual members about three candidates for political office, and in which properly pooled information could have led to what was clearly the best choice, candidate A.[37] In the first condition, each member of the four-person groups was given most of the relevant information (66 percent of the information about each candidate). In that condition, 67 percent of group members favored candidate A before discussion and 85 percent after discussion.[38] This is a clear example of appropriate aggregation of information. Groups significantly outperformed individuals, apparently because of the exchange of information and reasons. Here, then, is a clear illustration of the possibility that groups can aggregate what members know in a way that produces sensible outcomes.

In the second condition, by contrast, the information that favored candidate A was parceled out to various members of the group so that only 33 percent of information about each candidate was shared. As the condition was designed, the shared information favored two unambiguously inferior candidates, B and C; but if the unshared information emerged through discussion, and were taken seriously, candidate A would be chosen. In that condition, less than 25 percent of group members favored candidate A before discussion, a natural product of the initial distribution of information. But (and this is the key result) that number actually *fell* after discussion, simply because the shared information had disproportionate influence on group members.[39] In other words, groups did worse, not better, than individuals when the key information was distributed selectively. In those conditions, the commonly held information was far more influential than the distributed information, to the detriment of the group's ultimate decision.

From this and many similar studies, the general conclusion is that when "the balance of unshared information opposes the initial most popular position . . . the unshared information will tend to be omitted from discussion and, therefore, will have little effect on members' preferences during group discussion."[40] It follows that "group decisions and postgroup preferences reflect the initial preferences of group members even when the exchange of unshared information should have resulted in substantial shifts in opinion."[41] Nor does discussion increase the recall of unshared information. On the contrary, its major effect is to increase recall of the attributes of the initially most popular candidate.[42] The most disturbing conclusion is that when key information is unshared, groups are "more likely to endorse an inferior option after discussion than [are] their individual members before discussion."[43]

The Common-Knowledge Effect. These results are best understood as a consequence of the common-knowledge effect, by which information held by all group members has far more influence on group judgments than information held by one member or a few.[44] More precisely, the "influence of a particular item of information is directly and positively related to the number of group members who have knowledge of that item before the group discussion and judgment."[45] Under conditions of unshared information, group judgments have been found to be "not any more accurate than the average of the individual judgments, even though" – and this is the central point – the groups were "in possession of more information than were any of the individuals."[46]

As might be expected, the group's focus on shared information increases with the size of the group.[47] In a study by Stasser and colleagues designed to test judgments about candidates for office, involving both three person and six-person groups, all discussions focused far more on shared than on unshared information – but the effect was significantly greater for six-person groups. Most remarkably, the researchers write, "it was almost as likely for a shared item to be mentioned twice as it was for an unshared item to be mentioned at all."[48] And despite the failures of their deliberations, group members were significantly more confident in their judgments after discussion.[49]

DELIBERATIVE FAILURE 3: CASCADES

A cascade is a process by which people influence one another, so much so that participants ignore their private knowledge and rely instead on the publicly stated judgments of others. There are two kinds of cascades: informational and reputational. In informational cascades, people silence themselves out of deference to the information conveyed by others. In reputational cascades, they silence themselves so as to avoid the opprobrium of others.

Informational Cascades. Hidden profiles are closely related to informational cascades, which greatly impair group judgments. Cascades need not involve deliberation, but deliberative processes often involve cascades. As in the case of hidden profiles, the central point is that those involved in a cascade do not reveal what they know. As a result, the group does not obtain important information.

To see how informational cascades work, imagine a deliberating group that is deciding whether to authorize some new venture.[50] Let us also assume that the members are announcing their views in sequence, in a temporal queue, and that each member knows his place in that queue. Every member has some private information about what should be done. But each also attends, reasonably enough, to the judgments of others. Mr. Andrews is the first to speak. He suggests that the venture should be authorized. Ms. Barnes now knows Andrews's judgment; it is clear that she, too, should vote in favor of the venture if she agrees independently with Andrews. But if her independent judgment is otherwise, she would – if she trusts Andrews no more and no less than she trusts herself – be indifferent about what to do and might simply flip a coin.

Now turn to a third person, Mr. Carlton. Suppose that both Andrews and Barnes have argued in favor of the venture but that Carlton's own information, though inconclusive, suggests that the venture is a terrible idea. In that event, Carlton might well ignore what he knows and follow Andrews and Barnes. It is likely in these circumstances that both Andrews and Barnes had reasons for their conclusion, and unless Carlton thinks that his own information is better than theirs, he should follow their lead. If he does, Carlton is in a cascade. Now suppose that Carlton is acting in response to what Andrews and Barnes did, not on the basis of his own information, and that subsequent members know what Andrews, Barnes, and Carlton did. On reasonable assumptions, they will do exactly what Carlton did: favor the venture regardless of their private information (which, we are supposing, is relevant but inconclusive). This will happen even if Andrews initially blundered.[51]

If this is what is happening, there is a serious social problem: Those who are in the cascade do not disclose the information that they privately hold. In the example just given, decisions will not reflect the overall knowledge, or the aggregate knowledge, of those in the group – even if the information held by individual members, if actually revealed and aggregated, would produce a quite different result. The reason is that people are following the lead of those who came before. Subsequent speakers might fail to rely on, and fail to reveal, private information that actually exceeds the information collectively held by those who started the cascade.

Cascades often occur in the real world within deliberating groups or elsewhere;[52] they are easy to create in the laboratory. The simplest experiment asked subjects to guess whether the experiment was using urn A, which contained two red balls and one white, or urn B, which contained two white balls and one red.[53] Subjects could earn $2.00 for a correct decision, and hence an economic incentive favored correct individual decisions (a point to which I will return). In each period, the contents of the chosen urn were emptied into a container. A randomly selected subject was asked to make one (and only one) private draw of a ball in each round. The subject recorded the color of that draw on an answer sheet and his own decision about which urn was involved. The subject did not announce his draw to the group, but he did announce his own decision to everyone. Then the urn was passed to the next subject for his own private draw, which again was not disclosed, and his own decision about the urn, which again was disclosed. This process continued until all subjects had made draws and decisions. At that time, the experimenter announced the actual urn used. If the subject had picked the urn only on the basis of his private information, he would have been right 66.7 percent of the time. The point of the experiment was to see whether people will decide to ignore their own draw in the face of conflicting announcements by predecessors – and to explore whether such decisions will lead to cascades and errors.

In the experiment, cascades often developed and often produced errors. After a number of individual judgments were revealed, people sometimes announced decisions that were inconsistent with their private draws, but that fit with the majority of previous announcements.[54] More than 77 percent of "rounds" resulted in cascades, and 15 percent of private announcements did not reveal a "private signal," that is, the information provided by people's own draws. Consider cases in which one person's draw (say, red) contradicted the announcement of his predecessor (say, urn B). In such cases, the second announcement nonetheless matched the first about 11 percent of the time – far less than a majority, but enough to ensure cascades. And when one person's draw contradicted the announcement of two or more predecessors, the second announcement was likely to follow those who went before. Of note, the majority of decisions were rationally based on the available information[55] – but erroneous cascades nonetheless developed. Figure 14.1 shows an example of a cascade that produced an inaccurate outcome (the urn used was B):[56]

What is noteworthy here, of course, is that the total amount of private information – three whites and three reds – justified a 50 percent probability of the correct judgment (urn B). But the existence of two early signals, producing rational but incorrect judgments, led everyone else to fall in line. "Initial misrepresentative signals start a chain of incorrect decisions that is not broken by more representative signals received later."[57] This result maps directly onto real-world decisions by deliberating groups, in which people fail to disclose what they know, to the detriment of the group as a whole.

Reputational Cascades. In a reputational cascade, people think they know what is right, or what is likely to be right, but they nonetheless go along with the crowd in order to maintain the good opinion of others. Suppose Albert suggests that global warming is a serious problem and that Barbara concurs with Albert, not because she actually thinks that Albert is right, but because she does not wish to seem, to Albert, ignorant of or indifferent to environmental protection. If Albert and Barbara seem to agree that global warming is a serious problem, Cynthia not only might not contradict them publicly, but also might even appear to share their judgment, not because she believes that judgment to be correct, but because she does not want to face their hostility or lose their good opinion.

	1	2	3	4	5	6
Private draw	Red	Red	Red	White	White	White
Decision	A	A	A	A	A	A

Source: Willinger and Ziegelmeyet, "Are More Informed Agents," 291.

Figure 14.1. An Informational Cascade

	1	2	3	4	5	6	7	8	9	10
Private draw	Red	White	White	White	Red	White	White	White	Red	White
Decision	A	A	A	A	A	A	A	A	A	A

Source: Hung and Plott, "Information Cascades."

Figure 14.2. Conformity and Cascades

It should be easy to see how this process might generate a cascade. Once Albert, Barbara, and Cynthia offer a united front on the issue, their friend David might be most reluctant to contradict them, even if he thinks they are wrong. In the actual world of group decisions, people are, of course, uncertain whether publicly expressed statements are a product of independent information, participation in an informational cascade, or reputational pressure. Much of the time, listeners and observers undoubtedly overstate the extent to which the actions of others are based on independent information.

The possibility of reputational cascades is demonstrated by an ingenious variation on the urn experiment mentioned above.[58] In this experiment, people were paid $0.25 for a correct decision, but $0.75 for a decision that matched the decision of the majority of the group. There were punishments for incorrect and nonconforming answers as well. If people made an incorrect decision, they lost $0.25; if their decision failed to match the group's decision, they lost $0.75.

In this experiment, cascades appeared almost all of the time. No fewer than 96.7 percent of rounds resulted in cascades, and 35.3 percent of people's announcements did not match their private signal, that is, the signal given by their own draw. And when the draw of a subsequent person contradicted the announcement of the predecessor, 72.2 percent of people matched the first announcement. Consider, as a dramatic illustration, figure 14.2, which shows this period of the experiment (the actual urn was B):[59] This experiment shows that especially unfortunate results should be expected if people are rewarded not only or not mostly for being correct, but also or mostly for doing what other people do. The problem is that people are not revealing the information they actually have.

DELIBERATIVE FAILURE 4: GROUP POLARIZATION

There are clear links among hidden profiles, social cascades, and the well-established phenomenon of group polarization, by which *members of a deliberating group end up adopting a more extreme version of the position toward which they tended before deliberation began.*[60] The problem is especially severe for groups of like-minded people, who typically end up in more extreme positions as a result of deliberation. Group polarization is the typical pattern with deliberating groups, and it has been found in hundreds of studies involving more than a dozen countries, including the United States, France, Afghanistan, and Germany.[61] For example, those who disapprove of the United States and are suspicious of its intentions will increase their disapproval and suspicion if they exchange points of view. Indeed, there is specific evidence of the latter phenomenon among citizens of France.[62]

Group polarization occurs for matters of fact as well as issues of value, though it is easier to demonstrate the latter. If the question is whether a terrorist attack will occur in the United States in the next year, group polarization will not be easy to test, simply because the answer is either yes or no, and it is not simple to demonstrate greater extremism in binary choices. But suppose that people are asked, on a bounded scale of zero to eight, how likely it is that a terrorist attack will occur in the United States in the next year, with zero indicating "zero probability," eight indicating "absolutely certain," seven indicating "overwhelmingly likely," six "more probable than not," and five "fifty-fifty." In that event, the answers from a deliberating group will tend to reveal group polarization, as people move toward more extreme points on the scale depending on their initial median point. If the predeliberation median is five, the group judgment will usually be six; if the predeliberation median is three, the group judgment will usually be two.[63] Recall here that federal judges are highly susceptible to group polarization, as both Democratic and Republican appointees show far more ideological voting patterns when sitting with other judges appointed by a president of the same political party.[64] Juries polarize as well.[65]

Why does group polarization occur? There are three reasons.[66] The first and most important involves the now-familiar idea of informational influence, but in a distinctive form. People respond to the arguments made by other people – and the "argument pool" in any group with some predisposition in one direction will inevitably be skewed toward that predisposition. As a statistical matter, the arguments favoring the initial position will be more numerous than those pointing in the other direction. Individuals will have heard of some, but not all, of the arguments that emerge from group deliberation. As a result of the relevant arguments, deliberation will lead people toward a more extreme point in line with what group members initially believed.

The second explanation involves social influences. People want to be perceived favorably by other group members. Sometimes people's publicly stated views are, to a greater or lesser extent, a function of how they want to present themselves. Once they hear what others believe, some will adjust their positions at least slightly in the direction of the dominant position in order to hold onto their preserved self-presentation. They shift accordingly.[67]

The third explanation stresses that people with extreme views tend to have more confidence that they are right, and that, as people gain confidence, they become more extreme in their beliefs.[68] In a wide variety of experimental contexts, people's opinions have been shown to become more extreme simply because their views have been corroborated and because they have been more confident after learning of the shared views of others.[69]

Note that if it is understood in these terms, group polarization may well reflect rational behavior at the individual level.[70] Suppose that each group member privately assigns a significant probability, say of 0.6, to the truth of some hypothesis (say, that North Korea will have nuclear weapons within the next year). Suppose, further, that group discussion leads each group member to hear evidence largely supportive of the hypothesis, leading to a judgment in favor of a higher probability, say of 0.7. Rational updating may be entirely responsible for the shift. Now suppose all group members report after deliberation that they have each independently arrived at a probability of 0.7 for the truth of the hypothesis, based on the evidence they have received (and starting with a prior of 0.6). What this means is that there have been a total number of n independent items of evidence in support of the hypothesis (one such item for each of n group members), each of which has been sufficiently strong to support a Bayesian update from 0.6 to 0.7. The existence of these n independent items of evidence should then lead the group as a whole – and each group member post-deliberation – to assign a still higher posterior probability to the hypothesis, i.e., a probability well above 0.7.

Whether rational updating of this kind will produce accurate or inaccurate judgments depends on the antecedently held information within the group. Suppose that for people who are fully informed, the probability that the relevant hypothesis is true is in fact 0.3. If the group starts from a significantly inflated probability estimate, group polarization will lead them to make severe errors. Nothing in the phenomenon of group polarization demonstrates that deliberation will lead to blunders. But if the median predeliberation view is wrong, groups are likely to do worse than their individual members.

It should be clear that the four sources of deliberative failure can create serious problems for deliberating groups. What might be done in response? I have mentioned Hayek's suggestion that the price mechanism is an excellent way to aggregate dispersed information. Might the price system be enlisted as a supplement to, or even a replacement for, social deliberation?

PREDICTION MARKETS

Deliberation is one way to aggregate privately held information, but there are many other possibilities. An obvious alternative is to rely on the price signal, which has a similar aggregative function. As Hayek emphasized, the price mechanism is a kind of "marvel," because it combines widely dispersed information held by diverse people. And if an emphasis is placed on the information-aggregating properties of markets, it would seem plain that, to improve on the answer produced by deliberating groups, we might consider an increasingly popular possibility: *Create a market*.[71] Prediction markets, a recent innovation, have proved remarkably successful at forecasting future events; they seem to do far better, in many domains, than deliberating groups. Such markets are worth sustained attention, in part because they offer important lessons about how to make deliberation go better or worse, and in part because they provide a useful model for many private and public organizations.

Potential and Promise. A central advantage of prediction markets is that they impose the right incentives for diverse people to disclose the information they separately hold. Recall that in a deliberating group, members often have little incentive to say what they know. By speaking out, they provide benefits to others while possibly facing high private costs. Prediction markets realign incentives in a way that is precisely designed to overcome these problems. Because investments in such markets are generally not disclosed to the public, investors need not fear reputational sanctions if, for example, they have predicted that a company's sales will be low or that a certain candidate will be elected president. And because people stand to gain or lose from their investments, they have a strong incentive to use (and in that sense to disclose) whatever private information they hold; they can capture, rather than give to others, the benefits of disclosure. The use of private information will be reflected in the price signal. In these crucial ways, the problems that infect deliberating groups are largely eliminated in prediction markets.

Prediction markets also impose strong incentives for traders to ferret out accurate information. Traders do not trade blindly, and they are entirely able to stop trading, for a moment or more, in order to retrieve better information that will give them an advantage. In many deliberating groups, by contrast, participants cannot leave; they must continue deliberating, and the necessary information is, at best, dispersed and locked within individual participants. Well-functioning systems of deliberation encourage group members to act dynamically to acquire further information, just as markets do.

Of course, investors, like everyone else, are subject to the informational pressure imposed by the views of others. But a market creates strong incentives for revelation of whatever information people actually hold. And indeed, prediction markets have been found not to amplify individual errors but to eliminate them; the prices that result from trading prove reliable even if many individual traders err. In recent years, prediction markets have done more than to provide valuable information. In countless domains, their forecasts have proved extremely accurate.[72] The most dramatic finding is that prices generally operate as probabilities. When prices suggest that events are likely to occur with 90 percent probability, they occur 90 percent of the time; when the price suggest a probability of 80 percent, the events happen 80 percent of the time; and so forth.

Since 1988, the University of Iowa has run the Iowa Electronic Markets (IEM), which allow people to bet on the outcome of presidential elections. Before the 2004 elections, they did far better than professional polling organizations, outperforming polls 451 out of 596 times.[73] In the week before the four elections from 1988 to 2000, the predictions in the Iowa market showed an average absolute error of just 1.5 percentage points – a significant improvement over the 2.1 percentage point error in the final Gallup polls. In 2004, the Iowa market did even better. On midnight of November 1, it showed Bush with 50.45% of the vote and Kerry with 49.55% – very close to the final numbers of 51.56% for Bush and 48.44% for Kerry.

Prediction markets, aggregating diverse views, are flourishing in numerous domains. Consider the Hollywood Stock Exchange, in which people predict (among other things) Oscar nominees and winners as well as opening weekend box office figures. The level of accuracy has been extremely impressive, especially in view of the fact that the traders use virtual rather than real money. Among the most impressive achievements of the Hollywood Stock exchange to date is its uncanny accuracy in predicting Oscar winners, with correct judgments in twenty-two of the twenty-four categories for which trading was allowed in the last three years. The markets for the demand for gas outperform the experts on the demand for gas.[74] Many people believe that "you can't predict the weather," but the National Weather Service does quite well, and Orange Juice futures do even better.[75] A large prediction market focuses on the likelihood that economic data released later in the week will show specific values;[76] the market has performed even better than the consensus forecasts of a survey of about fifty professional forecasters.

Many companies are now using prediction markets to aggregate diverse views. Hewlett Packard (HP) and the California Institute of Technology initiated a project to study prediction markets as an information aggregation mechanism involving product sales.[77] In no fewer than six of the eight markets for which official forecasts were available, the market prediction was significantly closer to the actual outcome than the official forecast. For its part, Google has created a large set of prediction markets to help to forecast its own development.[78] The relevant markets predict launch dates for products, new office openings, and a range of other outcomes of importance to the company. The outcomes have been exceedingly accurate; prices have actually represented probabilities. Dispersed knowledge within the company has been accurately aggregated in this way. Many other companies, including Ely Lilly and Microsoft, have used prediction markets as well to supplement deliberation about future courses of action.

To be sure, prediction markets themselves involve a measure of deliberation. Many individual investors are likely to have deliberated with others before they invest. In some such markets, investors undoubtedly act as "teams," pooling resources after deliberating together about what to do. The point is that decisions ultimately come not from asking group members to come up with a mutually agreeable conclusion, but by reference to the price signal, which will have aggregated a great deal of diverse information. It is for this reason that prediction markets outperform deliberative processes.

Strategy, Manipulation, and Limitations. It is natural to wonder about whether and when prediction markets might fail. Some clues are provided by two conspicuous failures. Such markets found it more probable than not that Special Prosecutor Patrick Fitzgerald would indict White House adviser Karl Rove in 2005, and they found it exceedingly improbable that President George W. Bush would appoint John Roberts to the United States Supreme Court. The best explanation is that there was not a great deal of dispersed information about the particular decisions of Special Prosecutor Fitzgerald or President Bush. To be sure, investors knew that Fitzgerald would not indict Bush himself and that President Bush would not appoint Fitzgerald (or Tony Blair, Saddam Hussein, or John Kerry) to the Supreme Court; but they lacked the kind of information that would permit successful judgments about the probability that a particular movie would win the Oscars, or that a particular product would do well in the market, or that a particular candidate would be elected in a contested race.

There is an additional problem. Suppose that investors know that their "bets" might have a significant impact on the hypothesis that the market is supposed to predict. Investors might believe, for example, that the predictions of the Iowa Electronic Markets will affect the outcomes of political campaigns, by making certain candidates look promising or instead doomed. Such investors might pour immense sums of money into bets on their preferred candidates, and in the process hope to create a self-fulfilling prophecy. This danger seems nonexistent for genuinely exogenous events, such as a natural disaster or an unusual weather pattern. But for economic events, political campaigns, product success, and terrorism, the risk of manipulation cannot be ruled out of bounds.

Existing evidence does suggest that the risk may be more hypothetical than real. Several efforts to manipulate election markets have been made, and they have not succeeded: In a short time, canny investors see that prices are inflated or deflated, and the price rapidly returns to normal. More experience is required to know whether manipulation will work in other contexts.

Feasibility, Markets, and Deliberation Once More. I have suggested that prediction markets face a pervasive problem of feasibility. A deliberating jury, for example, could not enlist such markets to decide on questions of guilt or innocence. Among other things, there is no objective way to test whether the jury, or individual jurors, ended up with the right answer (and if there were, the jury might well be dispensable). More generally, it is not easy to see how prediction markets could be used on normative questions. At most, such markets could be used on the factual questions that are sometimes part of such questions.

There is another problem. When the relevant groups are small, effective markets may be impossible to create, simply because of the absence of sufficient numbers of investors. A certain number is necessary to ensure that prediction markets have enough information to aggregate. Nonetheless, government agencies might well enlist such markets to resolve a number of questions, and ambitious efforts are underway to examine how government might enlist them to answer an array of disputed questions.[79]

In fact governments might use prediction markets to help make projections about insolvency, budget deficits, and the costs and benefits of proposed regulations.[80] In each of these cases, the forecasts of prediction markets might provide a "reality check" for deliberative processes. Officials might take into account the markets' predictions of the anticipated damage from a natural disaster, the number of annual deaths from an actual or anticipated disease (such as mad cow disease or AIDS), the number of American casualties from a war effort, the existence of demonstrable harms from global warming by, say, 2010, the likelihood of scarcity of natural resources, shrinkage of tropical forests in the world, demonstrable deterrent effects from capital punishment or other severe punishments, increases or decreases in emissions of specified air pollutants, increases or decreases in concentrations of air pollution in the ambient air, and much more. In all these cases, private or public institutions might create markets to provide information on crucial questions, and public institutions might take that information into account in making judgments about policy.

The broadest point is that, even when prediction markets are not feasible, an understanding of their virtues helps illuminate the virtues and vices of deliberation – and helps show how to obtain more of the former and less of the latter. Such markets overcome the collective action problem from which deliberating groups suffer; they also give people a strong incentive to say what they know and to back their best-grounded convictions with money. It should be possible for deliberating groups to learn from the successes of markets, above all by encouraging their members to disclose their privately held information. When such groups do poorly, it is often because they fail to elicit the information that their members have. Good norms, and good incentives, can go a long way toward reducing this problem. Consider here a fundamental redefinition of what it means to be a "team player." Frequently a team player is thought to be someone who does not upset the group's consensus. But it would be possible, and a great deal better, to understand team players as those who increase the likelihood that the team will be right – if necessary, by disrupting the conventional wisdom.

The point applies to many organizations, including corporate boards. In the United States, the highest-performing companies tend to have "extremely contentious boards that regard dissent as an obligation" and that "have a good fight now and then."[81] Investment clubs have little dissent, and lose a great deal of money, when members are united by close social ties.[82] By contrast, the best-performing investment clubs lack such ties and benefit from dissent and epistemic diversity. When deliberating groups do badly, fear of social sanctions is often a major reason. When they do well, they resemble prediction markets in the sense that their members have a strong incentive to disclose their private information.

CONCLUSION

Groups often hold a great deal of information, and an important task is to elicit and use the information of their members. Deliberation is generally thought to be the best way of carrying out that task, but deliberative bodies are subject to serious problems. Much of the time, informational influences and social pressures lead members not to say what they know. As a consequence, groups tend to propagate and even amplify cognitive errors. They also emphasize shared information at the expense of unshared information, resulting in hidden profiles. Cascade effects and group polarization are common.

Prediction markets have significant advantages over deliberative processes, and in many contexts they might supplement or even replace those processes. Such markets tend to correct rather than amplify individual errors, above all because they allow shrewd investors to take advantage of the mistakes made by others. By providing economic rewards for correct individual answers, they encourage investors to disclose the information they have. As a result, they are often more accurate than the judgments of deliberating groups. To the extent feasible, many groups would often do well to enlist prediction markets in arriving at their judgments, above all because of the accuracy of the price signal. Much more broadly, deliberating groups might attempt to counteract the pressures I have explored, learning from the successes of prediction markets to reduce the risks of deliberative failure.

ACKNOWLEDGEMENTS

I am grateful to Christian List for valuable comments on a previous draft.

Notes

1 Irving L. Janis, *Groupthink*, 2d ed. (Boston: Houghton Mifflin, 1982), 7–9.
2 I explore these mechanisms from different directions in Cass R. Sunstein, *Why Societies Need Dissent* (Cambridge, Mass.: Harvard University Press, 2003),

and Cass R. Sunstein, *Infotopia: How Many Minds Aggregate Knowledge* (New York: Oxford University Press, 2006); I have borrowed from those accounts here.

3 Cass R. Sunstein, David Schkade, and Lisa Ellman, "Ideological Voting on Federal Courts of Appeals: A Preliminary Investigation," *Virginia Law Review* 90 (2004): 301.

4 See the comparison of democratic and nondemocratic regimes in Dominic Johnson, *Overconfidence and War: The Havoc and Glory of Positive Illusions* (Cambridge, Mass.: Harvard University Press, 2004): 180–83.

5 Roger Brown, *Social Psychology*, 2d ed. (New York: Free Press, 1986): 206–7.

6 Ibid.

7 Chip Heath and Rich Gonzalez, "Interaction with Others Increases Decision Confidence but Not Decision Quality: Evidence against Information Collection Views of Interactive Decision Making," *Organizational Behavior and Human Decision Processes* 61 (1995): 305.

8 See Robert Baron et al., "Social Corroboration and Opinion Extremity, *Journal of Experimental Social Psychology* 32 (1996): 537.

9 Daniel Gigone and Reid Hastie, "Proper Analysis of the Accuracy of Group Judgments," *Psychological Bulletin* 121 (1997): 149, 161; Reid Hastie, "Experimental Evidence of Group Accuracy," in *Information Pooling and Group Decision Making*, ed. Bernard Grofman, Guillermo Owen, et al. (Greenwich, Conn.: JAI Press, 1986), 129.

10 Robert J. MacCoun, "Comparing Micro and Macro Rationality," in *Judgments, Decisions, and Public Policy*, ed. Rajeev Gowda and Jeffrey Fox (Cambridge: Cambridge University Press, 2002), 116, 121.

11 Ibid.

12 J. Scott Armstrong, "Combining Forecasts," in *Principles of Forecasting*, ed. J. Scott Armstrong (Boston: Kluwer Academic, 2001), 433.

13 See Sunstein, *Why Societies Need Dissent*.

14 Caryn Christenson and Ann Abbott, "Team Medical Decision Making," in *Decision Making in Health Care*, ed. Gretchen Chapman and Frank Sonnenberg (New York: Cambridge University Press, 2000), 267, 273–76.

15 Robert L. Thorndike, "The Effect of Discussion upon the Correctness of Group Decisions: When the Factor of Majority Influence Is Allowed For," *Journal of Social Psychology* 9 (1938): 343.

16 *See* Jürgen Habermas, Between Facts and Norms: *An Author's Reflections*, 76 Denv. U. L. Rev. 937, 940 (1999).

17 *See* Jürgen Habermas, 'What is Universal Pragmatics?', in *Communication and the Evolution of Society* 1, 2–4, 32 (Thomas McCarthy trans., 1979) (discussing preconditions for communication).

18 *See* Amy Gutmann and Dennis Thompson, *Democracy and Disagreements* (Cambridge, Mass: Harvard University Press, 1997), 7–8 (outlining foundations of authors' vision of deliberative democracy).

19 *See generally* F.A. Hayek, 'The Use of Knowledge in Society', 35 Am. Econ. Rev. 519 (1945) (discussing dispersal of knowledge and its aggregation through markets).

20 For an overview, see Thomas Gilovich, Dale Griffin, and Daniel Kahneman, *Heuristics and Biases: The Psychology of Intuitive Judgment* (New York: Cambridge University Press, 2002).

21   Amos Tversky and Daniel Kahneman, "Judgment under Uncertainty: Heuristics and Biases," in *Judgment under Uncertainty: Heuristics and Biases*, ed. Daniel Kahneman, Paul Slovic, and Amos Tversky (Cambridge: Cambridge University Press), 1982, 3.

22   Paul Rozin and Carol Nemeroff, "Sympathetic Magical Thinking: The Contagion and Similarity 'Heuristics,'" in Gilovich, Griffin, and Kahneman, *Heuristics and Biases* p. 201

23   Tversky and Kahneman, "Judgment under Uncertainty," 3.

24   MacCoun, "Comparing Micro and Macro Rationality," 116, 121.

25   Mark F. Stasson et al., "Group Consensus Approaches in Cognitive Bias Tasks," *Japanese Psychological Research* 30 (1988): 68.

26   See Norbert L. Kerr et al., "Bias in Judgment: Comparing Individuals and Groups," *Psychology Review* 103 (1996): 687, 689, 691–93.

27   Janet A. Sniezek and Rebecca A. Henry, "Accuracy and Confidence in Group Judgment," *Organizational Behavior and Human Decision Processes* 43 (1989): 1. This finding very much bears on excessive risk-taking, including in the context of making war. See Dominic Johnson, *Overconfidence and War*, 180–83.

28   Edward L. Schumann and W. C. Thompson, "Effects of Attorney's Arguments on Jurors' Use of Statistical Evidence" (unpublished manuscript, 1989).

29   Glen Whyte, "Escalating Commitment in Individual and Group Decision Making," *Organizational Behavior and Human Decision Processes* 54 (1993): 430.

30   James W. Gentry and John C. Mowen, "Investigation of the Preference Reversal Phenomenon in a New Product Introduction Task," *Journal of Applied Psychology* 65 (1980): 715; Julie R. Irwin and James H. Davis, "Choice/Matching Preference Reversals in Groups," *Organizational Behavior and Human Decision Processes* 64 (1995): 325.

31   Whyte, "Escalating Commitment," 430.

32   Stasson et al., "Group Consensus Approaches," 68.

33   Garold Stasser and William Titus, "Hidden Profiles: A Brief History," *Psychological Inquiry* 14 (2003): 304.

34   Daniel Gigone and Reid Hastie, "The Common Knowledge Effect: Information Sharing and Group Judgments," *Journal of Personality and Social Psychology* 65 (1993): 959.

35   See Ross Hightower and Lutfus Sayeed, "The Impact of Computer-Mediated Communication Systems on Biased Group Discussion," *Computers in Human Behavior* 11 (1995): 33.

36   Patricia Wallace, *The Psychology of the Internet* (Cambridge: Cambridge University Press, 1999), 82

37   See Garold Stasser and William Titus, "Pooling of Unshared Information in Group Decision Making: Biased Information Sampling during Discussion," *Journal of Personality and Social Psychology* 48 (1985): 1467.

38   Ibid., 1473; see also Stasser and Titus, "Hidden Profiles," 304.

39   Stasser and Titus, "Pooling of Unshared Information," 1473.

40   Ibid., 1476.

41   Ibid.

42   Ibid.

43   Stasser and Titus, "Hidden Profiles," 305.

44   See Daniel Gigone and Reid Hastie, "The Common Knowledge Effect: Information Sharing and Group Judgments," *Journal of Personality and Social Psychology* 65 (1993): 959.

45   Ibid., 960.

46   Ibid., 973.

47   See Garold Stasser et al., "Information Sampling in Structured and Unstructured Discussions of Three and Six-Person Groups," *Journal of Personality and Social Psychology* 57 (1989): 67.

48   Ibid., 78.

49   Ibid., 72.

50   I draw here on David Hirschleifer, "The Blind Leading the Blind," in *The New Economics of Human Behavior*, ed. Marianno Tommasi and Kathryn Ierulli (Cambridge: Cambridge University Press, 1995), 188, 193-94.

51   Ibid., 195.

52   See ibid; also see Sunstein, *Why Societies Need Dissent.*

53   See Lisa Anderson and Charles Holt, "Information Cascades in the Laboratory," *American Economic Review* 87 (1997): 847.

54   See Angela Hung and Charles Plott, "Information Cascades: Replication and an Extension to Majority Rule and Conformity-Rewarding Institutions," *American Economic Review* 91 (2001): 1508, 1515.

55   Thus, 72 percent of subjects followed Bayes's rule in Lisa Anderson and Charles Holt, "Information Cascades in the Laboratory," *American Economic Review* 87 (1997): 847, and 64 percent in Marc Willinger and Anthony Ziegelmeyet, "Are More Informed Agents Able to Shatter Information Cascades in the Lab ?" in *The Economics of Networks: Interaction and Behaviours*, ed. Patrick Cohendet et al. (New York: Springer, 1998), 291, 304.

56   See Willinger and Ziegelmeyet, "Are More Informed Agents," 291.

57   See Anderson and Holt, "Information Cascades in the Laboratory," 847.

58   See Hung and Plott, "Information Cascades," 1515–17.

59   Ibid., 1516.

60   Roger Brown, *Social Psychology: The Second Edition* (New York, N.Y.: Free Press, 1986), 206–7.

61   Ibid., 204.

62   Ibid., 224.

63   Ibid.

64   Sunstein, Schkade, and Ellman, "Ideological Voting," 301.

65   See David Schkade et al., "Deliberating about Dollars: The Severity Shift," *Columbia Law Review* 100 (2000): 101.

66   Brown, *Social Psychology*, 200–45.

67   Ibid. It has similarly been suggested that majorities are especially potent because people do not want to incur the wrath, or lose the favor, of large numbers of others, and that when minorities have influence, it is because they produce genuine attitudinal change. See Robert Baron et al., "Social Corroboration and Opinion Extremity," *Journal of Experimental and Social Psychology*, 32 (1996), 537.

68   Baron et al., "Social Corroboration," 537.

69   Ibid.

70   I am grateful to Christian List for pressing this point; he should not be held responsible for my restatement of it here.

71   For valuable overviews, see Justin Wolfers and Eric Zitzewitz, "Prediction Markets," *Journal of Economic Perspectives* 18 (2004): 107; Michael Abramowicz, "Information Markets, Administrative Decisionmaking, and Predictive Cost-Benefit Analysis," *University of Chicago Law Review* 71 (2004): 933; Saul Levmore,

"Simply Efficient Markets and the Role of Regulation," *Journal of Corporation Law* 28 (2003): 589.

72 For early overviews, see David M. Pennock et al., The Real Power of Artificial Markets, 291 Science 987 (2001); David M. Pennock et al., The Power of Play: Efficiency and Forecast Accuracy in Web Market Games, NEC Research Institute Technical Report 1000–168 (2001). A wealth of valuable information can be found at http://www.chrisfmasse.com/

73 See Robert W. Hahn & Paul C. Tetlock, *Harnessing the Power of Information: A New Approach to Economic Development* 4 (AEI-Brookings Joint Ctr. For Regulatory Studies, Working Paper No. 04-21, 2004), available at http://www.aei-brookings.org/publications/ abstract.php ?pid=846.

74 See Robin Hanson, "Designing Real Terrorism Futures" (August 2005), available at http:// hanson.gmu.edu.

75 Richard Roll, *Orange Juice and Weather*, 74 Am. Econ. Rev. 861, 871 (1984).

76 See Wolfers & Zitzewitz, *supra* note 207, at 113–14.

77 See Kay-Yut Chen & Charles R. Plott, *Information Aggregation Mechanisms: Concept, Design, and Implementation for a Sales Forecasting Problem* 3 (Div. of the Humanities & Soc. Sci., Cal. Inst. of Tech., Social Science Working Paper No. 113, March 2002) (describing variation of this model employed by Hewlett-Packard), available at http://www.hss.caltech. edu/SSPapers/wp1131.pdf.

78 See Putting Crowd Wisdom to Work, available at http://googleblog. blogspot.com/ 2005/09/putting-crowd-wisdom-to-work.html

79 See Robert W. Hahn and Paul C. Tetlock, "Using Information Markets to Improve Decision Making," *Harvard Journal of Law and Public Policy* 29, No. 1 (Fall 2005): 213–289.

80 Michael Abramowicz, "Prediction Markets, Administrative Decisionmaking, and Predictive Cost-Benefit Analysis," *University of Chicago Law Review* 71 (2004), 933.

81 See Jeffrey A. Sonnenfeld, What Makes Great Boards Great, Harvard Business Review (Sept. 2002).

82 See Brooke Harrington, Pop Finance: Investment Clubs and the New Ownership Society (Princeton: Princeton University Press, 2006, forthcoming).

15

The Communication Structure of Epistemic Communities

Kevin J. S. Zollman

1.

Increasingly epistemologists have become interested in the relationship between social influences and proper epistemic behavior. The analysis of this set of issues comes in one of two forms. One form is to consider the proper response for epistemic agents when faced with evidence that comes via another person (or persons). This type of analysis remains focused on the traditional epistemic problems of individual belief formation and revision, but incorporates appropriate responses to data of a certain kind.

Another approach focuses more on the structure of epistemic communities. This second type asks, given certain assumptions about the individuals in communities, what sort of community structures best serve the epistemic aim of that community? Alvin Goldman (2009) calls this sort of epistemology "systems-oriented social epistemology." As an example of it, Philip Kitcher (1990, 1993) and Michael Strevens (2003a, 2002b) have recently looked at the impact that different methods for assigning credit have on communities of scientists. They conclude that our current method of assigning credit is best for achieving the desired results of science.

Here we will be interested in one among many potentially interesting features of communities, namely, the structure of communication. Specifically we will ask: what is the best way for information to be transmitted? In order to analyze this problem we will look at the prime example of an epistemic community, science. In order to do this, we will use a model first suggested by two economists, Venkatesh Bala and Sanjeev Goyal (1998). The surprising result of this analysis is that in many cases a community that withholds information from its members is more reliable than one that allows for fully informed individuals. One might expect that reducing information to scientists would also have the effect of making their convergence to the truth much slower, and our model confirms this suspicion. The model suggests that there is a robust trade-off between speed and reliability that may be impossible to overcome.

After presenting the model in section 2, the results from a computer simulation study of the model are presented in section 3. Section 4 discusses the limitations of the model as a model of science, and section 5 concludes by comparing the results of this model with another problem discussed by Kitcher and Strevens.

2. THE MODEL

Consider the following stylized circumstance. Four medical researchers are working on a particular disease. They are confronted with a new treatment method that might be better or worse than the current well-understood method of treatment. Work on the new treatment will help to determine whether it is superior. Since the old treatment is well understood, experimental work on it will not result in any new information about its probability of success; scientists' efforts will only refine delivery methods or reduce harmful side effects. Suppose these scientists, labeled A, B, C, and D, respectively assign the following probabilities to the superiority of the new treatment: 0.33, 0.49, 0.51, and 0.66. Then each pursues the treatment method she thinks best. Two scientists, C and D, pursue the new treatment option, and the other two, A and B, pursue the old treatment option. Suppose further that the new treatment is in fact better than the old but, as is perfectly possible, C's and D's experiments both suggest slightly against it.[1] After meeting and reporting their results to each other, all the scientists might now judge it to be more likely that the old treatment is superior.[2] As a result, none of them will experimentally pursue the new treatment; we have lost a more beneficial treatment forever.

This circumstance arises for two reasons. First, scientists in this example must pursue evidence, they are not passive observers. Second, they already have a good understanding of the old treatment, and further study of it will not help them to conclude anything about the new treatment.[3]

Even given this structure, the availability of the evidence contributes to the abandonment of the superior theory. Had D not been aware of C's result, she would still have believed in the superiority of the new treatment.[4] As a result, had she been unaware of C's results, she would have performed a second round of experiments, which would offer the opportunity to correct the experimental error and thereby to find the truth. In this toy example, it seems that the wide availability of experimental results was detrimental to the group's learning. Of course no general lesson can be drawn from this example. It is not offered as a general model for all scientific practice but is instead provided as a generalization of a learning situation that some scientists unquestionably face.

Two economists, Bala and Goyal (1998), present a very general model that can be applied to circumstances like the one faced by the medical researchers. Stated formally, in this model, there are two states of the world ϕ_1 and ϕ_2 and two potential experimental options to pursue A_1 and A_2. Option A_1 has the same expected return in both states, while A_2's is lower in ϕ_1 and higher in ϕ_2. The return from choosing an option represents the degree to which a particular experiment succeeds—a higher payoff represents a larger experimental success. Agents are aware of the expected payoff in both states, but are unaware of which state obtains. Agents have beliefs about the state of the world and in each period pursue the option that has the highest expected utility given their beliefs. They receive a payoff from their actions that is independently drawn for each player from a common distribution with the appropriate mean. Each agent observes the outcome of his choice and the outcomes of *some* others, and then updates his beliefs about the state of the world based on simple Bayesian reasoning.[5]

This model has multiple interpretations, but one of them is analogous to the circumstance discussed above. The agents are scientists, and their action is choosing which method to pursue. State ϕ_1 is the state where the current method is better, and ϕ_2 is the state where the new method is better. Bala and Goyal endeavor to discover under what conditions groups will converge in taking the best action in a given state. They consider two different restrictions: restrictions on priors and restrictions on information about experimental outcomes.

The second suggestion, limiting information about outcomes, will be our primary focus here. This restriction is achieved by limiting those other agents a given individual can "see" and thus restricting the information on which an agent can update. They do this by placing an agent on a graph and allowing her to see only those agents with whom she is directly connected.

Bala and Goyal consider agents arranged on a line where each agent can see only those agents to the immediate left and right of him. If there are an infinite number of agents, convergence in this model is guaranteed so long as the agents' priors obey some mild assumptions. Bala and Goyal also consider adding a special group of individuals to this model, a "royal family." The members of the royal family are connected to every individual in the model. When we now consider this new collection of agents, there is positive probability that the group will converge to the worse option! This is a remarkable result, because it contradicts a basic intuition about science: that access to more data is always better.[6] In this case, it is not.

The reason for this result is interesting. In the single line case, the probability that everyone receives misleading results becomes vanishingly small as the population grows to infinity. However, in the population with the royal family, this probability no longer vanishes. Negative results obtained by the royal family infect the entire network and mislead every individual. Once the entire population performs act A_1, they can no longer distinguish between the good and bad states because this action has the same expected payoff in both ϕ_1 and ϕ_2. As a result a population composed entirely of A_1 players will never escape.

One might worry about Bala and Goyal's results since they depend so critically on the infinite size of the population. For finite populations, there exists a positive probability that *any* population will not learn the correct action. One might wonder how much influence the "royal family" would have in these cases. Furthermore, it is unclear what moral we ought to draw from these results—many things are different in the two different models. In addition to increased connectivity, there is also unequal distribution of connections. If we are interested in evaluating the performance of actual institutions, it is unclear which features we should seek out. I will now endeavor to discover, using computer simulations, the influence that network structure has on reliable learning in finite populations and also to develop more detailed results regarding the relationship between network structure and success.

3. FINITE POPULATIONS

3.1. The "Royal Family" Effect

To begin, we will look at three graphs known as the cycle, the wheel, and the complete graph (pictured in fig. 15.1) and compare their convergence properties. The cycle is a finite analogy to Bala and Goyal's line. Here agents are arranged on a circle and only connected with those on either side of them. The wheel is a cycle, but one of the agents—Bala and Goyal's royal family—is connected to everyone else. The last network is one where everyone is connected to everyone.

We will, unbeknownst to our agents, make the world be ϕ_2, where the new methodology is better. We will then assign our agents random beliefs uniformly drawn from the interior of the probability space and allow them to pursue the action they think best. They will then receive some return (a "payoff") that is randomly drawn from a distribution for that action. The agents will then update their beliefs about the state of the

Figure 15.1. A ten-person cycle, wheel, and complete graph

world on the basis of their results and the results of those to whom they are connected. A population of agents is considered to be finished learning if one of two conditions are met. First, a population has finished learning if every agent takes action A_1; in this case no new information can arrive that will convince our agents to change strategies. (Remember that the payoff for action A_1 is the same in both states, so it is uninformative.) Alternatively, the network has finished learning if every agent comes to believe that she is in ϕ_2 with probability greater than 0.9999. Although it is possible that some unfortunate sequence of results could drag these agents away, it is unlikely enough to be ignored.

The results of a computer simulation are presented in figures 15.2 and 15.3. In figure 15.2, the x-axis represents the total number of agents, and the y-axis represents the proportion of ten thousand runs that reached the correct beliefs.[7] The absolute probabilities should not be taken too seriously, as they can be manipulated by altering the expected payoffs for A_1 and A_2. On the other hand, the relative fact is very interesting. First, we have demonstrated that Bala and Goyal's results hold in at least some finite populations. In all the sizes studied, the cycle does better than the wheel. Second, we have shown that both of these do better than the complete graph where each agent is informed of everyone else's results.

This demonstrates a rather counterintuitive result: that communities made up of less-informed scientists might well be more reliable indicators of the truth than communities that are more connected. This also suggests

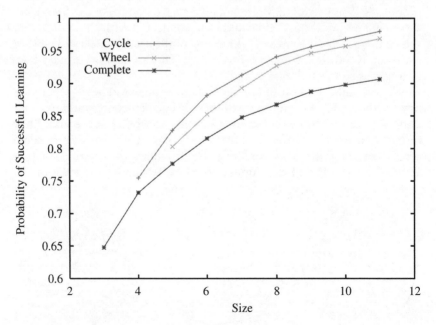

Figure 15.2. Learning results of computer simulations for the cycle, wheel, and complete graphs

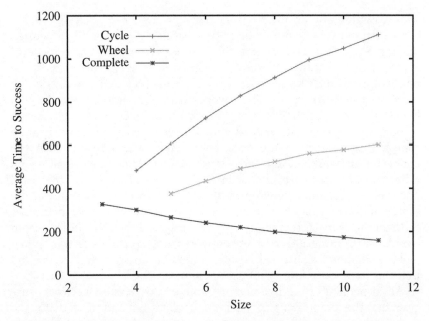

Figure 15.3. Speed results of computer simulation for the cycle, wheel, and complete graphs

that it is not the unequal connectivity of the "royal family" that is the culprit in these results. The harm done by the individual at the center cannot be simply overcome by removing their centrality.

There is a benefit to complete networks, however; they are much faster. Figure 15.3 shows the average number of generations it takes to reach the extreme beliefs that constituted successful learning among those networks that did reach those beliefs. Here we see that the average number of experimental iterations to success is much lower for the complete network than for the cycle, and the wheel lies in between. This suggests that, once networks get large enough, a sacrifice of some small amount of accuracy for the gain of substantial speed might be possible.[8]

3.2. Connectivity and Success

Why is it that less-connected networks, like the cycle and the wheel, are superior to more connected ones, like the complete graph? It appears that sparsely connected networks have a much higher "inertia." This inertia takes two forms. First, a less-connected network experiences fewer widespread changes in strategy on a given round than a highly connected network. The average number of people who change their strategies after the A_2 players receive an unlikely low return is four times higher in a highly connected network than a less-connected network. Second, unconnected networks are less likely to occupy precarious positions than connected ones. Conditioning on the network having only one A_2 player, a highly connected network is almost three times as likely to have no individuals playing A_2 on the next round. Since there is only one new piece of evidence in both cases, the difference between the two networks is the result of individuals having less extreme beliefs (i.e., closer to 0.5) in the connected network. Since all networks have the same expected initial beliefs, this must be the result of the information received by the agent.[9]

Both of these results suggest that unconnected networks are more robust with respect to the occasional string of bad results than the connected network because those strings are contained in a small region rather than spread to everyone in the network. This allows the small networks to maintain some diversity in behaviors that can result in the better action ultimately winning out if more accurate information is forthcoming. This also explains why we observed the stark difference in speeds for the cycle and complete networks in the previous section. When bad information is contained, so, too, is good information. In fact, we find that this trade-off is largely robust across networks.

An inspection of the five most reliable and five fastest networks suggests that the features of a network that make it fast and those that make it accurate are very different (see fig. 15.4). Four of the five most reliable graphs are minimally connected—that is, one cannot remove any edge without essentially making two completely separate graphs. Conversely, the five fastest graphs are highly connected, two of them are complete graphs, and the remaining ones are one, two, and three edges removed from complete graphs. Figure 15.5 compares the average time to success and probability of success for all networks of size 6. Here we find that there is a relationship between the accuracy of a network and its speed. In fact, this graph shows that sometimes a small increase in probability can result in a substantial increase in time to success.

This confirms the trade-off suggested earlier: in order to gain the reliability that limiting information provides, one must sacrifice other benefits, in this case, speed. In fact, the trade-off is even stronger than suggested

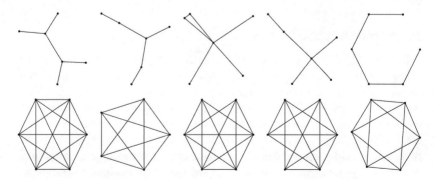

Figure 15.4. The five most accurate (top) and five fastest (bottom) networks

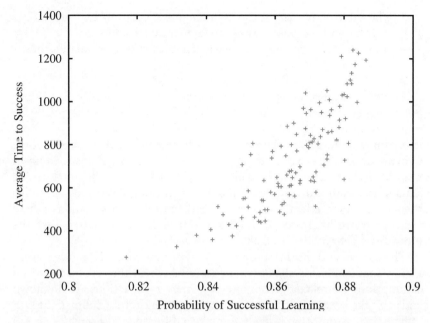

Figure 15.5. Speed versus accuracy for networks of size 6

here. These results are only for cases where we specify that the new method is better. When the uninformative action is better, convergence is guaranteed, but the connectedness of the graph determines its speed.

Ultimately, there is no right answer to the question whether speed or reliability is more important—it will depend on the circumstance. Although a small decrease in reliability can mean a relatively large increase in speed, in some cases such sacrifices may not be worth making. If it is critical that we get the right result no matter how long it takes, we will prefer groups where information is limited (without making the network disconnected). On the other hand, if speed is important and correct results are not as critical, perhaps a more connected network is desired. It is not the intention of this study to provide unequivocal answers to these questions, but to demonstrate that such trade-offs do exist and that one can achieve increased reliability by limiting information.

4. THE RIGHT MODEL

There are four assumptions that underlie this model that might cause some concern. They are:

1. The learning in this model is governed by the observation of payoffs.
2. There is an uninformative action whose expected payoff is well known by all actors.

3. The informative action can take on one of very few expected payoffs, and the possibilities are known by all actors.
4. Individuals are myopic—on each round they take the action they think is currently best.

The first assumption is of little concern. Here we use payoffs to symbolize experimental outcomes. Payoffs that are closer to the mean are more likely, which corresponds to experimental outcomes that are more likely on a given theory. The payoffs are arranged so that an individual who maximizes her expected payoff pursues the theory that she thinks is most likely to be true. This fact allows this model to be applied to learning situations where individuals are interested in finding the most effective theory (however effectiveness is defined) and also to situations where individuals are interested in finding the true theory. In either case the individuals behave identically.[10]

The second and third assumptions are less innocuous. In another essay, I show that similar results obtain in a model where the second and third assumptions are relaxed. Even in cases where both actions are unknown and can take a variety of values, information is harmful (Zollman 2009).

The final assumption is likely to make a difference, although as far as I am aware, there has not been specific investigation of variations along this line. In the model presented here the individual scientists are choosing the option that currently looks best; they are not considering the value that might be gained from pursuing the apparently suboptimal action in order to gain additional information. If an individual thinks we are probably in state ϕ_1 but is unsure, she might want to pursue action A_2 to ensure that her current belief is indeed correct. We exclude this possibility, but why should we?

First, I think the assumption of myopia more closely accords with how individual scientists choose methodologies to pursue. In situations of this sort, calculating when it is best to take a suboptimal action for the benefit of additional information can be *very* complex (see Berry and Fristedt 1985). The assumption of myopia corresponds to individuals who are willing to do some computation to determine the best course of action but not willing to engage in very complex calculations to do so. Second, myopic behavior is optimal when one cares significantly more about the current payoff and less about future payoffs. Information is only valuable when it will be put to future use. Since scientists are often rewarded for current successes (whether via tenure, promotion, grants, or awards), it is likely that scientists are at least close to myopic. Finally, even if this assumption is unreasonable, it represents an interesting starting point from which we can gauge the effect of making scientists less and less myopic.

These assumptions rest on a particular way of pursuing systems-oriented social epistemology. One type of social epistemology designs "scientific utopias" where everything—from social structures to individual behaviors—is in perfect harmony. The project of this essay instead takes its cue from Rousseau, who described his political philosophy as "taking men such as they are, and laws such as they may be made" (Rousseau 1791[1954]). We are interested in knowing what institutions make the best out of potentially imperfect individuals, so we will fix individuals' behavior in a reasonable way and compare how they do when placed in different social circumstances.

One might wonder if any situation faced by scientists actually fits this model. First, I believe this model very closely mimics Larry Laudan's (1996) model of theory selection. Laudan suggests that theory choice is a problem of maximizing expected return. We ought to choose the theory that provides the largest expected problem solving ability. Since we have often pursued a particular project for an extended time before being confronted with a serious contender, we will have a very good estimate of its expected utility. However, we will be less sure about the new contender, but we could not learn without giving it a try.

Even beyond Laudan, there may be particular scientific problems that fit this model. Bala and Goyal compare their model to crop adoption in Africa. There, a new seed is introduced, and farmers must decide whether to switch from their current crop (whose yield is well known) to another crop (whose yield is not).

Scientists often must choose between different methodologies in approaching a particular problem, and different methods have different intrinsic probabilities of succeeding.[11] In previous work, I connected this model of sequential decision-making to a case of medical research (Zollman 2009). For some time there were two prevailing theories about the cause of peptic ulcer disease. On one theory (the hypoacidity theory) peptic ulcers were caused by excess acid production in the stomach and treatment would involve finding various ways to reduce this acid. The other theory (the bacterial theory) claimed that peptic ulcers were caused by a bacterium that had to be eradicated in order to cure the ulcers. These two theories competed for some time before the hypoacidity theory won, to eventually be supplanted by the bacterial theory, which was resurrected almost fifty years after its initial abandonment. Scientists researching potential treatments for peptic ulcers chose experimental treatments on the basis of their belief about the underlying cause of peptic ulcers, and their beliefs about the underlying cause were influenced by the outcomes of these different treatments.

5. CONCLUSION

Preventing failed learning in this model is very similar to the problem of maintaining what Kitcher calls "the division of cognitive labor" (1990, 1993). This is the problem of encouraging scientists to work on theories they believe to be duds in order to secure an optimal community response.

Maintaining this division of labor prevents the abandonment of optimal theories when experimental results are misleading or priors are biased. Kitcher's solution to this problem is to appeal to the economic interests of the scientists by offering rewards to those who pursue other avenues. Kitcher (1990, 1993) and Strevens (2003a, 2003b) suggest that our current method of giving rewards to those who were the first to succeed has this effect.

This solution to the problem has the unfortunate consequence of being incompatible with our theories of good epistemic behavior for individuals. That is, scientists are doing well, under Kitcher's model, when they are actively pursuing the theory they believe to be incorrect with the hopes of gaining a big reward if the theory turns out to be true. In this essay I have another possible solution to the problem that does not rely on that type of epistemic impurity. Our scientists are genuinely pursuing those projects that they deem to be most likely to succeed, but the division of labor has been maintained sufficiently long by limiting the information available to our scientists.[12]

Even beyond the problem of maintaining the division of cognitive labor, this model suggests that in some circumstances there is an unintended benefit from scientists being uninformed about experimental results in their field. This is not universally beneficial, however. In circumstances where speed is very important or where we think that our initial estimates are likely very close to the truth, connected groups of scientists will be more reliable. On the other hand, when we want accuracy above all else, we should prefer communities made up of more isolated individuals.

Notes

The author would like to thank Brian Skyrms, Kyle Stanford, Jeffrey Barrett, Bruce Glymour, and the participants in the Social Dynamics Seminar at UCI for their helpful comments. Generous financial support was provided by the School of Social Science and the Institute for Mathematical Behavioral Sciences at UCI.

1 Specifically, suppose that all agree on these conditional probabilities:

P(The result of C's experiment | New method is better) = 0.4
P(The result of D's experiment | New method is better) = 0.4
P(The result of C's experiment | New method is worse) = 0.6
P(The result of D's experiment | New method is worse) = 0.6

2 Using the numbers above, A, B, C, and D would now assess the probability of the new theory being better as 0.1796, 0.2992, 0.3163, and 0.4632, respectively. This outcome is far from extraordinary. Given that the new methodology is better and the experimental outcomes are independent (conditioned on the new methodology being superior), the probability of getting this result is 0.16.

3 Had the scientists been passive observers, their beliefs would not have influenced the type of information they received. In that case, information about either treatment might still arrive, despite the fact that the theory has been abandoned. In addition, if experiments on the old theory were informative about the

effectiveness of the new theory, the fact that everyone pursues the old theory does not preclude them from learning about the new theory.

4 If D had only been aware of her own negative results, but not the results of C, her posterior belief in the superiority of the new treatment would have been 0.5621.

5 "Simple" here means that the agent only updates her belief using the evidence from the other's experiment. She does not conditionalize on the fact that her counterpart performed a particular experiment (from which she might infer the results of others).

6 Ellison and Fudenberg (1995) present a different model that comes to the same conclusions. In their model, the interaction structure is not fixed; individuals take a different random sample of fixed size in each time period. Because the individuals in their model have much shorter memories, it seems less appropriate for modeling scientific behavior (an application they do not consider). A similar conclusion can be found even for individual learning in the work of Herron, Seidenfeld, and Wasserman (1997). This work presents a rather different learning situation and will not be discussed in detail here.

7 Although it is possible for a population to continue unfinished indefinitely, no population failed to converge.

8 The results for both reliability and speed are robust for these three networks across modifications of both the number of strategies (and thus states) and the difference in payoff between the good and uninformative actions. Although these different modifications do affect the ultimate speed and reliability of the models, for any setting of the parameters the relationship between the three networks remains the same.

9 The statistics reported here are comparing one hundred runs of a complete six-person network with the most reliable six-person network pictured in figure 15.4.

10 This is not to say that true theories always have higher payoffs. Instead, this model is so general as to apply to either circumstance.

11 Success here can be defined in almost any way you like it. Different methods might have different probabilities of generating true explanations, adequate predictions, useful policy suggestions, etc. My hope here is to develop a model that appeals to people with varying commitments about what constitutes scientific success.

12 For a more detailed discussion of the cognitive division or labor, and the relation of this model to those problems see Zollman (2009).

References

Bala, Venkatesh, and Sanjeev Goyal (1998). "Learning from Neighbours." *Review of Economic Studies* 65, 565-621.

Berry, D.A., and B. Fristedt (1985). *Bandit Problems: Sequential Allocation of Experiments*. London: Chapman and Hall.

Bovens, Luc, and Stephan Hartmann (2003). *Bayesian Epistemology*. Oxford: Oxford University Press.

Ellison, Gregory and Drew Fudenberg (1995). "Word-of-Mouth Communication and Social Learning." *Quarterly Journal of Economics* 110(1), 93-125.

Goldman, Alvin (1999). *Knowledge in a Social World*. Oxford: Clarendon Press.

Goldman, Alvin (2009). "Systems-oriented Social Epistemology." In T. Gendler and J. Hawthorne (eds.), *Oxford Studies in Epistemology*, vol. 5. New York: Oxford University Press. (Reprinted here [chapter 1] under the title "A Guide to Social Epistemology.")

Herron, Timothy, Teddy Seidenfeld, and Larry Wasserman (1997). "Divisive Conditioning: Further Results on Dilation." *Philosophy of Science* 64, 411–44.

Hull, David (1988). *Science as a Process*. Chicago: University of Chicago Press.

Kitcher, Philip (1990). "The Division of Cognitive Labor." *Journal of Philosophy* 87(1), 5–22.

Kitcher, Philip (1993). *The Advancement of Science*. New York: Oxford University Press.

Laudan, Larry (1996). *Beyond Positivism and Relativism: Theory, Method, and Evidence*. Boulder, CO: Westview Press.

Popper, Karl (1975). "The Rationality of Scientific Revolutions." In *Problems of Scientific Revolution: Progress and Obstacles to Progress*. Oxford: Clarendon Press.

Rousseau, J.J. (1791 [1954]). *The Social Contract*. New York: Hafner.

Strevens, Michael (2003a). "Further Properties of the Priority Rule." Manuscript.

Strevens, Michael (2003b). "The Role of the Priority Rule in Science." *Journal of Philosophy* 100(2), 55–79.

Zollman, Kevin J.S. (2009). "The Epistemic Benefit of Transient Diversity." *Erkenntnis*, forthcoming.

Index